A Gathering of Wisdoms

TRIBAL MENTAL HEALTH:
A CULTURAL PERSPECTIVE

2ND EDITION

Swinomish Tribal Mental Health Project

A Gathering of Wisdoms

Tribal Mental Health: A Cultural Perspective

Second Edition

Swinomish Tribal Mental Health Project

Library of Congress Catalog Card Number: 91-066121

ISBN 0-9631016-0-9

The material in this book was originally produced by the Swinomish Tribal Community with assistance from the Skagit County Mental Health Center – with primary financial support from the Office of Human Development Services and the Administration for Native Americans. The current printing has been made possible by generous funding from the Indian Health Services, Portland area, and the Washington State Division of Mental Health.

For information please contact:
Swinomish Tribal Community
950 Moorage
LaConner, Washington 98257

Book design and production by:
Proforma Mountainview, Lynden, Washington

Dedication

To all the Healers and Helpers
traditional and modern,
spiritual and psychological,
medical and social,
who have given of themselves for
Indian People

And especially to Alex Paul, Jr.
whose healing spirit lives on in the drawings
throughout this book.

Contributors
to the First Edition
(Contributors to the Second Edition are listed in the Introduction to the Second Edition)

T*he following people have contributed to the original development of this book.*

MARK BACKLUND, M.D., of Skagit Community Mental Health Center, has provided psychiatric consultation to the Tribal Mental Health Program over the past fifteen years. He has contributed to the development of the ideas presented in this book and has provided extensive editorial assistance. His particular perspective can be found in Part 3, Ch. 17, along with those of all other members of the Tribal Mental Health Program Team.

JUNE BOOME, LPN (STALO) is a former Upper Skagit Tribal Support Counselor. Although originally from the Kilgaard Band in Chilliwack B.C., June lived in the Upper Skagit Community for many years. Along with the other Support Counselors, June made major contributions to the content of this book. In particular, June helped to focus discussions of boarding school experiences, of child rearing practices, of experiences of prejudice and of tribal social etiquette and communication patterns.

JENNIFER CLARKE, PH.D. was the Director of the Skagit Tribes' Mental Health Program from its beginning in 1984 until 1993, and was also the Director of the Swinomish Tribal Mental Health Training Project. Jennifer put together the views of all members of the Tribal Mental Health Team to develop the concepts and format of this book. She served as the primary organizer and scribe for for both the first and second editions of this book.

BERTHA DAN, (SWINOMISH ELDER), is the Cultural Consultant for the Tribal Mental Health Program. She was with the program from its beginning. Much of the cultural information and inspiration for this project came from Bertha. Her knowledge and her concern for the emotional and spiritual welfare of Indian people guided the development of program approaches. In addition, her dedication to spreading cultural knowledge and tribal mental health approaches has been crucial in maintaining team cohesiveness.

ALMEDA GILES, (SIOUX), was the Administrative Assistant for the Swinomish Tribal Mental Health Training Project in 1989-1990. In addition to typing most of the original manuscript, Almeda handled many details of layout and production of the original Book. She also participated in program seminars and meetings with cultural consultants.

JERE LAFOLLETTE, M.S.W., M.P.H., was the Executive Director of Skagit Community Mental Health Center from 1977 to 1998 and is now the Chief Executive Officer of the Associated Provider Network. Jere was instrumental in the development of both the Skagit Tribes' Mental Health Program and the Swinomish Tribal Mental Health Training Project. He assisted in the selection of the book's content and format. Jere's expertise in the community mental health system and his dedication to finding ways of adapting this system in order to meet tribal community needs are reflected in this material.

ALEX PAUL, JR. (COLVILLE), drew the designs for the book cover as well as most of those found alongside the text. In addition to being an artist, Alex was the speaker for the Skagit Valley Drummers and was a skilled dancer. We mourn his loss.

DARLENE PETERS, B.A., (Swinomish), was a Swinomish Tribal Support Counselor from 1985 until the Fall of 1988. She contributed knowledge of the problems facing young Indian people and ideas concerning culturally appropriate service delivery to this project. Although she is no longer with the Program, her contributions remain.

PEARL RODRIGUEZ, (SAUK-SUIATTLE), was an Upper Skagit Tribal Support Counselor from the beginning of the Program until 1994. Pearl made major contributions to the development of the Tribal Mental Health Program as well as to this book. Her expertise in extended family relations, the role of tribal elders, traditional spirituality and the problems facing young Indian people helped to guide the development of this book, especially Parts 1 and 2. Her viewpoint, as well as that of the other Tribal Support Counselors, can be found in Part 3.

DIANE VENDIOLA, **A.A.**, (Swinomish), was a Support Counselor for the Swinomish Tribal Community from 1988 until 1994, when she became the program supervisor/coordinator. Her background as an Indian culturally-oriented educator and trainer strengthened this Project. Diane's assistance in the development of a video on Tribal Mental Health to accompany this volume has also been invaluable. (See also Introduction to the Second Edition, p. 11)

Consultants
to the First Edition

(See introduction to Second Edition
for recent consultants)

The following persons served as Consultants to the Swinomish Tribal Mental Health Project. Each enriched our perspectives and helped us further develop our model.

LAURA EDWARDS, (SWINOMISH) was a widely respected tribal elder and the oldest living member of the Swinomish Tribe. She was the grandmother of almost 40 adults and the great-grandmother of over 80 children. Laura shared her wisdom and cultural knowledge in order to strengthen our understanding of the Indian extended family system, of Coast Salish child rearing practices, of the boarding school experience and of current problems facing Indian people. We hope that we have been able to communicate Laura's overall message of courage and hope for renewed family strength.

VI HILBERT, (UPPER SKAGIT), is a traditional story teller, teacher and elder. She has done much to preserve Coast Salish culture by recording the Lushootseed language and collecting traditional stories. Vi generously opened her home to us, commented on our program approaches and shared her understanding of connections between mental health, culture and language.

MAUREEN MARTIN, (SWINOMISH), is a traditional speaker, story teller and 'natural helper'. Her many interactions with the Tribal Mental Health Program over the years have made her an honorary member of our team. Maureen shared insights into traditional ways of helping, family values and strengths of the tribal community in coping with crisis and loss.

VIRGINIA MCKENZIE, (SWINOMISH), is a respected leader in the Indian Shaker Church. Her strong faith, beautiful voice and willingness to help those in trouble have made her a valued resource in the Swinomish Community. Virginia shared her perspective on traditional ways of helping and her views concerning the problems faced by young Indian people today.

BRUCE MILLER, (SKOKOMISH), has special combinations of abilities and knowledge: he is a Spiritual Leader, a strong spokesman for Indian culture, a story teller, has been the leader of a traditional dance troupe and is an expert in Indian education. His work in developing educational materials combining Indian cultural approaches with video, puppets and printed material were exciting and stimulating to us.

BRUCE MILLER, PH.D., is an anthropologist currently at the University of British Columbia, with particular expertise in Upper Skagit history and culture. Bruce shared insights into Coast Salish family patterns, communication style, and ways of dealing with conflicts. He also made a number of helpful suggestions concerning resources and background material.

KENNY MOSES, (SAUK-SUIATTLE), was a widely respected spiritual leader. He shared his perspective concerning problems facing Indian people, the close relationship between spirituality and mental health, and the nature of healing. His reassurance and encouragement of our program helped us face difficult challenges.

HARLAN SAM, SR., (UPPER SKAGIT), is a member of the Upper Skagit Tribal Council and a leader in the Shaker Church. He discussed educational, economic and vocational stresses which increase mental health problems for Indian people. He stressed profound cultural changes which have affected Upper Skagit families.

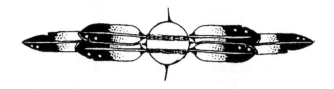

Acknowledgements

Many people have contributed to our project, some in ways they may not recognize. Our understanding has grown over some years, fed by many sources. We wish we could thank them all. The following people stand out in our minds as having been especially supportive.

Special thanks go to ROBERT JOE, SR., former Chairman of the Swinomish Tribal Community, to JOHN STEPHENS, Social Services Director for the Swinomish Tribe, and to MARILYN SCOTT, former Social Services Director Upper Skagit Tribe (and current assistant director for the Northwest Washington Service Unit of IHS), for their continuous support of both the Skagit Tribes' Mental Health Program and of the Swinomish Tribal Mental Health Training Project.

ISADORE TOM of the Lummi Tribe set an example for cooperation between spiritual, medical and psychological healers. We are grateful for his wisdom, kindness and encouragement, and we mourn his passing.

DR. AND MRS. NORMAN TODD of Chilliwack B.C. welcomed our troupe into their home, showed us their fabulous collection of Northwest Coast masks, and shared their deep knowledge of Coast Salish Indian culture and healing. Dr. Todd was also kind enough to present his views on the therapeutic benefits of Indian healing during our Tribal Mental Health Workshop at Swinomish in May of 1988.

FRANCIS PETERS of Swinomish joined BERTHA DAN in making a very powerful presentation concerning traditional ways of coping with grief and loss, also for our 1988 workshop. His comments helped crystallize our understanding.

During our 1985 workshop at Swinomish, DR. ROBERT

BERGMAN shared his experiences in working with Navajo traditional healers. MARY HELEN CAGEY of Lummi offered her perspectives on Shaker Healing. ROGER JIM of Yakima and LINDA DAY of Swinomish contributed their views concerning traditional culture and current needs in tribal communities. JOHNNY MOSES of Swinomish shared teaching stories, songs and traditional dances.

TERRY FARROW, M.S.W. (Umatilla) of the Indian Health Service joined JUNE BOOME and DARLENE PETERS (of the Tribal Mental Health Program) in offering personal insights during a panel discussion of the Advantages and Disadvantages of Mental Health Providers working in their own Tribal communities, also at our 1988 workshop.

ROBIN LA DUE, Ph.D., of the Cowlitz tribe journeyed to Upper Skagit to share her experiences in reservation-based mental health services with us in 1988.

GERALDINE KILDOW, R.N.; F.N.P., shared her experiences with the medical side of emotional problems, and in cooperating with traditional Coast Salish healers.

REENA BOLTON arrived from the far North (Terrace, B.C.) at a special time to give us helpful words about cultural roots and Indian identity.

THE SKAGIT VALLEY DRUMMERS have twice eased our minds with special prayer songs for our Programs' harmony and success.

Over the years a number of mental health specialists supported our developing program. In particular, NORINE MYERS M.S.W., of The Indian Health Service, FRANCIS KOHLER, M.D., JILL LAPOINTE, M.S.W., ANNE TAKAHASHI, M.A., MARJORIE PANEK, Ph.D. and DIANNA SANFORD, M.A. have offered insights and consultation concerning our program and client services.

MARY ELLEN CAYOU (Swinomish) deserves roses, our thanks and a pay raise for her cheerful secretarial assistance at the eleventh hour.

PAUL HANSEN proof read most of this material as well as patiently tolerating his wife's preoccupation and anxiety.

Skagit Tribes' Mental Health Program was developed with financial support from the Washington State Division of Mental Health. The program is one of seven ethnic mental health programs funded in order to develop culturally specific models of service delivery for minority groups. The staff of the other five "CREMS" programs were also helpful in stimulating exchange of ideas about connections between culture and mental health.

This material was developed by the Swinomish Tribal Mental Health Training Project with primary financial support from the Office of Human Development Services and the Administration for Native Americans. Additional support was provided by Skagit Community Mental Health Center and the Washington State Division of Mental Health. The first edition was printed in 1989 in a set of six booklets, jointly entitled the "Swinomish Tribal Mental Health Project." The first reprinting in a single volume was made possible by generous funding from the Portland Area Office of the Indian Health Service and from the Washington State Division of Mental Health.

Contents
A Gathering
of Wisdoms

Introduction 5
Introduction to the Second Edition: The
Gathering of Wisdoms Update Process 9

Book I

**THE BIG PICTURE: TRIBAL MENTAL HEALTH NEEDS,
CULTURAL CONSIDERATIONS AND STRENGTHS**

PART 1
OVERVIEW OF THE MENTAL HEALTH
STATUS OF INDIAN COMMUNITIES:
NEEDS and BARRIERS

Introduction, Book I, Part 1 19
Contents, Part 1 21
Chapter 1. The History of Indian-Non-Indian
Relations and Its Impact on the Mental Health
of Tribal Communities 25
Chapter 2. Interacting Problems Affecting the
Mental Health of Indian Communities 53
Chapter 3. Intergenerational Trauma in the
Tribal Community 77
Chapter 4. Barriers to Indian People Receiving
Mainstream Mental Health Services 115
Chapter 5. Mental Health and Related
Resources Currently Available to
Tribal Communities 119

PART 2
CULTURAL CONSIDERATIONS
FOR TRIBAL MENTAL HEALTH

Introduction, Part 2 141
Contents, Part 2 145
Chapter 6. The Importance of Culture
for Mental Health 149
Chapter 7. Tribal Family Systems 181
Chapter 8. Tribal Social Life 199
Chapter 9. Communication Patterns 223
Chapter 10. Native American Worldview:
Spirituality and Healing 235
Chapter 11. Traditional Healing Around the World:
A Cross Cultural Perspective 277
Chapter 12. Core Swinomish Tribal Values:
The Gathering of Wisdoms Update Process Report .. 283

Book II
PRACTICAL INFORMATION AND MODELS FOR
TRIBAL MENTAL HEALTH PROGRAMS

PART 3
A TRIBAL MENTAL HEALTH PROGRAM:
THE SKAGIT COUNTY EXPERIENCE

Introduction, Book II, Part 3 301
Contents, Part 3 303
Chapter 13. Overview of The Skagit Tribes'/Swinomish
Mental Health Program 307

Chapter 14. Therapeutic Framework: Cultural Congruence in a Tribal Mental Health Program 319

Chapter 15. Important Early Steps in Program Development 327

Chapter 16. Culturally Appropriate Service Approaches 333

Chapter 17. Perspectives of Tribal Mental Health Team Members 343

Chapter 18. Problems and Challenges Encountered in Program Operation 357

Chapter 19. Three Case Examples 369

Chapter 20. Tribal Mental Health Program Policies 383

Chapter 21. Program "Start-up" Ideas and Materials 403

Chapter 22. Information and Suggestions for Direct Service Providers 417

PART 4

RECORD KEEPING FOR
TRIBAL MENTAL HEALTH PROGRAMS

Introduction, Part 4 425

Contents, Part 4 427

Chapter 23. General Guidelines for Culturally Sensitive Record Keeping 429

Chapter 24. Sample Instructions for Tribal Mental Health Record Keeping 435

Chapter 25. Sample Record Keeping Forms 449

PART 5

TRAINING FOR
INDIAN MENTAL HEALTH WORKERS

Introduction, Part 5 471

Contents, Part 5 473

Chapter 26. Need for Tribal Mental Health Worker Training and The Skagit Tribes' Mental Health Worker Training Program 475

Chapter 27. Practical Suggestions for
Tribal Mental Health Training 485
Chapter 28. Sample Training Plan and Outlines 489
Chapter 29. Tribal Mental Health Conference
Materials and Exercises 511

PART 6

RESOURCE LIST FOR
TRIBAL MENTAL HEALTH

Introduction, Part 6 537
Contents, Part 6 539
Appendix One. Books, Papers, Monographs
and Articles from Books 541
Appendix Two. Journals, Newsletters, and
Journal Articles 549
Appendix Three. Indian Organizations and
Other Resources 551
Appendix Four. Native American Tribes 557

Introduction

Issues in Tribal Mental Health:
A Cultural Perspective

I ndian mental health workers have great knowledge about culturally appropriate mental health approaches. Unfortunately, the high service demands of most programs do not often allow the luxury of putting "experiential knowledge" into written descriptions which can be shared with other tribal mental health providers. We feel lucky that the Swinomish Tribal Mental Health Training Project allowed us to describe our own experiences and to discuss ideas with traditional consultants, as well as with other tribal mental health providers. We hope that this project will continue to stimulate exchanges of culturally oriented approaches and help build a supportive network among all tribal mental health providers within and beyond Washington State.

The information in this book is based upon the experience of the Skagit Tribes' Mental Health Program team in providing direct mental health services to members of two tribal communities and in implementing a training program for tribal mental health workers over the past 18 years. The goal of the initial project was to provide culturally "enhanced" mental health services to Indian clients. This program is administered by Skagit Community Mental Health Center through a cooperative agreement with the Swinomish and Upper Skagit Tribes. Client Services and many training experiences take place at tribal sites, where staff offices are located.

The success of this program in serving Indian people led to the award in 1988 of a special grant to the Swinomish Tribal Community from the Office of Human Development Services and the Administration for Native Americans.

The purpose of this Swinomish Tribal Mental Health Training Project was to share program experiences, cultural orientation and tribal service approaches with other tribes, Indian organizations, mental health and other interested agencies. This was done through the development and distribution of the first draft of this written material as well as through a series of inter-tribal/inter-agency "Healing Through Cooperation and Tradition" Tribal Mental Health Conferences (see Part 5). Additional support obtained from the Washington State Division of Mental Health allowed wider distribution of written materials and additional conferences. Some of the material in this volume was first printed in 1989 in a set of six booklets, jointly entitled the "Swinomish Tribal Mental Health Project." The reprinting of these booklets in a single volume with minor changes was made possible by generous funding from the Portland Area Office of the Indian Health Service and from the Washington State Division of Mental Health.

This book is designed for tribal administrators, tribal mental health/social services workers, college students in cross-cultural counseling courses, and other agencies interested in working with Indian tribes. This book is meant to be used as a resource manual: some sections will be more relevant to administrators, some to tribal staff and some to newcomers wanting to learn more about Indian community needs and values.

Book I, The Big Picture: Tribal Mental Health Needs, Cultural Considerations and Strengths

Book I, Part 1, "Overview of the Mental Health Status of Indian Communities" presents a broad introduction and background concerning Indian mental health status. Chapter One explores the impact of the history of Indian-non-Indian relations. Chapter Two presents the interacting problems and mental health needs of tribal communities. The impact of intergenerational trauma and treatment of trauma related conditions is presented in Chapter Three.

Chapters Four & Five describe barriers to Indian people receiving adequate mental health services, and mental health services currently available to tribal communities. Possibilities are suggested for inter-agency collaboration in funding, administration and service delivery. Particular emphasis is given to the importance of tribal control and location of culturally oriented mental health services. This may be particularly helpful to administrators and mental health workers who are not already familiar with Indian history, culture and mental health status.

Part 2, *"Cultural Considerations for Tribal Mental Health" explores the relation of culture and personal cultural identity to mental health and mental illness. The need for culturally congruent mental health approaches is emphasized. Later chapters address aspects of Native American culture which have particular significance for the mental health of Indian people such as tribal family systems, values, social norms, communication styles, worldview, spiritual healing practices and concepts of health and illness. The Gathering of Wisdoms Update Process Report summarizes core Swinomish values identified during GWUP community forums.*

Book II, Practical Information and Models for Tribal Mental Health Programs

Book II, Part 3, *"A Tribal Mental Health Program: The Skagit County Experience" describes one approach to providing culturally appropriate mental health services, as it has been developed in two small reservation communities, the Swinomish and the Upper Skagit.* This program's goals, accomplishments, therapeutic orientation, treatment techniques and cultural specifics are described. Other chapters present the viewpoints of Tribal Mental Health Team members as well as problems encountered in program implementation. Three case examples illustrate program services. *Part 3 ends with practical program materials, such as Tribal Mental Health Program Policies, Practical Suggestions for Program Development, "start-up" ideas, and information and suggestions for direct service providers.*

Part 4, *"Record Keeping for Tribal Mental Health" addresses challenges for culturally sensitive mental health programs which must also mesh with state and/or federal requirements for record keeping.* Record keeping must be adapted to meet tribal and cultural needs. The first chapter focuses on how record keeping in our Tribal Mental Health Program differs from most community mental health programs. The following chapters present instructions for use of this record keeping system and the actual forms developed for this tribal particular program.

Part 5, *"Training for Indian Mental Health Workers" presents a college-accredited Tribal Mental Health Training Program, along with practical suggestions for the development of similar training programs* and various practical training materials, including a two year curriculum, course outlines, plans for field placements, learning contracts and evaluation forms. Various materials for Tribal Mental Health Conferences are included, such as sample agendas, exercises, handouts, and evaluation forms.

Part 6, Resource List for Tribal Mental Health. Appendices One & Two contain an abbreviated list of books, journals, and articles. Appendices Three & Four list Indian tribes and Indian organizations. We hope that mental health and social services staff working with Indian people will find these resources useful.

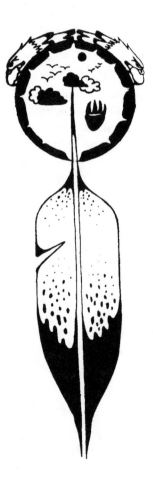

Introduction
to the
Second Edition
The Gathering of
Wisdoms Update Process

Since the publication in 1991 of <u>A Gathering of Wisdoms</u>, there has been a heartening response to this book from both Tribal and non-tribal communities. Tribal social services staff from around the country have written in praise of the book, it has been used in a number of college and university level cross cultural counseling and psychology courses, and a second printing of the first edition has sold out.

For some time we have thought that a second edition was needed, not only in order to address changes in the program, but also to strengthen the book with discussion of certain issues not adequately covered in the first addition. *The North Sound Regional Support Network for mental health services in Washington State provided special grant funding to allow the Swinomish Tribal Mental Health Team to undertake this project.*

The project, called the "Gathering of Wisdoms Update Process" (GWUP), was designed to:

1. Increase Swinomish Tribal Community awareness of the link between positive cultural identity and mental health,
2. Gather input from Swinomish Tribal Community members about traditional strengths, values and healthy Indian lifestyles

3. Incorporate this information into this new edition of <u>A Gathering of Wisdoms</u>.

We saw this project as a special opportunity to promote a sense of community pride and shared responsibility for the well being of the entire community. We hoped to create a sense of "ownership" not only of this book and of the Tribal Mental Health Program, but most importantly of the notion that mental health is CULTURAL and must be a fundamental tribal community concern.

Gathering of Wisdoms Update Process Committee

After initial discussions with tribal leaders, mental health staff and consultants, eight individuals were chosen to serve on a GWUP (Gathering of Wisdoms Update Process) committee. The purpose of the committee was to provide guidance and oversight to the entire Tribal Community GWUP process.

The following people served on the GWUP committee and through the course of our meetings evolved into a close working team.

Janie Beasley, (Swinomish) Tribal Realty Officer, Pentecostal Church Member and United States Airforce Veteran: Janie shared valuable perspectives on family relationships, grieving and the Pentecostal faith.

Larry Campbell, (Swinomish) Inter-Governmental Relations/ Cultural Resource Planner and Smokehouse representative: Larry provided a role model of commitment to serving the tribal community and respecting cultural traditions.

Jennifer Clarke, Ph.D., the original director of this Tribal Mental Health Program and primary author for <u>A Gathering of Wisdoms</u>: Jennifer returned from private practice to join in the GWUP committee meetings, community forums and to prepare this second edition of <u>A Gathering of Wisdoms</u>.

Josephine Finkbonner, (Swinomish) Shaker Church member and Instructional Aide for La Conner School District: Josephine offered her special insights into the needs of young people.

Kevin Paul, Swinomish Tribal Support Counselor from 1998 until 2001, traditional carver and member of the Skagit Valley Drummers: Kevin shared his prayers, humor, compassion and the perspective of a traditional artist.

Beverly Peters, (Swinomish/Musqueam) Youth Compliance Officer, Director of Spiritual Center and assistant to Father Pat Twohy: Bev shared her commitment to young people, concerns about parenting skills of young parents and offered insights into the role of the Catholic Church in this community.

Father Pat Twohy, Catholic Priest and Spiritual Advisor at Swinomish since 1986 (previously at Colville Reservation from 1973-1984) , author of <u>Finding a Way Home</u> and <u>Beginnings</u>: Father Pat brought insight to many sensitive issues and encouraged us to continue with this work.

Diane Vendiola, (Swinomish) AA, Supervisor/Coordinator of the Tribal Mental Health Program since 1994 and a Tribal Support Counselor in this program since 1988, and Swinomish Elder: Diane's loyalty, humor and excellent common sense kept this project on track. Diane coordinated all committee meetings and Tribal Community Forums and oversaw the execution of this project.

Other Special Helpers

In addition to the above committee members, several other individuals offered time and support to this project.

Bertha Dan, Swinomish elder and Tribal Mental Health Cultural Consultant since the beginning of the program in 1984, continued to stand by our side with her wisdom and unfailing support.

Brian Cladoosby has been Chairman of the Swinomish Tribal Community for the past four years. Brian's leadership has supported the Tribal Mental Health Program and the GWUP process.

Joe Dunn, Swinomish Alcohol Program Director since 1970, provided administrative overview for this project. Joe particularly shared his concerns for men's mental health issues.

Robert George, a respected elder from the Burrard Band in British Columbia, journeyed to Swinomish to help launch the first of the Tribal Community Dinner Forums. He shared his recollections of and love for Swinomish people. He spoke eloquently of the wisdom and importance of sharing and supporting one another.

Rudy Vendiola, BA, **Randy Vendiola**, MA, and **Shelly**

Vendiola, MA, all pitched in during community forums to help stimulate and facilitate group discussions. Rudy is the Director of Indian Education at the Ferndale School District. Randy is the Director of the Johnson O'Malley Program for the Lummi Tribal School. Shelly is an activist and consultant for the Indigenous Environmental Network. All three are the children of their very proud mother, Diane Vendiola.

GWUP Committee Process

The GWUP committee met on a monthly basis for a year. The first agenda was planning the overall GWUP process and the tribal- wide community Forums. *The mission was to involve the entire tribal community in an ongoing discussion about mental health as it relates to tribal realities and values.*

Considerable effort went into identifying key individuals who should be personally invited. In the tribal context, this means that someone must go to the home of those individuals, explain the purpose of the meeting, and invite them. Written invitations, even if personal, do not tend to be effective. In some cases, it is appropriate to personally offer to bring the invited person to the meetings, especially if they are an elder.

On a number of occasions, The GWUP committee meetings evolved into intimate discussions of personal cultural experiences. This small group became a safe place for exploring ideas and feelings related to the mental health of the Tribal Community. We experienced that special magic which sometimes happens when a group of people, however superficially different, are all committed to something they each hold dear: in this case the emotional and social well being of the Swinomish Tribal Community. *Many of the insights and ideas presented in the sections to follow reflect these team discussions.*

COMMUNITY FORUMS

This project proceeded in a typically Indian "organic" and somewhat unpredictable but lively manner.

Six Tribal Community forums were held, focusing on various aspects of Swinomish Tribal Community life and mental health. The intent was to build a sense of community belonging and common purpose in promoting positive mental health.

We especially hoped to increase recognition of the essential role of cultural identity in the mental health of individuals and the Tribal Community as a whole.

While most Tribal Community members may not have read A Gathering of Wisdoms, most are aware of the existence of this book and its' support of tribal values. There is a growing sense of pride at having "our" book, and a sense of excitement in having the opportunity to influence the content of this new edition.

The forums had a generally festive atmosphere, celebrating the values and integrity of this tribal community. The forums were conducted in a manner aimed at embodying community values related to gathering together, sharing and recognizing the importance of all tribal community members. The food shared and door prizes and games helped to make these events fun for both children and adults.

None the less, there was often a serious, even sacred tone. Prayers for the work of each evening and of the Gathering of Wisdoms Update Process opened each forum. There was a strong sense of support expressed for the work of the Tribal Mental Health Program and an acknowledgement of the increased community awareness of mental health issues and resources that has been slowly built over the years since the inception of the program.

Recognition and acceptance of mental health problems and services in this tribal community has been a long, slow process. The continuity and staying power of this program has achieved what short lived attempts to create rapid change have not:
Increased understanding of mental health needs and services,
More tribal members seeking services
The ability of many community members to engage in open and emotional dialogue concerning their deepest values, grief and hopes for this tribe.

The GWUP forums helped the community to see how far we have come, as well as how far we have yet to go.

The current edition of A Gathering of Wisdoms incorporates the ideas, values and cultural information discussed during these GWUP community forums. Many of the issues emphasized by community members reinforced information included in the origi-

nal edition of this book. New information has been added to the second edition. The "core Swinomish values" of spirituality, kinship, gathering together, sharing, interdependence and participation in traditional activities which were identified during the forums are presented in Part Two, Chapter 12. We have listened carefully in an attempt to convey the shared voice of the Swinomish people.

Many minor changes and additions have been made throughout this second edition, in order to update program and funding information or to clarify and strengthen the narrative. The resource lists in the Appendices have been much reduced. We concluded that a shorter list of especially relevant material would be more useful than the extensive and overly academic list provided in the first edition.

Considerable new material has also been added. The new Chapter Three, "Intergenerational Trauma in Tribal Communities", discusses the nature of trauma and trauma-related mental health conditions, presents the concept of "intergenerational" trauma", and addresses healing from traumatic experiences, with special attention to mental health treatment for Post Traumatic Stress Disorder. Ch. 6, The Importance of Culture for Mental Health has been expanded to include a description of the process of forming a positive cultural identity. The section concerning Native American worldviews, Spirituality and healing (Ch. 10), has been considerably expanded to include information on spirituality and spiritual healing. A new chapter (Ch. 11) provides a worldwide perspective on traditional healing systems. Recent developments in the Tribal mental health program and Swinomish Social Services are discussed in Ch. 13.

We wish to express our gratitude to the North Sound Regional Support Network for mental health services in Washington State, which has shown a commitment to tribal mental health not only by funding the GWUP process and second edition of <u>A Gathering of Wisdoms</u>, but also through their sponsorship of two intertribal mental health conferences over the past two years. We hope that this will become an annual event. This too is a "coming together" to promote a "gathering" of all our wisdoms.

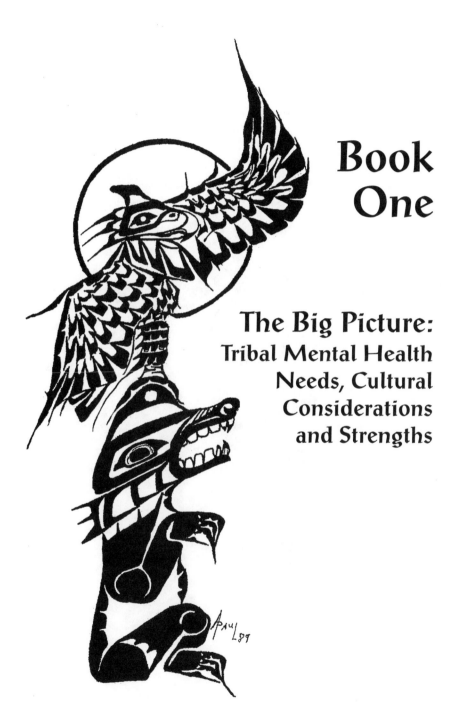

Book One

The Big Picture:
Tribal Mental Health Needs, Cultural Considerations and Strengths

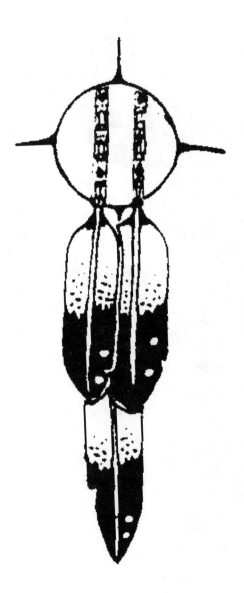

Part One

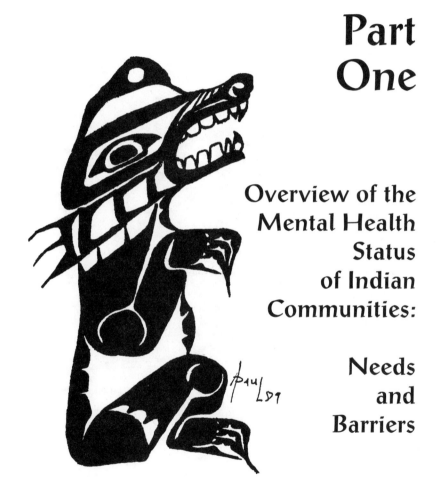

Overview of the Mental Health Status of Indian Communities:

Needs and Barriers

Introduction
Book One, Part One.

C*hapter One consists of a brief history of Indian-non-Indian relationships as they have affected the overall mental health status of Indian people.* A review of the significance of treaties, of shifting U.S. policies toward Indian people, of the systematic reduction of Indian lands, of the suppression of Indian religion, of the removal of Indian children from their families, of the effects of Indian education, and of the introduction of alcohol to Indian people provides a necessary background for understanding current mental health needs in tribal communities. This chapter should be particularly helpful for mental health administrators and providers who are not already familiar with Indian history and culture.

Chapter Two discusses mental health problems commonly encountered in tribal communities. The triad of depression, alcohol abuse and stress-related acting out is emphasized. Suicide, school problems, somatic difficulties, and child neglect are also discussed, as are cultural differences in patterns of disturbance. *Lack of a positive cultural identity is described as a mental health problem.* General suggestions about treatment are offered. This chapter may be helpful to both tribal and mainstream mental health and social services workers.

Chapter Three presents information about the range of trauma-related mental health problems and intro-

duces the concept of intergenerational trauma in tribal communities. Treatment for trauma related mental health problems is described. The importance of reconnecting with the community is emphasized. This chapter will be useful for both tribal and non-tribal mental health workers needing increased knowledge about trauma-based disorders.

Chapter Four discusses barriers which interfere with Indian clients receiving mental health services, with particular reference to the Community Mental Health system. Geographical, financial, attitudinal and cultural barriers are discussed.

Chapter Five provides an overview of mental health and related services available to tribal communities. Bureau of Indian Affairs, Indian Health Service, Tribal and Traditional services are discussed. Particular attention is given to an overview of the Community Mental Health System in the hopes of familiarizing tribal authorities and staff with this currently underused resource. *It is stressed that tribal mental health services must be tribally based and under tribal control in order to be effective.* It is suggested that tribes can draw upon the resources of both the Indian Health Service and the Community Mental Health System to develop collaborative, culturally oriented tribal mental health services.

Contents
Part One

Chapter One
**The History of Indian-Non-Indian
Relations and Its Impact on the
Mental Health of Tribal Communities**   25

Effects of Disease Epidemics 26
Treaties 26
Ethno-Centric Attitudes 28
Repeated Shifts in Federal Indian Policies 29
    Private Property and the Confiscation
    of Indian Land and Resources 30
    Indian Reorganization and the New Deal 31
    Termination and Relocation Policies of the 1950s . 32
    Tribal Resource Development and
    Self-Determination 33
    Recent Trends in Federal and
    State Indian Policies 35
Indian Child Welfare 37
    Removal of Indian Children from
    Families and Tribes 37
    The Indian Child Welfare Act 38
The Suppression of Indian Religion 40
Education of Indian Children
as a Means of Forced Acculturation 43

Removal of Indian Children to Boarding Schools .. 44
Public School Experiences 47
The Effects of the Introduction
of Alcohol to Indian Communities 49

Chapter Two
Interacting Problems Affecting the
Mental Health of Indian Communities   53

Stresses Placing Indian Communities
at Risk for Mental Health Problems 54
Interacting Mental Health Problems 55
The Triad of Depression, Alcohol Abuse
and Destructive "Acting Out" 56
   Depression 57
   Alcohol Abuse in Indian Communities 58
   Destructive "Acting Out" Behaviors 61
Problems Related to the Triad of Major
Disturbances 62
   Unresolved or Delayed Grief 63
   Sense of Personal Doom 64
   Suicide 66
   Violence 67
   Child Neglect 68
   School Problems 70
   Post Traumatic Stress Disorder 70
   Somatic Disturbance 71
   AIDS 71
   Personality Disorders 72
   Psychotic Conditions 73
Summary: Tribal Mental Health Problems
and Cultural Identity 74

Chapter Three
Intergenerational Trauma in the Tribal Community and Healing from Trauma 77

Intergenerational Trauma in the Tribal Community ... 77

Trauma: What It Is 78

    Child Abuse 81

    Sexual Abuse 81

    Damage Caused by Child Abuse 82

    Dissociation 83

    Negative Self Image 84

    Disturbances in Emotional Regulation
    and Self Injury 84

Patterns of Trauma Across Generations 86

Factors Determining the Impact of Trauma 87

Specific Trauma-Related Mental Health Problems 89

    Post-Traumatic Stress Disorder 90

    Dialectic of Trauma, Fragmentation of
    Experience and Memory Irregularities 93

    Borderline Personality Disorder 95

    Dissociative Disorders 96

    Complex Post Traumatic Stress Disorder 100

Mental Health Workers and
Secondary Traumatization 101

Healing From Trauma in Tribal Communities 102

    Giving Help After Acute Trauma 103

    Helping Children After Trauma 103

    Mental Health Treatment for
    Trauma Related Problems 104

        First Phase: Healing Relationship 104

        Middle Phase: Facing Trauma 106

        Final Phase: Reconnecting Mental Health
        Treatment for Children 110

    Traditional Treatments for Trauma 111

    Tribal Community-Wide Healing Process 113

Chapter Four
Barriers to Indian People Receiving Mainstream Mental Health Services   115

Barriers to Services 115

Chapter Five
Mental Health and Related Resources Currently Available to Indian Communities   121

Bureau of Indian Affairs Social Services 120

The Indian Health Service 121

The Community Mental Health System
and its Relationship to Indian Communities 124

History 125

Key Ideas Underlying a
Community Mental Health System 126

The Holistic Concept of Mental Health 126

Influences on Health 127

What We Mean by "Mental Health" and
"Mental Illness" 127

How the Community
Mental Health System Works 128

Types of Services Available From
Community Mental Health Centers 129

Crisis Services 129

Services for the Chronically Mentally Ill 130

Services for Severely Disturbed Clients 130

Funding for Community
Mental Health Programs 131

Community Mental Health Services
and Indian Communities 132

Traditional Healing Practices Relevant
to Mental Health Care 134

Diverse Funding for Tribally
Controlled Mental Health Programs 135

Community-Based Mental Health Initiative
for Indian People 135

Chapter One

The History of Indian-Non-Indian Relations and Its Impact on the Mental Health of Tribal Communities

T*hree centuries of trickery, theft, destructive and shifting governmental policies and racism have resulted in enormous destruction to tribal ways of life and, consequently, in widespread mental health-related problems among Indian people. In Washington state the picture is no less grim, although the time period involved is two rather than three hundred years.*

A basic knowledge of this history is a necessary background for mental health administrators and treatment personnel who wish to develop effective services for tribal communities. A full discussion of how historical factors influence the mental health status of Indian people is not possible here. Nevertheless, a brief review of the major events and trends in Indian-non-Indian relationships will orient the reader to the victimization, oppression and alienation experienced by Indian people in their relationship to the dominant society.

EFFECTS OF DISEASE EPIDEMICS

Even prior to the arrival of the first non-Indian explorers in the area which is now Washington State, a severe disease epidemic[1] had devastated the Indian population. Although the exact extent of the disaster is not known, it is clear that foreign diseases had greatly reduced the native population prior to the arrival of non-Indian settlers. This tragedy disrupted social, economic and ceremonial networks and left much of the Indian population stunned with loss.

The epidemic was probably spread from non-Indian traders to Indian traders who then brought the illness into the region along the Columbia River around 1790. As in other parts of the country, Indian people in what later became Washington and Oregon had no immunity to European diseases such as smallpox or cholera and therefore died at a much higher rate than non-Indians. *Estimates of the death toll in some villages in the area which is now Oregon and Washington are as high as 80 percent.*

The first non-Indian explorers and early settlers in the Northwest therefore encountered an Indian society not yet recovered from the effects of this staggering disaster. A second major epidemic swept the northwest around 30 years later, again taking a death toll estimated from between 30 to 70 percent of the Indian population.[2]

TREATIES

In 1846, the United States and Great Britain agreed that all territory below the 49th parallel (or what is now the U.S. Canadian border), would become the property of the United States. Not only was this done without the agreement of the Indian owners of what is now Washington state, it was done nine years previous to the Point Elliott Treaty of 1855, when several Puget Sound tribes ceded territory to the United States. Despite the irony of making a treaty with people whose land had already been claimed, the U.S. Government entered into six treaties with Indian people in Washington Territory between 1853 and 1868.

The effect of these treaties was that signatory Indian tribes relinquished their land in exchange for promises of reservations and a variety of other benefits to be provided by the federal government.

The history and consequences of treaties are a fundamental reality of Indian life. Treaties form the basis for legal protections of tribal property, resource rights, health and educational benefits, and for the sovereign status of tribes in relation to the federal government. Despite these advantages, treaties carry with them the legacy of deceit, loss of independence, failed promises and societal scapegoating.

The entire concept of a "treaty" was foreign to many Indian groups. Prior to the advent of the white population, the social and governmental organization of many Indian groups in the Northwest and elsewhere did not in reality conform to the European or American concept of a "tribe". Instead, large extended family groups maintained social, economic and ceremonial ties with a variety of other culturally similar groups. The rights of extended families, as well as of larger cultural groups, to territory and use of resources had become recognized and established through usage over time. Although some groups had hereditary headmen who were respected leaders, the social and political systems did not require a formal political or governmental structure.

Many tribal groups were forced to produce "chiefs" for the purpose of signing treaties with the federal government. "At the time of the Point Elliott Treaty of 1855, the United States government required each band to have a chief".[3]

Since many of the concepts of private property, title and governmental structures inherent in treaty negotiations were foreign to tribal representatives, it is easy to understand that some tribal treaty signers may not have had a clear understanding of what they were signing. In other cases treaty signers may not have actually had the right to represent an entire tribal group. Cases of purposeful manipulation of treaty negotiations by unscrupulous governmental representatives who offered Indian people large amounts of alcohol in the hopes of persuading them to sign were not unknown. A large proportion of treaty violations by Indian people took place either because these individuals had never in fact agreed to the treaty conditions or because they did not have a clear understanding of those conditions.

It is an established fact that the vast majority of treaty violations have been on the side of the U. S. government and of non-Indian settlers, rather than on the side of Indian people. In fact, the so-called "Indian wars" in western Washington between 1855 and 1859 were the direct consequence of "delays" in implementing the U. S. government's treaty obligations, as well as of repeated invasions of Indian territory by non-Indian settlers.

The ambivalence felt by many Indian people concerning treaties with the U. S. government can be easily appreciated. Treaties form the primary legal protection for tribal governmental and economic rights and, indirectly, for the protection of the Indian way of life. At the same time Indian people are acutely aware of the coercive and confusing circumstances surrounding the signing of many treaties. They have also had to contend with the repeated failures on the part of the U. S. government to fulfill their treaty obligations.

Often Indian people have found themselves in the position of having made enormous concessions of land and resources in exchange for restrictions of freedom, unwanted supervision and unfulfilled promises of enduring rights and benefits.

The unending need for Indian people to fight to receive even portions of their treaty rights has compounded the feelings of persecution and mistrust which many Indian people feel toward both federal and state government and toward mainstream American society in general. *Public lack of understanding, lack of support and often blatant hostility toward Indian treaty rights has been confusing and embittering to Indian people.*

ETHNO-CENTRIC ATTITUDES

In general, European and American society has held the opinion that their own way of life, values and institutions were superior to those of the Indian people, and that therefore they had some sort of inherent right to impose "civilization" on Indian people. To say that American society in general has lacked appreciation or respect for Indian culture and life ways is a gross understatement; in fact American society has in general assumed that the destruction of Indian culture was desirable and that the assimilation of Indian people into American society was inevitable.

The pervasiveness of this ethno-centric attitude has been so great that it is perhaps amazing that the United States government entered into treaties with Indian tribes at all. Certainly, it was and to some extent still is the view of the majority in American society that Indian culture should be obliterated and Indian people "saved", "educated", and "assimilated". The hostility underlying this assumed superiority is reflected in repeated official and unofficial attempts to annihilate the Indian race.[4]

The widespread American assumption that it was the "manifest destiny" of the United States to acquire and settle the entire American continent led to the passage of legislation in 1871 prohibiting any further treaties with Indian tribes. However, before that time the United States had entered into six treaties with Indian tribes in what is now the state of Washington, as well as many more treaties with tribes in other parts of the country. From the United States' point of view, these treaties paved the way for the settling of the northwest region and in fact large numbers of settlers poured into what is now the state of Washington during the 1860s and the 1870s.[5]

REPEATED SHIFTS IN FEDERAL INDIAN POLICIES

It has been said that the mainstream American society's attempt to assimilate or "civilize" Indian people has been pursued in three main ways: private property, education and religion (Hagan, 1961). To these could be added the introduction of alcohol, the removal of Indian children, and the systematic attacks on Indian languages. In all these realms, the mainstream society has generally assumed that American and European ways were not only superior to Indian ways, but were destined to prevail.

This underlying attitude has continually recurred, often resulting in the reversal or sabotage of those federal acts designed to uphold Indian treaty rights. The history of property and resource control, child welfare abuses, religious persecution, Indian educational policies, and introduction of alcohol must be examined in the context of periodic reversals in the direction of federal Indian policies.

Private Property and the Confiscation of
Indian Land and Resources

*The assumption that Indian people would either be extermi-
nated or assimilated into mainstream society was a convenient way
to justify taking their land. Indian people have been systematically
separated from their land through a variety of means both before
and after the signing of treaties. The widespread mainstream lack
of support for Indian treaty rights thinly masks a resentment of any
legal barrier to total absorption of Indian lands and resources.*

*Non-Indians have had enormous difficulty grasping the Indian
attitude towards land and resources: that each tribal group 'belongs' to a general area or tract of land which they hold in a sort of
sacred trust, but which they do not "own" per se, and therefore
cannot rightfully sell.* Land was traditionally used in common by
all members of the group without specific parcels being claimed
as the personal property of any individual.

This basic concept had proven workable for many generations of Indian society, based on each group acknowledging and
respecting the general territory of other groups. However, by the
mid 1800s it had become inescapably clear that non-Indians
would not respect Indian territorial customs. *Indian people signed
treaties with the explicit understanding that the treaties would protect at least a small portion of their land which would be in no way
further interfered with by non-Indian people.*

However, from the beginning, United States Indian policies
have been subject to bewildering inconsistencies and periodic
reversals. The invasion by non-Indian settlers into Indian land
actually increased following the signing of treaties. By the late
1880s, pressure from large numbers of settlers to acquire desirable
land in Washington Territory and elsewhere led to efforts to
break up the newly established reservations.

In 1887 the Dawes Act, also called the General Allotment Act,
was passed. The effect of this legislation was to break up the
reservations into individually owned parcels. Lands remaining
after this division were declared "surplus" and sold to non Indians, thereby greatly decreasing the tribal holdings.

The lack of vigorous Indian opposition to this movement was
due to the fact that most Indians did not understand either the
concept of private ownership nor the actual size of a 160 acre
parcel. Soon after this act, many Indian landowners were per-
suaded to either sell or lease their lands at very low figures. When

allottees died with many heirs, land was either divided into small sections or became practically unusable due to the difficulty of getting the consent of all heirs for use or sale.

In the period between the passage of the Dawes Act in 1887 and the passage of the Indian Reorganization Act in 1934, Indian people lost ownership and/or control over almost half of their remaining lands, usually the most desirable land. The division of tribal holdings into private property did a great deal to destroy the basic foundation of the communal lifestyle of Indian people.

Indian Reorganization and the "New Deal"

It was not until the 1920s that the attitudes of majority society toward Indian people began to shift. The outstanding record of Indian servicemen who volunteered during World War I6 (Indians were not subject to the draft, since they were not granted U.S. citizenship until 1924) led to increased popular concern for the welfare of Indian people. The federally commissioned "Meriam Report" in 1928 forcefully presented the devastating effects of forced acculturation on Indian society. The extreme poverty and severe health problems facing Indian people were publicly recognized. However, by that time the Indian death rate exceeded the birth rate, giving rise to the popular image of the "vanishing Indian".

Recognition of the disastrous failure of allotment policies led to a return in the 1930s to governmental policies supporting tribal community ownership of land and resources. Many remaining Indian lands were consolidated for tribal use and money was allotted for tribal purchase of lands.

The Indian Reorganization Act in 1934 gave increased power of choice to tribes and included provisions for tribal constitutions and business corporations. Tribes gained power of either approval or veto of disposition of tribal property and were authorized to take control of their own resources, to employ legal counsel and to negotiate with federal, state and local governments. *As Hagan (1961) points out, the most striking aspect of the Indian Reorganization Act is that the options it granted were not available to Indian people before 1934.*

During the 1930s and 1940s the loss of Indian lands was considerably slowed. Tribes began to develop more formal mechanisms for self government, including tribal incorporation and constitutions.

Termination and Relocation Policies of the 1950s

Developing mechanisms for Tribal self government were ham-pered when federal Indian policiies again took an abrupt shift in the 1950s with the era of "Termination". Essentially, the United States government attempted to end the special federal connection and responsibility towards Indian tribes.

Relocation of Indian people from rural reservations to urban areas was widely promoted as a method of speeding up the assimilation of Indian people into mainstream American life. Thousands of Indian people who were unable to find employ-ment on their home reservations were transported to urban areas where they were provided with minimal training and entry level jobs. However, little was done to assist these people in adjusting to the radically different urban lifestyle.

Language differences, social isolation and lack of familiarity with city life led to most relocated Indians returning to the reser-vation. Others remained in urban areas but developed serious and complex problems. Some Indian people merged into mainstream American society but relatively few were able to develop a satis-fying blend of Indian and mainstream beliefs and lifestyles. The assumption that the children of relocated workers would natu-rally disappear into American society has been shown to be plainly incorrect.[7]

The problems facing urban Indians in Washington State are eloquently addressed in the 1973 Report of the Governor's Indian Affairs Task Force, entitled The People Speak: Will You Listen? Lack of education, poverty and homesickness combined with discrimination on the part of the dominant society to cause fre-quent experiences of depression and isolation. Alcoholism in par-ticular became a major problem among relocated Indians in the cities.

A major aspect of the "termination" era was the movement to end federal responsibility forever for entire tribal groups. Lump sum monetary payments were offered to tribes in exchange for the tribes' accepting termination of their federally recognized tribal status. Although this was actually accomplished in only two cases, the threat of the complete withdrawal of federal trust and treaty responsibilities alarmed Indian people. *There was tre-mendous tribal resistance to this renewed attack upon tribal sover-eignty and Indian culture.*

Another major legal and political event of the termination era was the passage of Public Law 83-280. This law allowed states to impose their own civil and criminal laws upon tribes, thus overriding tribal codes and constitutions. The effect in some cases was an almost total repeal of the Indian Reorganization Act.

As one of the so-called "280 states", Washington claimed jurisdiction over a number of areas, including mental health, domestic relations, child welfare, juvenile delinquency, school attendance, and motor vehicles. Inconsistent federal laws as well as differing levels of tribal consent to state jurisdiction led to many confusing (and often still unresolved) legal situations. It had become clear to many Indian people that a transfer from federal to state jurisdiction represented a serious threat to Indian tribal survival.

Current jurisdictional circumstances vary widely between tribes even within the state of Washington. In some cases both the state and the tribe claim jurisdiction over the same matters. In other cases, the confusion has led to neither party actually exercising jurisdiction or providing services. Recent developments in the areas of child welfare and state recognition of tribal sovereignty have resolved some problems, but the unique situations of each tribe must be studied by those wishing to provide services to reservation communities.

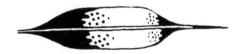

Tribal Resource Development and Self Determination

By the end of the 1950s federal policy had once again been revised to ensure that termination would not be forced upon tribes and that steps would be taken to protect land rights and cultural heritage.

During the 1960s federal policy began to place more emphasis upon tribal economic development. Attempts were made to locate light industry on reservations and to provide tribal governments with loans in order to establish tribally owned enterprises. However, during the 1960s the reservation Indian population began to increase approximately twice as rapidly as the average American population. Most reservations did not have adequate transportation, raw materials or power to attract industry or provide employment for the growing number of Indian workers. For the most part, reservation life continued to be marked by serious poverty and low employment.

The history of periodic reversals of federal policy, the partial transfer of jurisdiction from federal to state authorities, and the more than 5,000 statutes and treaties relating to Indian issues all combined to produce an enormously confusing legal situation. This made it easy for unscrupulous or uninformed non-Indians to disregard tribal rights to natural resources.

Confusion concerning state as opposed to federal or tribal jurisdiction was nowhere more painfully felt than in the serious disputes which arose which concerning fishing and hunting rights in Washington State.

Tribes, who had endured the repeated failures of the federal government and non-Indian society to honor past promises and who had survived the threat of termination during the 1950s, became both angered and organized over systematic attacks on fishing rights. The traditional and ongoing importance of salmon fishing in Northwest Indian economic and cultural life made fishing rights a natural rallying point for many Indian tribes.

By the end of the 1960s the pendulum had again swung in the direction of protecting tribal sovereignty. In 1974, both Public Law 93-638, called the "Indian Self-Determination Act", and the Boldt Decision in Washington state favorably affected tribal status. These legal events have had far-reaching implications for Indian people.

The Indian Self-Determination Act formally reversed the termination policies of the 1950s and greatly strengthened tribal control over programs and resources. Since 1975 this act has resulted in enormous growth in tribal capacity to develop and manage resources and in the development of a wide range of tribally-run and administered programs. Similarly, the Boldt Decision reaffirmed and defined treaty fishing rights which was of paramount importance in strengthening the economic situation of many tribal families.

Unfortunately the Boldt Decision has been a source of enormous controversy between Indian people and non-Indian commercial and sport fishermen. The lack of understanding and support by large segments of the non-Indian community has had repercussions for relationships between Indian people and the local non-Indian communities. Indian people once again found themselves in the position of having to defend their treaty-given rights to an unsympathetic majority of non-Indian society.

The fishing controversy further polarized the Indian and non Indian communities in parts of Washington State and left most Indian people convinced that only a careful and continuous watch can prevent their rights being further transgressed.

Recent Trends in Federal and State Indian Policies Toward Tribal Self Governance

The bewildering shifts in United States Policy toward Native American Sovereignty created an atmosphere of instability and distrust. Despite the gains of the 1970s in recognizing the rights of Native communities to control tribal property and resources, Indian people did not forget the long history of bad faith. Indications during the 1980's that the administration might be preparing to step back from federal trust responsibilities did nothing to reassure Indian people that the government would uphold tribal rights to Sovereignty.

Happily, over the past decade, positive trends have predominated. In Washington State, a Centennial Accord was signed in 1989 by Governor Gardner and a number of Indian Tribes. Partially in reaction to the anti Boldt decision backlash, this Accord reaffirmed the Government to Government relationship existing between Tribes and the State of Washington. The Accord requires the state Department of Social and Health Services to cooperate with Tribes in all areas of service, including mental health. With tribal input, DSHS developed statewide policies concerning how services are to be provided to Indian people. The Governor's office under Governor Locke instituted a "701" planning requirement. This specified annual meetings with each tribe to review policy and plans for service delivery. Plans are updated yearly.

The 701 requirement has also led to monthly meetings in Northwestern Washington between representatives of eight local tribes and the Tribal Liaison Officer of the North Sound Regional Support Network (RSN) for mental health services which are funded by the Washington State Department of Mental Health. These meetings have brought about much increased understanding and cooperation. Of particular importance, they have resulted in two successful Tribal Mental Health conferences sponsored by the RSN with major tribal input. These have been enormously well received, and it is hoped that they will become an annual event. *The RSN has been actively supportive of tribal efforts to improve mental health services to tribal members.*

Another area positively impacted by the Centennial Accord is Indian Child Welfare Services (see below). DSHS is required to work closely with tribal Child Welfare programs to ensure that the provisions of the Indian Child Welfare Act are met.

In addition, both the State Department of Alcohol and Substance Abuse and Juvenile Justice funding have been made available to allow tribes to design and implement culturally oriented prevention programs. (examples of such programs at the Swinomish Tribe are discussed in Part Three, Chapter Thirteen).

In 1992, Tribal Self Governance was further expanded with the beginning of "Compacting" agreements between the Federal Government and tribes. "Compacts of Self Governance" are intended "to transfer to the tribe the power to decide how federal programs, services, functions and activities .... shall be funded and carried out". They are intended to "strengthen the Government to Government Relationship and to uphold the United States' Trust responsibilities for the Tribe. (quoted from the "Compact of Self Governance Between the Swinomish Indian Community and the united States of America, April 1, 1997, Amended and Restated on January 1, 2002").

Many tribes have elected to enter into compacts which allow them to take over control of Indian Health Service Funds from which they derive benefit. Funding agreements are negotiated on a yearly basis which allow "reprogramming" of Indian Health Service funds at the Headquarters, Area and Service Unit levels to be redirected to allow expansion of tribally controlled direct health care services, including mental health. (see Chapter Thirteen for more information concerning tribally controlled health care services).

One negative note is that the long awaited Indian Health Care Improvement Act has remained pending in Congress for the past two years.

On the whole, it is clear that the era of Indian Self Determination is on the rise.

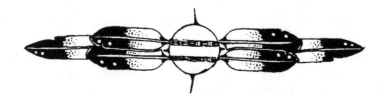

Four other aspects of the history of the relationship between Indian and non-Indian society have direct bearing upon the current mental health status of Indian people. Indian child welfare practices, religious persecution, destructive educational practices and the introduction of alcohol to Indian communities have each contributed to the problems facing Indian people today. Each of the these topics is briefly addressed below. While these topics will be further discussed in other sections, some understanding of these historical issues is needed in order to gain a beginning perspective concerning Indian and non-Indian relations.

INDIAN CHILD WELFARE

Removal of Indian Children from Families and Tribes.

The 1970s saw the passage of the Indian Child Welfare Act, PL 95-608. This crucial piece of legislation was designed to stem the flow of Indian children out of Indian homes and tribal communities. Prior to the passage of this act, the out-of-home placements of Indian children in foster care or adoptive homes was far greater than was true of non-Indian children. In Washington State, the adoption rate for Indian children was in fact 19 times that of non-Indian children.[8]

Prejudice against Indian lifestyles and lack of understanding of Indian religious systems and family networks led to systematically damaging practices by state caseworkers and non Indian court systems nationwide. Poverty of Indian families was often interpreted as sufficient cause for the removal of Indian children. Removals were made frequently without sufficient cause and without prior attempts to provide remedial alternatives.

Indian parents, unfamiliar with the state legal system, often were confused and frightened. They were rarely provided with adequate legal assistance. Indian children in foster care were legally freed for adoption at a far higher rate than non-Indian children. Many child placement agencies, caseworkers and special interest groups followed extremely unethical practices in coercing parents to place Indian children or relinquish them for adoption. In fact, certain religious groups made it an explicit policy to attempt to remove and "save" as many Indian children as possible.[9]

The massive removal of Indian children from their families and tribes was devastating not only to the integrity of Indian families and to the psychological and cultural identity of these children, but also to the vitality of entire Indian tribes. Despite their status as sovereign entities, tribes were denied any mechanism for monitoring the welfare and placement of tribal children.

It is important to point out that most Indian children placed in non-Indian homes did not make a good adjustment. *Far from providing these children with an improved chance for a "better life", non-Indian foster care and adoption has generally produced frustrated, confused and angry young Indians without a clear sense of belonging to either Indian or to non-Indian culture. Many developed serious social and emotional difficulties. An unusually large proportion of these adoptions have had to be legally terminated.*

Many adopted Indian children lost educational, health, fishing, enrollment or other rights. Adopted Indian children often grew up not knowing what tribe they were from or even whether or not they were Indian. This greatly hurt their chances of reintegrating with their tribal communities and functioning successfully as Indian adults.

The history of removal of Indian children is one of the factors contributing most strongly to the suspicion, fear and hostility with which many Indian adults view non-Indian caseworkers and other state authorities. Although hard data are not available, clinical experience suggests that the majority of Indian families have lost one or more children to the non-Indian child welfare system. Consequently, most Indian people have personal reasons for feeling that the involvement of state child welfare agencies with Indian children should be strictly monitored, and that control over child welfare and child custody should be maintained within tribal communities.

The Indian Child Welfare Act

The pain and grief of Indian people about the destruction of Indian family life led to political activity, much of which was centered in Washington state. The result was the passage of the federal Indian Child Welfare Act in 1978.

The Indian Child Welfare (ICW) Act provides a series of unprecedented protections for Indian children, families and tribes. The act enables tribes to exercise jurisdiction

over child welfare matters. Even when tribes do not choose to exercise exclusive jurisdiction, the act provides for tribal monitoring of child welfare matters at each crucial stage. Removal of Indian children was made more difficult. Standards of proof for establishing dependency or termination of parental rights were made stricter. Placement preferences giving priority to extended family and tribal members were legislated and careful review mechanisms were specified.

The Indian Child Welfare Act also provides the legal basis for congressional appropriation of funds to assist tribes in developing and operating child welfare programs. These funds are administered by the Bureau of Indian Affairs and awarded to tribes on a competitive basis.

Unfortunately, the funding level for these programs has never been adequate to meet the need. In spite of this, many tribes have developed successful programs which have done much toward reversing the flow of Indian children out of tribal communities, strengthening Indian families and developing tribally-based alternatives for Indian children in need of care.

A significant recent development in Washington State (as in some other states) has been the negotiation and signing of a state-wide Tribal-State agreement for the provision of child welfare services to Indian children. The agreement affirms and strengthens the Federal Indian Child Welfare Act and provides for a number of changes in the Washington State Department of Children and Family Services' involvement with tribes and Indian Children. *Tribal Mental Health providers should be familiar with this agreement as well as with local plans for implementation.*

THE SUPPRESSION OF INDIAN RELIGION

Misunderstanding of Indian ways and ethnocentric assumptions about the superiority of white culture have led to both active persecution and ongoing misunderstanding of Indian religious and spiritual practices. Few early settlers took the opportunity to learn about Indian religion. Instead, they projected their own fears and 'cultural demons' upon Indians, assuming that practices they did not understand were devil worship, ignorance or black magic.

Most non-Indians did not, and still do not, have any appreciation for the multiplicity and subtle complexity of Indian spiritual systems. Indian spirituality pervades many aspects of Indian culture. For thousands of years it has provided Indian people with a deeply spiritual outlook on life. These spiritual practices embody a deep contemplation of nature and the meaning of life and death and provide a set of socially constructive values by which Indian people traditionally conduct their lives.

Early in the history of Indian-non-Indian relations, Indians were visited by Christian missionaries from competing sects. Although some of these individuals meant well and appeared genuinely concerned for the welfare of Indian people, they were blind to the value of Indian religious ways, to their own ethnocentrism and to the damage caused by their missionary activities. *These missionaries told Indian people that they were "primitive", "ignorant", "heathen" and "doomed". They took advantage of the technological superiority of non-Indian culture to persuade Indian people that 'God was on their side'. Many Indian people were publicly "converted" early on, but still practiced and believed in Indian ways.*

Early Native American skepticism toward Christianity was fueled by competition and conflicts between the missionaries themselves. Catholics and Protestants of various denominations presented different versions of the truth, clearly disapproved of one another and competed for Indian converts. Indian attitudes toward this situation were summarized by Chief Joseph, who refused to allow missionary work among his people. *"They will teach us to quarrel about God as the Catholics and Protestants do....we may quarrel with men sometimes about things on this earth, but we never quarrel about God. We do not want to learn to do that."*[10] Which Christian denomination became established at which reservation was largely a matter of historical chance.

Non-Indian society struck two severe blows at traditional Indian religion:

1. The outlawing of the practice of Indian religion.

2. The religious indoctrination of Indian children in boarding schools and non-Indian foster and adoptive homes.

In the late 1800s it was made illegal for Indians to practice any aspect of traditional religions, spiritual dances or healing practices. The fact that this law was in direct violation of the constitutional right to worship after one's own manner was entirely overlooked. Courts of "Indian offenses" were established specifically in order to combat Indian religious ways. Indians were not only fined, but were actually jailed for such "offenses" as possessing traditional spiritual regalia or participating in a traditional dance. Indian police were used as spies to report such activities. Indian people who believed in traditional ways were made to feel guilty, primitive and evil.

The result of this persecution was that the practice of traditional Indian spiritual ways went underground. Indian elders still alive today remember having to practice spiritual and religious activities in hiding. Windows were darkened with blankets and only trusted friends were informed about the location of houses where traditional spiritual activities would be performed.

Many Indian children during this period grew up with very confused feelings and ideas about religion. Some Indian children were not able to develop an understanding of the real meaning of traditional ways: they often had a confused picture of the nature of Indian religious practices, pieced together from the comments of their elders, the secretive practices of their families and the negative propaganda taught them in the schools. In particular, children who were sent away to boarding schools or foster care were made to feel guilty about their families' traditional practices.

The suppression of Indian religion led to the loss of much valuable traditional knowledge. Indians who preserved spiritual knowledge became extremely reluctant to reveal what they knew, and sometimes even that they knew "anything" at all.

One of the particularly negative results of religious persecution was the loss of much medical and healing knowledge. Indian people have traditionally viewed spiritual well being as closely connected to physical, emotional, and social well being. Indian people have long had traditional ways of treating physical as well as spiritual problems; experts skilled in the treatment of physical problems were usually spiritual healers as well. Therefore, attacks on Indian religion also hurt Indian healing systems.

It was in the general context of persecution of traditional Indian religious practices that the Indian Shaker Church was born. The Indian Shaker Church (which has nothing to do with the New England Shakers), developed out of the vision and religious experience of a southern Puget Sound Indian man and wife, John and Mary Slocum. The Shaker Church combines Christian beliefs with many traditional Indian elements. In particular, the Shaker Church has a strong healing tradition. The Shaker Church provided many Indian converts in the Northwest with a way of following Christianity while still preserving their sense of Indian identity and cultural independence. Other uniquely Indian forms of Christianity have developed in other parts of the United States. (See section on Indian Shaker Church, Ch. 10, P. 271.)

Despite pressures to abandon traditional Indian spiritual practices, many beliefs and practices have not died out. They continue to be practiced, to be taught and to affect the world view and value systems of many, if not most Indian people.

Although "legal" persecution was gradually lessened from about 1935 onwards, the ban on the practice of Indian religion was not officially repealed until the passage of the Indian Freedom of Religion Act in 1978. By the middle of the Century much damage had been done. Some Indians had become ashamed of their Indian ways or had lost confidence in their traditions. Many others had learned that it was not safe to share their beliefs and experiences with non-Indians.

Most Indians combined some belief in traditional ways with the practice of Christian religion. A slow and cautious recovery of traditional practices began in the 1930s and 1940s. Then in the 1960s and 1970s there was a burst of renewed interest and participation in traditional Indian spiritual practices. It may be that the general political and social climate of the times, including the movement toward tribal self-determination, may have offered an atmosphere in which suppressed but still strong Indian spirituality could again flourish.

Today, Indian people are highly varied in their spiritual beliefs and religious convictions. Some are Catholics, some Protestants, some Bahai, and some Shakers. Others follow only traditional Indian spiritual practices. A large number, perhaps a majority, are involved in some combination of traditional Indian and Christian religion. (See Ch. 10)

Although to some degree these religious differences tend to fragment the Indian community, this is less true than might be expected by those not familiar with Indian society. Unlike mainstream Christians, most Indians are very tolerant of differences in belief systems and are quite willing to respect the right of others to worship in a way different from their own. *Indian people as a group have been remarkably successful in combining the new and the old in a manner which remains distinctly Indian.*

The history of religious oppression has left a bitter taste. Most Indian people are well aware of the antagonism of non-Indian society toward their spiritual ways. Many Indian people do not feel comfortable discussing any aspect of traditional Indian spirituality with non-Indians. Religious persecution has contributed to the stresses and mental health difficulties of Indian people. Repeated misunderstanding have also made it difficult for Indian people to trust non-Indian counselors or therapists.

One positive note was struck in 1987 when the Church Council of Greater Seattle wrote a formal letter of apology to all Indian people, admitting the past insensitivity of Christian churches and pledging future support for Indian religious freedom.

EDUCATION OF INDIAN CHILDREN AS A MEANS OF FORCED ACCULTURATION

One of the treaty rights granted to Indian people was an "education" for their children. It is doubtful whether many Indian treaty signers understood what was intended by this provision. Certainly Indian people have reason to question whether what they have received in the realm of education has been to their benefit. Without a doubt the treaty signers had no intention of giving the federal government the right to forceably remove Indian children from their parents and place them in distant boarding schools. Indian people certainly never agreed to an education which would attempt to eradicate their language, beliefs and values and replace these with those of the foreign, though dominant, white society.

Removal of Indian Children to Boarding Schools

The United States government seized upon their treaty obligation to provide Indian children with an education as an opportunity to pursue forced acculturation.[11] The Bureau of Indian Affairs (which had been recently transferred from the War Department into the Department of the Interior) was given responsibility for educating Indian children. During the last quarter of the 19th century and first half of the 20th century, the philosophy of education as acculturation was pursued by:

- forceably separating Indian children from their families and tribes
- placing Indian children in residential schools dedicated to de-Indianizing and Americanizing them
- prohibiting even non-English speaking children from speaking their own languages or using their own Indian names
- separating children who spoke the same language or were from the same tribe
- requiring participation in Christian religious practices
- forcing children to wear non-Indian clothes and hairstyles
- physically punishing evidences of Indian cultural orientation (such as being caught speaking Indian languages, following Indian spiritual practices, etc.)
- teaching Indian children subjects which bore no relation to their experience or culture

The BIA educational system was the main arm of federal acculturation policies. "Where cultural values conflicted, the superiority of the Bible, the primer and the plow were never questioned by whites and no attempt was made to compromise with Indian tradition" (Hagan, op. cit., p. 91). "...Indian Service Personnel generally agreed that a complete break with the home environment was desirable...youths were encouraged to shed their tribal culture as a relic of the past." Boarding schools were run like penal institutions. They were overcrowded and understaffed. Courses had little relation to Indian life. "If the student did not adapt to the school routine he was miserable; if he adapted he was miserable when he returned to his family" (Hagan, op. cit., p. 135).

It is no wonder that many Indian parents resisted sending their children away to boarding schools for months or years on end. Some parents hid their children.[12]. The BIA responded by denying food rations to uncooperative parents. In many cases "agency police were used to virtually kidnap children for schools" (Hagan, op. cit., p. 137).

One reason for parental resistance was the abnormally high death rate of Indian children in BIA boarding schools.[13] Although provided with minimally adequate physical care and nutrition, *many of these children were desperately lonely, frightened and suffering from acute culture shock at having to give up everything that they had known. Upon arrival, children were showered, de-loused, given haircuts and told not to speak Indian languages. These stressful experiences no doubt contributed to the high rate of depression, illness and death.*

Boarding schools were major agents in the loss of Indian languages. Children who were caught speaking Indian languages were rapped on the knuckles or made to stand in corners with rags tied around their mouths. Many children forgot their languages or became ashamed to even admit that they knew them.

Language is the major carrier of culture. Ideas and experiences are often not translatable between languages. A peoples' world view, beliefs and values are reflected in and inextricably embedded in their speech. When the language is lost, a great deal of the culture is lost also. Many things cannot be fully translated. With the words, sounds and rhythm of native speech goes the heart of the culture. *Nothing has done more to weaken Indian culture than attacks on Indian languages made in B.I.A. boarding schools.*

The effects on Indian society in general of the forced removal of children to boarding schools is only now being fully recognized. Children began to change in ways that their parents and grandparents could not understand, and often returned for vacations home expressing serious identity confusion. *Some children became ashamed of being Indian and bitterly disowned the values and lifestyle of their families. Others became rebellious, distrustful, withdrawn or depressed.*

Parents suffered from grief and worry over the fate of their children. They often felt helpless or guilty about not being able to protect their children. *Parents were denied the right to raise their own children in their own way and often missed out on virtually all of their children's childhood years. Deprived of their children and of the parenting roles, many families became less stable.* Elders were not able to pass on important family teachings. Some Indian people have suggested that the removal of children to boarding schools contributed to the increase in adult alcoholism on the reservations.

Many Indian children who spent their formative years in boarding schools grew up unable to fit comfortably into either Indian or non-Indian society. These children had essentially lost their parents and the chance of a normal family life. They had been subjected to rigorous discipline combined with attacks on their personal and cultural identity, and denied nurturing relationships with any adults. These children, well aware that they were different from their white teachers, had no adult role models with whom to identify. Sometimes they did not see an Indian adult from September til June. Many Indian children learned to "toughen up" and to expect that their emotional needs would never be met.

When and if these children returned to their tribes, they often had difficulty fitting into a family and tribal life which they did not completely understand. Having been denied normal Indian childhood experiences and role models, they were delayed in their social and emotional development as Indian people.14 A large number of these children developed severe problems in adulthood, such as alcoholism, depression or violent behavior.

One lasting consequence of the boarding school experience has been an upsurge in child neglect and a cycle of removal of successive generations of Indian children from their parents. Young Indian parents who had been virtually reared in boarding schools did not learn from their own families how to raise children. In particular, they received the non-verbal message that Indian people could not be good parents.

Alienated, angry and depressed, these young parents often were unprepared to care for children and to provide their own children with nurturing they had not received themselves. Although the Indian tradition of multiple adult caretakers for all children in the family has been extremely helpful in many cases, it is an inescapable fact of Indian life that entire generations of parents (now for the most part people in their late middle years) were denied the experience of a normal Indian family life.[15]

By the 1960s most authorities had realized that removing young children from their families had been a terrible mistake. It was also recognized that the education of Indian children needed to bear more relationship to the kinds of lives they would be liable to lead in the tribal community. States began to assume greater responsibility for the education of the Indian children, many of whom now attended public schools. In select cases, Tribes developed their own reservation-based schools.

Although BIA-run boarding schools still exist, they are fewer and are attended by a far smaller proportion of Indian children. Younger children are seldom sent to boarding schools. Frequently, children in boarding schools are those with serious family or behavior problems. However, *many Indian parents and grandparents alive today have bitter memories of boarding school experiences, which are inevitably conveyed to younger family members.*

Public School Experiences

Difficulties facing Indian children in the educational system have not been limited to BIA boarding schools. Indian students in the public school system have often faced prejudice from both teachers and from non-Indian students. They have been placed in the position of being directly compared with non-Indian students, many of whom come from homes with more money, more material possessions, better educated parents and a greater emphasis upon academic achievement. Often Indian students are not prepared to compete academically, either because of a less verbal orientation, less exposure to analytic problem-solving tasks or because of culturally-based disapproval of competition itself. *Indian children are taught at home to cooperate, listen respectfully without asking questions, and to not stand out from their peer group. They naturally feel bewildered and insecure when suddenly faced with an almost opposite set of expectations and requirements for success in the public school system.*

Although Indian children often do quite well in the early grades, they begin to fall behind their peers in third or fourth grade. By about sixth grade, many Indian children are below grade level, especially in areas such as reading and writing, which emphasize verbal skills.

Children at this age become acutely aware of cultural, racial and lifestyle differences. In addition, many Indian children find the versions of American history offered in the schools to be upsetting and alienating. For instance, Indian children in fishing communities in Washington state have often had to bear the brunt of non-Indian resentment over the 1974 Boldt Decision. *Lack of Indian oriented curriculum as well as lack of sensitive adaptation to different learning styles further alienate Indian students.*

One factor in the difficulty faced by Indian students is the lack of understanding on the part of school authorities of their home life and culture, as well as a lack of understanding on the part of their parents concerning the nature of their school experience. *Teachers often have little knowledge, respect or interest in Indian life ways and may convey the unconscious attitude that Indian ways are inferior to white ways.*

Indian parents, while verbally encouraging their children to get an education, may also convey a distrust and discomfort with the school system, based on their own childhood experiences with an insensitive educational system. Parents with a limited education may be unable to help their children with homework, may feel threatened when children learn things which they themselves do not understand, and may not appreciate the need for regular and quiet homework time.

Indian students caught between these two divergent sets of expectations often find no place for themselves. Frequently they become discouraged, angry and self destructive.

Indian teenagers in particular must not only grapple with identity issues common to all teens, but must also develop a clear cultural identity which somehow reconciles their history, family, lifestyle and cultural values with the mainstream values and the expectations which the school system presents to them.

Many Indian teens go through a period of rebellion against both Indian and non-Indian values and authorities. Such students may become involved with drugs, alcohol or other negative activities. An alarming number of Indian students drop out of school before completing high school. Estimates of the drop out rate in Washington state vary from 60 to 80 percent, with many leaving school by tenth grade.[16]

In some areas new programs and new attitudes are beginning to result in positive changes in this bleak educational picture. Enlightened and committed tribes and school districts are exploring new ways to bridge the cultural gaps through cooperative programs of cross-cultural exploration, communication between Indian parents and teachers and between tribal staff, tribal government, teachers and school administrators.

These programs, although far too few, demonstrate the possibility of constructive collaboration. Cooperative efforts require a great deal of hard work. They are necessary in order to reverse a century and a half of disastrous educational policies and disastrous oversights.

THE EFFECTS OF THE INTRODUCTION OF ALCOHOL TO INDIAN COMMUNITIES

It is important to see current problems caused by alcohol abuse in Indian communities in historical perspective. Alcohol not only causes severe problems in modern Indian life, it was also a tool of conquest and of cultural destruction.

With few exceptions, North American Indian peoples were unfamiliar with alcoholic beverages prior to encountering white traders. Indian people had no idea what to expect when they drank alcoholic beverages, and Indian society had no established norms for acceptable drinking behavior.[17]

Some of the earliest Indian experiences with alcohol took place during trade negotiations. Unscrupulous traders often plied Indians with strong alcohol, hoping to make advantageous trade deals. Many young Indian men found the experience of intoxication to be exciting. Some found that alcohol allowed a release of inhibitions and frustrations. Others at first thought that alcohol produced supernatural or divine experiences.

Almost from the beginning, Indian leaders recognized the dangers of alcohol and became alarmed by the irresponsible behavior caused by intoxication. Indian leaders tried repeatedly to stop the sale of alcohol to Indian people. In 1832, Congress first prohibited liquor traffic to Indian people, but this attempt to curb the availability of alcohol was for the most part a failure. *In 1902, it became illegal to sell any alcoholic beverage to Indian people either on or off reservation. This law remained in force for over 50* years.

Despite the ban on sale of alcohol to Indian people, problems with drinking steadily increased. Indian people faced enormous social, financial and personal problems, which tended to result in anger, frustration and depression. These problems increased the vulnerability of many Indian people to drinking related problems. Many Indian people also resented the prohibition on drinking, feeling this to be a further instance of prejudice, oppression and paternalism. Consequently, some Indians drank simply in order to defy the prohibition. Adolescents and young adults were particularly prone to rebel by drinking whenever the opportunity presented itself.

One consequence of the prohibition against Indian drinking was the development of a particularly negative drinking pattern. Indians who drank illegally and under the threat of discovery tended to drink quickly, gulping their drinks and consuming all of the available alcohol.[18] *A pattern was established of drinking for drinking's sake, of drinking associated with anger and rebellion, of drinking large quantities and of drinking with the goal of becoming intoxicated.*

Several aspects of Indian culture also influenced the patterns of alcohol use which developed during this period. Indian people have always valued sharing and group activities. Food and resources are generally shared with family and friends. When individuals have something special, or more than they need of something, they invite friends and family to share it with them. Group gatherings are also occasions for celebration.

The drinking of alcoholic beverages was naturally incorporated into traditional cultural patterns. Alcohol became seen as something special which one shared with friends and which could not be refused without risk of offense. When applied to alcohol, the cultural values of sharing, gift giving and group togetherness rapidly led to widespread and dangerous patterns of drinking.

Two other historical developments contributed to the spread of alcoholism among Indian people. During World War I, Indian soldiers who could not obtain alcohol at home often learned to drink heavily. Similarly, alcoholism became common among Indians sent to the cities through relocation programs. Self-destructive drinking patterns took root in Indian society, interacting in complex ways with the cultural breakdown and other social problems facing Indian communities.

In 1953, the federal ban on sale of alcohol to Indians was finally lifted. However, rather than improving the general situation, the sudden easy availability of alcohol both on and off reservations led to a further increase in alcohol abuse.

Some authorities have suggested a genetic basis to the apparently very high vulnerability to alcoholism among Indian people. Various inherited physical mechanisms have been proposed such as the lack of an enzyme in the liver necessary to efficiently metabolize alcohol. While it is not clearly established whether or not such an inherited factor may contribute to Indian drinking problems, it is certainly clear that the lack of cultural norms for 'social' drinking, combined with the enormous stresses inherent in Indian life are sufficient to place Indian people at high risk for alcohol-related problems.

Notes and References

1. Probably smallpox

2. See records of the Hudson's Bay Company for 1800-1830

3. Collins, June, *Valley of the Spirits*, 1974 p. 37

4. Anyone doubting the stark truth of this assertion is referred to any of a number of excellent texts which recount the history of the official United States policy towards Indian people, such as Brown, Dee, *Bury My Heart At Wounded Knee*; Hagan, William, *The American Indian*; Jackson, *A Century of Dishonor*; LaFarge, Oliver, *As Long As The Grass Shall Grow*.

5. *The People Speak: Will You Listen?*, Report of the Governor's Indian Affairs Task Force, 1973

6. Indians were not subject to the draft, nor were they U.S. citizens until 1924

7. *The People Speak: Will You Listen?*, Report of the Governor's Indian Affairs Task Force, 1973

8. Byler, William, "The Destruction of Indian Families," in Unger, Steven, *The Destruction of American Indian Families*, Association of American Indian Affairs, New York, 1977

9. Todd, Goldie Denny, "Indian Child Welfare", in *Indian and Alaska Native Mental Health Seminars*, Seattle Indian Health Board, 1982, p. 489

10. Hagan, T. *The American Indian*, 1966 p. 128

11. Meriam, Lewis, "The Problem of Indian Administration; 1928, p. 573-577. Bergman, Robert, "The Human Cost of Removing Indian Children from Their Families", in Unger, Steven, *The Destruction of American Indian Families*, Association of American Indian Affairs, New York, 1977

12. Coolidge, Dane, "Kid Catching" on the Navajo Reservation: 1930, in Unger, op. cit, 1977

13. Meriam, op. cit., 1928

14. Attneave, Carolyn, "The Wasted Strengths of Indian Families," in Unger, op. cit., 1977

15. Hollow, Walt, "Health and Mental Health", in *Indian and Alaska Native Mental Health Seminars*, Seattle Indian Health Board, 1982, p. 263

16. Swinomish Tribal Specific Health Plan, 1985

17. Weber, Richard, 'Alcoholism in the Indian Community', in *Indian and Alaska Native Mental Health Seminars*, Seattle Indian Health Board, 1982, p. 825-826

18. Weber, Richard, op. cit. p.826

Chapter Two

Interacting Problems Affecting The Mental Health Of Indian Communities

P erhaps the most serious problem facing tribal communities today is the insidious breakdown of Indian culture. Historical theft of Indian lands, outlawing of Indian spiritual practices, the massive removal of Indian children from their families, and the introduction of alcohol have all contributed to cultural loss, and have made it difficult for young Indian people to develop a healthy cultural identity. Many native languages have been lost. The imposition of non-Indian values has weakened traditional Indian culture and thereby jeopardized individual psychological health.

This chapter explores the range of mental health problems in Indian Communities, with particular attention given to the factor of cultural identity. It is suggested that a triad of depression, alcohol abuse and destructive "acting out" exists in which these problems tend to co-occur and are related to disturbances of cultural identity.

A related model for understanding a range of mental health problems is presented in Chapter Three, "Intergenerational trauma in tribal Communities." These two chapters complement one another, such that we suggest that they be read together.

STRESSES PLACING INDIAN COMMUNITIES AT RISK

Severe life stresses place Indian people at a high risk for a range of mental health problems. On a national level, Indian communities are affected by very high levels of poverty (reported at between 30-90 percent), unemployment (13-40 percent), accidental death (three times the national rate), alcoholism (30-80 percent), domestic violence, teen pregnancies, child neglect and suicide (2 times the national rate). At the Swinomish Tribe, 8 of every 13 students drop out of high school.[19] *Nationally, Indian people have the lowest educational level of any minority group.*[20] *The majority of Indian adults have not graduated from high school or obtained a GED.*

These tragic circumstances pose an obvious threat to individual and family stability. A typical Indian child is born to young parents who are high school dropouts, have little money, no jobs and poor job prospects. Such parents are prone to unhappiness, marital conflict and alcohol abuse. Children often suffer from poverty and are exposed at an early age to alcoholism, accidental death and frequent parental absence. Indian children are at a much higher risk for foster placement or adoption. *By age five, many Indian children have experienced significant losses or other traumatic life events which increase their risk for both childhood and adult psychiatric disorder.*

By the time Indian children enter public school they are frequently behind non-Indian children in academic skills, and are often labeled as learning delayed or disabled. As discussed in the previous section, Indian children often find the public school system to be foreign and confusing. Subtle prejudice on the part of school staff and other children is particularly damaging to the emotional well being of Indian children. These problems result in Indian children completing high school much less often than non-Indians, and increase the likelihood that they will continue the cycle of depression, problem drinking and unstable family life.

The "spiral of failure"[21] *described above results in Indian people experiencing high levels of emotional and social disturbance. Children, young adults and elders each have special needs which require culturally sensitive approaches.*

INTERACTING MENTAL HEALTH PROBLEMS

There is a substantial level of unmet need for mental health services in tribal communities.

Mental health problems in Indian communities are characterized by:
- **multiple and interacting family, financial, physical, legal and psychological problems**
- **acute symptoms often being masked by related problems (such as alcoholism, delinquency, violence or physical illness)**
- **diagnosis being complicated by different cultural values and symptom patterns**
- **the pervasiveness of depression in Indian communities**
- **a tendency to experience emotional and psychological problems as either physical illness or as caused by external stress only**
- **a high prevalence of chronic Post Traumatic Stress Disorder.**

Mental health problems in Indian communities tend to interact with one another, creating complicated situations which are difficult to resolve. Alcoholism and its longterm effects of family dysfunction have often been called the number one problem in Indian communities. Depression is the mental health problem seen most frequently in Indian communities, and alcoholism frequently complicates depression. Violence has also been clearly shown to be associated with alcohol abuse.[22] Furthermore, it has been demonstrated (DeBruyn, Hymbaugh and Valdez[23]) that chronic mourning, frustration, denial and hopelessness are associated with violence. Suicide, grief over tragic deaths, child abuse and family breakup are also frequently mentioned as interacting problems.

Recently, many authorities have begun to see psychological disturbances in Indian communities as not unlike the pattern of numbness, stimulus overload, preoccupation and hopelessness experienced by war veterans with chronic "post traumatic stress disorder." This model for understanding mental health problems in tribal communities is discussed in detail in chapter 3.

THE TRIAD OF DEPRESSION, ALCOHOL ABUSE AND DESTRUCTIVE "ACTING OUT"

In the Skagit Tribes' Mental Health Program, we have found that *depression, alcoholism and a variety of stress-related "Acting-Out" behaviors (such as fighting, rape, suicide, reckless driving, unsafe sexual activity, impulsive theft, and truancy) often occur together and seem to lead to one another*. When a client is experiencing problems with either depression, alcohol or destructive "acting out" behavior, we often discover that he or she also has problems in the other two areas, even if he or she does not initially mention these problems.

Therefore, *we have come to see depression, alcoholism and "Acting Out" as forming a Triad of Disturbance.* Many authorities have suggested that all three problems may have the same underlying cause or causes, but opinions differ as to which is the root cause.

Some authorities see violence (in the form of child abuse, battering, rape, or inability to control anger) as the root cause of other problems: They feel that childhood victims of abuse develop symptoms of depression, low self esteem and substance abuse in later life and often later become abusers themselves. (See detailed discussion of these issues in chapter 3.)

Other authorities focus on depression as leading to self defeating, fatalistic attitudes and behaviors, including alcohol abuse, suicide, school failure, etc.

Finally, many thinkers and therapists see alcoholism as the underlying cause of many mental health and social problems. They point out the depressant effects of alcohol on the body, the negative life events often resulting from alcoholism, and the correlation of alcohol abuse with violence, accidents, family dysfunction and death.

Each of these viewpoints has considerable merit. Each makes sense and is helpful in understanding and treating a certain percentage of cases. Since each view is reasonable, it may be that they are all correct. It may also be that these problems are united by a common factor underlying all

Indian people experiencing any of the problems in this triad often seem to have problems related to cultural identity. The history of attacks on Indian identity and culture (see previous chapter), along with the severe life stresses affecting Indian communities today results in widespread cultural identity confusion.

A negative cultural identity not only contributes to mental health problems, it is a mental health problem. An Indian person is unable to maintain psychological well-being without a sense of the cultural vitality and meaningfulness of Indian ways. For instance, the low self esteem often found in Indian teenagers is often tied to confusion about cultural identity and can contribute to self-defeating or dangerous behavior (such as drinking, fighting or suicide).

Lack of a strong and positive cultural identity can put Indian people at risk for any of a variety of mental health problems. *Cultural insecurity, (caused by past oppression and present life stresses,) creates the psychological condition in which the triad of depression, alcoholism and destructive acting out manifests itself.* The following diagram attempts to illustrate these relationships:

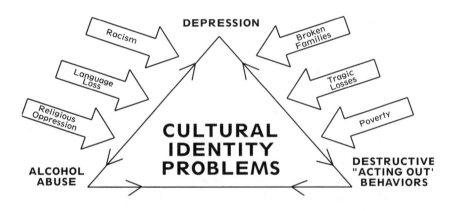

Each element of this Triad will be briefly discussed, with reference to its relation to the other two and to the influence of cultural insecurity. Other mental health problems common in tribal communities will then be reviewed, with an attempt made to show their relation to this core triad.

Depression

Acute depressive reactions, including suicide attempts, are frighteningly common Indian mental health problems. Chronic depression (called "dysthymic disorder" in the DSM IV diagnostic system) is even more pervasive and difficult to combat. Many "acting out" behaviors, such as drinking, reckless driving, and family conflicts can be seen as symptoms of widespread and underlying depression. Similarly, anxiety, fatigue, physical illness and pain, school and job failures, low self-esteem, low productivity and feelings of inevitable personal doom may also be manifestations of the "hopelessness and helplessness" syndrome of chronic depression.

Vague and pervasive depression is widespread in some Indian communities. Years of poverty, prejudice and cultural breakdown often lead to a loss of a sense of meaning and belonging and are therefore contributing factors in depression. This type of depression has been called "anomic" depression by some authorities (Jilek, 1982). Although certainly not all individuals in tribal communities are 'clinically' depressed, most people are, to a greater or lesser degree, personally affected by the historical and current traumas which complicate Indian life. *Multiple losses on a personal, tribal and cultural level all combine into much un-resolved grief and anger and ultimately into a deeply embedded depression. Depression may be stored up and turned against the self, causing guilt and depression.*

This type of depression may also be associated with an emotional numbing, such that it is difficult to fully respond to either problems or opportunities as they present themselves.[24] Since they are unable to imagine how things could really be different, depressed people tend to accept negative life circumstances as inevitable.

The task of a tribal mental health program is therefore not only to provide individual treatment for depression, but to support tribal communities in overcoming the history of tragedy and loss. We believe this can successfully be done only by promoting Indian cultural identity and strengthening the Indian way of life.

Alcohol Abuse in Indian Communities

Alcoholism and alcohol abuse are extremely pervasive and devastating problems in most Indian communities. The Indian Health Service has declared that alcohol abuse is the number one problem in Indian communities nationwide. Its overall impact among Indians has been very destructive, not only to individuals and families, but also to the fabric of Indian society and to the self-image of many Indian people.

Indian patterns of alcohol use and abuse tend to be quite culture specific. Although many Indian people do not drink at all, relatively few Indians are light or moderate "social" drinkers.

"Drinking" usually means heavy drinking, and often problem drinking. Drinking is usually done in groups, frequently at taverns or home "parties", and is most often weekend binge drinking, although some individuals drink more frequently. Probably the most noticeable and problematic aspect of Indian drinking is that Indians tend to drink to the point of intoxication, and frequently until losing consciousness.

It should be emphasized that many Indian adults do not drink at all, or only very rarely. Many Indians who previously have had a pattern of problem drinking have completely stopped drinking. In fact, clinical experience suggests that there may be a larger proportion of Indian alcoholics who are able to permanently stop drinking than is the case among non-Indian alcoholics. The reasons for this are not clear but may be related to the strong cultural tendency of Indian adults in their forties to take on more mature adult roles and community responsibilities.[25] A strengthening of Indian cultural identity in middle age may help individuals overcome problems with drinking.

It must be pointed out that drinking alcoholic beverages is strongly disapproved of in traditional Indian society and is contrary to traditional Indian values. Tribal elders and spiritual leaders are generally aware of and attempt to combat drinking problems. The use of alcohol is strictly prohibited during participation in traditional spiritual activities.

Alcohol abuse is a particular problem amongst two Indian groups: teens and young men. Indian children often begin drinking at an early age, sometimes even prior to their teen years. Alcohol abuse amongst teenagers seems to be associated with family conflict, parental alcoholism, problems in school, low self-esteem and cultural identity confusion. "...Some tragic things happened when they were young. Booze is a fine way of stopping the hurt. The trouble is it catches up and becomes the pain, the hurt."[26]

It has been suggested by some authorities that the loss of

culturally acceptable roles for men may contribute to drinking problems. Drinking may allow men to release built-up anger and frustration, sometimes in ways which would not be acceptable without the cloak of drunkenness. ***Drinking in Indian communities has been clearly shown to be associated with violence, accidents, sexual acting out and suicide attempts. There is considerable social pressure to drink, especially for Indian men.*** The following diagram illustrates the complex factors contributing to alcohol abuse in Indian communities.

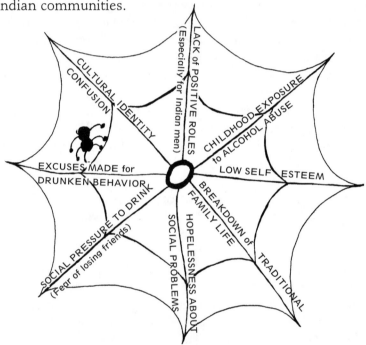

LACK of POSITIVE ROLES (Especially for Indian men)

CULTURAL CONFUSION

CULTURAL IDENTITY

CHILDHOOD EXPOSURE to ALCOHOL ABUSE

EXCUSES MADE for DRUNKEN BEHAVIOR

LOW SELF ESTEEM

SOCIAL PRESSURE TO DRINK (Fear of losing friends)

SOCIAL PROBLEMS

HOPELESSNESS ABOUT

BREAKDOWN of FAMILY LIFE

TRADITIONAL

Strands in the web of alcohol abuse

Each of the "strands in the web of Indian Alcohol Abuse" contributes to the development of drinking problems and also presents a barrier to overcoming alcohol problems.

Tacit acceptance of drinking as a method of handling stress contributes to problems with alcohol. Drinking is often excused as being the result of unbearable personal stress. Drinking is often attributed to financial problems, lack of a job, illness, death or marital conflict. Even people who strongly disapprove of drinking frequently seem to accept it as inevitable that someone may "go out" drinking when faced with a severe personal blow. This self-defeating expectation pattern is not unique to Indians, but it is unfortunately common in Indian communities. The dangers of tribal social acceptance of alcohol abuse must be recognized before the problem can be solved.

Happily, many Indian communities have come to recognize that alcohol abuse is a community-wide problem, not only the problem of individuals. Momentum is building to establish healthy tribal community expectations, including social pressure for abstinence and widespread tribal support for recovery and for non-drinking lifestyles.

New programs are being developed at many tribes which use both community and professional resources. Among these are: prevention programs for children and youth, and self-help groups such as Alcoholics Anonymous and Adult Children of Alcoholics. Awareness of the need to confront both hopelessness and denial is growing. Tribal mental health workers must be knowledgeable about alcoholism and drug abuse, and must work closely with tribal and community alcohol programs.

Destructive "Acting Out" Behaviors

Depressive reactions, alcohol abuse and "acting out" behaviors seem to be alternative and equally negative responses to an accumulation of life stresses. "Acting out" refers to any of a variety of destructive or self-destructive responses to stress including such things as:
- **impulsive suicide attempts**
- **domestic violence**
- **rape**
- **reckless driving or other dangerous actions**
- **sexual misbehavior or "unsafe sex"**
- **truancy**
- **fighting**

Impulsive violence against one's self and others presents a major mental health problem in Indian communities. Violence, accidents and suicide attempts are frequently associated with alcohol abuse. Although drinking increases the risk for such "acting out", these problems are not entirely the result of alcohol. *They also represent unhealthy ways of releasing tension and responding to stress.* As pointed out earlier, violence and self-destructive behavior may often be symptoms of hidden depression, or even of an unconscious attempt to avoid feeling emotional pain or becoming immobilized with depression. Thus, stress-related "acting out" behaviors complete the triad of disturbance along with alcohol abuse and depression.

Indian people experience a complex set of adverse social and economic conditions which cause severe stress. Effective mental health approaches must recognize and attempt to change these negative social conditions while at the same time attempting to help individual Indian clients to develop more constructive ways of handling real life stresses.

It is important to challenge the assumption that self-destructive and other impulsive acting out is unavoidable or "just the way it is". Cultural despair, anger and rebellion must be understood in their larger social and historical context. Defeatist attitudes must be questioned. Clients should be encouraged to explore more constructive ways of coping.

PROBLEMS RELATED TO THE TRIAD OF MAJOR DISTURBANCES

The triad of depression, alcohol abuse and stress-related acting out manifests itself in a large variety of other superficially different problems. Indian clients most often come to the attention of counselors or other tribal helpers because of specific problem behaviors, such as suicide attempts, violence or child neglect. Often these specific problem behaviors turn out to be either caused by or a slight variation on one or more elements of this triad.

For example, suicide is usually related to a *combination* of long term depression, anger and impulsive "acting out": suicide attempts occur when a person feels unable to "stand it" (cope with life stresses) any longer. Alcohol is very often involved, since it makes a person more depressed and also lowers inhibitions which normally prevent impulsive self-destructive acting out. Almost the same things could be said for other problem behaviors, such as domestic violence, child abuse or juvenile delinquency. Other problems, like child neglect, may have to do with two elements of the triad (depression and alcohol abuse), rather than all three. School behavior problems, truancy or dropping out may involve one, two or all three elements of the triad.

Unresolved or Delayed Grief

A significant number of Indian people have experienced staggering losses, often in rapid succession, such that a period of normal mourning, readjustment and recovery may not have been possible.

Losses or trauma experienced in early childhood are particularly hard to deal with. A history of early loss makes it more difficult for a person to resolve later losses. When significant losses follow one another in a relatively short period of time, it may become more and more difficult to deal with each successive loss. *Each new blow tends to call up feelings about previous losses, especially those in early life or which have not been accepted and resolved.*

Losses in early life contribute to adult depression. Similarly, unresolved losses contribute to depression and feelings of low self esteem, and therefore increase the dangers of alcohol or drug abuse, violence or other problems.

In order to resolve losses, it is necessary to go through a period of grief and mourning. A refusal or inability to admit and face the reality of a loss prevents normal mourning. Similarly, the belief that one must be strong at all times in order to protect others from one's own pain can interfere with normal expressions and resolution of grief. *Repeated losses can also lead to emotional numbness or chronic depression.*

Indian tradition provides important ways of coping with grief and loss and can be of enormous help in resolving losses and maintaining mental health. However, traditional methods of dealing with loss are sometimes insufficient to guide tribal members through repeated crises and losses. In these cases, counseling aimed at helping clients express grief, accept losses and say goodbye may be combined with traditional treatments.

The Sense of Personal Doom

When depression is complicated by unexpressed anger, guilt and exaggerated ideas of self importance, a sense of personal doom may result. This pattern seems to be rather common among younger Indian people who have problems with cultural identity. They see Indian culture as doomed by the attacks of non-Indian society. They are unable to identify with the strengths of traditional culture, nor can they identify with non-Indian society. Instead, they identify with the pain of Indian people. Since they see Indian culture as doomed, they cannot find personal meaning in traditional values; they can only find "fulfillment" in a sense of personal doom.

The sense of personal doom is far more than a passive acceptance of negative life circumstances. It is a powerful self image with an almost mythic dimension: certain Indian people feel personally destined to a life of tragedy, failure and early death. Their self concept and in fact the meaning they see in their lives is directly tied to living out this negative personal destiny.[27]

In fact, it is very often Indian people with exceptional ability, charisma and potential who develop a sense of personal doom. These are people who seem to be naturally 'cut out' for success, but who may feel that the path to success is blocked for them. When they find themselves unable to stand out for their successes, they sometimes unconsciously 'decide' to stand out for their failures. The thinking goes something like this: "If I can't be the *best*, I'll be the *worst*".

It is as if these people have decided to live up to society's (or their parents' or their teachers') worst fears and expectations: They decide to destroy themselves through alcoholism, accidents or suicide. This "solution" to life's problems graphically expresses not only their low self-esteem and hopelessness, but also their rage.

The sense of personal doom is one manifestation of the triad of depression, alcohol abuse and destructive acting out. Anger and discouragement about negative social realities facing Indian people can lead either to a numb acceptance of tragedy or to rebellion. *The sense of personal doom combines both these responses: tragedy is embraced in a defiant way; rebellion gives a driven and powerful quality to the underlying depression.*

Violence and alcoholism too often are accepted as inescapable conditions of Indian life: in fact, some Indian people find a sort of negative but none-the-less powerful cultural identity in their sense of being doomed *because* of being Indian.

This attitude of personal doom is seen in a number of younger Indians. It was verbalized most tragically by a young man who had been raised in a rather rigid and conservative non-Indian foster home, where he had been repeatedly told that Indians were "no good", "drunks" and "failures". As soon as he could, he returned to his reservation, where he began drinking heavily and getting into various kinds of legal trouble. He said "I always knew I wasn't white. I had to prove myself as an Indian. They kept telling me that Indians all drink, so I drink". This unusually verbal and insightful young man described his feeling in this way: "There is no way out for me as an Indian; life for Indians is pretty hopeless, so my life is hopeless too." Two years later, this young man killed his young wife and then killed himself.

Feeling personally doomed to tragedy is a mental health problem. Thinking that one is marked for failure because one is an Indian, or believing that it is ones inevitable fate as an Indian to be alcoholic or a victim of violence is a sign of serious depression and negative cultural identity.

It is a serious mistake to think that this fatalistic attitude is merely the result of real negative life circumstances: It is also different from the attitude of "non-interference", acceptance or receptivity toward life's ups and downs which has been described by many Indian people and which has contributed to the survival of Indian people and cultures.

Not all Indian people feel personally doomed, regardless of how much personal tragedy they have experienced. Many people find strength and meaning in Indian culture. In fact, it appears that **the more a person values traditional Indian culture, the less likely they are to become overwhelmed or to decide that they are doomed to meaningless tragedy. Since traditional values seem to offer some protection against an exaggerated sense of personal doom, it may be that a renewal of traditional orientation and building a positive cultural identity may be crucial components in the treatment of this problem.**

Suicide

Suicide is an unfortunately common mental health problem in the Indian community, generally estimated at twice the national average.28 Suicide is one of the tragic consequences of the triad of depression, alcoholism and destructive 'acting out'. It is important to note that depression alone does not usually result in suicide. It is when alcohol abuse, anger, frustration and impulsive "acting out" occur in the context of chronic, though often unrecognized depression, that suicide often results.

Young Indian men between the ages of 15 and 40 seem to be particularly at risk for suicide, both because of their frequent lack of satisfying roles in the modern Indian community and because of their tendency to use more violent and deadly methods of attempting to kill themselves, (such as hanging or shooting). Many authorities feel that a high proportion of fatal car accidents and alcohol-related deaths in general may also be unrecognized suicides.

While in many respects what we know about suicide in general also applies to Indian suicides, *Tribal mental health workers should be aware of certain differences between Indian and non Indian suicides, including:*

- *the involvement of alcohol in over 90 percent of Indian suicides*
- *the much greater vulnerability of younger Indian men to suicide (in contrast to the greater vulnerability of older men in non-Indian society)*
- *the greatly increased risk of an impulsive suicide attempt following a rejection or disappointment*
- *the fact that talking about wanting to join dead relatives, or having an experience of being visited by the dead, may be a clue to an impending Indian suicide attempt*

As in non-Indian society, a history of suicides in the family, as well as a personal history of previous suicide attempts, greatly increases the risk of a completed suicide. *Most suicide attempts are impulsive acts.* Most people surviving a suicide attempt do not go on to kill themselves. Therefore, it is extremely important to develop community systems for responding to suicide threats and attempts. Because suicide attempts are impulsive and often occur outside of office hours, tribal community members need to have basic information about suicide and about resources for crisis intervention.

Treatment of suicidal clients must also address underlying prob-

lems such as cultural identity confusion, alcoholism and depression. Since suicidal clients are frequently angry, alienated from mainstream society and "hard to reach", it is particularly important that culturally acceptable methods of treatment be offered.

Violence

Frustrations and anger about unjust social conditions combine with depression, alcohol abuse and social acceptance of "acting out" behaviors to make violence a major problem in many Indian communities. Similarly, depression, hopelessness and fear of revenge often make it difficult for families and communities to take a stand against violence and abuse.

Family and community expectations and responses have a major impact on violent behaviors. Violence tends to "cluster" in certain families, such that it is often possible to trace violent patterns over two or more generations. Children in some families see their parents physically fighting, and so learn that violence is an 'acceptable' way to express and release frustrations.

Families where violence is common tend to share an unspoken belief that violence is 'normal' and inescapable. Although some families do not think violence is good, they unintentionally allow it to go on by accepting it as "something we have to put up with". *In contrast, families who expect conflicts to be handled without violence generally have far less violence.*

Violence in Indian communities, like other destructive and self destructive behaviors, tends to be associated with low self esteem, frustration and alcohol abuse. Negative social conditions (like poverty or prejudice) make people feel angry and frustrated. Nonetheless, when people feel worthwhile and competent they can usually channel their frustration and anger into attempts to change things. However, when people feel badly about themselves or helpless to make changes, they often lash out against themselves or others close to them.

Alcohol lowers inhibitions: it makes it more likely that people will do things which they would not otherwise do. When drinking, people tend to do foolish or dangerous things, including fighting, rape or other violent crimes. Some people more or less intentionally use alcohol to "let off steam" in violent ways.

If family and friends excuse violent acts "because he/she was drunk" and "not responsible", the person is more likely to continue to use violence to release frustrations and is less likely to learn more mature ways of handling these feelings.

Like alcohol abuse, violence is a community-wide problem, call-ing for community-wide solutions, including:

- **protection for victims in crisis**
- **services which help both victims and abusers explore positive alternatives**
- **social disapproval of violence and confrontation of abusers**
- **education for non-violent choices and lifestyles**

Child Neglect and Abuse

Neglect of Indian Children has be-come a serious problem in some tribal communities. Indian parents usually love their children and have a very warm relationship with them. None-theless, some parents do not provide their children with adequate nutrition, medical care or supervision. Physical and sexual abuse of Indian children have also become frequent in recent years, as is the case in the non-Indian population also.

Neglect seems to be related to three things: poverty, parental alcohol abuse and lack of adequate knowledge about parenting in today's world. In particular the fact that many Indian parents were themselves raised in foster homes or boarding schools pre-vented their experiencing a normal Indian family life or learning how to be good Indian parents. These are major factors contribut-ing to the neglect of Indian children.

It is crucial for both child welfare and mental health workers to be able to differentiate this type of neglect from a lack of caring and from active abuse of children. So long as a warm and involved relationship between the parent and child exists, it is often possible to help parents develop new skills and resolve patterns of neglect.

Mental health workers can play a key role in:
- **evaluating the strength of the parent-child relationship**
- **advocating for the family with child welfare workers**
- **providing support to Indian parents**
- **helping children express and work through emotional difficulties resulting from family conflict, neglect or out of home placements.**

There is good evidence that physical punishment of children was extremely rare in traditional Indian societies, where children tended to be indulged, given considerable freedom and taught to conform through social pressure rather than through punishment.

Many Indian children encountered physical punishment for the first time in B.I.A. or church-run boarding schools, where physical punishment was sometimes frequent and severe. When grown, these children "imported" these methods back into Indian communities when they themselves became parents. Young parents without a stable family background or adequate preparation for parenthood sometimes rely on physical methods of discipline. When combined with alcohol abuse and severe life stresses, physical discipline sometimes becomes abuse.

Sexual abuse has become a serious problem in some, though not all, Indian communities. It seems to be very closely associated with alcohol abuse in the family. Some tribal mental health experts have estimated that as many as 90% of Indian women psychiatric patients were sexually abused as children.[29] This does not demonstrate how frequent or rare sexual abuse may be in Indian Communities, but it does suggest a very high correlation between sexual abuse and other mental health problems.

Sexually abused children tend to develop many other problems, including low self esteem, school failure, depression and alcohol or drug abuse. Early identification and treatment programs emphasizing extended family resources and positive identification with healthy Indian culture are needed.

Adults who were sexually abused as children also have particular mental health needs: they may need sensitive help in facing the true nature of certain early experiences and their own buried feelings. They often need to evaluate the impact of abuse on their lives and to have help in developing more open and hopeful expectations about relationships.

The nature and psychological consequences of child abuse are explored in more detail in chapter 3, which presents a trauma model for understanding intergenerational problems in tribal communities.

School Problems

Mental health workers in Indian communities are frequently called upon to evaluate and treat problems experienced by Indian children in the school system. Learning problems, behavior problems, withdrawal, truancy and dropouts are common. *Mental health workers who are sensitive to cultural misunderstandings and are aware of the various problems facing Indian children may be able to help Indian children adjust to the school system in a way which gets their personal and educational needs met.*

In addition, the mental health needs of depressed, neglected or abused children are often first identified within the school system. *Close working relations with school systems can increase early identification of problems and can allow mental health workers to educate school authorities about the personal and cultural needs of Indian children.* Experts with a variety of diagnostic, remedial and therapeutic skills need to work as a team with tribal mental health workers who have cultural knowledge and access to extended family resources.

Post-Traumatic Stress Disorder

"Post-traumatic stress disorder" (P.T.S.D.) (also called "delayed stress syndrome") provides a diagnostic concept relevant to problems experienced by many Indian clients. People who have been battered, raped, sexually abused as children, or who have been in fatal car accidents often show the continuing anxiety, emotional numbness, preoccupation, or "flash backs" typical of post-traumatic stress disorder victims. This concept has proven particularly helpful in understanding the problems of Veterans of military combat, especially those who fought in the Vietnam war.

In a less obvious way, people who have experienced repeated or chronic violence, tragedy and culture loss as well as people who were raised in alcoholic or abusive families, also experience similar symptoms. The concept of post-traumatic stress disorder may help tribal mental health workers understand the experiences and reactions of some clients and develop treatment plans aimed at helping them resolve past traumatic experiences. Treatment for victims of sexual abuse, of repeated domestic violence and adult children of alcoholics all focus on helping clients recognize the nature of traumatic abuses and the impact of these experiences on their personalities, ability to trust, make longterm commitments and handle conflict in constructive ways.

These issues are explored in greater detail in chapter 3.

Somatic Disturbances

Indian people often do not think of themselves as experiencing emotional problems such as "anxiety" or "depression". Instead, they often experience such problems indirectly as physical problems. Fatigue, headache, back pain and stomach upset may be caused by psycho-social problems, such as family conflict or unresolved grief. *The tendency to experience distress in the body seems to be due to three things:*

- **greater social acceptance of physical as opposed to mental illness**
- **cultural understanding that the mind and body are not separate, (such that physical problems have an emotional side and emotional problems have a physical side)**
- **the occurrence of spiritual problems which sometimes create bodily symptoms**

Many Indian people feel more comfortable expressing their problems in terms of physical illness. They may not verbalize emotional distress even when they are fully aware of it. Tribal health and mental health workers must therefore be alert to the possibility that physical problems may well have an emotional or spiritual component which also needs attention. Multiple and recurring physical problems in particular are liable to have an emotional component.

Often these types of problems can be successfully dealt with by referral to a traditional spiritual healer. Many times counseling can also help clients identify underlying feelings and concerns. Learning to express concerns verbally and through appropriate action can help prevent physical illness.

AIDS

Although Auto Immune Deficiency Syndrome or 'AIDS' is not in and of itself a mental health problem, it often creates mental health problems which must be responded to by mental health workers. The number of AIDS cases so far diagnosed in the Indian community is relatively small. However, the Indian Health Service has expressed concern that the Indian population may be at particularly high risk in the AIDS epidemic.[30] This is because:

1. The rate of occurrence of other sexually transmitted diseases is very high in the Indian community.
2. Impulsive behavior while drinking may lead to unplanned and unsafe sexual activity.
3. The generally poor health status of Indian people may increase vulnerability to the AIDS virus.
4. The highly contagious and lethal AIDS virus could potentially devastate small and relatively self-contained Indian populations.

Despite the fact that most Indian communities have not yet had to grapple with any substantial number of AIDS victims, many Indian leaders are concerned that the AIDS epidemic could result in catastrophic losses to Indian people similar to the destruction caused by small pox and cholera epidemics of the 19th century.

Indian Health Service and Tribal authorities have recently developed programs to provide AIDS education to the Indian community, and particularly to young Indian people. The Northwest Indian Health Board, tribes, and IHS have cooperated in educational efforts aimed at preventing tragic illness and death.

Tribal mental health workers must be equipped to help AIDS victims and members of their extended families to cope with the consequences of this illness. Much work needs to be done in developing culturally appropriate ways to meet the emotional and mental health needs of Indian people effected by the AIDS epidemic.

A Note Concerning "Personality Disorders"

A "Personality Disorder" is a long standing behavior and personality pattern which is (1) substantially outside of the social norm for a given society and (2) which causes the individual to have recurrent problems. The DSM IV (the standard manual of psychiatric categories and diagnoses) describes a number of specific personality disorders.

These diagnostic categories pose special problems for all minor-

ity groups, including Indians. This is because culture exerts a major influence on the development of personality. Norms of culturally acceptable behavior differ considerably between cultures. What is acceptable and normal in one culture may be considered deviant in another. Therefore, it is quite difficult for a person from one culture to accurately assess the normality of the personality patterns of an individual from a different culture.

For these reasons, mental health workers should be cautious in applying diagnostic labels and concepts such as "Dependent Personality Disorder" or "Passive Aggressive Personality Disorder" to individuals from a culture other than that in which these behavior patterns were identified and described.

In cross-cultural diagnosis there is great risk of mistakenly labeling individuals whose behavior and personality style we do not understand as being "sick" or "disturbed". There is even a risk of labeling entire cultural groups as "paranoid", "schizoid" or "histrionic".

The concept of "Personality Disorder" could be helpful in tribal mental health work if culturally accurate descriptions of Indian personality disturbances were developed. In the absence of such an addition to the diagnostic system, *mental health workers should be cautious in the use of such labels. Only diagnosticians familiar with Indian culture should risk using such diagnoses, and then only with consultation with Indian mental health workers.*

A Note Concerning "Psychotic" Conditions

Despite high rates of indicators for risk of mental disorders, outright psychotic conditions appear to be relatively rare among many tribes.[31] *Although schizophrenia, manic depressive illness and other psychotic reactions are apparently fairly common in certain tribes, they are unexpectedly rare in others, including a number of Washington State tribes. It is unclear whether the problems are in fact less common than in the general population, or whether they are underdiagnosed. Several explanations are possible.*

First, clinical experience (from both tribal and I.H.S. mental health workers) suggests that many Indian individuals who are experiencing borderline psychotic states tend to abuse alcohol or act in other destructive ways. Their drinking may in turn be seen by the Indian community as the cause of their problems. This way of responding to problems may 'mask' some psychiatric conditions and therefore make accurate diagnosis difficult. Disturbed people who drink heavily or do impulsive or self destructive things may also be more likely to die early and so never be diagnosed or treated.

Second, some people who are having psychiatric problems may interpret their experiences as spiritual problems and therefore seek help from traditional spiritual healers rather than from mental health specialists. At times, Indian spiritual leaders diagnose the person as having a mental problem and suggest that the person seek counseling or psychological help. Other times traditional help is given which relieves the client's fears and provides them with family support and guidelines for coping with their problem. It may be that many Indian clients only become identified as having a "mental health" problem if traditional treatments fail to relieve their distress.

Third, variations in the incidence of major psychiatric illnesses may also be due to variations in genetic vulnerability between Indian populations.

Until reliable data from controlled studies are available, no firm conclusions can be drawn concerning Native American vulnerability or relative invulnerability to the more severe and psychotic mental disorders.

SUMMARY: TRIBAL MENTAL HEALTH PROBLEMS AND CULTURAL IDENTITY

The mental health problems described above are not exhaustive, but merely attempt to call attention to problems commonly encountered in tribal communities. Each tribal community differs in its patterns of disturbance. ***Local cultural factors should be considered in diagnosis and treatment. Local cultural consultants are of great value in this effort.***

Since cultural identity problems can contribute to many other mental health problems, it is obvious that treatment should attempt to resolve cultural confusion and support the development of a positive cultural identity. This can be done by helping clients to recognize the unique values inherent in traditional Indian cultural experience and by actively supporting tribal cultural activities. Some specific ways this can be done are discussed in Parts II and III.

Notes and References

19. Swinomish Tribal Specific Health Plan, 1985

20. Office of Minority Health Testimony before Senate Select Committee on Indian Affairs on 7/7/88

21. Dr. Craig Vanderwagon, Director, Division of Clinical and Prevention Services, Indian Health Service, Testimony before Senate Select Committee on Indian Affairs on 7/7/88

22. Skagit Community Mental Health Center

23. Bates, Edward, Promotion of Indian Health, from *Indian and Alaska Native Mental Health Seminars*, Seattle Indian Health Board, 1982, pp. 289-290

24. Debruyn, Hymbaugh, and Valdez, op. cit., 1988

25. Weber, Rick, Alcoholism in the Indian Community, *Indian and Alaska Native Mental Health Seminars*, Seattle Indian Health Board, 1982, p. 821

26. Steltzer, U. and Kerr, C., *Coast of Many Faces*, 1979, p. 114

27. In psychoanalytic terms, this sense of destiny would be considered a negatively "inflated" self concept indicating a "narcissistic" personality structure. In Jungian analytical psychology, the sense of personal doom would be thought of as "identification with an archetype", i.e., the person would be seen as having psychologically equated themselves with a mythic figure of the Fated or Doomed Hero. A third mainstream theory, transactional analysis (T.A.), would refer to this problem as the result of a negative "life script" which has "chosen" in childhood because it seemed like the most reasonable alternative at the time.

28. Debruyn, Hymbaugh and Valdez, 'Helping Communities Address Suicide and Violence', *American Indian and Alaska Native Mental Health Research* 1 (3), March, 1988, p. 56

29. Testimony of Phyllis Old Dog Cross before Senate Select Committee on Indian Affairs, 7/7/88. U.S. Government Printing Office, Washington, 1988, p. 21

30. AIDS in Indian Country: Caution, Health Education and Prevention, National Indian Health Reporter, 1987

31. Testimony of Dr. Scott Nelson, Chief of Mental Health for IHS. before Senate Select Committee for Indian Affairs, 7/7/88

Chapter Three

Intergenerational Trauma in the Tribal Community

This chapter addresses the nature of trauma, the range of trauma-related mental health problems, and the critical tasks involved in treatment and healing. Although much of this information is not specific to tribal communities and is available elsewhere, it is provided here because of the high prevalence of trauma related problems among Indian people. *There is a pressing need for mental health and other social service workers in tribal communities to become educated about trauma-related problems.*

Horrible events damage people, families and communities. Trauma creates distance, distrust and disconnection between people. Healing is about reconnection, reconstruction and finding meaning.

The normal response to truly awful experiences is to avoid them, including trying to forget or deny them. Both victims and witnesses to terrible events have difficulty telling what they have seen. Society as a whole avoids, denies, dissociates and tries to forget. *Tribal societies are no different in this regard than other societies.*

Yet remembering, telling and reconnecting with others is necessary for healing. The person harmed by trauma must make sense of what has happened and understand the impact on his/her life before he or she can move past the grip of the trauma. A person who has become isolated behind a wall of silence must tell the story, in order to experience support and acceptance and especially in order to no longer feel alone with the pain.

Tribal communities are traumatized communities. Not only do individual tribal members need help and healing, but the tribal community as a whole needs a healing process. The core of this healing is to reconnect with one another and with all that is meaningful in Indian culture. This process requires facing the truths about harm done, not only by outsiders, but sometimes by parents, aunts and uncles, brothers and sisters, husbands and wives.

Tribal culture provides outstanding models for community healing. The values of sharing, coming together, kinship and resilience in the face of grief and loss make tribal cultures potentially models for communities worldwide. This potential will be fulfilled when tribal communities bring forth their healing strengths to recover from the multiple wrongs done to Indian people as a whole and also from the violence, self destructiveness and breeches of trust which occur within the tribal community itself. *Recovery from multiple and intergenerational trauma is the most important task facing tribal communities.*

TRAUMA: WHAT IT IS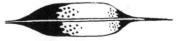

Traumatic events change people, permanently. Trauma shatters the basic sense of safety in the world. It creates fragmentation of the self and of social bonds.

Once we have undergone an acute trauma, we know, in an inescapable, visceral way, that terrible things can happen anytime, to anyone. We can never go back to who we were before the trauma happened or be the person we might otherwise have become. The awareness of personal vulnerability alters how we see our place in the world. *We can no longer assume that events are predictable and controllable or that others are trustworthy. Even when we are able to recover and go on with life, safety and control over one's fate can never again be taken for granted.*

Traumatic experiences are extremely frightening and often life threatening events which almost all people would find distressing. Although the Diagnostic and Statistical Manual of the American Psychiatric Association (DSM IV) refers to such events as "outside the range of normal human experience", this is in fact not the case: Studies have shown that between 30 and 75% of the general population has experienced at least one serious trauma. The percentage is likely to be much higher in Indian populations, due to the multiple risk factors outlined in the previous chapter.

When a person believes that they or someone else may be about to die or be severely hurt, they are "traumatized". The initial reaction is often to feel numb or immobilized with shock, but feelings of terror, anxiety, anger and despair soon follow. Lasting effects may include ongoing anxiety, inability to relax and enjoy life, chronic depression, guilt, substance abuse or suicide.

For instance, being badly beaten, raped, shot or stabbed, or witnessing this happening to someone else would be very traumatic. Serious accidents or injuries may produce trauma related symptoms. Being in a fire, flood or earthquake can be traumatizing, as can medical emergencies and conditions, including prolonged pain. Learning of the death or near death of a family member can also be traumatic. Many people who watched the recent attacks on the World Trade Center on television developed symptoms of acute stress.

Trauma caused by other people is especially damaging. War, combat, bombings, witnessing or committing atrocities, and torture all produce feelings of intense helplessness and horror. This is often complicated by feeling betrayed or experiencing a loss of meaning and trust in basic human decency. These types of trauma were particularly common among Vietnam veterans, who were first traumatized by their war experiences and then again by the shock of being blamed, attacked and shunned by many people upon their return home. Studies have shown that twenty years after the war, 15% of Vietnam veterans still suffered from Post

Traumatic Stress Disorder (Kulka et al, 1990)

Rape is an unfortunately common event in the US, with an estimated lifetime prevalence for women of 14-20%. Although we generally think if women as the rape victims, in fact 5-10% of sexual assault victims are male. Shame at reporting is likely to lead to under-estimations of this problem. Rape victims experience fear, anxiety, depression, anger, sexual dysfunction, physical symptoms, substance abuse, dissociation and Post Traumatic Stress Disorder. In fact, *approximately 94% of rape victims meet diagnostic criteria for Post Traumatic Stress Disorder 13 days following the rape, and 13% still suffer from PTSD 15 years later.*

When the perpetrator of violence or abuse is a trusted family member of the victim, the psychological harm done is often severe.

Battering and domestic violence are very common traumas in Indian as well as non Indian society, with violence occurring between perhaps as many as 30% of couples. Domestic violence ranges from ongoing verbal abuse to extreme torture or killing. The battering is usually cyclical: there is a repeated pattern of explosion (the trauma) followed by apologies and forgiveness, a "honeymoon" period, then building tension preceding the next attack.

Once a close relationship has become violent, this is likely to continue and to worsen unless there is effective intervention, most often involving both the legal and the mental health systems. The impact upon the battered partner may include depression, fear, guilt, low self esteem and a sense of learned helplessness.

Refugees have often experienced physical torture, resulting in Post Traumatic Stress Disorder (PTSD), depression, sleep disturbance, psychosis, sexual problems or suicide. Amnesty International estimates that over 60 nations continue to permit torture for purposes such as eliciting information, punishment or setting an example to control others.

Torture includes such things as beatings, near strangulation, application of electric shock, sexual abuse, exposure to extreme temperatures, threats of death and mutilation, forced nakedness or other humiliation and being made to feel responsible for harm done to others.

Child Abuse

Child abuse and neglect deserve special attention because of their prevalence in both Indian and non-Indian communities, and because of the lasting damage often caused.

Physical child abuse ranges from unwanted tickling to intentional killing of children. Forcing a child to stand in a corner for long periods, "spanking" with objects such as hairbrushes, belts or sticks, beatings, tying or confining a child and forced ingestion of disgusting things are other forms of abuse.

Neglect may be even more damaging than physical abuse, especially when a child is deprived of basic attention and a loving bond with the parent. Neglect involves such things as not providing basic food, clothing, and medical attention. It also involves failing to supply a child with affection, interactions with others, and teaching. *Every child needs to be held, comforted, talked to and noticed for who they are as a person. When this does not happen, children are psychologically handicapped.*

Sexual Abuse

Child sexual abuse may be the most damaging type of child abuse, due to the severe damage done to the child's feelings about him/her self.

Sexual abuse takes many forms, ranging from exposure to age inappropriate sexual pictures, jokes, or comments, witnessing the sexual activities of adults, sexual fondling and intrusive touching, to repeated oral, genital or anal rape.

Up to 30% of women and 10-15% of men in America are known to have been sexually abused. Some authorities believe that the problem is even greater in some Indian communities. This could be due to widespread alcoholism and a resulting lack of adequate parental supervision.

Among mental health clients, up to 70% percent of women report having been sexually abused during childhood. *A staggering 92% of homeless women report histories of sexual and physical abuse, as do 81% of non-homeless women who live in poverty (Harris, 1994)*

Damage Caused By Child Abuse

Abused children may distrust all adults and expect to be abused. They learn to be constantly alert and watchful. They become abnormally "tuned in" to the emotional state of the abuser, in order to try to avoid or prevent further episodes of abuse.

Children who have been exposed to severe harm or threats of death to themselves, family members or pets, experience terror and numbness. Often *these children seem "frozen" and withdrawn,* not talking freely to adults or playing cooperatively with other children.

They may make excessive efforts to be "good" in the hope of avoiding further abuse. They may try to be inconspicuous so that the abuser will not notice them.

Abusers generally try to isolate their victims from others in order to keep the abuse hidden. They may not allow the child to play or have friends and may threaten them with further harm if they tell anyone about the abuse. Children in such situations may work very hard to "look normal".

Children abused within the family are at the greatest risk. They are dependent upon and often deeply attached to the abuser, not only because of their need for love, but also because they may feel that their very survival depends on pleasing the abuser, whom they may see as having absolute, unchallengeable power. Some children even think that their abusers can read their thoughts.

The effects of childhood sexual abuse on mental health are severe. Victims often have lifelong difficulties with trust and intimacy. Many develop serious mental health problems, including depression, anxiety disorders, Borderline Personality disorder, Post Traumatic Stress Disorder and Dissociative Disorders.

Studies have shown that as many as 75% of clients with Borderline Personality Disorder have histories of childhood sexual abuse. Severe child sexual abuse has been reported in 96% of clients diagnosed with Dissociative Identity Disorder. Between a quarter and a half of all people admitted to mental hospitals have a history of childhood sexual abuse. Childhood sexual abuse increases the risk of developing full blown Post Traumatic Stress Disorder if exposed to trauma in adulthood.

Sexual abuse within the family (incest) may be the most particularly hurtful of all. Betrayal by a loved and trusted family member leaves a child feeling that there is no safety in the world and no one to turn to. Abuse may start so gradually that small children do not realize what is happening and may be very confused.

Incest within the family tends to be ongoing and repeated, leaving the child trapped in a situation from which there is no escape. Most serious, child victims of sexual abuse feel terrible guilt and shame and often develop harmful self concepts, such as "It was my fault" , "I am bad", etc.

Abused children blame themselves rather than the abusers. Doing this allows them to preserve their emotional tie to the abuser. In a paradoxical way, believing that he/she is bad preserves some hope and sense of power: If she is the bad one, and her parents are good, then there is some hope, because she can try to become "good". "If I am good enough, they won't hurt me". This allows the child to hold onto some sense of personal control and to the hope of love and protection from those upon whom she must depend.

Dissociation

Child abuse may lead to a reliance on dissociation as a coping strategy. Since a child cannot leave or make abuse stop, the only choice may be to "escape" psychologically through dissociation. The child may try not to remember or be aware of the abuse. They may enter self-induced trance states, such as fantasizing that they are someone else or that the abuse is not happening to them. *Abused children often report "going away" in their minds to some safe place, or feeling "outside of their body", such that they observe but do not feel involved in what is happening.*

The more severe the abuse, the greater the dissociation. Some children become such good dissociators that they can ignore pain and can become totally anmestic for the abuse. If they are asked if they are being hit or sexually touched they may say no. Sometimes this is purposeful concealment out of fear or to protect the abuser and family, but often the child truly has no conscious memory of being hurt.

Some abused children enter dissociative states automatically and involuntarilly without later memory for this. The "other" state may feel alien or different from his/herself. In extreme cases of early, severe, and ongoing abuse, separate personality fragments may develop. The developing personality of the child may fail to coalesce into a normal single "center of identity", but may

instead take the form of "parallel selves". These compartmentalized "self parts" hold specific painful memories, feelings or psychological functions. In this way, a child caught in an unbearable
situation may be able to cope with the abuse by not "knowing"
about it. (See discussion of Dissociative Disorders, below).

Negative Self Image

*The most damaging aspect of child abuse is a negative self
image. Many abused children develop a deep sense of personal
"badness", worthlessness or shame.* Abused children almost always believe that they are to blame for the abuse. They may feel
inherently "bad" and that their badness is the cause of the abuse.
In many cases abusers tell child victims that they caused the
abuse (e.g. by being naughty or wearing a short dress, etc.).
Children naturally believe what adults tell them. However, children do not have to be told that they are at fault for them to form
this mistaken belief.

All small children are ego-centric: they believe that they are
the cause of whatever happens around them. For instance, if they
feel loved, they think that positive things happen because they
are lovable. When bad things happen, (such as parents fighting or
divorcing), children almost always believe that it is their fault.
*Abused children usually think that they deserve to be badly treated
because they are "no good" or "worthless".*

*Social bonding is such a basic human need that children and
even adults will choose an abusive connection over no connection at
all.* The only real attention an abused child may receive is the
abuse itself or "special" attention associated with it. Unfortunately, abused children may come to see closeness and love as
always involving abuse or violence.

Later in life, abused children often continue to carry the self
image of being bad, dirty, worthless or no good. Even if they do
well in life and are well liked, they may be convinced that if
people "really" knew them, that they would be despised.

Disturbances in Emotional Regulation and Self Injury

*Healthy Indian parents comfort their babies and young chil-
dren. When children are fed, held and given loving attention, they
feel safe and worthwhile. Parents normally help children deal with
upsetting feelings like fear or anger by talking to them to calm them
down, perhaps holding them, telling them a story or suggesting that*

they take a nap or a time out. However, when parents do not provide modeling and teaching, children may fail to learn how to manage their own feelings.

Food and sleep are usually comforting experiences for children. If meal times or night time are scary, children may develop eating problems, sleep difficulties or bodily symptoms. They may fail to develop self- care habits necessary for self "regulation" of their emotional states.

When children do not learn how to "sooth" themselves or get over upsetting feelings, they may learn to escape painful feelings through abrupt and drastic acts, such as cutting or burning themselves. *There is a well established connection between repetitive child abuse and repetitive self abuse in adulthood.* One study found that 100% of 87 psychiatric patients who purposely injured themselves had histories of severe childhood abuse or neglect (van der Kolk et al, 1991).

Some traumatized children develop habits of physically hurting themselves by cutting, burning, hair pulling, etc. Usually, these behaviors are aimed at escaping feelings that seem unbearable. These children unconsciously learn to use one type of pain to block out another. Other times, a person may feel 'numb' or "unreal" and may hurt themselves in order to be able to feel again. *In most cases, self injury is a way of changing a feeling state that is extremely uncomfortable into one that is more tolerable. People who self injure usually report feeling relieved and calm afterwards.*

Self injury is often misunderstood to be either "manipulative" attention seeking or a suicide attempt. However, people who hurt themselves usually feel ashamed and try to hide their behavior . Rather than wanting to die, these people want to stop the pain they are feeling and to feel better and in more control. Once this is understood by client and therapist, they can work together to end the emotional pain in more constructive ways.

There are many other negative and self destructive ways of trying to manage distressing feelings, such as purposeful vomiting, compulsive sex, drug use or taking foolish risks. These acts are usually attempts to escape bad feelings.

Self-injury usually begins in childhood, increases during adolecense, and becomes a very entrenched way of coping with stress by adulthood. It is important for mental health workers to ask clients directly if they ever hurt themselves, because unreported self harm generally continues or worsens over time.

PATTERNS OF TRAUMA ACROSS GENERATIONS

 *Many wise thinkers have observed that if we were able to stop child abuse throughout the world, we could largely stop violence, crime, prejudice, discrimination, war, drug abuse, alcoholism, prostitution, academic failures and even unhealthy political competition. People would be happier, more productive, more creative and more tolerant.*

This is because child abuse never ends with the harm done to an individual child victim: it impacts that person for life and effects all their interpersonal relationships. An abused child often grows up with severe difficulties trusting others, with a painfully negative self image and sometimes with severe self destructive urges. Lack of self confidence may lead to serious social and personal limitations.

Too often abused children grow into angry, violent and dangerous adults. Although studies have shown that the majority of abused children do not grow up to become abusers, it is also true that the vast majority of abusive adults were themselves abused as children. People who were loved and well cared for as children simply do not suddenly turn on children or other people when they become adults. **People who hurt others have almost always had a history of childhood mistreatment or violence.**

Those who do go on to become abusive parents often deny that they were mistreated as children, or at least deny that mistreatment had any serious effects. None the less they may be preoccupied with feelings of rage, anxiety, depression and shame.

Interestingly, non abusive parents tend to acknowledge whatever pain or abuse they experienced in early life and to have reached an understanding of it's impact. This process frees them to make new decisions about the kind of parents they want to be and empowers them to learn positive ways to teach, discipline and interact with their own children.

We naturally learn the parenting methods and behaviors of the people who raised us. If we grow up in violent, neglectful or chaotic environments, this is what we learn and unconsciously tend to consider "normal". Unless we are lucky enough to have some powerfully life changing experiences, we tend to act according to the models we were exposed to as children.

When children grow up in an atmosphere of loss, violence,

neglect and/or abuse, these wounds deeply effect their self image and understanding of other people. Their ability to trust and take constructive risks is compromised: if their experiences have taught them that life is dangerous and sad, they are less likely to strive for personal goals and may have little hope for warm and trusting personal relationships.

This is the basic template for the concept of "intergenerational trauma". Trauma in one generation is often passed on to the next generation. This concept explains why certain groups of people have higher levels of interpersonal trauma, including child abuse, violence, suicide, substance abuse, etc. than some other groups.

Children growing up in Indian communities have a much higher than average risk for trauma, including family alcoholism, suicide, child abuse, neglect, and violence. *Too many Indian people suffer from the cumulative effects of repeated personal and intergenerational trauma.*

However, Indian cultures are not intrinsically more violent or dysfunctional than other cultures. Given the extreme stress visited upon Indian people since the beginning of contact with American/European people (see Ch. 1), it seems reasonable to assume that *much of the trauma in Indian communities is directly or indirectly the result of contact with Euro-American society.*

FACTORS DETERMINING THE IMPACT OF RAUMA

While trauma is always painful, the extent of harm varies enormously. In general, the greater the violence, the greater the risk of lasting psychological problems. This makes intuitive sense.

However, *the way a person perceives a situation may be even more important than exactly what happened.* For instance, if they think "I am going to die" they may experience more psychological effects than if they thought "someone will rescue me". Or "I can get away". Two people in the same circumstance often have quite different perceptions of the level of danger and also of their personal ability to influence the situation. A person who sees an oncoming vehicle before it hits them may have greater difficulty getting over the event than someone who did not know an accident was about to occur.

The experience of helplessness is a hallmark of the traumatic experience: The traumatic experience is one in which no effective action is possible. The more helpless a person feels, the greater the impact of a trauma. One is caught in a terrible situation from which no escape is possible.

Another crucial factor in the severity of post traumatic responses is the interpersonal context. People recover more easily from terrible events which are accidental or natural disasters, especially if they receive immediate help and support. In accidents, fires, earthquakes, etc., people usually are helped and comforted by others quickly.

Also, they may have shared the terrible experience with others, and thus do not feel entirely alone. The caring of family and community greatly lessens the impact of the trauma. Most importantly, the experience, however terrible, does not cut the person off from the human community.

However, when a traumatic experience is caused by others, especially in an intentional or malicious way, the harm is great. This kind of trauma leaves a person feeling deeply unsafe. *The closer the perpetrator of harm is to the victim, the greater the impact and the more severe the long-term damage.* Thus, violence perpetrated by strangers is ultimately easier to cope with than violence by a trusted loved one. Sexual abuse of a child by a neighbor is usually less damaging than sexual abuse by a family member. This is because of the severe psychological harm caused by disruptions of family bonds, trust and the sense of basic safety.

Violence or abuse within the family is especially damaging because it is likely to happen many times. When a child is trapped in a violent or sexually abusive family, the abuse may dominate the child's entire psychological world. The abuse may be frequent and may go on for many years.

The age at which a person first experiences trauma has a great deal to due with the ultimate effects. In general, *the earlier the trauma, the worse the effects.*

People with early trauma are more psychologically vulnerable to later trauma. For instance, Vietnam veterans with a history of child abuse were more likely to develop PTSD than those without such a history. In other words, people who already feel vulnerable and damaged may react more strongly to new trauma than those who have reached adulthood feeling reasonably safe and positive about themselves.

Women and minorities have a higher incidence of Post Traumatic Stress Disorder, most likely because of the increased risks of abuse and violence faced by these groups.

When people survive a trauma in which others were killed or severely hurt they often suffer from "survivor guilt": they feel somehow responsible, as if they should have done something to save the others. The burden of living with the memory of what happened to others can be terrible, especially if they were family members.

SPECIFIC TRAUMA-RELATED MENTAL HEALTH PROBLEMS

Clients with Post Traumatic Stress Disorder have a broader range of symptoms, more secondary diagnoses, greater service utilization, and higher mortality rate than clients in most other diagnostic categories.

Research has demonstrated that many mental health difficulties are directly or indirectly related to trauma. Not only PTSD, but depression, anxiety disorders, eating disorders, borderline personality disorder, and dissociative disorders may all be trauma- related, at least in many cases. *This may be especially true in tribal communities because of the prominent experiences of personal and cultural trauma.*

There is a wide spectrum of severity of post traumatic conditions. The earlier the age of onset, the more violent the trauma, the more frequent and the greater duration, the further up the continuum the victim is likely to be.

"Acute Stress Disorder" is a short term reaction to a single trauma, involving the following symptoms within three months after the trauma:

* dissociative symptoms (such as feeling numb, detached or without emotions, in a daze, as if things are not entirely real, or not being able to recall some important parts of the trauma),

intrusive re-experiencing

avoidance of situations which are similar to the trauma,

marked anxiety and physiological arousal.

This is a highly treatable condition which usually resolves in less that three months without permanent problems.

POST TRAUMATIC STRESS DISORDER

Post Traumatic Stress Disorder is a serious mental health condition previously known as "shell shock", "battle fatigue" or the "Vietnam syndrome".

The DSM IV official criteria for a diagnosis of PTSD include:
Exposure to *a terrible event,* during which the person experienced intense fear, helplessness or horror
Persistent *intrusive re-experiencing* of the event
Persistent *avoidance of reminders* of the event and *numbing* of overall responsiveness
Persistent increased *physiological arousal*
Symptoms continue for more than a month and cause clinically *significant distress or impairment in social and occupational functioning*

Symptoms may begin soon after the trauma ("acute onset"), or may not begin for six months or longer ("delayed onset"). PTSD is often a chronic disorder lasting many years.
It is important for tribal mental health workers to become familiar with the three "symptom clusters" of PTSD. Traumatized people usually have at least some of these symptoms, even when they do not meet diagnostic criteria for PTSD.

I. *Intrusive re-experiencing of the "imprinted" trauma is a frightening symptom of PTSD. Individuals with PTSD suffer from repeated and sudden memories, thoughts or visual images of the trauma.* They may experience sensory perceptions such as hearing noises or smelling smells associated with the trauma. Recurring nightmares about the trauma may lead to the person awakening screaming. These people may be afraid to go to sleep because of the nightmares, which have a repetitive and terrifying quality. Severe insomnia can result.
"Flashbacks" are extremely vivid experiences in which the person actually feels as if he or she were reliving the trauma or some aspect of it. Flashbacks can include hallucinations, full dissociation from the here and now and acting as if one were actually experiencing the trauma, such as an enemy attack or a rape, at that moment. Exposure to reminders of the event causes both

physiological reactivity and intense psychological distress.

People with PTSD feel as if the trauma were happening over and over again. Even small reminders may lead to big reactions and vivid memories. The person is "fixated" on the trauma, as if frozen in time. This may be because at the time of the trauma, they were "flooded" with adrenaline. The intensity of the experience and of their extreme physiological arousal metaphorically "burns in" the images and sensations of the traumatic experience. *Traumatized people may have disturbing bodily sensations or visual images even if they are not able to describe in words what happened to them.*

In young children, re-experiencing often takes the form of abnormally repetitive play. The child acts out themes related to the trauma over and over, as if they were unable to think of anything else. This is so even though they may not be able to talk about it. Children may also have repeated frightening dreams with no identifiable content.

II. *Numbing of feelings and avoidance of reminders of the trauma may lead to the person withdrawing from activities and relationships. It is as if they are desperate to avoid the intrusive, unwanted reliving of the trauma.* People with PTSD try not to think about the trauma or let themselves experience feelings about it. They may avoid anything that reminds them of the event, such as certain people, places topics of conversation, etc.

If the person is unable to block out the re-experiencing through avoidance or dissociation, *they may turn to substance abuse to escape the pain.* One study of veterans showed that 85% of veterans with PTSD developed substance abuse problems after their return from Vietnam.

At times people with PTSD are unable to recall all or part of the trauma. In fact, it is possible for traumatized people to entirely forget the event, even though they usually have significant problems in living. Some experiences may be too overwhelming for a person to consciously know about, so the mind seals off those memories, away from everyday awareness.

People who have been repeatedly traumatized in childhood are more likely to have amnesia than those who live through a single trauma in adulthood. Sometimes the memory returns much later when the person encounters something that triggers the recollection. Such experiences can be extremely sudden and terrifying.

People with PTSD may feel detached from other people and

surroundings, almost as if they were just going through the motions of life rather than really participating. In fact, many trauma victims retreat from life and relationships, loosing interest in people and activities they previously enjoyed. They may have a very restricted range of emotional expression and have difficulty with close or intimate relationships. Sometimes these people cannot see any hope for the future, so they don't make plans and may expect not to live long.

III. *People with PTSD suffer from an ongoing over arousal of the autonomic nervous system: their bodies are overly tense and "on alert".* They may have difficulty falling or staying asleep. They may feel restless, on guard or "hyper-vigilant", as if always expecting danger. *It is as if the person were constantly in the state of "emergency"* in which they feel much as they did at the time of the trauma, unable to relax or feel safe.

This state of readiness for "fight or flight" is the normal human response to acute danger. The bodies of people with PTSD repeatedly experience this state when there is no actual danger. The person may have no idea why this is happening to them. Because there is no present danger or actual emergency, there is no way the person can use this "readiness" to cope.

This constant alertness for possible dangers can lead to the person having difficulty concentrating on anything else. He or she may be irritable and prone to sudden outbursts of anger or rage, which of course cause relationship and employment difficulties. Their "hair trigger" startle response is difficult for them and others to live with. Being in a constant state of irritable alert is exhausting.

Dialectic of Trauma

Trauma related disorders can present with a bewildering assortment of symptoms, many of which seem contradictory to one another. Judith Herman, in her milestone book, <u>Trauma and Recovery</u>, highlights the central paradoxes of PTSD: *traumatized people may be unable to remember, or may be unable to stop remembering.* Intrusive symptoms and intense emotions alternate with constriction, withdrawal and apathy. Herman refers to this as "the dialectic of trauma".

Fragmentation of Experience

Trauma causes lasting changes to the person's physiological arousal patterns, emotions, thinking, beliefs and memory. Conscious perceptions are often fragmented. For instance, they may experience a sudden intense emotion without knowing what it is about, or they can have a horrible memory without any feeling at all about it. Thus, emotions and memories may be "disassociated" from each other.

Memory Irregularities

Trauma causes disturbances in memory. Traumatized people remember either too much or too little: they are either amnestic for the trauma or are suddenly caught up in reliving it.

Bessel Van Der Kolk, a leading trauma researcher, has suggested that *traumatic memory is not "encoded" in the same way as is "normal" memory.* When a person is overwhelmed with terror, shock and pain, different brain chemicals (neurotransmitters) are released. Different parts of the brain are active than during normal experiences. These changes may interfere with memory formation during a traumatic experience. Rather than storing an orderly narrative of the event, various aspects of the experience may be "stored" in separate "compartments". The person may not have been able to gain a clear understanding of what was happening during the trauma itself, and so cannot later access a "story" to explain what happened. Instead, *memory fragments may return as intrusive visual pictures, strange bodily sensations, sounds, smells or thoughts which do not seem to make sense.*

In normal memory, the person can recall what happened more or less in chronological order, and can remember the emotions involved, the physical sensations they experienced, and can recall the context and meaning of the event. For instance, I may remember that I went to my sister's house for Thanksgiving dinner, and that we ate a delicious turkey and had a good time together and that I felt full and sleepy afterwards. I remember what happened, how I felt, what I did and what it meant to me. The memory does not frighten me.

In contrast, if I was in a boating accident during which someone else died and I almost drowned, I might have a very confused memory of the episode later or I might not remember it at all. It is also possible that I might be toubled by suddenly feeling terribly

cold, or feeling scared all the time, or by hearing someone screaming for help, or I might "see" the rescuer's hand reaching out to me
but not remember what the person looked like. If I did not
remember that I was in a boating accident at all, these memory
fragments would be even more disturbing.

Most people are extremely frightened when fragments of "disso-
ciated" memory suddenly invade their awareness. Often they fear
that they are "going crazy" because the things they are experiencing do not appear to make sense. Clients may seek therapy at this
time in a state of great emotional turmoil. Sometimes they feel
flooded with feelings and memory fragments of which they cannot make any coherent sense.

Post Traumatic Stress Disorder Can Become Chronic

Initially, intrusive symptoms are the most evident and cause
the greatest distress. These symptoms tend to fade over time, but
they may be suddenly reactivated by some reminder or event.
Many people with post traumatic conditions experience "anniver-
sary reactions": they experience a return of intrusive symptoms on
the anniversary of some terrible event.

When a new trauma happens to people who have experienced
earlier trauma, the new trauma "reactivates" the old. It is as if the
recent trauma acts as a sort of psychic magnet to attract feelings
and memories which may have been long dormant, either due to
being avoided or entirely out of awareness. People with PTSD
can experience an abrupt return of intense distress even many
years after a traumatic event.

When PTSD becomes chronic, the intrusive symptoms tend to
decrease while the avoidance and numbness increase. People with
lasting PTSD may seem chronically depressed. *Long-term use of*
alcohol or other substances to block memory and emotional pain can
mask the underlying problem.

Chronic PTSD often leads to suicide attempts. Studies have
shown the one fifth of rape survivors attempt suicide, and as
many as 19% of Vietnam veterans who experienced active combat have made suicide attempts. Unresolved feelings of guilt over
participation in horrible events can lead to self hatred. Sometimes
the brush with death during a trauma eventually leads to chronic
preoccupation with death, often with recurrent fantasies or threats
of self imposed death.

These people feel that they have lost the meaning of life and are often profoundly disconnected from others. Sometimes they feel that a part of themselves has "died" or is lost. They may appear emotionally detached or cold. The person may be seen as simply withdrawn, passive, unmotivated or lacking ambition. *These "constrictive" or "numbing" symptoms of post traumatic conditions are often missed by therapists, even though they are the predominant symptoms of chronic PTSD.*

Chronic PTSD with numbing of feelings, social withdrawal and lack of hopes or ambitions may be especially common in tribal communities.

Borderline Personality Disorder

Borderline Personality Disorder (BPD) is a another common and severe mental health problem which is often trauma related. BPD is characterized by an ongoing pattern of instability in interpersonal relationships, self image and emotional control. There is marked impulsiveness, beginning by early adulthood. Relationships are often intense but unstable and explosive. These people alienate others yet are terrified of abandonment. The title of one book about BPD, "I Hate You; Don't Leave Me" captures the "feel" of BPD. These people experience almost continual distress, including chronic feelings of emptiness.

People with BPD suffer enormously from depression, self- harm, such as repeatedly cutting themselves, and from suicidal impulses and attempts. When under stress, they are likely to act out impulsively or self destructively in an attempt to escape what feels to them like unbearable emotional pain. They tend to have intense anger which is not well controlled and may erupt in quite inappropriate ways. It is as if these clients live in a state of ongoing crisis and chaos, which serves the purpose of keeping the deeper pain at bay, out of awareness.

Clients with BPD have been seriously stigmatized in the mainstream mental health system. These clients are hard to treat, such that they are often "written off" as untreatable. *The label BPD has become something of an insult or excuse for the failure of the mental health system to help these people. In effect, they are blamed for their own difficulties.* Borderline clients have the reputation of being manipulative and having an uncanny ability to "split" helpers into those who support them and those who do not, often with the result of misunderstandings and tension among treatment staff.

Many recent studies have established a clear link between BPD and a history of severe child neglect and abuse, especially sexual abuse. This strongly suggests that BPD is in fact a post traumatic condition. However, many times clinicians fail to explore the trauma histories of these clients, and therefore never help the client to face underlying problems hidden beneath all the upheaval and "dysfunction" in their lives.

Dissociative Disorders

Dissociation is defined as "a disruption of the normally integrative functions of consciousness, memory, perceptions or identity". That is, one or more aspects of one's experience is separated or "cut off" from usual consciousness. The word "dissociation" can refer to a very great variety of experiences, including everyday experiences, symptoms occurring in various mental health conditions, and religious or spiritual experiences such as trance states.

All people experience some degree of dissociation. Experiences of absorption in daydreams or a creative project which are so consuming that a person looses "touch" with there surroundings for a time are normal. "Highway hypnosis" when a person realizes that they have been driving for a period of time without really being aware of what they were doing or where they were is another case. *Only when dissociation causes emotional distress and difficulties in living is it considered a "disorder".*

The "dissociative disorders" are a group of highly varied diagnoses, with a large range in the type and severity of symptoms. *Dissociation may refer to "spacing out" or "going away" in one's mind, or to experiences of abrupt and more or less complete alterations in the experience of self identity, emotional state or memory.* Dissociation can be a "psychic defense" used to escape or deny the impact of disturbing information or events.

Most authorities believe that Dissociative Disorders develop as a direct consequence of extreme and early trauma. Almost all people with dissociative disorders report a history of child abuse, combat, concentration camp internment, sexual assualt or other severe trauma. Clinical experience with dissociative clients usually reveals a clear connection between the specific symptoms and the client's trauma history. *Traumatic information is received and stored in an abnormal way, set apart from ordinary memory.*

"Depersonalization" is a very common human experience, even

though people rarely discuss it, perhaps because it is difficult to describe. People may feel as if they were not really "there", present or "real". Instead they may have the feeling that they are just observing events and their own actions from outside. It is not considered a problem unless it is severe and chronic, interfering in daily life. When depersonalization occurs on a regular basis it can be very distressing. *"Depersonalization Disorder" is a stress related and underdiagnosed condition in which the primary symptom is chronic feelings of abnormal detachment.*

"Dissociative Amnesia" is an inability to recall important personal information. It generally occurs following an overwhelming trauma. For instance, forgetting one's name, age, all of one's childhood or major life events such as a marriage or combat experience indicate dissociative amnesia. Usually the information forgotten is connected to the trauma, such as war, torture, rape or child abuse.

Many people with severe child abuse, especially early sexual abuse, have periods of partial or complete amnesia for these experiences, and often for large blocks of their childhood. A study in which 206 women were interviewed 18 years after having been treated in a hospital emergency room for childhood sexual abuse showed that 38% had no memory of the experience (although some did recall other experiences of sexual abuse). (Williams, 1994) *Missing memories may or may not ever be recovered. If the memory is stored in a very fragmented way, it may be impossible to ever form a coherent picture of the event.*

"Dissociative Fugue" is a dissociative disorder which involves sudden and unplanned travel away from home with an inability to recall some or all of one's past life. The individual may either be very confused about who they are or have no memory at all of their former life and may even assume a new identity. This is a rare condition, associated with extreme stress and trauma.

"Dissociative Identity Disorder" (DID; formerly known as Multiple Personality Disporder) is the most severe and best known of the dissociative group of mental health problems. This condition involves the individual having two or more distinct identity states with enduring patterns of feeling and behavior. The compartmentalized "self states" serve important psychological functions, such as containing unbearable memories or expressing otherwise unacceptable feelings.

It is estimated that 95% of DID cases are linked to quite severe child abuse. The death or loss of a significant other or witnessing intentional killings have also been implicated in some DID cases, as has severe childhood neglect or extensive childhood medical trauma.

These states or "alters" take recurrent control of the person's consciousness and behavior. There is some degree of loss of memory by the "host" self for these "other self" episodes. The extent of amnesia present in DID is quite variable, but usually there are some blockages in the person's awareness. There may be periods of total memory gaps or "lost time", ranging from a few minutes to days or even years. People with DID are often unable to account for some of their time and for activities which other people tell them about.

Other symptoms suggestive of DID are hearing voices which seem to come from inside one's head. These voices may argue or comment on the person's activities, character or relationships, often in a hostile or derogatory way. They may give advice or orders. Sometimes they are helpful. Other voices may sound like frightened children or very powerful beings. "Dissociative voices" are quite different from voices found in psychotic conditions such as schizophrenia. They are usually organized, do not seem to come from outside of the person, and may be able to carry on sensible conversations.

Sometimes people with DID find things in their possession which they cannot account for. They may find evidence that they have done things which they not only don't remember, but cannot imagine doing. They may find writings they obviously produced, but in strange handwriting and expressing views very different from "theirs". Other people may tell them that they sometimes act in extremely different ways from usual and tell them of things they have said or done which they not only do not remember but find incomprehensible, embarrassing or frightening.

DID is a condition of hiding. These people learned early on how to escape from the pain of traumatic experiences and how to hide the abuse from others. People with DID may not know about their "self parts", and generally try very hard not to let other people discover this. Nevertheless, these people do know that something is very wrong, and they expend a great deal of energy trying to look "normal".

People living with DID are experts at "covering up". They

may "come to" in places or situations they do not understand. For instance, they may find themselves in an unfamiliar place, with no memory of how or why they went there. This can obviously be very frightening. They may suddenly realize that they have no idea what has been said during several minutes of a conversation, or even what the conversation is about or who they are talking with. Generally they get very good at pretending that they know what is going on.

DID is a very complicated condition. It is quite treatable, given a knowledgeable therapist, great commitment by both client and therapist and circumstances which support lengthy and intensive treatment.

There is great controversy about this diagnosis, with some clinicians believing that this condition either does not exist at all or is caused by patient suggestibility from media exposure or irresponsible therapy. However, there is extensive evidence that this condition not only occurs but is relatively common, perhaps as common as one person in a hundred. Scientifically validated structured interview techniques (SCID-D-Revised, Steinberg)have been developed which increase the rate of accurate diagnosis.

"Dissociative Disorder Not Otherwise Specified" (NOS) is a sort of catch-all diagnosis for conditions in which dissociative difficulties seem to be the main problem, but which don't fit into the other recognized categories. Often these are cases of partial DID or where it is not yet clear what the correct diagnosis is.

No data are available concerning the prevalence of dissociative disorders in Native American communities. Although there are clinical reports of a number of cases, it seems likely that most cases are never identified. This may be due to the reluctance of many Indian people to seek treatment and to the fact that many mental health workers are not sufficiently trained in recognizing post traumatic and dissociative conditions.

It is also likely that dissociative conditions in Indian cultures may take rather different forms than in mainstream American society. Different cultures certainly experience trauma and express symptoms in differing ways.

In many cultures, somatic and dissociative symptoms are far more common and accepted than in Western societies. Some authorities consider "culture bound disorders" to be dissociative condi-

tions which fulfill cultural needs and express cultural meanings and conflicts. "Culture bound disorders" occur only within a specific cultural framework, are culturally accepted, are time limited in their acute manifestation, and may result in resolution of personal psychological difficulties or improved social status. (see Ch. 12, Traditional Healing Worldwide). These experiences are therefore something like "existential crises". It is questionable whether they should be considered disorders at all.

Complex Post Traumatic Disorder

Readers may have noticed that many of the mental health conditions discussed above have a great deal in common. There is reason to question whether PTSD and Dissociative Disorders are very different conditions at all. There is always a trauma history and some post traumatic symptoms in Dissociative Disorders, and there is always a degree of dissociation in PTSD.

The diagnosis of Post Traumatic Stress Disorder developed out of the experience of veterans in the Vietnam War, including Native American veterans, many of whom developed symptoms of PTSD. On the other hand, the renewal of interest in the dissociative disorders emerged following the women's movement of the 1970's and the resulting increase in awareness concerning child abuse and it's consequences. It may be a historical accident that research concerning these two conditions proceeded along parallel lines for some time before researchers and clinicians recognized the similarity.

Because these disorders all appear to be trauma related, and have many symptoms in common, several leading authorities have proposed that they should be reclassified in the DSM V as "Trauma related disorders", rather than as an anxiety disorder (PTSD), a dissociative disorder (DID) and a Personality disorder (BPD).

The terms "Complex PTSD" or "Disorders of Extreme Stress" have also been proposed to refer to cases in which people experience both the PTSD symptoms of intrusive re-experiencing, avoidance, numbing and hyper-arousal discussed above, and also significant dissociation, bodily symptoms, depression, anxiety, identity distur-

bance, and dysfunctional interpersonal relationships, often with chronic interpersonal violence. Substance abuse and self injury are also common in clients with this type of complex PTSD. These are the most serious trauma-related conditions and result from severe, prolonged and repeated stress, especially interpersonal violation and abuse.

Very often such clients are diagnosed with Axis II personality disorders, especially Borderline Personality Disorder, and both the trauma and the dissociation are ignored. It may be more useful and less stigmatizing to approach the client's problems as consequences of their trauma, rather than as somehow due to a "faulty personality". Observations of severely traumatized clients have tended to blur the usual distinction between Axis I and Axis II disorders.

Mental Health Workers and Secondary Traumatization

Mental health workers and other helpers who spend time every day with traumatized clients often develop some "secondary" or "vicarious" trauma symptoms. They listen to, visualize and "take in" a certain amount of their client's experiences.

Over time, this can lead to problems for the helper. He or she may to have difficulty sleeping, have nightmares, or become preoccupied about "man's cruelty to man". They may begin to see trauma everywhere, even where it is not.

Some counselors also experience "burn out". This means that they are no longer able to really feel for their clients or give them undivided attention. They may dread going to work and generally not be able to do as good a job as they should.

It is critical that people in helping roles learn to take care of themselves. This means setting limits on how much they take on, and making sure that they take time for themselves to relax, have fun and connect with loved ones.

Mental health workers need to know and respect their personal limits, both in order to stay emotionally well themselves, and in order to be able to continue this important work of helping others heal.

HEALING FROM TRAUMA IN TRIBAL COMMUNITIES

Trauma breaks basic human connections. Self image and images of others are shattered, as is the belief in the basic goodness of life and sense of personal safety.
Most people take for granted that they are reasonably safe in their daily lives. Trauma destroys this assumption and leaves people feeling very vulnerable. When in extreme terror, people may cry out for their mothers or to God. When there is no answer or relief, they may feel abandoned. Later, this can lead to a sense of alienation and disconnection from all relationships, from community and often from spirituality. Religious assumptions may be shattered if the person feels abandoned by God.

Healing must repair connections with others, self image, values and beliefs. Healing comes in many forms. Individual counseling or therapy, spiritual help, and group or whole community gatherings are all important aspects of the healing process. With the right kinds of help, most people can become more psychologically and emotionally healthy.

Giving Help Immediately After Acute Trauma

The first thing needed by a person having just experienced trauma is to feel safe from further harm. It is best to get physically away from the harmful situation. Other people should reassure the person that it is over and that they are now safe and will be protected.

Social support at the time of a traumatic experience or very soon afterward may help lessen the impact. The victim may feel protected, comforted and understood when others respond with support and caring. People who have just been traumatized, whether in an accident or by abuse, should not be left alone.

Acutely traumatized people should not be forced to talk about what has happened, but they should be allowed to talk about it as much as they want. *Telling somebody else what happened may help them take in the reality of the event and also grasp that it is over now.*

***Spiritual help may be needed, especially when the trauma has
been very shocking*** or has left a person feeling "lost" or that the
bad experience is "sticking to them". Prayers or "brushing off" the
bad influences may bring immediate relief.

Sometimes trauma survivors cannot stop thinking, dreaming
or talking about a trauma. Other times they may try very hard to
avoid any mention of it. In either of these cases, mental health
services should be offered. ***Early intervention can often prevent the
development of serious or lasting problems.***

Helping Children After a Trauma

Children react to traumatic events differently than adults. Most
importantly, they react not only to what they themselves have
experienced, but also to how they see their parents and other
adults responding.

***When a child sees his or her parents as overwhelmed and
helpless, the impact of a trauma is far greater.*** When children
perceives their parents as able to cope with the trauma and still
continue with daily life, they are better able to handle or "integrate" the event.

***For both children and adults, the most important element in
recovery from trauma is to rebuild attachments and relationships.***
Unless the trauma has been caused by a family member, the
child's main need is to be close to family and to be reassured that
they will be taken care of. Small children need physical closeness
after a traumatic experience.

Children have to be helped to understand what has happened. It
is important for parents, aunts, uncles, grandparents or whoever
is closest, to talk to the child about the tragedy, accident or
disaster. Children may have very confused or mistaken ideas
about the nature and causes of such events. Adults need to help
the child understand the actual nature of the event, and especially
that it was not their fault.

***Young children will re-enact a traumatic event over and over in
their play.*** Older children or adults can help by suggesting different outcomes or ways of mastering terrible events. Older children
may draw or paint aspects of a trauma, but may be reluctant to
discuss it. ***Adults can help them bring forth their feelings by openly
discussing what has happened and how it effects the family.*** It is
important for adults to show children that "life goes on" by

providing meals and other basic care and by talking about how the family will cope with the loss or trauma.

MENTAL HEALTH TREATMENT FOR TRAUMA RELATED PROBLEMS

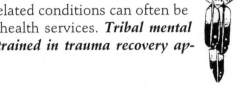

People with trauma –related conditions can often be greatly helped by mental health services. ***Tribal mental health workers should be trained in trauma recovery approaches.***

The tasks of healing are:
- *Building relationships that allow a healing process to begin*
- *Recognizing, "owning", and "processing" the trauma*
- *Grieving one's losses and assimilating the impact*
- *Reconnecting with loved ones, community and culture.*

Treatment occurs in three general phases, though of course they overlap to some degree.

First Phase: Establishing a Healing Relationship

There is a saying among mental health professionals that "It's the relationship that heals". This is especially so when working with traumatized people. It is not fancy techniques or specialized knowledge that is most important; it is the "therapeutic alliance". People who have been harmed by others must feel connected to a caring and consistent helper before they can face the trauma and the ways they have been injured.

It can enormously stressful and frightening for many people to begin to tell about their trauma. It is very important for counselors to make it clear that they are not in a role of authority and will not interrogate the client. Therapists should establish a collaborative style of interaction that helps the client feel that they are partners in the therapy. *The counselor should show respect and a willingness to hear whatever the client is ready to tell. The client must feel that they have control over the therapy process.*

Indian clients may have particular difficulty telling non-Indian therapists about experiences which they find shameful. They may fear that the therapist will be disrespectful or judgmental. Survivors of abuse often expect to be further betrayed, and this may be compounded by the general sense of distrust for non-Indians which many Indian people feel.

The counselor or therapist must respect the client's boundaries and have clear boundaries of their own. This is especially important with clients who were hurt by boundary violations, such as sexual abuse.

Before they can address their issues, clients must feel that the counselor is reliable and emotionally trustworthy. Counselors and therapists must show that they will be available on a regular basis and will do what they say. Clients must experience the counselor as respectful, caring and non-judgmental. They must be able to trust that the counselor will hold confidential what is discussed.

Counselors should respect the client's healing process. Therapy must be at the client's own pace. It cannot be rushed. Pushing traumatized people into material they are not ready to deal with is re-traumatizing and may endanger their well being. There is another saying among those who do this work: "It takes as long as it takes". This means that the counselor cannot set an arbitrary time table for therapy. Treatment of severely traumatized people is usually a lengthy process, often taking several years. Therefore, one characteristic required of therapists is the ability to "hang in there" with the client.

For all of these reasons, it is best not to ask for a detailed description of traumatic experiences too soon.

Instead, the first phase of treatment should inform the client about the nature of trauma and trauma reactions. **Survivors of terrible events need to learn that their symptoms are caused by trauma and are normal for someone who has been through what they have.**

They also need to develop hope that they can heal. The therapist "lends hope" to the client until the client is able to experience his or her own hopefulness. Clients need to learn what treatment is all about, what to expect, and that treatment can help them to move past feeling stuck in the past.

Early treatment should focus on "stablization" and symptom management. Clients can be taught ways to reduce anxiety and physiological arousal, such as deep breathing, relaxation or stretching excersizes, visualizing a private "safe place", using prayer or meditation, etc. Detailed safety plans should be made with clients who are still in dangerous situations or who are at risk for self harm. Skills for healthy living can be taught and clients can be encouraged to improve their support networks.

Sometimes medications are useful for symptom relief. They can help decrease anxiety and uncomfortable hyper-arousal of the nervous system, and they may help with sleep problems and depression. However, they do not provide a cure, and they do not help with the painful sense of alienation, detachment or self blame.

Middle Phase—Facing the Trauma

People who have been badly hurt need to "tell their story". They must share with at least one other human being all of what has happened to them. During the middle phase of treatment (which may be lengthy) the client and therapist explore in detail what happened, and how it impacted the person throughout their life.

Often people who have experienced terrible things are told to "try not to think about it", "get over it" or "it's all in the past, just let it go". This advice may work for getting past
minor upsets or disappointments, but it does not help people recover from major trauma-related disorders. As discussed earlier, it is the very nature of traumas that they "keep coming back" in one way or another. The person cannot get away from it or "over it".

Talking about past trauma can help in several ways: First, it helps people to "make sense" of what may feel like a confused jumble of feelings and memories. Talking about it allows the person to gradually form a clearer understanding. It is as if "getting it out" where they can "look at" what has happened to them, rather than just avoiding or feel overwhelmed by it, lets them see things somewhat more objectively.

The client learns that it is not "too awful to talk about" and that the therapist can stand to hear it. This helps the client not to feel overwhelmed, ashamed and isolated. In many cases, people with trauma related mental health problems have not talked about their terrible experiences with anyone, at least not in a comprehensive way. They usually feel all alone with their distressing memories and feelings. Telling someone about it relieves some psychological pressure, it helps the person feel more "connected" to the human community and it helps them find some coherence to their life story.

Mental health workers must be able to tolerate hearing some very terrible things. This means that they must be able to listen with an open heart and mind. The therapist must show the client that it is possible to face what has happened without being destroyed. The counselor must not cut the client off or shy away from discussing any aspect of the trauma, no matter how hard it may be to know about cruelty, tragedy, horror, degradation, humiliation and terror in intimate detail.

Traumatized people may have cut off their feelings and need to reconnect with their emotions. *Very intense fear, rage, shame, disgust or hopelessness may emerge as the client explores their memories.* It is essential that the client know that the therapist understands how badly they feel. However, the counselor must never assume that he or she knows what clients are feeling or what "really" happened to them. "I know how you feel" is usually not a helpful response, and may even be seen as belittling. *Clients are the experts on their own experiences, not the therapist.*

It is never helpful to tell someone that his or her feelings are wrong, no matter how much you may wish that they felt differently. Sometimes it can be helpful to share with a client that it makes you sad to see them feeling so ashamed or hopeless, or that you would like to help them move from feeling so terrible to feeling strong and safe.

The job of the mental health worker is to "witness" the healing work of the client. Often what is helpful is simply to reflect back to the client what you see and hear. For instance, you might say, "you look so sad when you talk about your grandmother", or "I think you mean that you are too scared to talk about it right now. Is that right?" Witnessing also means standing by the person as they move through the healing process.

Sometimes talking about the trauma provokes very painful flashbacks or memories. The client may re-experience aspects of the original trauma during the therapy process. *It is the job or the therapist to provide a sort of "anchor" to the here and now, so the client does not feel lost back in the middle of terrible events.*

Often it is helpful to focus on what the client is experiencing physically. As discussed in the previous section, traumatized people experience a great deal of hyper arousal of the nervous system. They may feel so tense and irritable that they feel as if they were going to explode. At other times they may feel numb or not in their body. Therapists should ask how clients are feeling physically, acknowledge that these are feelings that trauma survivors often have, and help clients learn to "reground" themselves by doing such things as breathing deeply, bringing the discussion back to the here and now or doing a "sensory check" where they simply notice what they are seeing, hearing, smelling or touching right then.

When victims blame themselves for abuse or other trauma, it is best to avoid overly quick reassurances or simple platitudes such as "it wasn't your fault". First the survivor needs to be heard.

Later they can be helped to examin and reevaluate negative or harmful beliefs in order to gain a more helpful perspective. **Traumatized people must rebuild a positive view of themselves as competent and lovable.** Cognitive-behavioral therapy methods offer particularly effective tools to help people change self destructive beliefs and thought patterns. **The goal is to "empower" the client to solve their problems and embrace life.**

It may be extremely difficult for the traumatized person to fully "assimilate" what has happened and put it in perspective. The counselor tries to help the client "integrate" whatever happened, by naming it, facing it, understanding how it has changed her life. Survivors must come to terms with how the trauma has impacted their self image, view of others, sense of personal safety, values and beliefs, physical health, sleep and eating habits, emotional health, and ability to trust and be close to other people.

It is important to identify the specific problems, that have resulted from abuse or trauma, such as an eating disorder, a tendency to blow up at others, avoiding getting close to anyone, or giving up on things too easily. Then the therapist can help the client make changes in these specific areas. But until the client has processed the trauma emotionally and verbally, he or she may not be able to make needed life changes.

Losses from trauma must be mourned. This includes mourning the loss of loved ones who have died, mourning the loss of productive or happy years due to the trauma, and mourning the loss of "what might have been". It includes loss of innocence, of the sense of safety and the loss of trust in others.

Mourning is a process that takes time. The individual must be allowed to experience and express all of the feelings they have about their losses, including grief, anger, guilt or shame. Tribal social support and traditional rituals for dealing with loss may assist healing.

Every client has strengths, and it is up to the mental health worker to help the client find them. Many times traumatized people have great difficulty recognizing what is positive about themselves. Asking what the person did to get through the hard times may help them to see their personal history as not only about trauma and loss, but also as about resiliency and personal strength..

Identifying strengths and choices helps the person understand that they are more than what happened to them. For instance, exploring how they coped in awful situations may lead to the discovery that they are brave, determined, able to keep going no matter what, that they tried to protect others, that they have not lost their ability to love, etc. Recognizing personal strengths builds the self esteem and confidence needed to go on living in positive ways.

Final Phase of Treatment—Reconnecting and Finding Meaning

During the end phase of treatment, the focus is primarily on learning to live in healthy ways in the here and now. Clients who have felt alienated and detached need to reconnect with family and tribal community. They need to experience a sense of belonging and having common interests. Making commitments to family and community pulls the client out of themselves and into the stream of life.

It is very important for the survivor to feel "empowered" to take control of their own life. Whereas they may have been helpless as a child or unable to prevent the trauma from happening, they do have choices now. They can choose to talk about it or not to. They can choose who to spend time with. They can leave a situation which feels unsafe. They can ask for help and support when they need it.

Clients who have suffered chronic trauma-related problems may never have learned to set personal goals. Now they may need to assess their needs, interests and options.

The goal is not to forget the past, but to be able to live with it in a healthy way. Healing results in the trauma survivor being able to tell the story without re-experiencing it. People who have recovered from trauma no longer feel a need to either run away from it nor to focus their attention on it. They are changed because of what they have gone through, but the trauma no longer dominates their lives. They have found a perspective that allows them to go on with the business of living.

All survivors need to grapple with difficult questions about the meaning of their experiences. Most survivors eventually move from a preoccupation with the question of "why" the trauma or abuse happened to a focus on "what does it mean to me?" *The meaning a person finds in their experience to a large degree determines how they will fare in later life.*

People who have healed from trauma experience a sense of personal integrity: they know who they are, what they value, and they feel basically good about themselves, personally and culturally. They feel able to face the future and competent to pursue what is most important to them. Often trauma survivors find a sort of personal "mission" to help prevent the kind of abuse or trauma that they experienced, to give expression to their experiences through creative work, or to help others recover. Helping others brings a sense of meaning and purpose.

Mental Health Approaches to Trauma Treatment for Children

Treatment for traumatized children differs considerably from treatment for adults. Children do not process their experiences primarily in words. Very young children hold memories mainly in their "somatosensory systems", i.e. in their bodies.

Slightly older children express and work things through in play. Therefore, *"play therapy" is used to help these children explore feelings, give expression to what they have gone through, and help them discover possible ways to cope.* Dolls and other props may help children "show" what has happened, what they think it means, and how they feel.

Role playing of different scenarios can help children understand what has happened and what it means. Role playing can help them see how adults should behave, as well as learn skills to say no and to seek help. Children may be taught about "good" and "bad" touch and about when to seek help. (see also p. for further discussion of play therapy).

TRADITIONAL TREATMENTS FOR TRAUMA-RELATED PROBLEMS

In a very real sense, all traditional healing approaches are forms of trauma treatment. They incorporate the very elements that are most important in helping people recover from traumatic experiences: a renewal of hope, positive self image and spiritual beliefs, renewal of family connections, and reaffirming one's place in the human community.

In fact, tribal healing approaches often recognize the relationship between terrible experiences and emotional and physical symptoms much more clearly than do mainstream mental health views. Perhaps this is due to the massive trauma which has been visited upon tribal people over the past two to three hundred years. The discussion of spiritual healing found in Part 2, Chapter 10, provides specific Coast Salish examples of how traditional approaches are aimed at helping people recover from severe life stresses.

Traditional story telling makes use of myth and metaphor to speak to the unconscious in non-threatening, non-confrontational and culturally meaningful ways. Traditional healing can bring about a sense of meaningfulness in the person's life, culture and relationships. *Most important is the experience of cultural continuity, connection to ancestors and living kin, and the experience of emotional support.*

The purifying rituals involved in many traditional healing ways (cleansings, restrictions on certain activities, prayerful preparation, etc.) may help a person let go of terrible memories and feelings. *They are helped to enter into a "sacred (psychological) space" where healing may occur.*

Talking circles (discussed in Chapter 10) offer an exceptionally powerful traditional approach to trauma recovery. Talking circles emphasize respect for every member of the circle, and promote a sense of belonging. They allow the individual to share just what they are ready to share. There is no pressure to move beyond their comfort level. The other members of the circle offer their presence, witness and (mostly silent) emotional support. Common experiences of trauma and resilience are often shared, promoting a sense of belonging and hope.

The Talking Circle, like other forms of traditional healing, offers a "holding environment" somewhat similar to mainstream psychotherapy: the material discussed is not to leave the group, or even to be discussed later between members of the circle. It is a special situation and time, set apart from ordinary life, devoted to airing deep personal concerns. These special "boundaries" make it possible for very disturbing personal information to be revealed. The boundaries of the "holding environment" create the safety needed to approach traumatic material. The presence of caring but non-intrusive witnesses is crucial, as it is in therapy.

Talking Circles carry great cultural and spiritual meaning for Indian people, allowing the power of cultural symbols to aid the healing process. In tribal communities, many people share similar histories and psychological issues. Therefore, Talking circles can be especially effective in decreasing the sense of isolation, detachment and alienation which are prominent symptoms of trauma-related conditions.

It almost seems that Talking Circles were designed specifically to help Indian people heal from traumatic experiences.

The Sweat Lodge is another traditional Indian healing method especially effective in helping people recover from trauma. A small enclosed hut encircles a bed of hot stones on which water is thrown, creating heat and steam. This is rather like the Finnish sauna.

The Sweat Lodge is a sacred experience approached in a reverent manner. Small groups of men or women enter the Sweat Lodge and sit together in the darkness. As they experience the heat and purifying sweat, they may talk about what is on their mind. *Often highly personal and difficult material is aired in this intensely personal and protected environment. Like the Talking Circle, it is understood that what is discussed may not be revealed to anyone afterwards.*

The Sweat Lodge has been used in treatment programs for Native American Vietnam Veterans, with considerable success. It mirrors ancient practices for purging warriors from the contamination of violent experiences in order to allow re-entry into civilized society. Interestingly, the Sweat Lodge has not only been helpful in treatment of Native American Veterans with PTSD, but it has also proven helpful with non- Indian veterans. This is a prime example of the potential value of Indian healing traditions for the human community worldwide.

Every tribal culture has specific healing ways which have grown

out of centuries of experience. Thoughtful analysis of these tradi-
tions always reveals the healing wisdom ("therapeutic processes")
underlying the ritual procedures ("therapeutic techniques") em-
ployed. Mental Health workers in tribal communities should seek
to understand just how these traditional healing ways work.
Descriptions of spiritual, practical and herbal medicine are available for many Native American cultures. However, the interested
mental health worker will usually not find what they seek in the
standard psychological literature, but instead in ethnographies,
"medical anthropology" or "cross-cultural psychology" literature.

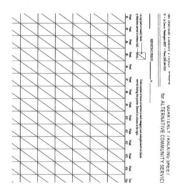

TRIBAL COMMUNITY-WIDE HEALING PROCESS

Indian spiritual and political leaders have recognized the perva-
siveness of personal and cultural trauma in tribal communities. The
mental health needs of tribal members have become a priority.
Many tribal communities are exploring creative ways to blend men-
tal health and traditional healing approaches.

Awareness in Indian country about the interconnections between
mental health problems, trauma and culture loss has increased
greatly. There is widespread understanding of the destructive pat-
terns of intergenerational trauma as they have effected entire Indian
tribal communities.

At Swinomish, there is a growing feeling that the entire tribal
community is engaged in a healing process. Elders are concerned for
the children and young people and want to find ways to reach them.
Tribal leaders are supportive of mental health and related services.
There has been a huge increase in culturally-oriented "prevention"

activities for youth. This development stems from the recognition of the crucial importance of a positive cultural identity for mental and social health.

The Talking Circles, community dinners and tribal-wide "forums" (described earlier, which were a central part of the process leading to the second edition of this book), have offered occasions for open sharing of grief, difficult personal life experiences, and hopes for the future. We hope that these types of activities will continue. There is a sense of positive momentum building towards greater mental health.

Many Indian people have long spoken out against alcohol and drug abuse. Now many people are finding the courage to speak out against domestic violence, child abuse and other hurtful behaviors. If violence, child abuse and alcoholism were eradicated in Indian communities, many other problems would soon disappear.

Tribal Community healing can only come from the inside: each tribal community must take responsibility for the mental health of its own people. Funds are short, but can be found with persistence. Many of the most important healing activities do not require funding.

Indian culture provides models for community healing. The core tribal values of coming together for sharing, laughter and emotional and spiritual support are values which support positive mental health. These values and activities are explored throughout this book.

What is most needed is for individual tribal members to commit their time and energy to supporting one another and to building healthy lifestyles. We must never give up!

The tribal community has the creative and healing resources necessary to bring about mental health and cultural growth. That is what this book is about.

Chapter Four

Barriers To Indian People Receiving Mainstream Mental Health Services

D espite the existence of serious mental health problems, Indian people have historically received only very limited mental health services. Community mental health centers have generally been unsuccessful in serving Indian people, despite their state mandate to do so. This is still true in most places today. Both low availability and under utilization of services account for this situation. Barriers to services may be geographical, financial or cultural.

Services theoretically available to all have not in practice been accessible to Indians in many cases. The geographical isolation of many reservation communities, the lack of transportation and the inability of many Indian families to pay even small fees charged by agencies with sliding scales all limit the accessibility of "mainstream" services.

Cultural barriers to mainstream mental health services are even greater. *Despite repeated attacks on Indian culture, there is still a resilient cultural life that forms the basis for Indian identity. Many Indian people live within the boundaries of the Indian world; their social ties are primarily with other Indians. This helps to preserve traditional practices, values and beliefs.*

Although many Indian languages have been lost, communication barriers between the tribes and surrounding mainstream communities have by no means been eliminated. Indian people share assumptions, practices, and linguistic meanings to which non-Indians are not privy.

Most Indian people resist being absorbed into the mainstream American culture. Mainstream mental health services, which are predicated or dominant cultural assumptions, are unacceptable to and ineffective with many Indian people.

Services offered by state and county agencies are often not appropriate for Indian clients. When mental health providers are unfamiliar with tribal lifestyles, family values or communication style, there is a high probability of misunderstanding. *Frequently, non-Indian providers misinterpret Indian quietness and reserve as hostility, resistance or indifference.*

Indian clients often feel uncomfortable in dealing with non tribal agencies. Bureaucratic complexity and impersonal atmospheres may confuse and alienate Indian clients. Historical oppression and prejudice make it difficult for Indians to trust non-Indians. Indians are frequently angered and puzzled by the emphasis on regular weekly appointments. "Insight" and verbal exchanges emphasized in most mainstream mental health counseling are inappropriate for many Indian clients. Indians may also perceive long waiting periods, extensive paper work and repeated appointments as intentional rebuffs and may give up in disgust.

Many non-Indian providers are not even aware that important value differences exist. This lack of awareness increases the danger of Indian clients being misunderstood, labeled or rejected.

Even non-Indians who consider themselves unbiased often

harbor unconscious stereotypes and ethnocentric assumptions about normalcy, maturity and mental health which are incompatible with Indian values.

For instance, Indians tend to place a higher priority upon cooperation with family than upon individual autonomy. It is seen as more important to help a family member in difficulty than to keep an appointment. Financial resources are generally shared among a number of extended family members. This is seldom understood by non-Indian agencies.

Differences in religious beliefs and practices can create barriers to Indian people receiving mental health services. Traditional Indians often make time commitments incomprehensible to non-Indians, such as spending much of their time, energy and money during winter months in ceremonial activities. This can disrupt appointments, jobs or school attendance. Some Indians also fear that mental health therapy may interfere with their spiritual well-being.

Historically, culturally adequate theoretical and service models have either been lacking or have not been recognized by mainstream agencies. Too few effective programs have been developed. Little has been done by state and local mental health agencies to develop tribal mental health approaches or to train tribal members as service providers. ***Mental health services to reservation communities are currently inadequate to meet the pressing needs.***

There is a growing awareness of Indian mental health needs on the part of tribal authorities, the Indian Health Service, state officials and many Indian people. Increases and improvements in services are urgently needed. Existing resources are discussed in the next chapter. One approach to a tribal mental health program is presented in Part III, along with suggestions for resource development.

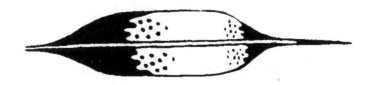

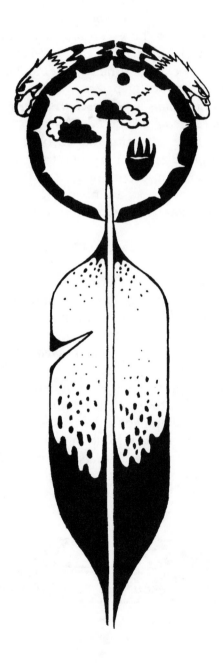

Chapter Five

Mental Health
And Related Resources
Currently Available To
Indian Communities

It has never been entirely clear how responsibility for mental health and social services to Indian people should be distributed among federal, state and tribal agencies. Ambiguity and false assumptions that some other agency is responsible tend to contribute to Indian people remaining underserved. At the time treaties were signed, mental health services were nonexistent and social services were limited to religious charities. Although most treaties made reference to some sort of health care, it was a long while before federal authorities began to extend their interpretation of health to include mental health.

While for many years the Bureau of Indian Affairs had almost total responsibility for managing the resources, education and general "welfare" of Indian people, the social services they offered were minimal and often more controlling than helpful.

The Indian Health Service took over primary responsibility for health care of Indian people in the 1950s, and added limited mental health care more recently. However, funding and staffing restrictions meant that services were generally insufficient to meet the needs, either in quantity or in cultural orientation.

While state and locally funded mental health and social services programs are theoretically available to all residents, in actuality "mainstream" mental health agencies have generally not been successful in serving Indian people.

Because the high level of need in Indian communities is not being met by mainstream programs, and because effective mental health care for Indian people requires special knowledge and different service approaches, many tribes are interested in developing tribally operated programs to address the mental health needs of their own people.

This chapter provides an overview of the main existing services available to tribal communities. Suggestions are made for the development of collaboratively funded programs under tribal control.

BUREAU OF INDIAN AFFAIRS SOCIAL SERVICES

The Bureau of Indian Affairs (B.I.A.) is a branch of the Department of the Interior. Although the B.I.A. has considerably less control over Indian communities and tribal resources than was the case prior to the 1950s, the B.I.A. still serves as a trustee for tribal lands, forests, soil, etc. The B.I.A. oversees roads, tribal legal codes and often holds lands in trust for particular families, and distributes income from leases on a periodic basis. Despite increasing tribal control and self-determination, the B.I.A.'s powers and responsibilities remain far reaching.

Although the stated mission of the Bureau of Indian Affairs is to serve the interests of Indian people, their actions have not always been perceived by Indian people as being for their benefit. Many Indian people have quite ambivalent feelings about the Bureau of Indian Affairs. On the one hand, they recognize the importance of the federal trust responsibilities with which the B.I.A. is charged. On the other hand they resent the B.I.A.s bureaucratic mode of operation and the control it has exerted over tribal affairs. The B.I.A. has been described as "a most efficient octopus, reaching into the lives and homes of most American Indians".[32]

After the transfer of health services from the Bureau of Indian Affairs to the Indian Health Service in the 1950s, the two remaining B.I.A. responsibilities which are most relevant to mental health care for Indian people are education and child welfare. The B.I.A. offers educational services, including: boarding schools for some high school age students, grants for attendance at four year colleges, assistance with vocational education, and special programs for handicapped students. Most other education has been transferred to the state public school systems. (Federal assistance is made available to school districts having a large number of Indian children through Johnson O'Malley and Title IV funds earmarked for Indian education).

As mentioned in Chapter 1., the B.I.A. administers and monitors Indian child welfare grants to tribes. A percentage of the available money is allocated to each Area Office (the Area Office for the Northwest is in Portland) where decisions are made about which tribal programs in their area will be funded. Each Area has a number of Agency Offices, staffed by a social worker who monitors the grants of local tribes. Agency Social Workers may also provide tribal staff with consultation, referrals or arrange for special services for children with particular needs.

The B.I.A. also maintains enrollment records and family trees for tribes in their region. The B.I.A. can be helpful in verifying enrollment, in tracing ancestry or in locating missing parents.

THE INDIAN HEALTH SERVICE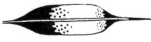

The Indian Health Service (I.H.S.) is the branch of the Department of Health and Human Services (D.H.H.S.) which has broad responsibility for the prevention and treatment of health, (including mental health) problems facing Indian people nationwide. In recent years IHS direct services have been drastically reduced, to be replaced by tribally-run services funded through Federal/Tribal Compacting Agreements. Most funds are now channeled thru I.H.S. to tribes. I.H.S. continues to provide consultation and technical assistance.

The overwhelmingly poor health status of most tribal communities at the time that I.H.S. took over Indian Health care in the 1950s dictated that primary emphasis be placed upon improving physical health. Tuberculosis was a particular problem for Indian people, as was frequent malnutrition, a high infant mortality rate, pneumonia and other respiratory diseases, diabetes and alcohol-related illness such as cirrhosis of the liver.

The Indian Health Service and tribal communities collaborated to successfully improve the overall health status of Indian people. For instance, the incidence of tuberculosis was dramatically reduced.

Despite these improvements, the overall health status of Indian people remains a major problem. Rates of injury and death from non-disease causes are the highest of any minority group.[33] Unintentional injuries, cirrhosis of the liver, homicide, suicide, pneumonia and diabetes are the six leading causes, in order of greatest contribution, to "excess" deaths occurring in the Native American population. *These statistics clearly point to major mental health problems in the Indian community.*

Mental health services came relatively late into the Indian Health Service delivery system, starting in the 1960s. During the 1970s a number of Service Units employed mental health workers who provided outpatient counseling to tribal members. *The Indian Health Service began to employ and train para professional Indian mental health technicians to reduce cultural barriers and to facilitate access of Indian people to professional counselors.*

The Indian Health Service also explored cooperation between mental health providers and traditional Indian spiritual healers on the Navajo Reservation. I.H.S. funds were used to provide stipends to apprentice Medicine People working with recognized Navajo Diagnosticians, Singers and Sandpainters. In addition, I.H.S. hired Medicine Men and other Traditional Healers as consultants.

However, despite these valuable efforts, severe staffing and funding constraints have generally limited both the extent of direct

mental health services and opportunities for cultural innovation.
Treatment and prevention of alcohol and drug abuse has been a
major I.H.S. priority for several years. I.H.S. has worked with
Tribal Coordinating Committees to develop Tribal Action Plans
to combat alcohol abuse.

Over the past two decades the interrelationship between mental health, substance abuse and physical problems has become
increasingly clear. The Indian Health Service increased the priority placed upon mental health services for Indian people. *The top
administrative levels of the Indian Health Service recognized the
importance of mental health services which are responsive to cultural values and of the need for increased tribal input and control.*

*However, the Indian Health Service system was not been able to
meet the pressing needs for direct mental health care, either in
quantity or in cultural sensitivity. This was true for three reasons:*
- **the size and structure of this federal bureaucracy
  prevented adequate local control over the development
  of service approaches unique to Indian culture.**
- **inadequate funding and severe staffing constraints
  limited the volume and range of available services.**
- **the primarily 'medical model' approach of I.H.S. was
  not effective in dealing with the complex and
  interacting mental health, substance abuse and social
  problems.**

A brief review of the Indian Health Service structure and
staffing patterns should illustrate these problems. The Indian
Health Service is divided into twelve Area Offices, each with
administrative responsibility for a number of Service Units. Each
of twelve Area Offices has either a full or part time mental health
consultant. However, in many of these offices the mental health
consultant doubles as the social services consultant and may also
serve as substance abuse consultant.

The I.H.S. services delivery system has proven woefully inadequate to meet pressing needs for service.

Most Indian Health Service mental health care was provided
on an outpatient basis either in I.H.S. facilities or in tribal offices.
The primary model of service was individual or family weekly
appointments lasting approximately one hour. Specialized services were "minimal to non-existent" due to staffing constraints.
Inpatient services are still provided either through contracts with

local hospitals, through referral to state psychiatric hospitals or in one of two Indian Health Service inpatient psychiatric facilities nationwide, both of which have long waiting lists.

In addition to direct services, the Indian Health Service has recently developed important activities including:

- a quality assurance program which reviews Service Unit activities for compliance with mental health program standards.
- a national mental health plan for American Indians and Alaskan Natives.

In summary, the Indian Health Service is still an important resource for Indian people in the mental health field, as well as in other areas of health care. I.H.S. can be helpful in providing contract funds, consultation and research assistance in addition to direct services.

However, both the limited resources and the difficulties inherent in the federal bureaucratic structure have made it impossible for the Indian Health Service to meet the level of need existing in tribal communities today. An increasing number of tribes are electing to contract directly with I.H.S. in order to operate their own programs with greatly increased tribal control of services and monetary resources. *Frequently, Indian Health Service resources can be creatively combined with tribal, state and locally funded mental health resources to produce integrated, tribally based programs suited to the cultural needs of Indian people and under the control of tribal government.*

THE COMMUNITY MENTAL HEALTH SYSTEM AND ITS RELATIONSHIP TO INDIAN COMMUNITIES

The state-funded mental health system represents a major resource for mental health care which has been generally underutilized by Indian people. This chapter presents an overview of the community mental health system and its relevance to Indian communities.

A brief history of the development of community-based mental health care will be presented. This will be followed by a discussion of key ideas underlying community mental health services. The types of client problems seen in a community mental health center, services offered and the relationship between community mental health programs and Indian communities will be discussed.

History

Before the Civil War, there was little organized mental health treatment, even for the most seriously mentally ill. If a mentally ill person could not be cared for at home, he/she was often left to wander from community to community, begging for food and shelter. Mentally ill people were often jailed or imprisoned.

After the Civil War large state institutions were established in order to provide more humane treatment. By about 1900, all states had residential institutions for the chronically mentally ill. However the quality of treatment varied greatly. The best state institutions provided decent food, clothing and housing. But in poorer or less progressive states the conditions were often terrible; patients were mistreated by attendants, they were often put in dark, damp or padded cells, and were often restrained in strait jackets for long periods of time. Budgets for some mental health facilities were so inadequate that decent food was not even available. All this was made worse by the fact that there no known effective treatments for mental problems. The needs of less severely disturbed people were hardly recognized at all.

During the second World War, a group of new medicines (such as Thorazine) were discovered which relieved many of the most severe symptoms of major mental illnesses, such as extreme fears, distorted thinking and misperceptions of reality. Patients who had spent many years in institutions were suddenly able to return to their communities. While these medications did not "cure" severe mental illnesses, they did make it possible for most mentally ill people to live outside of hospitals.

The release of large numbers of people with psychiatric problems back into the communities made it necessary to develop community support and outpatient treatment systems. At the same time, concepts of "mental health" and "mental illness" began to change: models became less strictly medical and more "holistic". Mental health services came to be seen as helpful for people who were not perceived as "crazy". The mental health needs of people who were not actively psychotic became better understood.

During the 1950s and 1960s "community mental health centers" began to develop across the nation. Community mental health centers were designed to provide community-based treatment: including alternatives to hospital care, follow-up services and services designed for clients with a broader range of mental health problems.

Key Ideas Underlying a Community Mental Health System

Three ideas are basic to an understanding of the community mental health system:
• The Holistic Concept of mental health
• Multiple Influences on Health
• What We Mean by Mental Health and Mental Illness

The Holistic Concept of Mental Health

There are several alternative ways to look at mental health:
• The "medical model" sees emotional problems as caused either by something outside the body attacking the person or by the malfunctioning of a body part, leading to physical disorder.
• The "biological model" sees problems as inherited.
• The "environmental model" sees imbalances and poisons in the world around us as causing mental health problems.
• The "interpersonal model" sees family and social relationships as causing mental and emotional problems.
• The "holistic model" emphasizes the inter-relationship between physical, social, spiritual and environmental systems.

Community mental health programs are usually designed on the holistic model because it considers all the points of view. The "holistic model" recognizes the need to treat the whole person in order to keep an overall balance. It does not arbitrarily chop a life up into separate pieces.

The holistic view sees all parts of life as interrelated. Our spiritual life, our family relations, our emotions, our thinking, and our physical health are related to each other and to our environment. There is a constant give and take between the physical, the mental, the spiritual and the emotional, and between the individual, the family and culture.

When the holistic view is adapted to the cultural context, it is consistent with most Indian philosophy. For instance, Indian people have long understood that environmental problems such as destruction of natural resources or contamination of water sources can lead to physical, spiritual or emotional illnesses.

Influences on Health

According to the holistic view, health and mental health are influenced, for better or for worse, by many things. Our health is influenced by our behavior, our spiritual lives, our family relations, our heredity and our environment. The availability of health and mental health care also affects our health, particularly when there are serious, longterm or emergency mental health problems.

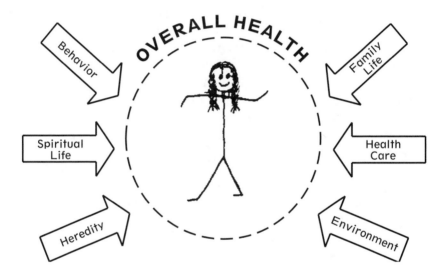

What We Mean By "Mental Health" and "Mental Illness"

Our "mental health" is just one part of our total being. All aspects of life must be in balance for good physical, spiritual and emotional health.

Qualities often associated with good mental health include:
- **being able to express a full range of emotions, including sadness, anger, joy and contentment.**
- **positive interpersonal relationships.**
- **ability to give as well as receive support from others during times of trouble.**

- **ability to concentrate on a particular task.**
- **leading a balanced life: that is, enjoying both work and play, not abusing alcohol or drugs, respecting one's self and others, and facing problems without becoming either overwhelmed or totally preoccupied by them.**

When any of the above characteristics of "mental health" is missing, emotional/psychological problems or "mental illness" can develop. For instance, child neglect, cruel discipline, a lack of positive nurturing in childhood, or environmental deprivation can negatively effect the development of the personality. This can result in an inability to empathize with others, insecurity or a lack of confidence, distrustfulness or chronic anxiety.

More severe problems, such as Schizophrenia or Manic Depressive Illness, appear to be related to chemical abnormalities in the brain. Studies of extended families show that chemical imbalances are strongly influenced by heredity and genetic makeup. The characteristics of these "major mental illnesses" include:

- extremely confused thinking / confusion about what is real
- hearing or seeing frightening things which are not seen or heard by other people and which do not have spiritual meanings
- severe depression or withdrawal from other people
- being too confused or upset to take care of ones self physically
- a desire to harm ones self
- inability to sleep
- extreme worry or unrealistic fears

None of us are without some "quirks" or problems that cause us anxiety and worry. Likewise, no one is without some strengths or positive resources. All of us deal with what could be called "mental health" or family problems. Although most of the time we do not need professional help, some types of problems cannot be handled by the individual or the family. Problems like schizophrenia, manic depressive illness and severe depression require the help of a counselor, psychiatrist or mental health center.

HOW THE COMMUNITY MENTAL HEALTH SYSTEM WORKS

Most mental health services today are provided in outpatient counseling clinics rather than in state hospitals, even for the acutely and chronically mentally ill. When hospital care is needed, this care is closely coordinated with community mental health care. Individuals suffering from acute mental health emergencies are generally treated in local hospitals for very short periods of time. This is true even for involuntarily detained patients. Individuals who require longer term care may be referred to state hospitals for varying lengths of time. Most hospital stays last less than one month. Clients are then referred back to the community mental health center nearest their home for "out-patient" follow-up care.

Types of Services Available from Community Mental Health Centers

Community mental health centers provide a wide range of services to various client groups. These services can be broken down into:

- crisis services
- services for the chronically mentally ill
- counseling programs for less seriously disturbed people

Crisis Services

All mental health centers provide services to individuals and families in acute crises. Most mental health centers provide 24 hour telephone crisis lines, open every day of the year. When needed, telephone contact may be followed by a face-to-face meeting. This may take place at the mental health center, the emergency room of the local hospital, or in some cases in the client's home. Emergency crisis services focus on defining the client's problem, developing a plan for dealing with the immediate crisis, and making arrangements for ongoing treatment if needed.

If a person is found to be suicidal, a danger to themselves in other ways, or if, through their mental illness, they pose a life-threatening danger to other people they may require emergency hospitalization in a local general hospital. *Hospital care is used primarily in emergency situations. Here a client can be protected from harm, and may receive medication, rest, appropriate nutrition, and counseling. In most cases a hospital stay lasts only a few days, with referral to out-patient services through the mental health center following discharge. If an individual requires longer hospitalization, he or she can be transferred to the State Hospital system, as discussed above.*

Services for the Chronically Mentally Ill

State laws require that state funds be used to serve those individuals having the most severe problems. Therefore, most community mental health programs focus a great deal of attention on working with the chronically mentally ill. Services for the chronically mentally ill include:

- An evaluation to see if a client needs medication, and if appropriate, prescribing medication and seeing the client regularly to monitor the effects and dosage.
- "Day treatment" programs where clients participate in group therapy, in classes directed toward improving social adjustment, in pre-vocational training, and in recreational activities.
- Community support services provided by individual case managers who assist clients with everyday living, including nutrition, shopping, finding a place to live, dealing with DSHS, Social Security or other agencies, and helping with vocational training and employment if appropriate.

Services for Less Severely Disturbed Clients

In addition to State funded emergency services for the acutely disturbed and programs for the chronically mentally ill, **community mental health centers often have specialized programs for other client groups. These specialized services must usually be funded through United Way, private fees, or special grants.**

The particular programs available from community mental health centers vary greatly from place to place and state to state. This is due to the different levels of funding in various states and to the success of each community mental health center in obtaining special resources to meet needs in their local communities.

For instance, in Skagit County, some of the special counseling services for individuals who are not chronically mentally ill or in acute crisis include:

- Counseling services for Vietnam veterans.
- Special treatment programs for the victims of child abuse and neglect and their families.
- Anger management and anger control counseling.
- Home based counseling for the elderly.
- Multidisciplinary case assessment services for the elderly.
- Volunteer peer counselors for the elderly living in their own homes.

- Counseling to families in crises referred from the Division of Children and Family Services.
- Special counseling in conjunction with local school districts.
- A variety of substance abuse treatment services.

This list gives an example of the variety of treatment services available through mental health centers.

Funding for Community Mental Health Programs

Funding for community mental health programs comes from a variety of sources. This includes State and local government, Medicaid reimbursement, private fees and insurance, special grants from State agencies or private foundations, and donations.

In the case of Skagit Community Mental Health Center, the State of Washington, (through its Division of Mental Health, and the Northwest Regional Support Network or RSN), provides about one third of the agency's total financial support. The State requires that all funds they provide must go to meeting the needs of the chronically and acutely mentally ill as the first priority. Since the cost of services provided to these mentally ill clients exceeds the funds provided by the Division of Mental Health, there are little State funds remaining to serve other less severely disturbed groups. Thus, the Mental Health Center must seek funding from other sources to provide services to individuals other than the acutely disturbed or chronically mentally ill. A similar pattern could be found in all other states.

However, the Washington State Division of Mental Health also makes it clear that specific "priority populations" should receive mental health services. These include children, the elderly, and minority populations.

The reason Washington State has placed special emphasis on children, the elderly, and minority groups is that mental health services are not used as actively by these groups as by non minority people between the ages of 18 and 60. This under utilization of services by minorities, children, and the elderly is due in part to the failure of mental health programs to design and develop mental health services which are appropriate for or able to reach these groups.

For example, few mental health centers have developed special services for the elderly. Since elderly people generally will not come to mental health centers for service, special approaches must be developed to meet their needs. It is our belief that to effectively serve elderly clients, program services must emphasize extensive outreach. A similar situation exists for children and minorities.

Although community mental health centers are required by state law to serve minority groups in their service area, they have generally not been successful in doing so. In the past, most mental health centers have provided services along conventional clinic or "mainstream" patterns. Minority people have felt that this type of service did not meet their needs.

Different cultural perspectives and beliefs regarding the cause and treatment of mental illness call for different approaches to service delivery. Home-based or reservation-based services that are truly accessible are a prerequisite for effectively serving Indian clients. Services must be provided in the language of the client and in a manner which is respectful of traditional values and beliefs.

Mental health centers must work closely with each minority population to design effective programs that can meet the particular needs of each group.

Community Mental Health Agencies and Indian Communities

Most community mental health centers have not developed specific programs or models for serving Indian clients. While they may have had contact with tribes to explain their services, they have generally expected Indian people to use services in the same way as non Indians. This has resulted in under utilization of services by Indian people.

The State provides mental health funds to Community agencies on various levels of local government. These local comprehensive mental health plans are generally developed for geographic areas that should take into account the special needs of minority populations. *Indian tribes should negotiate with local agencies and government officials to ensure that appropriate and accessible services are provided to members of Indian communities.*

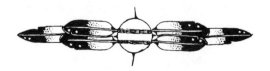

Each tribe must assess its own needs, help decide how services will be provided and what types of mental health programs will most effectively meet the needs of Indian people. Due to the important resources available through community mental health centers, these centers can often be helpful in the planning and assessment process. Collaboration can ensure that tribes control what happens within their reservations. In this way community mental health programs can successfully serve Indian people. *Only by a process of sensitive accommodation can community mental health centers become more accessible to Indian people, to other minorities, and to the community at large.*

As discussed in Part 3, Skagit Community Mental Health Center has worked closely with the Swinomish and Upper Skagit Tribes to develop a tribally-based mental health program. This program emphasizes the employment of Indian staff, reservation based services, close coordination and consultation with tribal officials and religious leaders and the provision of a wide range of services chosen by the clients themselves. A special 'Minority Program Development Grant' from the Division of Mental Health has enabled the Mental Health Center to develop this special culturally oriented program in conjunction with local tribes.

This model of service has proven useful in meeting the mental health needs of Indian people in Skagit County. However, we recognize that there are many other possible models for providing effective mental health services to Indian communities.

In Summary

Community mental health services are relevant to Indian communities in the following ways:

1. *State funds are available to serve Indian tribal communities.* In fact, state law requires that community mental health centers provide services to all population groups in their local area, including Indian tribes. Since most Indian communities are 'underserved', this often represents an untapped resource.

2. *Community mental health centers have great mental health expertise, especially in services to the acutely and chronically mentally ill.* Every community mental health center has a variety of staff, trained to treat a wide range of personal and family problems. No single individual employed by a tribe or by Indian Health Service can provide the range of services available through a community mental health center.

3. *Community mental health centers have access to a variety of resources for the treatment of mental health problems.* Although these outside resources may be less familiar to tribes, it is important that Indian people have access to these needed services. These resources include:

- emergency/crisis services
- involuntary detention of suicidal and acutely mentally ill people
- hospitalization and treatment for severe mental illness
- intermediate care or halfway houses for clients in transition from hospital care back to their own communities
- access to various support services, such as vocational training, veterans services, parenting training, etc.
- transition from hospital care back to their own communities

Each tribe must decide if and how they wish to work with the community mental health system and how they will coordinate among Indian Health Service, community mental health agencies and tribal programs in providing services to their communities.

TRADITIONAL HEALING PRACTICES RELEVANT TO MENTAL HEALTH CARE

Most tribal communities have traditional Indian healing specialists or spiritual leaders who form an important component of physical and mental health care for Indian people. These healing practices are embedded in thousands of years of Indian culture and healing/spiritual knowledge. Many Indian people have deep faith in these methods of help and receive unquestioned benefit from the services of traditional specialists. *Often traditional healers resolve mental and emotional problems, such that these situations never come to the attention of conventional mental health providers.*

Despite these facts, traditional healers have rarely received either financial support or professional respect from the mental health system. *It is of great importance to the mental health of Indian people that traditional healers be recognized, respected and invited to participate in the provision of mental health care. Spiritual leaders can be very helpful as consultants regarding client needs and cultural factors.* At times, it is possible for mental health providers to actively collaborate with traditional healers. Because of the cultural sensitivities involved and the need to personally know the local traditional healers, cooperative approaches can best be developed by tribally based programs.

DIVERSE FUNDING FOR TRIBAL CONTROL OF MENTAL HEALTH PROGRAMS

Some tribes have made creative use of a variety of funds to develop tribally-based mental health programs. Tribal Mental health workers may be funded partially by Indian Child Welfare grants, by "equity" funds from the Indian Health Service, by contracting with I.H.S. for mental health funds, by funds from tribal enterprises, by funds earmarked for educational purposes or through cooperative agreements with local mental health centers.

An increasing number of tribes are recognizing the need for programs which are not only physically located in the tribal community, but which are designed in order to meet specific local needs and to conform to the values prevalent in each tribal community. *In the opinion of many tribal authorities, the era of tribal control over mental health programs has begun.*

COMMUNITY-BASED MENTAL HEALTH INITIATIVE FOR INDIAN PEOPLE

Over the last decade there has been an encouraging growth of national awareness in the area of Indian Mental Health needs. In 1989, Indian mental health experts from around the country gave testimony before the Senate Select Committee on Indian Affairs concerning the need for a "Community Based Mental Health Initiative" for Indian People. The record of this makes testimony fascinating reading[37] for anyone interested in the status of Indian mental health needs and services.

Senator Daschle of South Dakota referred to "the incredible severity of the problem". After noting that the Indian Health Service Mental Health budget for 1989 was $13.091 million, he further said that "how in the world you ever begin to address the problem with that limited a budget boggles my mind."[38]

When asked about the backlog of un-met mental health needs, Dr. Scott Nelson, then Chief of Mental Health Programs for I.H.S., replied that a little less than half the mental health needs were being met. Senator Daschle replied that "it's encouraging for someone in your position to tell us that you actually believe you are meeting 40 percent or more of the needs of Indian health. I am troubled by that answer, but if that's your answer, we'll accept it."[39] Discussion during these hearings focused on:

- the growing violence, alcoholism and harm to children
- on the need to address these types of problems on a family system level
- on the need for Indian groups themselves to identify models for improving their health status

The fragmentation of services between tribal programs, I.H.S. and other (non-Indian) programs was emphasized by a number of those giving testimony. The need for cooperative working relations, spurred by administrative, financial or political incentives was emphasized. Fragmentation between tribally-run health, mental health, alcoholism and social services programs was also identified as a problem. Finally, the need for cultural relevance of services was discussed, especially in terms of approaches which combine western medicine with traditional Indian cultural healing systems and values. "One would have to develop the rapport or establish some connection to the tribe, and work closely with the community on how to integrate what's already being utilized by the tribe, and then to make it available within the Comprehensive Mental Health Centers."[40]

Recommendations made during these hearings were broad and wide ranging, but can be summarized as:

1. Develop Indian mental health programs under local Indian control.

2. Develop legislation aimed at improving coordination of services between tribal programs, Indian Health Services, National Institute of Mental Health, State and County Mental Health Agencies and between tribally run mental health, alcoholism, health, education and social services programs.

3. Fund programs which involve entire family systems in treatment.

4. Explore the effects of cultural oppression and attitudes toward Indian culture and spirituality on the mental health of Indian people.

5. Develop holistic models of mental health, capable of ad-

dressing complex and interacting problems.

    6. Fund programs which encourage cooperation with Traditional Indian Healers or Medicine People.

    7. Provide intensive mental health training to Indian professionals and natural helpers and to others working in Indian communities.

These recommendations are consistent with the goals and philosophy of the Skagit Tribes Mental Health Program. Over the last decade there has been a marked increase in inter-system and inter-disciplinary programs, often combining federal (Indian Health Service), Tribal, and often state or special grant funds to develop creative culturally-oriented prevention and treatment programs throughout Indian Country.

Notes and References

32. Burton, J. Indian Heritage, Indian Pride, Norman, OK University of Oklahoma Press, 1974.

33. The testimony of the Office of Minority Health at the 7/7/88 ZOversight hearing of the Senate Select Committee on Indian Affairs

34. From the testimony of Dr. Scott Nelson, Chief, Mental Health Programs, Indian Health Service, before Senate Select Committee on Indian Affairs on 7/7/88

35. From the testimony of Dr. Scott Nelson, Chief Mental Health Programs, Indian Health Service before the Senate Select Committee on Indian Affairs on 7/7/88

36. DeBruyn, Hymbaugh and Valdez, "Helping Communities Address Siucide and Violence: The Special Initiatives Team of the Indian Health Service", American Indian and Alaska Native Mental Health Research 1(3) March, 1988, pp. 56-65

37. pub. #90-354 of the U.S. Government Printing Office, Washington: 1989

38. page 12 of above sited document

39. op. cit. p.14

40. op. cit. testimony of Marlene Echo Hawk, p. 45

41. op. cit. p. 55

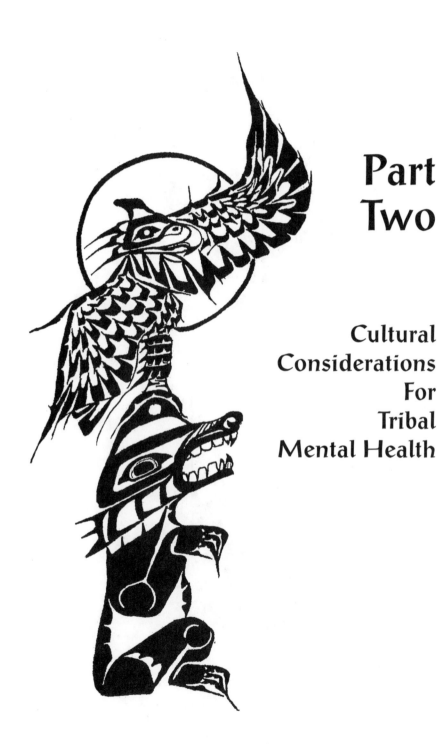

Part Two

Cultural
Considerations
For
Tribal
Mental Health

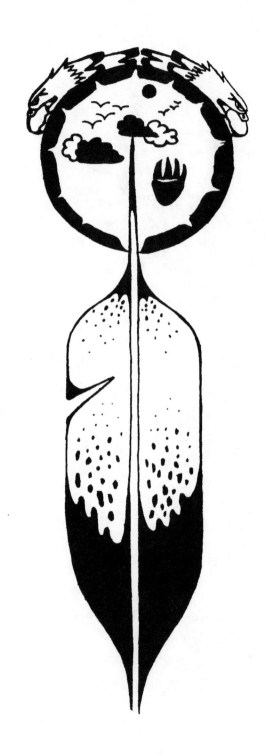

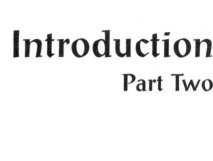

Introduction
Part Two

Chapter Six presents a general orientation to the relation of culture to mental health. *Culture influences all human experiences. It particularly affects mental health and the various forms which mental health problems take among different cultural groups. Positive cultural identity helps prevent mental health problems. The process of Indian identity formation is discussed, followed by a model of cultural congruence aimed at supporting cultural identity and values. Guidelines for culturally appropriate mental health services are presented.* Stereotypes about culturally different people need to be identified and corrected.

Chapters 7 through 12 attempt to orient the reader to those aspects of Native American Indian culture which have particular significance for the mental health, social/emotional problems and mental health care of Indian people, such as family relations, values, social norms, communication styles and worldview, spiritual orientation, healing practices, and concepts of health and illness. The GWUP Report on core Swinomish values summarizes community views elicited during the tribal forums in preparation for this second edition.

Fully describing any culture is an impossible task: culture is a pervasive experience which must be lived to be appreciated. Written descriptions are always limited. But they are useful if aimed at a particular audience and confined within clear limits.

The following discussion is directed primarily at mental health and social services workers who need to develop a basic familiarity with Indian culture. We anticipate that many of our readers will be non-Indian, and that some may have a very limited background in Indian culture(s).

Most Indian readers will be quite familiar with the aspects of Native American life described in the following sections. *Some Indian readers may find the discussion either over-simplified or over-generalized. Indian readers will certainly find some points which do not fit their personal, family or tribal experiences. We hope that these imperfections will be accepted in the spirit of providing a useful orientation for health and social service workers.*

Although generalizations are sometimes necessary, they can also be dangerous. While there are some deep similarities underlying the cultures of most Indian people, there are also definite cultural differences.

In Washington State alone there are roughly thirty federally recognized tribes, many of which include two or more culturally distinct native peoples. In fact, at the time of original contact with non-Indians, there were approximately fourteen language families and seventy tribes in the area which is now Washington state.[1] Although this book does not attempt to describe aboriginal Indian cultures, *it is important to remember that cultures are living and evolving systems with ancient roots. Cultural differences exist not only between tribes, but also between Indian people of different generations and extended family groups.* In addition, enormous cultural pressures have caused rapid cultural changes, especially among Indian people who have lived for a time in urban areas.

All generalizations run the risk of being in some way inaccurate, or even offensive to certain people. However, it is not possible to discuss the vital role of culture in mental health without making certain generalizations. We hope that any one discovering an inaccuracy in these booklets will understand that it is not possible to be completely accurate in discussing anything so complex as Indian culture.

While the contributors and consultants involved in the preparation of this book include Indian people from a wide range of

Tribal groups, there is a concentration of focus on Coast Salish, Lushootseed and Swinomish cultural experiences. For this reason, some matters discussed in this booklet and its companion volumes may be more applicable to Coast Salish groups than other Indian cultures. Whenever we have been aware that a certain aspect of culture was specific to Coast Salish culture, we have said so. However, we realize that differences also exist among the various Coast Salish Tribes and extended family groups.

Readers should understand that the cultural matters presented are only specific examples of Indian cultural experiences. Examles are generally more powerful than theoretical statements about culture in general. For instance, while many Plains Indian people greeted the Ghost Dance religion eagerly because of its promise of bringing back their dead ancestors, this religious movement failed among the Navajo precisely because of a deep-seated cultural fear of ghosts and the dead. Unlike the Sioux, the last thing most Navajo people wanted was a massive return of their dead. In this example, the same element (The Ghost Dance prophesies) had an almost opposite effect on these two very different Indian cultural groups.

Knowing about these specific reactions increases ones understanding of the power of culture in general. It also illustrates that most Indian people have strong feelings about their ancestors and about how to behave toward the dead. While this generalization may not be universally applicable, it is a generally useful thing to know in dealing with most Indian people.

While specific examples give life to generalizations, it must at the same time be clearly understood that no specific cultural belief or practice is universal. It is in this spirit that readers should regard all cultural information presented in this book.

Readers who work with Indian people should seek additional ways to become knowledgeable about the particular Indian cultural context in which they are working. This can best be done by observation, interaction, and by talking with Indian people about their viewpoints, rather than by making assumptions. This is most possible through long-term and close daily interaction with Indian people, preferably in a family, group or tribal setting rather than only with isolated individuals. This is an invaluable training experience for any non-Indian wishing to learn about Indian culture.

In addition, workers providing services to a given Indian tribal community should seek out ethnographies and other information specific to that particular group. Tribal authorities may be able to suggest materials. The books and articles listed in Part VI may also be of help.

Above all, it is crucial that mental health workers recognize that Indian culture is neither lost nor dead. It is a vital and changing reality which determines how Indian people see the world and relate to others.

Rapid cultural change has been forced by contact with non-Indian society. The results of this contact have often been extremely negative. *Although current social and economic circumstances limit the choices open to many Indian people, the resilience and richness inherent in Indian cultures have provided Indian people with a distinctive world view and a capacity for inner strength. In spite of obstacles and long periods of suppression, there are many signs of Indian cultural renewal.*

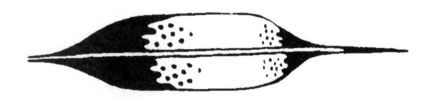

Contents
Part Two

Chapter Six
**The Importance of Culture
for Mental Health**   149

The Role of Cultural Identity in Mental Health 149
Forming a Positive Indian Cultural Identity:
Process and Pitfalls 152
    Basic Conditions for Positive Cultural Identity 155
    Child Logic & Negative Self Image 158
    Ongoing Conditions for Positive
        Cultural Identity 159
    Summary 161
Cultural Congruence in Mental Health Services 163
    Need for a Broad Conceptual Framework 163
    Cultural Congruence in Ethnic Mental Health 163
    The Concept of Cultural Predominance 164
    The Concept of Cultural Congruence 168
    Dimensions of Culturally Congruent Services 170
    Guidelines for Culturally Congruent Services 172
    Summary 173
Stereotypes and the Experience of Prejudice 175
A Word About Cultural Deprivation 178
A Word About Acculturation and Biculturation 179

PART TWO   Cultural Considerations for Tribal Mental Health

Chapter Seven
Tribal Family Systems   181

The Extended Family 181
Childhood 184
Teaching 185
Individual Gifts 186
Male and Female Roles 186
Names and Naming 188
The Role of Elders 190
Problems Facing Indian Elders 193
Respect for Ancestors 196

Chapter Eight
Tribal Social Life   199

Lifestyles 199
Structure of Tribal Government 201
Social Etiquette -
The Unspoken Rules of Tribal Relationships 203
    Respect 204
    Informality and Social Involvement 205
    Social Status 207
    Inter-Family Relations 208
    Togetherness, Hospitality and Sharing 209
    Gift Giving 211
    Decision Making 212
    Non Self Assertion and Non Interference 213
Social Pressure and Social Controls:
Gossip, Ignoring and Shaming 214
Attitudes Toward Time 217
Traditional Ways of Dealing with Grief and Loss 219

Chapter Nine
Communication Patterns   223

Native Languages 224
Indian English.. 224
Verbal vs. Non-verbal Communication 225
Eye Contact 227
Handshakes 228
Thank-you/Give Honor Gesture 229
Expression of Emotions 230
Humor 232
Storytelling 233

Chapter Ten
Native American Worldview:
Spirituality and Healing   235

Introduction 235
Spiritual World View 236
   Spiritual Privacy... 240
   Spiritual Healing Tradition 242
   Prayer, Music and Song 243
   Spiritual Tolerance and Variety............................ 245
   Traditional Concepts of Health............................ 247
   Traditional Ways of Helping and Healing 251
   Traditional Expectations of Helpers 252
The Smokehouse Way 254
   Spiritual Disturbances 255
   Spirits and Songs 256
   Resistance to Spiritual Call 257
   Entering the Smokehouse...................................... 258
   Initiation 259
   Smokehouse gatherings 261
   The Work: Memorial as and Namings 262
   Singing, Drumming and Dancing.......................... 264
   Living the Smokehouse Way 264

Risks of Participation 266
Misuse of Smokehouse 267
Benefits of Smokehouse Life 268
Summary 269
Indian Christianity 270
Catholicism at Swinomish 270
Indian Shaker Church 271
Pentecostal Church 273
Talking Circle 274
Summary 275

Chapter Eleven
Traditional Healing Around the World
A Cross-Cultural Perspective

277

Traditional Healing Around the World:
A Cross Cultural Perspective 277
Summary 281

Chapter Twelve
Core Swinomish Tribal Values
Promote Mental Health

283

The Gathering of Wisdoms Update Report 283
Spirituality 284
The Central Value of Kinship 285
Gathering Together 286
Sharing and Interdependence Promote
    Community Wellness 287
Participation in Traditional Activities 288
Traditional Uses & Significance of Cedar 288
Resurgence of the Canoe Culture 289
Drum Making and Drumming 292
Bone games or Slahal 294
Traditional Occupations 294

Chapter Six
The Importance of Culture for Mental Health

The Role of Cultural Identity in Mental Health

S tarting in infancy, we learn how to be 'human' through interactions with other people. Without social stimulation, love, modeling and communication with others, a child cannot grow into a recognizably 'human' creature; he/she will not develop language, emotional expressiveness, social responses or 'personality'. All these human experiences and social interactions are culturally determined: culture is "the integrated pattern of human behavior which includes thought, communication, actions, customs, beliefs, values and institutions of a racial, ethnic, religious or social group."[2]

A person learns to be a person in a particular culture. Personality is always effected by culture. In fact, culture is so basic to human experience that it cannot be separated from humanness or from personality: there is no such thing as a basic, pre-cultural or 'blue print' human being.

Although it is possible to change our attitudes and level of understanding of our culture, it is not possible to totally separate ourselves from our cultural roots.

One way of explaining culture is to say that it is all the things we take for granted. Not only our conscious values, but our assumptions about the way things are come from our early culturally determined experiences. Most human beings are extremely ethno-centric or culturally self centered: We all tend to take for granted that OUR WAY is the BEST WAY, if not the only way.

Generally, people only learn about the nature and personal importance of their own culture through encounter with other cultures.

Personal identity is deeply tied to cultural identity. We often believe that we are destined to be a certain way because of who our parents, grandparents and great-grandparents were. ***Even when we are not aware of it, we are the carriers of our cultural heritage, and this forms an essential part of our personal identity.***

Indian people, by and large, have become quite conscious of themselves culturally. This is because Indian people have been constantly confronted with a very different culture, i.e. that of 'mainstream America'. The experiences of invasion, domination, prejudice and the utterly overwhelming numbers of non-Indian Americans have made cultural differences obvious to most Indian Americans.

Unfortunately, many Indians have been taught to devalue their culture, and therefore, to devalue themselves. The 'dominant' culture has often either assumed that differences were weaknesses or has been blind to differences altogether. American culture is plagued by a 'one-size-fits-all' mentality. The 'melting pot', once a democratic ideal, has become a sort of cultural tyranny imposed on ethnic peoples by the mainstream majority. The most tragic aspect of this is that many ethnic people, Indian included, have come to judge themselves by this narrow and biased yardstick.

Many Indian people experience an identity crisis. Many old ways have been lost. Others have been threatened or at times even outlawed. For instance, the centuries-old traditional whaling practices of the Makah Indians were outlawed, thus seriously destabilizing Makah culture. Whole generations of Indian children have been separated (by boarding schools and state child welfare systems) from their natural 'caregivers', the extended family. Young people are often caught between the traditional values of their elders, the loss of traditional cultural values by many of their parents' generation, and the promised but too often unobtainable success supposedly available in the (non-Indian) mainstream world.

Indian children are often given ambivalent messages by their own people as well as by mainstream society. They are told to follow the old ways, but also to learn the white ways. They may be told to get an education, but not be encouraged to study. They may be told to get a good job, but be resented and thought 'uppity' if they appear to know things their parents don't or to make more money than their Indian peers. Coast Salish people have a poignant joke which illustrates this point: Two crab fisherman were returning home with full crab pots. The crabs in the non-Indian pot kept climbing out, so the non-Indian fisherman had to keep putting them back in. Finally, he asked his Indian companion, "How come your crabs stay in the pot but mine keep getting out?" The Indian fisherman said, "these are Indian crabs." "What do you mean," said the non-Indian? "Everytime one of 'em gets up, the others pull him back down."

At the same time, mainstream society gives Indian children contradictory or confusing messages. They may be told to work hard in order to succeed, but also told that Indians are 'lazy' or can't ever 'make it'. They may be told to value themselves but also that their beliefs or culture are not worthwhile.

Indian children are in effect put in a no-win situation: they cannot meet both sets of contradictory expectations. Therefore, they often feel doomed to failure. If they stick to the traditional Indian ways they may be seen as failures by white society and may feel rather insecure themselves, but they will at least gain the respect and acceptance of many family and tribal members. If they choose the 'white' way, they are liable to do so at the expense of family and tribal approval and often of their own psychological well being. *Most Indian people choose some mixture of traditional and mainstream value orientations, but only exceptional people are able to completely transcend the confusion, self doubt and frustration created by the conflicted social environment in which they find themselves.*

A positive cultural identity is crucial for mental health: we must feel at ease with who we are and we must basically like and accept our culture. This does not mean idealizing our culture, only feeling comfortable with our heritage and having a sense of cultural belonging.

Cultural identity is of particular importance for Indian people precisely because it has been disrupted by loss of cultural knowledge, attacks on Indian ways and destructive social conditions. **A negative or confused cultural identity is in itself a mental health problem, often leading to unhappiness, low self-esteem, indecisiveness and self destructive behavior. Cultural identity is relevant for all mental health work in the following ways:**

• Assessment of each client must include an evaluation of his/her cultural background and identity.

• The client cannot be helped to change without first understanding his/her cultural values.

• Treatment approaches should be congruent with the client's cultural values and lifestyles.

• The cultural aspects of the therapist-client relationship should be considered and often need to be discussed during treatment.

• A positive cultural identity should be a treatment goal whenever ambivalence, conflict or a devaluation of the self or culture group exists.

FORMING A POSITIVE INDIAN CULTURAL IDENTITY: PROCESS AND PITFALLS

There are three primary characteristics of Indian people who have achieved a positive cultural identity: They have a general knowledge of their own tribal culture, they know their personal roles in the family and tribal community, and they have a basically positive emotional acceptance of themselves as members of their culture group. These three qualities are discussed in turn.

I.   **General Cultural Knowledge** *means having context and perspective about one's culture.*

People with a positive cultural identity have a general understanding of their cultural history: they are aware, at least in general terms, of the tribal and larger cultural/ linguistic group history. They have a basic understanding of past and current life ways, material culture, family life and beliefs typically held by their people (regardless of whether or not they personally share these beliefs).

Furthermore, they are at ease with the language spoken by tribal members. If the language has been lost, they have at least as much knowledge of what it sounded like as do most tribal members, and they are liable to know at least a few words. Most important, these people are comfortable with current spoken norms, whether in English or a Native tongue. This means that *they "get" most jokes, innuendos and nuances of meaning. They generally understand what in-group expressions or sayings mean.* The level of sophistication of course varies with the intelligence and experiences of the individual. The key point is that they feel at ease with the common norms of conversational give and take in their cultural group.

People who have a positive identification with their culture are familiar with the commonly accepted beliefs held by cultural group members. They know what is generally held to be true, important, right and good, what behaviors will bring respect, and what is considered dangerous or bad. They need not agree with all these beliefs, but they must have familiarity and general comfort in negotiating interactions with others who do.

Finally, those with positive cultural identities know the tribal traditions. They are knowledgeable about typical tribal activities and role expectations. In other words, *they know "how we do things".*

II. *People with a positive cultural identity know how they personally fit into the cultural context.*

A person with a positive cultural identity knows his or her family ties, social roles and responsibilities: for instance, this person might be able to say "I belong to a family who are Shakers (or Catholic, or Smokehouse, etc), and who are (or are not) directly involved in tribal politics, etc.

Such a person can identify his or her role in the family. For instance, "I am the eldest son, so I will likely become the family spokesperson as an adult", or "As a younger daughter I am expected to cook and serve visitors", or "I am an auntie who cares for children", or "As a grandfather, I teach and guide my grandchildren".

People who have achieved a positive cultural identity generally understand their "cultural" responsibilities, even if they do not totally accept or agree with them. For instance, the person might say or think: 'because of my role in the family and community, it is my job to care for a disabled or aging relative, or help with funerals, or speak in public for my family, or share food and money with those in need in my family, or assist family at important times (such as confirmation, "give aways", Smokehouse initiation or sports events), etc.

The person's particular cultural role might require that they learn, remember and bear "witness" to names given, or learn family songs and other special family spiritual property, such as teachings about healing, ceremony, proper food, or family stories. Each family in Coast Salish society has its own teachings, and certain younger people are given the responsibility to hold these teachings for the family.

III. *The third quality of individuals with a positive cultural identification is a basically positive feeling about their culture and their own place in it. In other words, this person feels comfortable, natural, and has a sense that "I belong".* They may have areas of disagreement with cultural norms, or even major areas of doubt or criticism, without this disrupting their overall feeling of "connectedness": It is not necessary that the person glorify their own culture or think that it is better than other cultures, or be particularly focused on cultural matters. It is not always the person who surrounds him/herself with traditional music, art or cultural objects, or one who attends many cultural events who has the healthiest cultural identity: It may be the person who is relaxed, able to joke, may even be culturally "unconventional" in some of their beliefs and activities who has the more positive cultural identity. *The key thing is whether or not a person feels inwardly at peace with "who I am" culturally.*

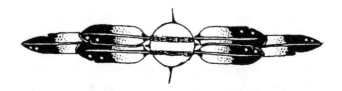

BASIC CONDITIONS FOR DEVELOPING A POSITIVE CULTURAL IDENTITY:
What Is Needed and What Can Go Wrong

Basic Trust

All little humans need food, warmth, cleanliness, physical contact and comforting. When these things are provided, babies tend to flourish. Ideally, when the baby cries, he is picked up and comforted. When she is hungry, she is fed. When he is wet, he is changed. When she is scared, she is comforted. *The people around the baby interact in ways which make the baby feel good.*

Under these circumstances, the baby learns the basic (nonverbal and unconscious) *lessons that 'The World is a Safe Place,' 'People are OK,'* (i.e. trustworthy and sources of nurturance), *and 'I am OK and Lovable.' This lesson is the root of all positive identity. Once learned, it sets the tone for later identity and personality development.*

This is what is often called "Basic Trust" and "Basic Self Worth". It is the key developmental "task" of infancy, and it predicts to a great degree how the person will fare in later life. The sense of Basic Trust is established mostly during the first year of life.

This basic experience is pretty much the same in all cultures. However, *even very early, cultural differences can make lasting impressions. What the young child experiences is likely to determine the conditions under which they later will feel safe and at ease:* We all tend to feel most comfortable with what we know best. There is a basic psychological law that *'What is learned first is learned best.'*

The infant and toddler take in the basic patterns and rythms of the language they hear, even before they understand the meaning of the words. They take in and respond emotionally to the music they may hear. Whether or not one hears music early in life, and what kind of music may well effect how a person responds to music for the rest of their life. There is also some reason to believe that hearing music early on may have other positive effects on the developing brain.

Young children are deeply effected by how much they are held and other experiences of physical closeness and nurturance.

The responses of adults to a baby's crying, laughing, etc. may teach that child how emotions are handled and expressed in their culture.

Cultures differ in the number and variety of caretakers young children interact with. No pattern is necessarily "better" than another, but the psychological results differ. Cultures in which children are raised mainly by a single primary caretaker, (usually but not always the mother), tend to produce children who are primarily bonded to their parents. In contrast, cultures in which young children are exposed on a routine basis to a number of caretakers tend to produce children who are psychologically bonded to the group or tribe rather than only to their parents. This difference has implications for the way an individual views him/her self throughout life: one may see oneself primarily as an autonomous individual, or may identify primarily as a member of a larger social unit, such as a family or tribe.

Cultures differ greatly in the amount of physical stimulation children experience in play, the amount of physical touch provided by grown ups, in the number and varieties of toys, etc. Food preferences may be set very early in life. In fact some researchers have suggested that babies may 'learn' to like certain foods as a result of ingesting the mother's milk during breast feeding.

All of this demonstrates the central importance of the quality and variety of experiences, especially interpersonal experiences, during the first one to three years of life. *Hopefully, by age two or three, a child has a strong sense of basic trust, self worth, and belonging. This is the ground from which a positive cultural identity can grow.*

Predictability and Control

A sense of predictability and control is the next building block of healthy identity and self worth. Predictability refers to the idea that things are reliable and can be counted upon to happen in a certain way. It is the opposite of chaos.

When a child internalizes a sense of a predictable world, they believe that 'If this, then that'. For instance, 'when I am hungry, I am fed', 'when I cry, I am picked up and comforted'. This sort of *consistency leads to a child internalizing hopefulness, because they have learned that good things can generally be expected to happen and discomfort will be alleviated.*

A consistently predictable environment tends to promote self confidence. This is because the child learns that 'What I do makes a difference', 'my own behavior influences what happens to me'. 'If other people are predictable, then I can depend on them to respond to me in a certain way.' 'If this is so, I can plan because I know what to expect and I know that I have some degree of control.'

Unpredictable Environments

Unfortunately, many children do not grow up in predictable environments. For instance, some babies and toddlers learn that sometimes they are picked up or comforted if they cry, but other times they are not. Sometimes they are fed when they feel hungry, but other times they have to wait a very long time.

The 'lesson' a child learns in an unpredictable environment is 'I can't depend on or trust people. I cannot predict what may happen and I have no power to impact events.' This view of life obviously leads to difficulties in self confidence, low motivation for future planning, and self doubt.

Alcoholic families tend to be unpredictable environments in which to grow up. Meals may be irregular, rules and schedules may be chaotic, the physical and emotional availability of caretaking adults may be erratic. Children growing up in such unpredictable environments may have difficulty trusting others and may have low self confidence.

It is important to point out that the presence of a number of people coming and going in a household does not mean that the environment is unpredictable. Nor does a high noise level. These may be normal lifestyle experiences, which children can adapt to without problems. But abrupt changes from established patterns can indeed be unsettling to young children. A sudden and unusual influx of visitors, or a sudden absence of people with whom a child usually interacts can both be disturbing.

The Dangerous Environment

Some households are more than unpredictable; they are dangerous: children may be actively and intentionally hurt, passively endangered or emotionally attacked. These may be homes where children are beaten, sexually abused, seriously malnourished, exposed to dangerous conditions such as hot fires, toddlers left to play in the streets, or situations where children are verbally abused. ***In such circumstances, the child learns 'Don't trust', 'Expect to be harmed by people' and 'I am bad'.***

It is fairly obvious why children in actively dangerous environments learn to not trust and to expect harm. It may be less obvious why children in such situations conclude that they themselves are bad, rather than (more accurately) thinking that those who hurt them are at fault. However, this is a nearly universal outcome of being raised in a dangerous household, and sometimes results from being raised in an unpredictable home.

Child Logic and a Negative Self Image

Small children are "ego centric": they believe that they are the cause of what happens around them and to them. This is developmentally normal. Small babies do not differentiate themselves from the environment at all: so far as they know, they ARE the world. Only gradually does the baby discover where his or her body ends and other people and things begin. Learning the limits of their psychological influence takes much longer.

Child logic says: 'I cause everything: good things happen because I am good. If bad things happen, it is because I am bad'. Small children believe that they cause illness, death, divorce. One version of this is to believe that parents leave them because they were bad or unlovable. "If she loved me, how could she have died?", etc.

As discussed above, children have a fundamental need to feel safe and to feel that they have some sort of self efficacy, i.e. to feel that 'I matter and I have some control'.

Imagine how terrifying it would be to be a small child living with hurtful, rageful or neglectful adults: you would be little, unable to leave or escape, and unable to change the situation. The child is faced with the really unbearable fact that 'The people I am totally dependent on hurt me or ignore me'. This perception is terrifying, in fact, it is too terrifying to fully 'take in.'

If the child in such a situation fully understood that they were helplessly trapped in the control of very dangerous people, their plight would be intolerable: if they grasp that their parents (or uncle or sister, etc.) are responsible for the danger and hurts (i.e. is/are the "bad" one(s)), then they would feel hopeless and would know that they might not survive at all.

However, if they think 'I am the bad (or responsible, wrong,

defective) one,' then there is some hope: 'I can be better, I can try really, really hard to be 'good', to be quiet, to do what he wants me to, to protect my little brother,' etc. This psychological shift of blame preserves a flicker of hope. It gives the child a more tolerable way to see their situation and also preserves their desperately needed emotional bond to the abusive or neglectful caretaker.

Virtually all children in abusive circumstances develop some deeply held beliefs like 'It was my fault', ' I am no good', 'I deserved it' or 'I am unlovable'. Even though this is an understandable defense and even a survival technique, this leads to the very worst damage resulting from child abuse. A negative self image outlasts bruises, broken bones or the years during which the child is actually being hurt: it impacts how the child sees him or herself for life.

ONGOING CONDITIONS FOR POSITIVE CULTURAL IDENTITY

As children move beyond babyhood, their needs become more complex. It is after about age three that the cultural components of personal identity become more prominent. Being talked to, given attention and emotional interactions all teach cultural identity.

Children must be talked to, helped to learn to talk, and listened to. This attention not only helps them learn communication skills, but especially helps them learn the unique sounds, intonations, pacing of speech and norms of communication in their particular culture group. By talking and example, children learn how to get the things they need and want. This may be by direct asking or through more indirect means of communicating. They acquire cultural assumptions and 'know-how!'

Children also need both verbal and non-verbal interactions with others. Smiles, corrections, laughter, and frowns all teach the cultural "rules" for proper behavior. Children form relationships, first with their care takers, next with extended family and then with peers. All these relationships are "culturally embedded" in that they convey the values and role expectations for people of certain ages, sex, social status, family membership, etc. *Without ongoing opportunities to interact and form relationships with people of their own culture group, a child will not be able to learn the roles, norms and cultural values of their culture. Therefore, they will have an impaired personal and cultural identity.*

"Mirroring" is a particularly powerful type of interaction in identity formation. Mirroring refers to ways that other people, especially close adults, reflect back to a child 'who they are.'

It is easy to observe mirroring by watching mothers with their infants. There is a back and forth interchange of facial expressions, sounds and behaviors which 'communicate' to the baby that his or her emotional and other experiences are understood. This in turn helps the baby and small child begin to be able to identify just what they are feeling and experiencing, and to begin to understand how others perceive them.

For instance, when the baby laughs, the mother or other care taker laughs back. When the baby "coos", the mother coos back. If the baby cries, the mother makes some sort of sympathetic sounds. If the baby makes early talking sounds, older family members often encourage this by repeating back what they heard or perhaps what they hope the baby was trying to say (modeling). If a baby claps his hands, adults often clap back.

All this mirroring lets the baby know that they have been seen and understood. It is a demonstration of empathy and 'being in tune' with the child's experience. To the extent that the empathy is 'on target', this process communicates to the baby that he matters: someone has paid attention, understood and communicated back. The child begins to experience being in a relationship with another person who values him.

This experience helps children develop a self image of being worthwhile. In addition, the mirroring helps shape the child's gradually developing understanding of what kind of person they are. For instance, when a toddler yells, a parent might say "Boy, you're really mad!" in a tone that might convey acceptance, irritation or possibly pride. Repeated over and over, such a message may lead to a child concluding that "I am an angry person, and that is good (or bad)."

As time goes on, the important adults in a child's life may say (or other wise convey) things like "you're really pretty" (or smart, or stupid, or fat, or a good artist, or a rascal or a tomboy, etc.) In other words, they tell the child who they think he or she is. They may say "You look like your grandfather", "This kid is really tough", "This girl is really shy", or "You're Dad's little buddy!," or "You don't have any respect!", etc.

Other people, especially family, teach us who we are, by what they say to us and about us, and how they treat us. If we are treated as valued and respected, we feel worthwhile. If our needs are routinely ignored or we are humiliated, we feel unimportant or ashamed.

We develop our picture of who we are as we see it mirrored in the words and actions of others. ***The younger we are, the greater the impact.***

To a great extent, people become what the important adults around them expect them to become, both good and bad. "You're going to be lazy just like your father" may be a self fulfilling prophesy, and the child comes to believe that this is true. "When you get to college, you'll meet all sorts of people and see all kinds of new possibilities for your life" tells the child that they are someone who is likely to go to college and that this will be a certain type of good experience. "Learn French! You can't even talk English!' conveys a very different impression of who the child is.

As children grow older, 'mirroring' merges with 'messages' as 'feedback' becomes less physical and more verbal. Increasingly specific value statements and instructions are given. 'Messages' are less descriptive of who the child is than is 'mirroring,' and are more directive about who the child ought to be.

Messages greatly impact school age children and teenagers. They come from family, community members, school, media and peers. ***By school age, Indian children are receiving multiple and often contradictory messages about who they are, about the value of Indian culture, and about what they "ought" to do*** (and what they are expected to do, which are not necessarily the same!)

SUMMARY

A positive cultural identity is formed when children experience basic trust and safety, self worth, and a feeling of belonging in family and culture. A predictable environment leads to a sense of personal efficacy and an ability to hope and plan for the future. Caretakers who themselves have a positive cultural identity are able to model this for children. Since children naturally identify with the important adults in their lives, this helps the child to feel good about who they are culturally.

People with a positive cultural identity have a basic understanding of their culture as well as of their personal place and role in that particular cultural context. They feel at ease and able to navigate the intricacies of social interactions in their cultural setting, and they experience a sense of belonging.

A number of things can interfere with the formation of a positive personal and cultural identity. Not getting one's basic needs met in infancy can result in a child experiencing the world as unsafe, others as untrustworthy, and themselves as worthless. In very unpredictable environments, children cannot learn cause and effect or that their own actions matter. If there is active harm or abuse, children may develop an internal image of themselves as BAD.

When caretakers have had life experiences which deprived them of the opportunity to develop a positive personal and cultural identity, they are handicapped in their ability to help their children and grandchildren feel culturally comfortable. Experiences such as loss of Indian languages, myths, stories, songs and ceremonies negatively impact cultural security. How a people think about themselves and the world is embedded in language. Therefore, loss of Indian languages is an especially huge loss for Indian elders who grew up speaking languages which are no longer commonly spoken.

The intergenerational legacy of tragedy and violence, beginning with the epidemics of the 1790's and 1820's, and continuing through loss of lands, racial discrimination, outlawing of traditional spiritual and healing practices, forced separation of children from families and tribes through mandatory boarding schools or foster care all contributed to loss of cultural knowledge and integrity. An entire generation of Indian people were forcably removed from their families and tribes and indoctrinated with anti-Indian philosophy. They were not allowed to speak their own languages, their elders were mocked, they were told that traditional beliefs were "the work of the Devil", and they were punished and humiliated for being Indian.

Throughout this book we explore the impact of these horrible historical experiences and their impact on mental health and cultural identity.

The goal of this program is to take steps toward overcoming this problem and bringing about a stable renewal of positive Indian cultural identity. The following article presents a theoretical and practical model for mental health services which support cultural identity.

CULTURAL CONGRUENCE IN MENTAL HEALTH SERVICES

Jennifer Clarke, Ph.D.

Introduction - The Need for a Broad Conceptual Framework

Mainstream mental health approaches have generally not met the needs of ethnic minority populations. This is due in part to the lack of a theoretical approach able to encompass broad cultural issues yet flexible enough to be adaptable to specific cultural contexts. This chapter suggests an approach to this problem.[1]

There is a wealth of fascinating literature relevant to ethnic mental health. Interestingly, much of it comes from outside the fields of psychology and mental health. Valuable anthropological knowledge has rarely been integrated into practical service delivery approaches.

Psychologists who have addressed ethnic mental health issues have tended to focus on 'cross-cultural' counseling rather than on 'ethnotherapy' or broad culturally-oriented approaches. Although they have identified many crucial cultural variables, much of this work has remained focused on improving the cultural sensitivity of mainstream therapists rather than on developing culture-specific approaches for service delivery.

It is certainly important to increase the awareness and sensitivity of mainstream therapists and to highlight pitfalls common in cross-cultural counseling. However, only within-culture therapeutic approaches are liable to adequately meet the growing needs of ethnic minority populations. This is because traumatic losses, culture shock, cultural isolation, depression, alcoholism, somatoform and anxiety disorders and unique culture-bound syndromes often call for specific, culturally-oriented treatments.

The key elements of effective ethnic mental health services must be identified. A model for practical integration of these elements is needed. A useful theoretical approach must also deal with the impact upon culturally distinct ethnic groups of contact with modern Western society.

Cultural Congruence in Ethnic Mental Health

The Cultural Congruence model provides a theoretical framework for mental health care in a variety of cultural contexts. This model attempts to clarify what is meant by the term 'cultural appro-

priateness:' All elements of mental health service delivery must be culturally specific in order to achieve 'cultural appropriateness'. Each culture must be understood as an organically functioning system into which mental health care must be naturally and harmoniously integrated if it is to be accessible, acceptable and effective.

The Cultural Congruence model includes two closely related concepts: 'Cultural Predominance' and 'Cultural Congruence'. Cultural Predominance asserts that culturally-specific services should have priority over mainstream services; Cultural Congruence asserts that all service elements must be derived from and harmoniously integrated into the overall cultural context. These two concepts will be outlined, followed by a brief discussion of specific functional elements which make up Culturally Congruent mental health programs.

The Concept of Cultural Predominance

It has often been mistakenly assumed that services to ethnic and racial minority populations could be provided merely by adding on circumscribed 'enhancements' from the ethnic culture to the existing mainstream service system. Figure 1 illustrates this approach.

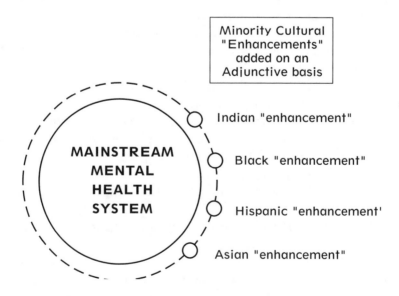

Figure 1.
Mainstream Mental Health Model of Service Delivery
to Ethnic Minority Populations

In this model, circumscribed culturally 'enhanced' services are simply added on to mainstream mental health services in the hopes of making services relevant to ethnic minority populations. Basic mental health assumptions and services remain unchanged.

Such cultural 'enhancements' might include:

- having a minority person on an agency advisory board
- using translators in therapy
- hiring minority persons trained in mainstream mental health approaches to deliver case management or psychotherapy
- printing agency brochures in the language of the ethnic culture

Although well-intentioned, the above types of isolated cultural 'enhancements' or attempts at 'cultural sensitivity' have been only partially successful. This is because mental health services derived from the assumptions and concepts of one culture can be of only limited effectiveness in another. Western mental health concepts and practices are culture-specific, having been derived from a particular historical and cultural background. *Attempts to merely transplant Western approaches to other cultural groups lead to confusion, misunderstanding, therapeutic failure and even damage to clients.* While adapting services and increasing therapist sensitivity are positive steps, they fall short of achieving cultural congruence.

'Enhancement' measures may be adequate for more acculturated or assimilated members of ethnic groups. However, they are clearly inadequate to meet the mental health needs of more traditional populations. The success of such measures tends to be in inverse relation to the degree of cultural integration in the ethnic group to be served. *The more culturally intact, integrated and traditional an ethnic group is, the less likely it is that simply 'tacking on' cultural elements to mainstream mental health services will be successful.*

The concept of Cultural Predominance helps clarify the appropriate starting point for ethnic mental health services: *belief systems, lifestyle, perceived problems and culturally identified service needs should determine the choice of services to be provided.* This position requires a re-orientation away from conventional mental health practices toward services derived from the culture of the group served. Since standard mental health approaches have been shown to be ineffective for ethnic clients, the mental health system must come to terms with this reality. Ineffective approaches should not be the basis for services to ethnic minorities.

We must challenge the definition of 'basic' mental health services. Culturally-oriented services derived from the cultural context are fundamental to effective ethnic mental health programs. These services can no longer be regarded as mere 'enhancements' to mainstream services. Culturally Predominant services require a new relationship between cultural programs and the mainstream mental health system. Figure 2 illustrates what this relationship might look like.

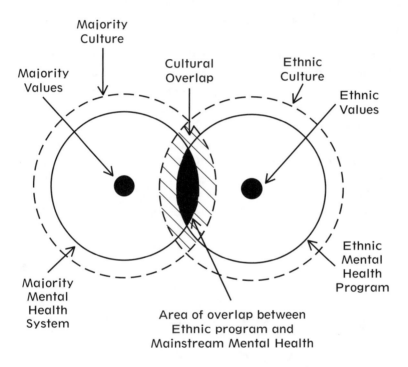

Figure 2.
Cultural Predominance From a Systems Viewpoint
Ethnic mental health programs should be founded on cultural values and designed to meet the needs of the ethnic group served, rather than being conceived of as adjuncts to mainstream mental health services (as was illustrated in Figure 1.). The focal point of an ethnic program differs from that of a mainstream program; ethnic cultural values, experiences and needs should predominate. Some overlap of the ethnic program with the mainstream system allows constructive linkages, so that needed 'mainstream' services can be available to ethnic clients.

A culturally oriented mental health approach is not a mere frill: it is the heart of effective services to any ethnic population. Each ethnic group's perceptions of mental health, mental illness and appropriate treatment must be the foundation of service delivery to this group.

Cultural Predominance contrasts with the prevailing community mental health system model. ***Instead of culturally unique services being considered 'enhancements', mainstream services become 'enhancements' or adjuncts to culturally congruent services.*** When specific mainstream services, such as psychotropic medication, hospital stays, day treatment, or a neurological exam are needed in individual cases, these can be added to supplement the basic cultural program. Services outside of the core cultural program are secondary or adjunctive to the primary cultural services. (see Figure 3).

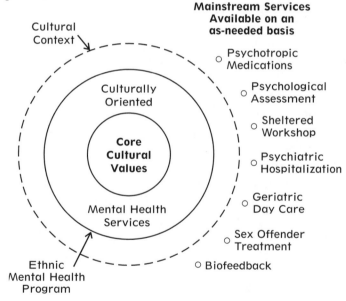

Figure 3
Cultural Predominance: Ethnic Prioritization of Services
This figure shows a program based on cultural values, from which culturally-specific services are derived. Services which meet the needs of the ethnic community take priority over mainstream services. Specific mainstream services are integrated into the culturally oriented program only when the needs of individual clients cannot be met through culturally oriented services alone.

Cultural Predominance involves a shift in perspective as to which services are fundamental and which are 'enhanced'. Although apparently a simple concept, it is one with profound implications. It is crucial that this perspective difference be grasped.

The Concept of Cultural Congruence

The concept of Cultural Congruence is closely related to that of Cultural Predominance. Cultural Congruence asserts that all aspects of mental health service delivery must be consistent with the specific cultural context in which service is being provided.

The culturally congruent mental health program is integrated into the overall cultural context. Program structure and services are consistent with cultural values. Program elements may be described as 'functional elements' in order to suggest their dynamic quality as interrelated and interacting parts of a living cultural system. Thus, program elements are congruent within the overall cultural context, as well as with one another. The relative importance of each element depends on the particular cultural meaning and emphasis.

This approach recognizes that cultures are living and functioning whole systems, complete with norms, values, standards of behavior, social systems and culturally dictated interaction patterns. Most significant, each culture has unique concepts of birth, death, health, illness and healing.

Culturally congruent mental health services must not merely 'consider' such things as client belief systems, spiritual practices, extended family relationships and child rearing patterns, but must be directly derived from the cultural base of the group being served. The entire cultural system itself is the foundation from which mental health concepts and practices are developed.

Among the elements which must ideally be congruent are: the language spoken, religious and cultural beliefs, the cultural identity of direct service providers, the setting in which services are provided, the structural components of service such as intake procedures, time availability and duration of sessions, charting procedures, therapeutic goals, therapy techniques, and the involvement of traditional healers in treatment. For example, culturally congruent mental health services for Hispanic people should be provided in Spanish by Hispanic therapists, at time and places convenient for migrant workers, and may at times involve folk healers or priests. Specific service elements vary according to the group being served.

To the extent that all dimensions of the therapeutic approach are culturally congruent and mutually compatible, mental health services will tend to be effective. When any one of these elements is incongruent with any one of the others, a cultural barrier is introduced which must be overcome in order to provide effective mental health services. For instance, even a Spanish speaking Hispanic therapist may be looked at askance by some Hispanic clients when encountered in the context of a mainstream mental health agency. More time may be needed to develop trust than would be necessary if the same therapist were met in the ethnic community or in an Hispanic agency.

Mental health services lacking complete cultural congruence are not necessarily doomed to be totally ineffective. However, each element which is incongruent with the culture will tend to introduce an obstacle to smooth therapeutic interaction. *The greater the cultural congruence, the greater the therapeutic effectiveness; conversely, the greater the number and extent of incongruent elements, the greater the resulting therapeutic difficulties.* Thus, the Concept of Cultural Congruence provides a principle which is both comprehensive and practical.

The Cultural Congruence model allows for flexibility in designing services which meet the needs of given cultural subgroups. The degree of traditional orientation and exposure to mainstream society must be assessed for each client population as well as for each individual client. Appropriate mental health services for highly homogeneous and stable traditional ethnic groups differ from appropriate mental health services to ethnic groups having a wide spectrum of cultural identification, racial, religious and national background. For instance, *appropriate culturally oriented mental health services to Indian people living in small, rural reservation communities can differ considerably from appropriate services to the more diverse Indian populations found in urban areas.*

In many ethnic groups a so-called 'acculturation continuum' exists, such that individual members of the cultural group differ considerably from one another in their degree of traditional orientation, as well as in their degree of familiarity and comfort in dealing with mainstream society. For instance, 'Southeast Asian culture' includes very traditional and monolingual tribesmen, highly educated professionals who relate primarily to western values and social norms, and fully "bicultural" individuals comfortable in both traditional ethnic and mainstream society. It is important to realize that what is culturally congruent for one such subgroup may not be so for another.

In Summary, the concept of Cultural Congruence is useful in that:

1. It provides a standard for the development and evaluation of effective mental health services to specific cultural groups. Programs may be designed to emphasize cultural congruence, as can evaluation tools.

2. It assists in pinpointing and remedying specific problems which develop in ethnic mental health service programs.

3. The Cultural congruence model is flexible enough to be usefully applied to mental health services in a wide spectrum of cultures and of cultural subgroups.

Dimensions of Culturally Congruent Mental Health Services

The unique cultural factors of each ethnic group must be considered in designing a successful mental health approach for that group. However, there are a number of general dimensions in any mental health service system which must be harmoniously integrated in order to achieve cultural congruence.

Twenty general dimensions of a mental health program are shown in Figure 4. These are not meant to be exhaustive nor to exclude the possibility of other equally important dimensions being identified. ***The relative importance of these components varies from one cultural context to another. Attaining a balance between these factors which fits unique cultural values is the key to achieving cultural congruence.***

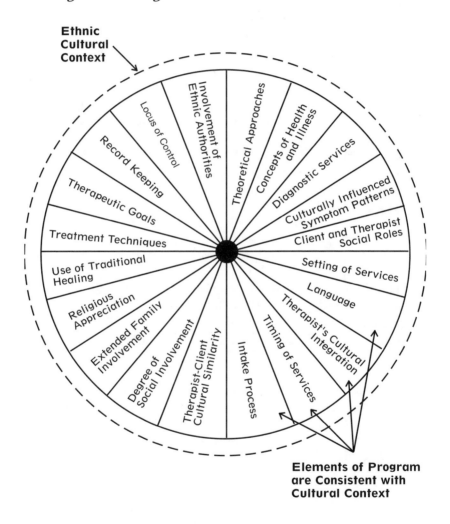

Figure 4.
Culturally Congruent Mental Health Services
Twenty components of a Culturally Congruent Mental Health Program are shown. These aspects of service delivery must be congruent with the culture and with one another.

Guidelines for Culturally Congruent Mental Health Services

For mental health services to be effective, the following dimensions must be congruent with one another and with the culture of the group being served:

1. Theoretical approaches should be culturally oriented.
2. Cultural concepts of illness and health should be understood and incorporated into treatment.
3. Diagnostic or classification systems should be culturally accurate and acceptable.
4. Culture-specific symptom patterns should be recognized.
5. Client-therapist pairs should be culturally similar.
6. Service providers should have achieved a positive personal cultural integration.
7. Services should be provided in the client's native language.
8. Settings of services should be easily accessible and culturally familiar to clients.
9. The nature and timing of the intake process should reflect cultural priorities and not be offensive to clients.
10. Services should be provided at convenient times and in lengths which conform to cultural expectations.
11. The role of extended family members in the therapeutic process should reflect cultural values.
12. Provider and client should be socially related such that therapeutic rapport is possible.
13. The degree of social involvement or enmeshment of mental health workers with the client should be culturally determined.
14. The client's religious beliefs should be understood, supported, and, if culturally appropriate, integrated into the therapeutic process.
15. Traditional healing practices and traditional healers should be integrated into the therapeutic process when culturally appropriate.
16. Treatment techniques should be culturally comprehensible and acceptable.
17. Therapeutic goals should be consistent with the client's cultural values.
18. Therapeutic expectations should be consistent with cultural biases toward inner or outer control (locus of control).
19. Record keeping systems should be minimally intrusive and culturally accurate.
20. The support of appropriate ethnic authorities or institutions must be obtained.

Readers interested in a discussion of the overall significance of each of these components of ethnic mental health programs are referred to the chapter on Cultural Congruence in Multi-Ethnic Mental Health Services: Six Demonstration Programs in Washington State.[3] (See listing in Part 6, Appendix One.)

Part 3 of this book presents a particular Tribal Mental Health Program based on the Cultural Congruence model. Readers will find a discussion of how each of these twenty program elements are addressed in this particular tribally-based program.

Summary

This chapter has outlined a theoretical model for culturally oriented mental health services, based on two overlapping concepts, the concept of Cultural Predominance and the concept of Cultural Congruence.

The concept of Cultural Predominance challenges the assumption that mental health services can be made 'culturally appropriate' merely by 'enhancing' mainstream services with cultural activities, ethnic minority providers, or other circumscribed 'adjuncts'. Instead, an inverse relationship is needed. *Culturally oriented services are the core of effective ethnic mental health programs, to which various mainstream services can be added when needed in individual cases.* The concept of Cultural Predominance challenges long held mental health system assumptions by asserting that culture-specific services should take priority. *This concept involves a basic shift in perspective as to which services are primary and which secondary.*

The concept of Cultural Congruence defines the relationship among culturally-specific services within the context of the culture of the group being served: *cultural values determine the nature and emphasis placed upon various services.*

Culturally congruent programs are embedded in the cultural context. Program services are consistent with the values of the culture, which form the 'core' or 'heart' of the program. Services are adjusted to one another, in order to form a program whole which is meaningful in terms of the cultural context. For this reason, service dimensions may be referred to as 'operative elements', in order to emphasize their function in the culture by the use of an organic metaphor.

Twenty operative elements have been identified and described. These are not necessarily the only elements possible in a culturally oriented mental health program, and their relative importance differs between cultures.

The Theory of Cultural Congruence posits that to the extent that these operative elements of mental health services are congruent with one another and with the cultural context, the therapeutic process will tend to be a smooth one. To the degree that these elements are culturally incongruent, barriers to smooth therapeutic interaction will be introduced.

Clients receiving culturally congruent mental health services receive an overall message of personal and cultural validation not possible when services are culturally incongruent. This message is conveyed both verbally and nonverbally. Cultural congruence ensures that the client's value system, life experiences and expectations about the therapeutic process will be integrated into the therapeutic process even when the client is not fully conscious of these factors. ***When mental health services are culturally congruent, the full weight of the cultural system can be brought to bear in support of the healing process.***

STEREOTYPES AND THE EXPERIENCE OF PREJUDICE

When any group of people has limited knowledge of another, stereotypes tend to develop. When a group with greater socio-economic power holds stereotypes about a minority group, the stereotypes tend to become used as justifications for oppression and discrimination.

All stereotypes are de-humanizing, both to those who are the 'objects' and to those who hold these views. This is true regardless of whether the stereotypes are 'positive' or 'negative'. Although 'positive' stereotypes or idealizations may not seem as destructive or dangerous on the surface, they are in fact just as de-humanizing as negative stereotypes. This is because all stereotypes are, by definition, over-simplifications which make people into abstract 'types' or 'things', rather than people.

In fact, all prejudice, discrimination, and ethnic oppression is based on stereotypes. In order to oppress or victimize another person or group of people, it is first necessary to (mentally) strip them of their humanity. *By ignoring complexity, ambiguity and individuality, and by exaggerating differences from oneself and ones own group, one can make the other group seem flat, unreal and non-human.*

It follows than an essential step in combating prejudice against culturally different people is examining and correcting stereotypes. This is not always easy. Stereotypes can be deeply rooted beliefs which may seem to be accurate or harmless. Probably everyone has stereotypes about some other groups. Examining ones own stereotypes requires open mindedness and courage.

Stereotypes about Indian people are common and have often been destructive. In order to offer effective mental health services to Indian individuals, stereotypes must first be dismantled. *Some common stereotypes about Indians are listed below, along with more accurate information.*

Stereotype

1. Indians live on reservations because...
- they can't make it on the outside
- they are undereducated
- they have no choice

Fact

1. There are many reasons why Indians may live on reservations, including:
- it is their own land and home
- to be with their own people
- to maintain their culture and way of life
- to maintain a family feeling
- to avoid outside interference
- to shield children from the prejudice of outsiders
- fear of outside prejudice or of being alone

Stereotype

2. Indians would naturally want to leave the reservations.

Fact

2. Many Indians prefer to live on reservations. Many who have lived away return because they consider it their home. Many Indians are proud of their tribe and feel that it is important to maintain their tribal community.

Stereotype

3. Indians all get 'per capita' checks from the government just for being Indian.

Fact

3. Nobody gets paid 'for being Indian'. Members of certain tribes or native corporations receive periodic dividends from the sale of resources or from jointly held stocks. Some families have leased land from which they receive income. Usually the amounts are small. In any case, most Indian people do not receive substantial per capita dividends or lease payments. Those who do, are entitled to them in much the same way that any non-Indian stock holder or heir is entitled to his/her income; because of legal ownership, not because of race.

To object to Indians receiving such payments for their own property is tantamount to objecting to Indians owning property or making money from their holdings. When non-Indians question these earnings or suggest that they are charity, Indian people naturally tend to feel angry and insulted at the message that they do not have the same rights as others to inherit property or to have holdings in a corporation.

Stereotype

4. Government programs for Indians are charities.

Fact

4. Government programs, such as the Indian Health Service, Bureau of Indian Affairs educational services, etc., are attempts to fulfill obligations for services guaranteed to Indian people by treaties. These services were guaranteed in exchange for vast territories and natural resources ceded to the U.S. Government. A variety of laws have been passed and programs instituted in order to protect and administer these rights.

Stereotype

5. All Indians drink and are alcoholic.

Fact

5. Many Indians do not drink at all or very little. Patterns of drinking are strongly influenced by culture and vary from tribe to tribe. Although alcohol abuse is a serious problem in many Indian communities, there are also Indian people who do not have problems with alcohol.

Stereotype

6. Indians are careless and wasteful of money and property.

Fact

6. Many Indian people share resources among extended family members. Many Indians feel that it is wrong for some people to have a great deal more than others, since this is unfair and destructive to cooperation among the group as a whole. Therefore, possessions beyond what are immediately needed are often distributed among others in need. This serves to preserve the cohesiveness of the group and earn community respect. Sharing is valued over saving, which may be seen as selfish hoarding. Since the future is often felt to be unpredictable, saving up for the future is seen by some people as foolish. The best insurance is the goodwill by ones fellows. When you give, it comes back to you double.

Stereotype

7. Indians are lazy and can't work hard or keep a steady job.

Fact

7. Indians tend to have somewhat different priorities than do mainstream whites. Not only is accumulation of wealth less valued, but hard work is not usually valued in and of itself. Instead, family or spiritual needs may be placed above work, with the consequence that jobs may be lost. Some Indians prefer seasonal jobs which allow them periods of time to devote to other interests. Indians often work hard at things they enjoy, such as fishing, or to get things they need. However, some Indian people do not see the value of continuing to work once they have obtained what they need.

Stereotype

8. Indian families are usually separated and have little cohesion.

Fact

8. Family is very important to Indians. Family ties and loyalties are usually very strong. Although educational and child welfare institutions have weakened some families, many have maintained cohesiveness in spite of such interference. Families are larger and may be somewhat more fluid, in that people may move around between family homes, while still maintaining great internal cohesiveness.

A WORD ABOUT 'CULTURAL DEPRIVATION'

The term 'culturally deprived' has been widely misused in an ethno-centric (culturally self-centered) way. It was commonly used in the 1960's to refer to poor and/or minority people whose heritage, values and lifestyle were neither understood nor respected by middle class white educators, social workers and politicians. They assumed that people who did not share mainstream cultural values and experiences were lacking in any culture. Most of the people who were called 'culturally deprived' were not deprived at all; they were culturally different. As cultural awareness has become more widespread, these ethno-centric and naive views have become somewhat less obvious, but they often still exist.

Mainstream American culture is only one of many cultures. Lack of familiarity with the majority culture does not make a person 'culturally deprived'. Many ethnic minority persons have richer and more vital cultural lives than does the average American.

Nonetheless, true cultural deprivation does exist: it is the condition of having been cut off from or having become emotionally alienated from ones own culture. This can happen to foster children raised away from their own ethnic group, to refugees, or to any people who have experienced breakdown and loss of their culture. It also happens frequently to middle-class Americans who lead mobile, rapidly changing lives, and whose family, home or social roots have become too shallow to nurture them.

The truly culturally deprived person is a person in limbo, a person without a sense of belonging, a person who neither knows nor accepts himself. True cultural deprivation not only increases the RISK of mental health problems, it IS a mental health problem in itself. *At best, a culturally deprived person is out of balance, incomplete and vulnerable. At worst he is confused, depressed, anxious, or amoral.*

Cultural deprivation complicates mental health problems. Treatment for people who are culturally deprived should address ethnicity, cultural identity, roots or rootlessness and ability to make commitments. Treatment should help clients know and accept themselves and their personal cultural heritage.

A WORD ABOUT ACCULTURATION AND BICULTURATION

The anthropological term 'acculturation' originally meant a process of interaction between members of two different cultures, resulting in increasing familiarity and exposure to the foreign culture, exchange of ideas, goods and technology and consequent change in each culture. In practice, one culture usually dominates and tends to take over the other.

Typically, contact between technologically-oriented Western cultures and non-Western people has resulted in a greater or lesser degree of destruction of the latter's culture. Words like 'primitive', 'advanced' or even 'pre-industrial' and 'pre-literate' imply an inherent superiority of Western culture as well as an inevitable direction of cultural change from 'primitive' to 'civilized', 'advanced' and 'Westernized'. Although anthropologists did not intend this term to carry such smug, ethnocentric implications, this is how the term has generally come to be interpreted. In fact, the term 'acculturated' tends to carry with it an unspoken bias of more advanced than 'non-acculturated'.

Ethnic minority people and students of culture change have challenged the assumption that loss of native cultures is either inevitable or desirable. Many people have come to see 'acculturation' as something undesirable, as meaning 'de-culturation' or a loss of one's culture. Instead, it has been suggested that the term 'bi-culturation' better describes a positive model for cultural identity and adjustment under conditions of cross cultural interaction. 'Bi-culturation' refers to a process of dual cultural competence, in which the original culture is positively valued and actively maintained while at the same time comfort, familiarity and competence in mainstream culture is also achieved.

The bi-cultural person does not lose his/her original cultural identity, beliefs or values when he or she learns to function in and enjoy mainstream society. *The bicultural person is one who has achieved a mature ability to cope constructively with mainstream society while at the same time remaining firmly rooted in his/her native cultural tradition. This ability to balance both traditions reflects psychological and emotional maturity; it is indicative of good mental health.*

Notes and References

1. This chapter combines new material with material from a previous article also written by Dr. Clarke and included in Ethnic Mental Health Services: Six Demonstration Projects in Washington State, published by the Culturally Relevent Ethnic Minority Services Coalition in cooperation with Skagit Community Mental Health Center, 1989.

2. Terry Cross, "Cultural Competence Continuum," Focal Point, Fall, 1988.

3. Information on to how to obtain this booklet may be requested from the Culturally Relevent Ethnic Minority Services Coalition or from Skagit Community Mental Health Center.

Chapter Seven
Tribal Family Systems

The Extended Family

Family tends to be both more important and differently defined for most Indian people than for most non-Indian Americans. The extended family comprises the basic social unit in most tribal societies. Whereas it might be said that in mainstream America the individual is the basic social unit, in tribal society the family is the basic social unit. Who one is (personally and socially) is strongly influenced by which family one belongs to, and of ones precise place in that family. This is true not only of children but of adults also.

*Members of Indian extended family groups tend to share exten-
sive responsibility for the welfare of the entire family.* This includes
more than shared concern for the emotional well- being of family
members or providing help in times of crisis. It involves a day to
day sharing of financial resources, belongings, child care responsibilities, etc.

In many Indian cultures, the great majority of ones time is
spent with family members. From birth to death, ones compan-
ions are usually members of the extended family. Indian people
tend to live with family and spend a great deal of time talking
with them and going places with them. Family members often
form ones primary social group to an extent usual in non-Indian
American society.

*Indian families are generally bigger and more inclusive than are
non-Indian nuclear families. Grandparents, aunts, uncles and cousins are often just as important and emotionally close as are parents
and siblings. At one time or another most tribal children live in the
same household with grandparents, aunts, uncles or cousins.*

In some traditional tribal societies, all relations of ones
grandparent's generation are called "grandmother" or "grandfather". This is a sign of respect and also expresses the emotional
and psychological relationship existing between individuals of
different generations. Similarly, relations of ones parents' generation are often called either "mother", "father", "aunt" or "uncle",
depending on the degree of social and emotional closeness. Cousins are often regarded and addressed as "brother" or "sister".
Relatives of 2nd, 3rd, 4th and even 5th degree (e.g. 3rd cousins)
are often recognized as members of ones family. In many traditional Indian societies, it is not acceptable to date or marry anyone who is known to be even distantly related. For this reason, it
is very important to know who one is related to.

Indian families are not only larger and more inclusive, but are
in some ways more flexible. How 'close' a relative is considered
to be is determined not only by blood relation, but by many
social and emotional factors. For that matter, whether someone is
recognized or 'claimed' as a family member is to some degree
dependent on social factors. At least in Coast Salish Society,
individuals have some degree of choice as to whom they recognize as their relations and as to how close they are considered to
be. *To 'claim' a person as a 'close' relation is a sign of respect,
approval and of a desire to maintain ongoing family ties. Likewise,*

to fail to recognize a person as ones relation can be way to show disapproval or even to give offense.

In some tribal communities, everyone is considered to be a relative, to a greater or lesser degree. Sometimes this may be literally (biologically) the case, and is certainly often an emotional and social truth.

In many Indian societies, people who are not biologically related may become formally or informally adopted into the family. Not only children, but adults who for one reason or another regularly associate with a given family may come to be accepted as family members. Jay Miller in his enlightening book <u>Lushootseed Culture and the Shamanic Odyssey</u> gives this example: "I call him 'nephew' because he calls my close cousin 'aunt'." (p. 126)

Elders in particular may 'adopt' children or younger people, especially if they lack strong family ties. Similarly, younger people at times adopt someone as their 'grandma' or 'grandpa'.

Family membership can be an important way of defining who is 'in' and who is 'out' of ones social group. In fact, in more traditional tribal societies, it can be difficult to become really close to anyone who is not in some sense a part of ones family. As one of our Tribal Support Counselors put it, it is rather like being on a team: "you're either in or you're out."

Indian family systems can be somewhat confusing for non-Indian newcomers to tribal communities. For instance, newcomers tend to assume that someone addressed as "auntie" is in fact the speakers' biological aunt. However, this may or may not be the case. Even more commonly, new-comers may fail to take proper note of the complex family ties existing between tribal members.

In order to begin to understand tribal relationships, social exchanges, and politics, it is first necessary to have an understanding of family membership, family social standing and inter-family relations. In most cases, non-Indians will need a patient tribal member to tutor them in these matters. (See also Chapter 12 Swinomish Core Values: The GWUP Report.)

Childhood

Indian children are born into a particular family system, which will largely determine their personal and tribal social identity. From parents, aunts, uncles and especially from grandparents, they learn 'who they are', i.e. who they are related to and the important family history. This gives children a sense of belonging to a family group and to the tribe. Knowing who you are related to and 'what you come from' is an extremely important part of knowing who you are in tribal life.

Tribal children grow up with a group of siblings and cousins of roughly the same age. These children often form a lifelong cohort who play together, learn together and take care of one another. Very often all of the others in ones cohort are considered 'brothers' and 'sisters'. Older children often look out after younger ones. Indian people often are intensely loyal and protective of these relations. When they grow up they may help one another financially as well as helping to care for each others children.

Indian parents are often loving and indulgent with young children. Children are often permitted greater freedom at an earlier age than are non-Indian children. Children are respected as individuals who generally know what is good for them. Strong likes and dislikes are generally honored, even about such things as whether or not to go to school or where to live. Of course, other values also influence such decisions. For instance, some Indian families may think that it is more important for a child to learn to fish or to participate in a traditional gathering than to go to school.

In strong Indian extended families a child may have several equally safe, loving family homes to choose from. They may move freely among the houses of their parents, aunts and uncles.
Indian children may be taught or disciplined by any adult, and often have close emotional ties to several adult relatives. While all adults in the family may share some degree of responsibility for all the children, in some tribes aunts and uncles have special roles as caretakers, teachers or disciplinarians.

Grandparents are often of enormous emotional and practical importance in the lives of Indian children. Not only are they often caretakers and disciplinarians but above all they are the emotional nurturers and teachers.

Children are generally expected to learn by watching, listening and imitating. Traditionally, they were not encouraged to ask questions or interrupt adults, but instead to listen to the stories and teachings of their elders. Often, children are included in adult activities to an extent unusual in non-Indian society.

While tribal children are seen as having their own individuality and unique gifts, they are also seen as a reflection on their family. Thus, a well behaved child who demonstrates good 'teaching' is seen as a credit to all of his/her family. A misbehaving child (or adult) can bring shame to the entire family. Often Indian parents tell their children, "If you do wrong, it's not you people will talk about, it s me." There is often considerable pressure to live up to family responsibilities and standards.

Discipline of children in many Indian communities is more social than physical. Misbehavior is often handled by withdrawal of approval, shaming or by ignoring. Desired actions are rewarded by approving looks and comments, or by public recognition. Many Indian people first encountered physical punishment in schools. Adults who were physically punished in boarding schools sometimes did not learn traditional Indian forms of discipline.

Teaching

Many Indian families have special family 'teachings', 'advice' or knowledge which is kept within the family. Children are taught 'who they are', 'what they come from', how to live and any special responsibilities carried by their family. Often, a strong Indian upbringing is seen as preparing children to cope with the outside world and with rough times.

Traditionally, grandparents told children stories in the evening. Teaching stories were more than entertainment; they contained messages about life and how to live. Animal figures and powerful images enriched childrens' lives, though certain stories could be very frightening.

Teaching stories are designed to make children and adults think about things in a new way. They do not provide simple solutions.

Elders sometimes spoke very sternly or forcefully to children, who were expected to listen quietly. Moral messages were often repeated many times, so that they became deeply ingrained.

Individual Gifts

People are born with special gifts. These form an aspect of individual destiny and should be carefully cultivated. Some people have the gift of clear public speaking. Some are able to heal the spirit through their personal power. Others may be able to receive special visions or premonitions or to 'see' the nature of an illness.

Indian people accept that individuals differ in their special gifts and abilities. People are not expected to excel in every area, but are instead valued for their unique ways of contributing to the group. Individual differences do not necessarily set people apart from the group. On the contrary, they are seen as complementary gifts which tie individuals to the whole. Since each person is different, each has a special contribution to make. *Each individual brings something special to the group and is at the same time dependent upon others for those strengths, skills or knowledge which he/she lacks.*

In this way, both individual uniqueness and group solidarity are valued. Uniqueness is of value precisely because of its special contribution to the whole.

Male and Female Roles

Indian cultures differ in the roles they give to men and women. Therefore, the following generalizations may not apply to all Indian groups. In many Indian groups, social pressures and cultural changes have led to some disruption in traditional sex roles.

Women tend to assume responsibility and adult roles at a younger age than do men. Especially if she has a child, a girl may take on many adult roles when she is still a teen-ager. Women tend to have primary responsibility for home and children. Women are often expected to devote themselves to their family and to their husbands. Their education may be seen as less important than a boy's. In many Indian groups, men eat before women.

However, women's roles are not necessarily strictly controlled and they do not generally have less real power or status than men. In some Indian cultures, women are the primary property owners. *Frequently women, especially older women, are re-*

spected decision makers and family leaders. Grandmothers often have special respect as teachers and heads of extended families.

Boys often are not expected to assume adult responsibility as early in life as are girls. In some Indian groups, men are seen as "young" until they are in their forties, regardless of whether they are married and have children. Irresponsible and impulsive behavior may be more accepted in young men than in women.

Traditionally, men were the hunters, fishers and providers, as well as warriors. As traditional economies were disrupted, many Indian men lost their way of contributing to the family economy and of achieving self respect. Since steady jobs and taking orders are seen in some Indian societies as below the status of men, some Indian men have had difficulty accepting the types of jobs actually available. Many Indian men prefer fishing and other seasonal jobs. They may earn money in lump sums but not have a stable income.

Often, women have been more willing to take routine or unskilled jobs or to become trained as office workers, aides, etc. Consequently, *in some Indian communities there has been a shift away from men being the main providers to women.* In some Indian communities women not only run the home, but also earn the money.

When this is so, an imbalance in power may result. In some tribal societies, women tend to contribute more and have more power than men. This can be problem for both men and for women. Women may resent their double load of responsibility and feel resentful that their men do not make a greater contribution. Men may feel ashamed as well as resentful of women who have assumed wage earning roles. A shift in status and respect may result, with women gaining greater overall power. In some cases, relationships between men and women may become strained.

It is critical that young men find ways to gain respect and assume adult roles. More attention needs to be given to the needs and dilemmas facing young men. New opportunities for culturally-acceptable employment must be found. Older men must actively mentor younger men.

Men are generally seen as having stronger spiritual powers than women, though this is not universal. Men often have important social and ceremonial roles. Middle aged men are the public speakers, masters of ceremony, acknowledged heads of families, etc.

On important public occasions men often dominate the scene and   receive public recognition.
However, this does not necessarily mean that
they are the primary decision makers, planners
and organizers of these events and gatherings.
Women are often active behind the scenes in
determining what will take place and how.

*In Coast Salish Society, it is generally under-
stood that although men receive greater public
recognition, this recognition includes the entire
family. It is well understood that women are full
partners in all important events. Women have considerable quiet power.*

Names and Naming

*Indian people often have several names, including baby names,
nicknames, 'white' names and Indian names, for use with different
groups and for different occasions. Thus, names are in some ways
more complicated and meaningful than is typical for mainstream
Americans.*

Traditionally, most Indian groups gave babies and young children temporary names for use in early childhood. In some Indian
societies children were not named at birth, but acquired a name
only when some unusual event or quality of the child brought a
name into use. In other Indian societies, babies were named soon
after birth by an elder or medicine person, but this name was held
in reserve and not commonly spoken.

Today, Indian children usually are given an American name at
birth. However, many Indian children were affectionately known
as 'baby' for several years, perhaps until the arrival of the next
child. This name reflects the child's social role in the family.
Although non-Indian social workers and teachers are sometimes
dismayed by what they see as a lack of appreciation for the
child's individuality, the term 'baby' carries with it enormous
love, respect and acceptance of the child into his/her family.

Many Indian children and teens are given nicknames. They
are generally fond references to some quality of the person, and
may be used only by family or friends. These nicknames may last
throughout life, alongside more formal names used at school or in
dealing with non-Indians.

Some names can be easily recognized as Indian. Not only

names like 'Jack Strong-Bull' or 'Winona White-Fawn', but names which reflect the history of contact with English, French or Spanish invaders and immigrants can often be recognized as belonging to Indians. For instance, American missionaries, educators and BIA officials often assigned American names to Indians whose Indian names they either could not or would not be bothered to pronounce. Thus, many Indian people came to be called 'Henry', 'John', 'Joseph', 'George', 'Bill', 'Jack', 'Mark', etc. Many times 'family' surnames were created by school officials who asked children what their fathers' names were. When told that Jimmy's father was named 'Joe', Jimmy came to be called 'James Joe'. Many Indian surnames today are borrowed American first names.

Although most Indian people use American names for everyday interactions, they often have separate Indian names which they regard as their real names. As one Indian woman explained it, English-American names are more or less conveniences. On the other hand, ones 'Indian name' is often a prized personal possession.

In Coast Salish culture, Indian names are family names, previously 'carried' by an ancestor or older relative, and passed on to a younger person as a gift or mark of recognition. Generally, only one individual carries a certain name at a time. Family elders decide who will receive which family name. *Acquiring an Indian name tends to increase an individual s status in the Indian community. Considerable planning and ceremony may be involved in conferring a name.* Respected guests must be called to witness and later testify to the bestowal of the name. *A person who receives an Indian name also receives the responsibility of upholding the honor of that name.* The actions of the person who 'carries' a certain name will either enhance or diminish the value of that name.

Indian names connect a person to their ancestors, to their family, and to future Indian generations in a way that borrowed American-English names, often acquired by chance and kept or shed according to convenience, can never do.

Non-Indian newcomers in Indian communities are liable to have some difficulty understanding Indian uses of names. The common practice of switching back and forth between nicknames, common names and occasionally even 'Indian names' in the same conversation may be confusing to the non-Indian who assumes that separate individuals are being discussed.

Another source of confusion is the use of family names. People are often thought of as belonging to the family group into which they were born, regardless of where they were raised or whether they were married into another family. Thus, if Jimmy was born into the Joe family but raised in the Edgar family, he may be known either as Jimmy Joe or as Jim Edgar. If Elmira was born into the Lucas family but married into the William family, she may be called either Elmira Lucas or Ellie William. For a person not intimately familiar with the local families and naming system, it can take quite some time to figure out just who is being referred to. The use of nicknames further complicates the picture.

Role of Elders

Elders have a unique and honored place in Indian society. Attaining the status of 'elder' is to a large degree an individual matter, dependent upon personal standing and family circumstances as well as upon age. The oldest members of a generation in a given family may be regarded as that family's elders, even if they are only middle aged. In addition, certain people become widely acknowledged as tribal elders, due to a combination of great age, social contributions, family standing, wisdom and continued ability to contribute to the group welfare. While all older people theoretically should be shown respect by all younger people, in practice certain individuals gain greater respect than others.

Elders are the teachers and the carriers of tradition. The transfer of cultural knowledge is their special responsibility. Their greater life experience, historical perspective, spiritual knowledge and closer ties to the old ways of tribal ancestors make them a valuable resource for younger people. They alone know the "right" way to do things and may be the only ones who know the native language, geneologies, and the important people from other tribal communities. Elders are in the unique position of being able to interpret traditional moral and cultural truths. What they say is generally regarded as truth which is not to be questioned.

Since elders are regarded as both knowledgeable and morally right, they tend to have considerable social power. This is not to say that their views are always accepted, followed or respected. However, they are seldom challenged directly. Elders often confront or correct younger people, sometimes in a very firm or stern manner, and often in public.

Older people, especially grandparents, are often the primary teachers of children, and not infrequently are their primary care givers. Traditionally, extended families lived together. While young adults were at work, their children were often left at home with grandparents. This pattern has been somewhat disrupted by the mainstream emphasis upon the nuclear family, reinforced by the size and design of modern houses, federal regulations for subsidized housing which limit the number of adult occupants, the nuclear family unit recognized by welfare agencies, etc. Nevertheless, it is still common for Indian children to spend a considerable amount of time in the home of their grandparents.

Even when children do not live in the same home with them, *grandparents generally have the role of teachers and advisors. They teach young children what they need to know about tribal culture, about family history and relationships, and about socially expected behavior. They often stress respect for others, sharing and togetherness.* Grandparents are generally consulted about major decisions. *Even middle aged adults regularly seek advice from their parents, aunts and uncles, especially at times of crisis.* Very often, though not always, this advice is followed.

It should be pointed out that the people who are recognized as ones elders are not always ones biological grandparents, grand aunts or grand uncles. Because of the large and often fluid nature of the Indian extended family, many older people have a hand in raising children. When one is young, all adult relatives and many non-blood relations are (literally) ones 'elders'. In traditional tribal communities, all adults shared in child raising responsibilities, at least to the extent of being able to give advice and/or reprimands. In such a situation, *children grow up with multiple 'psychological' parents and grandparents.* When they themselves become adults, all the surviving parenting figures from their childhood continue to be their 'elders'.

The individuals who one person recognizes as 'my elders'

may differ from those recognized as elders by other people, even by those of the same age or family. *'My elders' are not only older people who have had a hand in teaching or raising me, they are also those whom I most respect.* Thus, a person can, to a large degree, choose to recognize or not to recognize certain people as their elders. The degree of respect shown to an older person reflects social approval for how they have lived their life.

When a person has helped others, raised children and contributed to the welfare of the family and tribal community, they can expect to be rewarded by a position of honor and respect in old age. In general, people attain greater status, social privilege, and public respect as they get older. At the same time, a person is expected to 'earn' this respect by a lifetime of proper behavior. People who have been socially irresponsible are generally given less recognition in old age.

Many Indian people feel that elders have a responsibility to speak out to the community about important matters and to help younger people face life's journey. An "Elder" is not merely an old person: Elders have knowledge and wisdom and take seriously their responsibility to share this.

A number of factors go into determining the degree of respect given to older people, including:
- Their age
- Their ancestry
- Their past achievements and contribution to the welfare of others
- Their current helpfulness to younger people
- Whether or not they are respected by their own family
- Their spiritual and traditional knowledge
- The overall social standing of their family members
- The size of their family

Respect may be shown to elders in a variety of ways. When they enter a building, younger people often go out of their way to welcome them, shake hands and talk. Younger people give up their

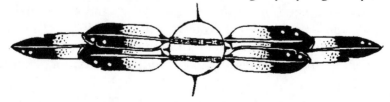

chairs or bring chairs to elders. Elders are served first at meals. Often, younger family members bring them their plates. When younger people have extra fish or other food, they often send some to the homes of elders. Young people seek advice from elders and visit them. Most important of all, younger people are expected to listen to elders whenever they wish to talk, without interrupting, until the elder has finished talking.

Just as younger people without elders may be considered 'poor', older people without younger people to care for them and give them recognition are also 'poor'. Since much important knowledge is family knowledge, only elders from ones own family can teach a younger person what they most need to know to become respected themselves.

Similarly, ***elders need younger people to whom they can pass along important family knowledge. Elders generally choose who in the family is 'next in line' to receive particular knowledge or responsibilities.*** Elders watch youth for signs of leadership qualities, which they then encourage and mentor. Youth watch elders for indications of approval and disapproval. When Swinomish elders agree with someone has said, they may say "O Si ⁷ ab," which is a Lushootseed term of respect. This lets the speaker know that the older person agrees with and respects what they have said.

Thus, older and younger family members are in a sense mutually dependent upon one another, not only for love and physical care, but also for the means of acquiring and maintaining knowledge, status and respect. Loss of elders can bring great stress to middle-aged people who must then "step up" into the role of family elders.

Problems Facing Indian Elders

The modern trend toward youth losing respect for older people has become a major source of disappointment and bitterness for some Indian elders. Some elders feel "pushed out" by younger peole who want to assume leadership positions or do things in new ways. As in all cultures, leadership transitions pose delicate challenges for all concerned.

Many elders complain that young people no longer "listen." Elders may become offended if not shown proper deference during public gatherings. When they feel disrespected, some elders withdraw into silence. Over time, this may rob the community of much-

needed advice, wisdom and role models.

As discussed above, it is a valued cultural norm for grandparents to teach and often care for children. However, in cases where parents have died or are unable to care for their children due to such problems as substance abuse, the total burden of raising grandchildren may fall on grandparents. When these older people are ill or tired, this can be terribly stressful. *In healthy Indian societies, elders have great responsibilities for children, but not total responsibility.*

Contrary to the Indian social ideal, some Indian elders, like many mainstream elderly, have become socially and physically isolated. As nuclear families have become more common, there has tended to be more conflict between elderly mothers and their daughters' in law, who often expect to be the mistresses of their own households.

As Indian society has changed, it has also become less clear who has financial and personal responsibility for older people. As breakdown of larger extended families occurs, responsibility for older family members is less likely to be evenly spread among a group of adult children. Sometimes, one son or daughter may find it necessary to assume primary responsibility.

Indian elders are less likely than younger Indians to seek mental health services. This may be due to language barriers, to a preference for traditional medicine, to a lack of familiarity with the goals and methods of mental health care, or to feelings of uneasiness about having to seek help from a younger person. Accordingly, elders may not be seen by mental health workers unless they develop severe cognitive and behavioral symptoms, such as severe memory loss, disorientation, nightmares or marked irritability.

Too many times, mental health intervention results in the elder being removed from the Indian family and tribal community and being placed in a nursing home. This results in deprivation of the daily support of family, tribal social roles and of the respect accorded elders in Indian communities. Not surprisingly, Indian elders are often very fearful and reluctant to go into nursing homes, even when their physical and medical needs are not being met at home.

Depression is a major mental health problem for all elderly people. For Indian elders, the losses of cultural meanings and language, the common history of early separation from parents and extended family, and the frequent experience of multiple losses of family members through tragic death all tend to place older Indians at high risk for depression. The diminished respect actually accorded elders (in contrast to the cultural ideal) is a major factor in the depression affecting Indian elderly.

Prevention and treatment of depression for Indian elderly must involve a strong cultural component. Maintaining tribal social involvement, teaching the young, and giving advice and approval concerning family matters are of primary importance. Younger tribal members demonstrating respect for their knowledge, experience and service to the tribal community is essential for the well being of Indian elders.

If at all possible Indian elders should remain in the Indian community, either in the homes of extended family members or in tribal housing for seniors. Continued participation in familiar and valued social and cultural events is important. Daily interchange with younger family members is crucial in allowing Indian elders to fulfill their cultural duty: to pass along cultural and family knowledge to the younger generation.

Young Indians cannot learn their traditional heritage except from Indian elders. Indian elders cannot experience the gratification of passing along important stories, family history and sacred knowledge without daily involvement with Indian children and youth. Thus, the mental health needs of the young and the old are in many ways complementary. Special programs designed to promote regular and meaningful interaction between elders and young people can be very helpful in meeting the socio-cultural needs of young and old alike.

Indian society has the potential of presenting a model for the rest of the world concerning graceful and dignified ways of aging. Tribal governments and social service administrations can play an important role in designing modern systems to help maintain traditional values related to age, teaching and extended family interactions.

Respect for Ancestors

Most Indian cultures have special beliefs and prac-tices relating to ancestors. Although attitudes vary from fear and a desire to maintain a safe separation to a wish to communicate with the departed, probably all Indian cultures place a high value on honoring the dead.

Ancestors are part of one's family. They determine who one is and their deeds reflect on one's identity. Some-times a person's name has been passed down from a dead ancestor. Often, spiritual powers, songs or sacred knowledge have been handed down from deceased relatives. Generally, an-cestors are thought to have been more knowledgeable of tradi-tions and sacred ways than are living people. Therefore, they represent an important connection to ones Indian past and cul-tural heritage.

Most Indian people do not regard the deceased as simply 'dead'. They have changed their form of being, but have not ceased to exist altogether. By virtue of having passed on to 'the other side', ancestors have acquired a special, semi-spiritual, status which no living person can share. They have been initiated into the mys-tery of death and have taken on a new form of being. In this, they have preceded the living and pointed the way to the spirit world. Often, the dead are thought to watch over and protect living relatives.

The recently dead are in a marginal, ambiguous and dangerous category. They are not far removed from the social ties, feelings and concerns of life, yet they have entered the spirit world. They may continue to affect the living, not only because of the grief of the living, but also by their own spiritual powers. Therefore, *all actions which might effect the dead or bring the living into contact with the dead must be undertaken with great care.*

In some cases, the dead can be dangerous. Among the pos-sible dangers are:

- that the spirit or ghost may remain near family members and cause them emotional or spiritual trouble,
- that the spirit may attempt to take family members with it in order to ease their grief,
- that spirits may make family members sick if their possessions are not burned (and thereby sent with them),

- that spirits or ghosts may come out after dark, especially near burial places, and could harm anyone who is out at night,
- that ghosts could haunt a house and bring harm to people living there,
- that spirits of people whose gravesites have been disturbed may cause sickness or other misfortune.

Thus, there are several reasons for showing respect to the dead, including:
- to remind the living of their connection to family members who have passed on,
- to uphold family honor and traditions,
- to make sure that ones ancestors will be pleased and will not cause harm to oneself or ones family.

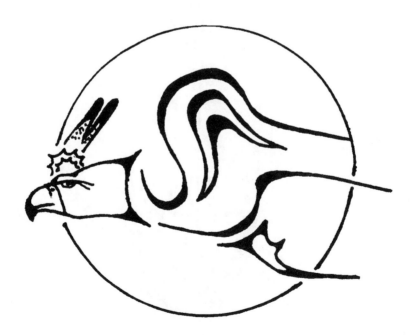

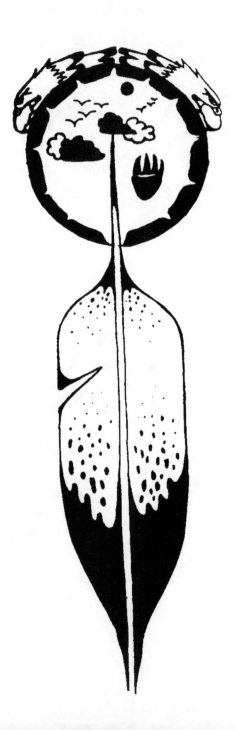

Chapter Eight
Tribal Social Life

Lifestyles

There is a resilient and pervasive socio-cultural life that forms the basis of tribal identity. Despite superficial adaptations to non-Indian culture, many Indian people maintain functionally separate social, and to a large degree economic, lives. Some Indians avoid all but superficial exchanges with non-Indians. They meet their social needs within the Indian community and may have very limited experience dealing with non-Indians. Their social ties are with Indians and these ties perpetuate traditional values, practices, beliefs and cultural/linguistic meanings to which non-Indians are not privy.

Whereas 'culture' is usually understood to mean the values, ideals, beliefs and norms of a people, 'lifestyle' generally refers to everyday habits, problems and realities. Lifestyle might be seen as a specific and perhaps somewhat transient manifestation of a broader underlying culture.

Indian life styles today have both positive and negative aspects, including: a strong family-orientation, sharing, exchange and reciprocity, the experience of prejudice, intensive social pressures, large public gatherings and meals, generally limited material resources, frequent traveling within a culture-specific circuit, a seasonal rhythm to life, a crisis-orientation, religious and spiritual activities, the presence of alcohol abuse and its results, and the effects of repeated tragic deaths and losses.

Both non-Indian prejudice and Indian distrust of non-Indians accentuate lifestyle differences. Even non-Indians who consider themselves unbiased often harbor unconscious stereotypes and ethno-centric attitudes. *Repeated negative experiences have led many Indian people to develop a pervasive distrust of non-Indian American society.* The history of persecution, prejudice, death, destruction of families and loss of language is an inescapable backdrop to Indian life.

Although socio-economic realities of poverty and limited opportunities cannot be easily separated from culture, these stresses and realities are not the whole of Indian culture. *Indian culture has survived in spite of these negative influences because it contains within itself constructive and resilient ways of responding to loss and misfortune.*

For instance, despite the pressures of non-Indian society to conform to a twelve month, forty-hour-a- week work world and nine month school year, many Indian people continue to follow a seasonal work pattern and lifestyle. Whole tribal communities shift gears with the changing seasons. For instance, in Coast Salish cultures, during the winter the emphasis is on spirituality, inner strength, sharing and family relations. During the summer, Coast Salish people fish, work, play sports and lay in food for the year. Many people travel to yearly events, such as Powwows, Bone games or rodeos. In these ways, responsiveness to the seasons and the natural world is maintained.

While a receptive or even fatalistic life view may be intrinsic to some Indian cultures, poverty, alcoholism and social alienation are not. While many Indian people face severe economic and social

conditions, these conditions must not be confused with Indian cul-
ture. If Indian people are to find their way past current problems to
a secure future, Indian culture must provide the key.

This chapter and the next chapter review several of the social
and interpersonal characteristics of everyday Indian life. Although
no hope or pretense is made of a comprehensive description, this
discussion is offered to provide a general introduction to Indian
social realities. Those with a serious interest in specific Indian
cultures or communities should avoid taking these generalizations as facts and should seek specific and concrete information
about particular Indian groups.

STRUCTURE OF TRIBAL GOVERNMENT

Mental Health workers and others who deal
with Indian people need to develop an under-
standing of Tribal political and governmental
principles and realities. Most basic, it is critical to
understand that **Indian Tribes are sovereign**
Nations. *This is a psychological and historical*
reality which has been officially and legally recog-
nized by treaties between Indian Nations and the United States Govern-
ment. From this basic fact many other realities of tribal life are deter-
mined.

Traditional tribal societies had a considerable variety in forms
of political organization. While some groups were organized in a
formal manner, many were quite informal. Certain leaders were
recognized as heads of family groups or as having authority in a
particular area of life, such as hunting, warfare or ceremonies.
Depending upon the tribe, leadership roles could be either hereditary or earned. Social norms, rather than formal laws, generally
controlled behavior. Often decisions were either family matters
or were made by consensus between representatives of extended
family groups.

As discussed in Part I, contacts with non-Indian society led to
widespread disruption of tribal forms of self government. Epidemics weakened social cohesiveness, theft of lands disturbed
systems of resource use, and United States military actions tended
to weaken tribal authority. Non-Indian society generally did not
understand Indian systems of decision making and self govern-

ment. They often ignored, misinterpreted or actively attacked tribal systems. Treaties, governmental proclamations and legal acts tended to disrupt tribal control.

Much control and legal responsibility for tribal affairs was assigned to the Federal Bureau of Indian Affairs, as was also discussed in Part I. This enormous bureaucracy has exerted extensive control over many areas of Indian life over a period of several generations. *The B.I.A.'s actions have often not been in the interests of Indian people. Taken as a whole, they have tended to weaken tribal self regulation. Paternalistic attitudes, combined with strict supervision of tribal resources, undermined tribal self government.*

Federal Indian policies have alternately advocated tribal termination and supported tribal self government. The Indian Reorganization Act of 1934 gave tribes an opportunity to regroup, set political goals, and organize formal governmental bodies and legal codes. However, the 'Termination' era of the 1950's hampered the development of many tribal governments.

The Indian Self Determination Act of 1975 finally provided a firm legal basis for tribes to build governmental, judicial and law enforcement structures to exercise Tribal Sovereignty. Most tribes and Indian people are firmly committed to the concepts of Tribal Sovereignty and Self Determination. Many tribes have taken impressive steps toward exercising full jurisdiction and self government.

Each tribe has a somewhat unique governmental organization, depending upon historical and cultural differences, tribal size, etc. Generally, tribal constitutions summarize the legal basis of their existence and outline the structure of tribal governments. Constitutions of Federally Recognized Tribes are approved by the B.I.A.

Most tribes have elected Tribal Councils which set policy, review budgets, approve tribal business ventures and contractual agreements and exercise ultimate authority over tribal programs. The number of Council members, their terms of office and exact roles vary between tribes. Most often, Councils have from 7 to 15 members, with staggered terms of office from two to five years, and include a Chairperson, Vice Chair, Treasurer and general members who sit on a variety of tribal committees, such as Health and Social Services, Education, Law Enforcement, Fisheries and Wildlife, Resource Development, Tribal Enterprises, Tribal Code Development, etc. The degree of involvement of Councils in day to day tribal program operations varies.

The role of Tribal Chairpersons deserves special comment. The Chairperson is not a 'chief' in the stereotypic sense, although in a few cases chairpersons may also be recognized as hereditary chiefs. Tribal chairpersons do not have broad personal authority, either to set policy or to make independent decisions. Instead, they function as members of the Tribal Council, sometimes with tie-breaking vote power. Their general roles are:

1. To participate as a member of the Tribal Council
2. To represent the Tribe on official occasions
3. To sign contracts, tribal enactments, resolutions and other official documents
4. To keep informed about a broad spectrum of Tribal and community affairs which affect the tribe.

Despite their somewhat restricted legal powers, ***tribal chairpersons can play very important roles in supporting or not supporting tribal mental health programs,*** in mobilizing public opinion and in lending emotional support to tribal mental health staff.

Mental health providers serving tribes need to develop relationships with tribal government and administration. The proper procedure and level of tribal operations will differ between tribes. Consultation should be sought from tribal staff.

SOCIAL ETIQUETTE - THE UNSPOKEN RULES OF TRIBAL RELATIONSHIPS

In order to provide effective mental health services, it is necessary to carefully consider the spoken and unspoken 'rules' of tribal social etiquette. Although most Indian people have never put the 'rules' of tribal social life into words, their early training and experiences have taught them how to get along in tribal society. Likewise, most non-Indians can get along in their own culture without giving it much thought. However, non-Indians are at times unable to figure out what is 'really' going on in tribal society. At worst, they are not even aware that they don't understand and may blunder along misinterpreting things, being misunderstood, or even insulting other people.

Respect

Respect for others is of great importance in tribal life. Indian people recognize the importance of getting along with others, maintaining complex social relationships throughout entire lifetimes and avoiding giving offense. Norms for social politeness and demonstration of respect can be very subtle, complex and are often difficult for non-Indians to comprehend.

'Respect' has wider connotations in many Indian cultures than in mainstream American culture. For Coast Salish people, respect includes knowing ones proper place in the social structure, and that of other persons. Respect implies recognizing family ties and prerogatives. In particular, respect implies polite attention to ones elders. *It is seen as very important to publicly recognize elders and not to put oneself forward in their presence.*

Another aspect of 'respect' is recognition of individual differences and private experiences. In some Indian cultures, such as Plains culture, individuality is highly developed and many of life's most important experiences are personal and private, such as spiritual vision or power experiences. What is right for one person may well be wrong for another. Furthermore, no one is qualified to judge what is right for another. While this quality of tolerance or 'non-interference' is less salient in certain other Indian cultures, *it is generally considered disrespectful to tell other people what to do, or to pry too deeply into the thoughts, feelings or inner experiences of others.*

Clearly, this is very important for mental health workers to understand. *It may come as a surprise to non-Indian and mainstream-trained therapists that some Indian clients find attempts to 'understand' them or help them 'express their feelings' to be intrusive and downright disrespectful.*

This is an area of enormous individual and inter-tribal differences. Therefore, it is probably wise for mental health workers to be cautious in asking personal questions, claiming to understand the clients' experiences or trying to elicit feelings. It is best to take the cue from the client as to the appropriate level of exploration of feelings and inner experiences. *Indian clients often prefer to 'let you in' when they are ready, rather than to have you delve into aspects of their experience which you think are important.*

Indian people are taught from early childhood how they must speak to and treat their relatives, their elders and members of other families. The maintenance of these often unspoken rules is necessary in order to preserve social harmony.

Tribal community members naturally understand the socially 'right' way to treat different people, depending upon their family and social status. Although it is not always easy (or culturally appropriate) for the rules of social etiquette to be verbalized, their observance makes a great deal of difference in determining whether or not mental health services will be successful, or even accepted to begin with.

Mental health programs which seek to deliver services in a manner which is consistent with tribal social norms must rely heavily on tribal members to guide program services. Since the exact ways of showing respect vary from one Indian community to another, there is no substitute for having cultural insiders providing direct treatment services.

Informality and Social Involvement

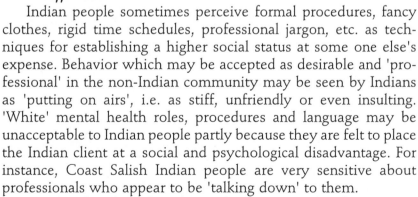

Another social value of relevance for tribal mental health programs is that of informality. Informality does not mean either disrespect or casualness. Instead, it refers to a style of interaction which does not impose artificial barriers or emphasize status differences.

Indian people sometimes perceive formal procedures, fancy clothes, rigid time schedules, professional jargon, etc. as techniques for establishing a higher social status at some one else's expense. Behavior which may be accepted as desirable and 'professional' in the non-Indian community may be seen by Indians as 'putting on airs', i.e. as stiff, unfriendly or even insulting. 'White' mental health roles, procedures and language may be unacceptable to Indian people partly because they are felt to place the Indian client at a social and psychological disadvantage. For instance, Coast Salish Indian people are very sensitive about professionals who appear to be 'talking down' to them.

A related, informal and non-threatening style of interaction protects the client's dignity by doing nothing which might make the client feel insulted or intimidated.

Thus, informality is related to respect. Both qualities, as practiced by Indian people, serve to protect the client's self-esteem and to help maintain positive social relationships. As with respect, Indian mental health workers naturally know how to demonstrate an appropriate and friendly degree of informality. Although non-Indians can learn how to conduct themselves properly in Indian society, this is a time consuming process which may never be fully mastered.

The essence of respectful informality is to conduct oneself in such a way so as to demonstrate that the client and the provider are more or less 'the same' in power and social status as well as in many, though not necessarily all, aspects of lifestyle and values. For instance, workers are most likely to be accepted if they dress in a manner commonly accepted in the tribal community, i.e. more or less the way the client dresses.

An informal conversational style is more likely to be effective than a technical or 'professional' approach. Often, Indian people feel uncomfortable when asked a set of formal questions. Indian providers usually understand many things without having to be told, and therefore don t need to ask the client extensive interview questions. Further, they generally know what questions would be unacceptable to ask.

Tribal workers and clients may live in the same small community, share a social network, and often find themselves in situations where they must relate outside of the therapeutic context. Therefore, it would be artificial to attempt to structure all contacts with clients in the way usually done in mainstream mental health programs. A worker who does not insist on a particular setting or time (such as a pre-scheduled office appointment) in order to talk with the client is more liable to be accepted.

Tribal mental health workers must be skillful in handling the transition to a 'helper' role, so that the client does not feel awkward or 'put down'. While the tribal mental health worker gives full attention to the client and to the client's problems, he/she does not attempt to restrict or direct the conversation in quite the same manner found in conventional mental health treatment. For example, the Counselor does not avoid discussing his/her own relationships and does not object to mingling some friendly chatting or even casual community gossip with 'counseling'.

Considerable involvement in the client's life, or 'enmeshment' is characteristic of tribal mental health program approaches. It shows up in more fluid program structure, less defined and more flexible service boundaries and in complex client-provider role relation-

ships. While multiple social, family and provider roles may not seem unusual to many Indian readers, they may be seen by mainstream mental health professionals as presenting unacceptable conflicts of interest. These issues and their implications for tribal mental health programs are discussed further in Part III.

Non-Indian American society encourages specialization and differentiation. Compartmentalization of various aspects of life is more or less taken for granted, such that one's family life may not overlap greatly with work life or even social life. A non-Indian person may have several quite separate social circles, such as church, school, special interest and neighborhood groups, and the individual's roles may be quite different from one setting to the next without causing any real discomfort.

In particular, it is expected in mainstream American society that professional relationships will be kept separate from social relationships. This is nowhere more true than in the mental health field, where clear boundaries between clients and therapists and between the treatment setting and social life are thought to be of primary importance for the well-being of clients and workers alike.

Mental health providers working in tribal settings need to understand that mainstream mental health expectations may not be appropriate in the tribal situation. Without a thorough re-examination of cultural assumptions about social roles, and therapeutic boundaries and structure, both Indian and non-Indian mental health workers are liable to have difficulty in the tribal setting. Either they will feel resentful and frustrated when the tribal realities do not conform to their expectations, or they will feel guilty and professionally inadequate for adapting to the tribal system and not upholding the accepted rules of the mainstream mental health system.

Social Status

In some Indian societies, social status plays a particularly important role in determining individual self esteem and relationships with others. Respect and social recognition may be valued above popularity. Public shame may be feared over illness, pain or poverty.

The status of family members, including ancestors, contributes to each individual's social standing. Similarly, ones own behavior reflects on other family members. Maintaining ones family name is considered extremely important. Generosity, helpfulness, traditional knowledge and upholding family responsibilities are important in determining status. Physical appearance and financial success are generally less important than in mainstream non-Indian society. Older Indian people are liable to be particularly conscious of the social hierarchy and status of family groups. They keep track of who is related to whom.

Coast Salish culture and social relationships can be better understood once one develops an appreciation of the status system. Behavior related to social status subtly colors most social interactions. People are generally highly motivated to uphold the honor of their name. *If people are not accorded the degree of respect which they feel is appropriate, they may feel insulted and emotionally hurt.* Maintaining a proper balance between personal social recognition and respect for others is of crucial importance for the mental health of Coast Salish people.

Inter-Family Relations

Many tribal communities have one or more strong families who have great social and political influence. Almost all tribal members are influenced by subtle and not so subtle family loyalties, obligations and conflicts. Political and social ties, as well as spiritual and career choices are often determined by which extended family a person belongs to. Tribal mental health workers must not only understand how the extended family system functions, they must also know the family membership and affiliations of their clients.

Since the extended family tends to form the social nucleus in many tribal societies, relationships with members of other families tend to be somewhat more distant. Although considerable gossip may occur in private, *public exchanges between families tend to be polite.* In general, people are careful not to offend people belonging to other families, especially if the other family has high social standing.

One reason why it is important not to offend other families is that inter-family rivalries, once begun, can be difficult to end. Tension between two people may involve their entire extended family groups in an ongoing series of unpleasant exchanges. For instance, an affair between one woman's husband and a second woman may result in the second woman being beaten up by the first woman's sister. This could then lead to the son of the first woman's sister being insulted in school by the second woman's nephew. Later, the second woman's brother might not be hired for a job by the first woman's cousin.

Obviously, this can all get quite confusing. After a period of time, it may no longer be clear to anyone just why these two families don't get along. However, *a pattern of suspicion and dislike may be perpetuated for quite a long time, possibly for generations.*

This sort of thing also occurs among non-Indian families. The primary differences are that tribal communities tend to be small and relatively closed social systems, so that most tribal families know one another and are liable to interact over long periods of time. Intense family loyalties, as well as close identification of the individual with the family, make inter-family tensions more likely.

Factors that affect relationships between families include:
- the relative social status of each family
- whether the families are related through marriage
- the religious affiliations of the two families
- the degree of traditionalism of both families
- their history of friendly or of unfriendly relations

Personal friendships may be less important in determining relationships than is typical for mainstream Americans. The maze of family relationships can be complex. Without a cultural insider for a guide, it can be very difficult for non-Indian mental health workers to understand the inter-family relationships which affect individual feelings and reactions.

Togetherness, Hospitality and Sharing

Gathering together, visiting with family and friends and sharing food, stories and songs is a key aspect of traditional life for Indian people. The values placed on togetherness, hospitality and sharing continue to be important in most Indian communities. (see also Ch. 12)

Before contact with European/American culture, Coast Salish people lived in communal long houses where most possessions and resources were shared. Trade and exchanges among kin were the foundation of the economy and social stability. *Sharing, hospitality and gathering together are traditional Coast Salish values.*

Occasions of any importance are marked by large gatherings, usually involving a meal. Birthdays, graduations, sports, picnics, and religious events bring large extended family groups together. Sometimes a family or tribal community will invite hundreds of people to help commemorate a special event.

In Coast Salish Society, people who live quite far apart from one another often maintain strong family and inter-family ties. Long visits and large gatherings help maintain these ties by providing occasions for people to come together, exchange news and renew friendships.

Hospitality is highly valued by most Indian people. Opening one's home, sharing what one has and giving gifts to guests are of great cultural significance. The value placed on togetherness and the value placed on sharing and contributing to the welfare of the group are both shown in Indian hospitality.

When visitors come to an Indian home, they are almost always welcomed and offered food or at least a cup of coffee. In traditional Indian society, it would be shameful to send someone away hungry. Creative cooks find ways to stretch meals, even when visitors are unexpected. Indian children learn to share their beds and their possessions.

Respect and honor are generally gained by giving, not by keeping. Hoarding food, money or possessions is regarded as selfish and small-minded. Financial wealth in itself does not bring status and respect. Instead, *people who help others, give generously and share gain respect, even if they are financially poor.* When a family member, neighbor or even a total stranger is in need, Indian people often share their food and possessions, even if they themselves have very little. The practice of helping the needy is especially apparent at the time of a death, when people bring food and contribute money to help pay for the costs of the funeral.

Indian people sometimes refer to sharing with others in need as 'Indian insurance'. Reciprocal exchange and community support guarantee that individuals and families will not be left alone to deal with personal or financial crises. Although no strict records are kept, people who are generous in helping others usually receive more help when they themselves are in need. This does not imply a precise 'pay back', but is instead a way of showing that one remembers and appreciates previous help.

Gift Giving

Gift giving is somewhat more complex in some Indian societies than in mainstream non-Indian society. Gifts may be given for many reasons, including:

- To help others in need
- To thank others for their help
- To show respect
- To 'even out' a status imbalance
- To blot out a shame, mistake, dishonor, or insult
- To demonstrate superiority
- To pressure others to do something
- To please someone by giving them something they have admired.

Gift giving can either be a way of honoring others, thanking them, or in some circumstances, even insulting or shaming them. In many Indian societies, gifts are often given publicly, as a way of honoring guests or thanking others for emotional help, spiritual help, ceremonial assistance or advice. Presenting gifts in public brings honor to both the giver and to the receiver. It lets people know something about the relationship between the two persons or families, and serves to cement their relationship.

Gifts are often highly valued possessions, since they represent the meaning behind the gift as well as the object itself. People may give special things to others which they would never feel they could buy for themselves.

However, too large a gift can imply that the other person is needy and can put the other person in the uncomfortable position of being in ones debt. *In Coast Salish Society, when someone gives a large gift they tend to gain status and social advantage. If the recipient can not return a gift of approximately equal value, they may feel ashamed, in debt and 'hurt'. In some cases, they may feel morally and socially obligated to the other person.*

Even if a gift is felt to be too large, it cannot be refused. In many Indian societies, *it would be a grave insult to refuse a gift or the offer of food.* Even if one is not hungry, it is necessary to eat a little in order to avoid offending ones host. To refuse food implies that one thinks oneself too good to eat with the host, thinks the food is bad, or that one is an enemy. Similarly, to refuse a gift implies that one thinks oneself so superior that one cannot have social dealings with the other person.

In some Indian cultures, social protocol demands that when someone admires something, several times, the owner must give it to him. Thus, if someone admires a bracelet or jacket, the wearer may take it off and give it to him. This may be done in a spirit of generosity, in that the giver may be genuinely glad to be able to give a gift which they know will be appreciated. On the other hand, if over-used, this method of 'getting something off' someone can cause resentment. Some Indian people believe that if you fail to give away what has been admired, you will soon lose or break it anyway. In some Indian groups, the necessity to give something away does not arise until the object has been admired four times.

Non-Indians are well advised to seek input from Tribal members concerning appropriate gift giving.

Decision Making

As a broad generalization, Indian people are less likely than are non-Indian Americans to believe that they have (or should have) personal control over their lives. Indian people may be more interested in fitting in with life, people and events than in directing events. In many Indian cultures, independent decision making is valued less than social cooperation. Many Indian people feel that their own wishes and plans must be balanced along with the needs and wishes of family members.

Cultural differences in how decisions are made can cause misunderstandings between mental health workers and Indian clients. Mental health workers are often taught to encourage clients to 'take responsibility', 'evaluate options', and make decisions. Workers from cultural traditions where rapid and firm decision making is a valued individual trait may find Indian decision making styles bewildering and frustrating.

Indian decision making styles may differ from non-Indian American styles in any of the following ways:
1. *Decisions are often made by family as a whole rather than by the individual alone.*
2. *Decisions are often made by consensus only after all members of*

the group have come to agreement, rather than by authority figures or by voting.

3. *Decision making may take quite a long time.*
4. *Individuals may prefer to accept the advice of an elder rather than make an independent decision.*
5. *Decisions may not be made at all; instead events may be allowed to unfold in their own way.*

It is important for mental health workers not to attempt to impose their own decision making styles on Indian clients. At times, it may be quite difficult for non-Indian workers to distinguish normal, healthy Indian decision making from immobilization, low self esteem, and a sense of helplessness associated with depression. It is often appropriate for mental health workers to help clients explore their realistic options, and to ask them how they usually make decisions or what needs to happen before a decision can be reached. But it is inappropriate to pressure clients, especially young people, to make rapid or independent decisions, and it may be quite inappropriate to label people who have more receptive or passive decision making styles as 'dependent', 'immature', 'confused' or 'passive-aggressive'. This is an area where non-Indian workers often need consultation from Indian co-workers.

Non-Self Assertion and Non-Interference

Indian people value group cohesiveness over individual achievement. In many Indian cultures, children are taught not to compete against one another or stand out from their peer group. Indian adults may avoid excelling over others, for fear of hurting their feelings or appearing 'uppity'. Those who stand out too much may be rejected or punished by gossip and social disapproval. Therefore, Indian people as a general rule do not 'put themselves forward' or 'toot their own horns'. However, they may be quite comfortable accepting praise or honor on behalf of their whole family or tribal group.

In most traditional Indian societies, it is considered extremely impolite to tell other people what to do or directly attempt to control them. Indian people usually try not to intrude on each others business, and are particularly reluctant to interfere with other families.

The value on 'non-interference' is shown in traditional child rearing. Children may not be directly punished, but are instead taught through story and example. Often, children are taught by 'natural' consequences: things are allowed to run their course in the belief that people learn best from experience. For instance, a mother may not warn her child not to pull the cats tail; instead, she may watch quietly while the cat scratches the child, believing that the child will learn more effectively from this experience than from being lectured.

Indian people are often hesitant to confront others or interfere with their behavior. Traditional values on non- interference are also complicated by distrust of non-Indian authorities, including police, teachers and child protective service workers. This combination of factors makes it quite difficult for many Indian people to report or take active steps to stop even very destructive behavior of others.

Social control is more often maintained through more indirect social mechanisms, such as gossip, shaming, withdrawal of approval, or through humor and teasing.

Social Pressure and Social Controls: Gossip, Ignoring and Shaming

As a general rule of human and social organization, tight-knit communities exert greater social control over their members than do larger, more diverse and more mobile communities. In tribal communities where everyone knows one another, and where relationships are multigenerational in scope, community opinion and social approval tend to be very powerful motivating forces.

The Indian population in the United States is relatively small, averaging about one percent or less of the total U.S. population. Nonetheless, many Indian people associate primarily with other Indians. For reservation Indians social relationships are often primarily with tribal members and others having an ongoing relationship to the tribal community.

Indian people living in tribal communities tend to be highly responsive to the opinions of other tribal members. Tribal community opinion exerts social pressure on members of that community to conform to its norms and unspoken rules. Some of the social 'rules' commonly found include:

- Respect your elders
- Be loyal to your family members
- Do not stand out as different
- Value Indian tradition; do not be too 'white'
- Contribute to the community good
- Participate in community gatherings and events
- Share your time, your money and your possessions
- Respect religious and spiritual leaders and beliefs
- Don t be too assertive; know your place
- Recognize your relations
- Don t hurt other people's feelings

Like all societies, tribal communities have ways of enforcing their norms. In Coast Salish culture, the use of honor and example, gossip, ignoring and shaming are powerful ways of maintaining social conformity. Public opinion and social pressures seem to be more compelling than formal rules, laws or punishments.

In some Indian cultures, children or adults may be publicly praised or admired for desired actions. On the other hand, misbehavior may be punished by public 'shaming'. This can take the form of a more or less pointed refusal to look at, speak to or recognize a person, or may be expressed through public reprimands or ridicule.

Desired behavior is often pointed out by using the example of others. When someone has done something helpful or important, they are often publicly recognized, thanked or honored. A speaker on a public occasion may mention his/her accomplishment or help, a dinner may be held in his/her honor, or he/she may be given a gift. This system makes the person who is recognized feel good and more liable to continue to act in the respected manner. Perhaps even more importantly, it holds up to others an example of desirable behavior, which they will hopefully follow.

The principal can be stated this way: positive (desired) behavior brings honor and respect; negative (undesired) behavior brings disrespect. Gossip, ignoring and shaming are ways of showing disrespect and of bringing social pressure for behavior change.

Gossip is widespread in many tribal communities. People are naturally interested in each others' activities and may spend a good deal of time discussing what others are doing. Like everywhere, people enjoy talking about others but may not like being talked about themselves. The threat of disapproving gossip can prevent undesirable activities and the reality can often cause people to change their behavior. *Indian people sometimes show disapproval or dislike by pointedly ignoring others.* People may pretend not to see someone, refuse to answer them, not say hello etc. Not recognizing someone is a more common way of expressing disapproval than is direct confrontation. However, Indian people rarely miss the point.

Shaming is a more severe way of expressing disapproval. *Elders sometimes reprimand or scold people in front of others or even at large public gatherings,* such that the scolded persons are embarrassed and lose face. There is very little that a person faced with such treatment can do, since to protest would be an act of disrespect and would likely make things worse.

Sometimes an elder or other person in authority may tell a story designed to point out another person's failings without actually naming them. Both the object of this censure and others generally get the point. (This strategy may fail to work with ignorant outsiders who fail to realize that they are being 'shamed'. However, since other tribal members generally do get the point, this may not be terribly important.)

Non-Indian new-comers to Coast Salish tribal communities may be taken aback by the often very public nature of both praise and criticism. Where a non-Indian may feel embarrassed by lavish public praise (or even by being a witness to it), Coast Salish people may feel honored and pleased. Where a non-Indian might feel mortified and speechless if faced with a public scolding, Indian people are often able to take this in stride, and, on occasion, even learn from it.

Gossip, ignoring and shaming not only help to maintain social conformity and positive behavior, they are also ways of releasing anger and aggression without violence or other acts that might lead to breakdown of social relationships. *In tribal societies where there is a high degree of mutual inter-dependence, it can be very*

***important to avoid direct confrontation which could disrupt ongoing
social and economic interactions.*** Less direct methods of releasing
anger and showing disapproval can serve a positive social function.

It is important for mental health workers to understand these
cultural realities. Since mental health problems usually involve
interpersonal relations, mental health workers often need to help
clients resolve social conflicts, respond to family and social pressures, and define themselves in relation to the larger social group.
Mainstream mental health workers are often trained to encourage
assertiveness and constructive confrontation as ways of resolving
conflicts. It is extremely important to understand that direct confrontation may not always be a constructive response. In some
tribal communities, too direct or assertive behavior can have
lasting negative consequences. Newcomers must therefore become familiar with the unique social norms of the tribal community in which they plan to work.

Attitudes Toward Time

The joke that Indian people operate on 'Indian time'
points to very real and important cultural differences in
attitudes toward time between most Indian and non-Indian
Americans. Many Indians resent being rushed or having to
adjust to time pressures. Scheduling, precise appointments,
regularity and being 'ruled by the clock' are seen by many
Indians as foreign, unnatural, unhealthy and destructive of
proper relationships and life rhythms.

'Indian time' refers to doing things at a natural pace. The pace
tends to be more relaxed, with activities adjusted to fit with what is
happening, rather than with a pre-set timetable. It is more an
unfolding than an ordering or structuring of events. Things are less
planned. Instead, they occur when the time is right, i.e. when all
the necessary aspects of a situation naturally come together.

Of course, this does not mean that things are never planned,
only that they are usually not planned on a rigid schedule. Indian
people tend to be patient, in the faith that things will work out as
they should. This attitude may result in some things taking longer
than is the non-Indian norm. For instance, meals, visits and meetings may involve more time than is typical in non-Indian society.
Indian people tend to be 'process-oriented' rather than 'product-

oriented'. For instance, meetings may be allowed to develop naturally rather than expected to achieve a specific pre-set task. Many Indian people prefer to see how the day develops rather than to plan ahead what must be accomplished.

While being 'on time' is not considered as important by many Indian people as by most non-Indians, it is considered very important to be present during important tribal events, i.e. to "be there when it s happening". It is felt to be particularly important to be with family members during times of crisis, even when this conflicts with appointments, school or jobs.

Social responsibilities, such as helping family, listening to elders talk, or visiting with guests often take priority over appointments. These different priorities can create cultural conflicts. For example, Indian families who travel out of town to visit sick relatives may consider it more important to stay with them than to return home in time for work or school. Children sometimes miss school because of attendance at spiritual gatherings. If someone's car is blocking the driveway, an Indian person may miss a counseling appointment rather than risk being impolite by asking someone to move it. When family or friends from out of town drop by unexpectedly to visit, the host or hostess may well drop previous plans to spend time with the visitors.

Just as Indian people will often drop what they are doing if someone asks them for help, many Indian people expect those in helping roles to respond immediately to requests for service. Unless a mental health worker is obviously with another client, some Indian people may feel insulted if they are asked to wait before being seen. Paper work, phone calls, or meetings with co-workers are considered far less important than responding to clients, even when the client drops in unexpectedly at a busy time. Non-Indian workers in tribal settings who fail to adjust their priorities to Indian expectations may be considered rude, uncaring and high-handed.

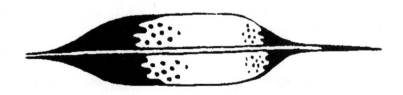

Traditional Ways of Dealing with Grief and Loss

Death, grief and traditional ways of dealing with loss are of great importance for tribal mental health work. Multiple and unresolved losses can put Indian people at high risk for depression, thus making them particularly vulnerable when a further death occurs. Tribal communities are often faced with tragic deaths of young people, as well as with the loss of elders. Death of a tribal member creates a crisis or imbalance which affects the entire community.

In most Indian cultures, death brings both grief and a feeling of dangerous imbalance to the family and community. Because of the close family ties, family members of the deceased are seen as particularly at risk, both emotionally and spiritually. People in mourning may lose part of themselves if they get stuck in grief.

Indian cultures differ in their specific attitudes toward death and ways of dealing with grief. However, all traditional Indian cultures provide special ways of coping with death, as well as of strengthening the family and the community as a whole.

From the point of a death through the funeral and the period of mourning, Indian cultures provide ways of protecting, strengthening and restoring mental health. At each stage of the grieving process, specific events and activities guide the family toward an acceptance of death and a renewal of tribal social life. Traditional grieving processes reaffirm tribal relationships and help set things right.

When a death occurs in Coast Salish Society, family and friends immediately gather together to support the family. People come to the family home to bring food and offer help. Although they may not say anything in particular, they stay with the family to show that they care and share their grief.

From the point of death until after the funeral, family members are given enormous social support. They are rarely left alone. Togetherness is felt to be the primary source of strength at the time of a loss. Coast Salish people feel that the presence and prayers of many people are extremely important. Since family members are seen as weak and vulnerable at this time, friends lend them their own emotional strength.

Certain helping roles are carried by specific individuals. These are strong and knowledgeable people who have prepared themselves over a period of years to guide family groups at such times. Often, these roles are handed down within certain families. The people holding these roles are generally middle aged or older.

These "grief helpers" are expected to immediately step in and begin talking to the family and explaining what steps need to be taken. Often, they help deal with authorities or guide the family in making funeral arrangements. They also advise the family about how to care for themselves and provide enormous moral support.

Other people begin to cook for the family and visitors. *From the point of death until after the funeral, people bring food and cook for groups ranging from ten to several hundred people.*

Non-Indians may not understand tribal etiquette at the time of death. *Whereas in non-Indian society deaths are often seen as private times when families should not be disturbed, Indians often feel that visiting the family is the best way to show support.* Whereas many non-Indians prefer small private funerals, Indians generally prefer large funerals. Even people who did not know the deceased personally may attend funerals to show their support. Whereas in non-Indian society, friends and neighbors often bring hot dishes to leave for the family, in Indian society the family of the deceased generally consider it their responsibility to feed those who attend the funeral.

Prayer services and vigils are often held each night. People sit with the body and with the family. People pray together, share memories and express their concerns.

Funerals usually take place on the third or fourth day after a death. Funerals often take place at a tribal building. Tribal work and social activities are canceled in order to show respect for the dead. The funeral may be attended by people who have come from long distances to show their respect and strengthen the family by their presence.

Funerals often incorporate Christian services with traditional Indian ways. Community leaders assist with the actual funeral, as well as with graveside prayers and speeches. Respected elders often speak during funerals, at the graveside, or during the meal following the burial. They discuss problems facing the community, mention the accomplishments of the deceased and of family members and stress the importance of traditional values. People are thanked for attending and showing their support for the family.

Sometimes the family and other younger community people are given advice about how to deal with grief and carry on living. The grieving family may be told to leave their tears at the grave, so as to allow the spirit of the deceased to leave in peace. Crying too long is sometimes thought to upset the dead and hold them to this earth. Excessive mourning may be seen as dangerous for family members, since the spirit may pity them and try to take them along to the land of the dead.

After the funeral, guests are invited to share a meal with the family. A table may be spread for up to several hundred people at funerals of well known people. This meal signifies a return to life and more normal social relations. People talk more freely, smile and visit with old friends. Speeches are made and friends donate money to help cover expenses.

Frequently, the meal is followed by a 'give away'. Blankets, clothes, money and household items are given to the cooks, casket bearers, grave diggers and others to thank them for their help.

Many Indian people have traditional ways of cleansing themselves and their homes of the presence of death or the spirits of the deceased. This may be done by spiritual healers 'brushing' off the person or 'sweeping' out the house. This serves to remove dangerous influences, purify the house, protect people from harm and strengthen their personal spirits.

Some families also hold a traditional Burning after the funeral. This may be held at any time which is convenient for the family. The clothes and favorite possessions of the deceased are burned in a traditional manner, or sometimes are given away to friends and community members. This serves several purposes:

1. The family are helped to accept the reality of the death by clearing out the deceased's possessions. This frees them to go on to a new phase of life.

2. The Burning gives recognition to the dead and may be seen as a way of giving them back their favorite things, so that they may go in peace to 'the other side.'

3. The belongings of the deceased are sometimes are distributed to others who can use them.

Each family and each tribe have somewhat different views of the Burning. Some do not believe in this at all, or have other ways of taking care of these spiritual and emotional needs.

Coast Salish and certain other Indian people often hold a 'Memorial' for the deceased four years after the death. This is a time of remembering, honoring and completing the period of mourning. It is a kind of final goodbye to the deceased, which may be prepared for over a two or three year period.

Although funerals and memorials are certainly times of sadness and grief, they are also times when family ties are renewed. The relationship of individuals to family and ancestors is acknowledged and hopefully strengthened.

Family and community support shown at times of death and during the grieving process contain cultural strengths and healing. Mental health workers should attend funerals and community meals. It may also be appropriate for mental health workers to spend time with the family during the crisis period, to attend prayer services, Burnings, spiritual healings and memorials.

Two important points to emphasize about Indian funerals are the amount of time often required and the great importance of family members being involved throughout the entire process.

Family members may devote four, five or six days to funeral activities. Non-Indian employers or supervisors need to understand why considerable leave time is necessary for family members and also why mental health staff should attend these events.

Chapter Nine
Communication Patterns

Many Indian groups have patterns of communication which differ from the non-Indian norm, as well as from other Indian groups. The languages spoken, rhythm and intonation, subtle differences in meaning, gestures, facial expressions, humor, story telling and the use of silence are all important aspects of communication. Among many Indian groups, what is not said may be as important as what is spoken.

NATIVE LANGUAGES

Some native languages have been partially or completely lost. Others are still widely spoken. Older people are more likely to speak their native languages, especially when discussing emotionally or spiritually important matters. Many tribes are making efforts to revive their native languages by teaching children. Even when languages have been largely lost, certain native words may have remained in common use and be interspersed with English.

Language has enormous cultural meaning for all people. We learn to think and express ourselves in a particular language. Some ideas or feelings may not be translatable between languages. Important cultural information, attitudes and meanings are embedded in language.

For these reasons, the loss of a native language is enormously painful and destructive to culture. Indian people who have lost their languages often feel a deep sense of loss, sadness, anger and even shame. This is liable to be particularly difficult for elders, though it also effects younger people. The fact that Indian children in schools were forbidden to speak their languages has had lasting negative consequences for Indian people.

Many Indian people today feel that native languages bring out their deepest feelings. Native languages are often used for prayer or during spiritual activities. Some people feel that this is critical in order to communicate with the spirits of the deceased. Many people feel that young Indians need to hear their peoples native language in order to absorb a deeper sense of identity and culture than can be conveyed in English.

INDIAN ENGLISH

Verbal communication includes more than the use of a particular language. Although some native languages have been lost and most Indian people are fluent in the English language, communication barriers have by no means been eliminated. Indian ways of speaking English sometimes differ considerably from the brand of English spoken in surrounding non-Indian communities.

One reason that Indian ways of speaking English are unique is that many Indian people either learned English as a second language or learned English from grandparents whose primary language was not English. Differences in accent and rhythm can persist over several generations.

Many Indian groups use somewhat different terms and phrases than do non-Indians. In addition, rhythm and intonation of speech may differ. The fact that many of these differences are very subtle make them all the more important for understanding and rapport. For instance, when, following the death of a family member, an Indian person says that he or she needs to have "some work done on the house", this is liable to refer to the need for spiritual treatment to remove lingering spirits or dangerous forces, not to carpentry repairs. Not understanding the meaning of such expressions can lead to missed therapeutic opportunities or even to bad feelings.

It is beyond the scope of this report to present a full description or linguistic analysis of these speech and meaning differences, but it is crucial to point out that they exist. *A mental health worker not familiar with the speech patterns and expressions common in the Indian community may misinterpret what an Indian person says, and may also be misunderstood by the Indian client.*

VERBAL VS. NON-VERBAL COMMUNICATION

It is something of a misunderstanding to say that Indian people tend to be less verbal than non-Indians. It is more accurate to say that Indian cultures often have different norms about verbal behavior than is the case in non-Indian American culture. Oral traditions and story telling are highly developed in some Indian cultures. Non-verbal communication may also be as important, or more important, than verbal communication.

In certain situations, Indian people may prefer longer silences than are comfortable for most non-Indians. Periods of silence may be valued as opportunities for 'feeling' out other people, for thinking about what has been said, for showing respect, or for maintaining privacy. Sometimes Indian people feel that non-Indians chatter all the time, sometimes without saying anything important. On the other hand, non-Indians sometimes feel that Indians are withdrawn, unfriendly or passive because they talk less. In fact, Indians may at times be quiet in order to show acceptance and respect or in order to wait and see before saying something.

Other times Indian people are silent because they do not want to directly express disagreement, especially with their elders or people in authority. Indian people are generally cautious about what they reveal to non-Indians, and silence may indicate an unwillingness to discuss certain topics.

However, Indian people can in fact be quite talkative. Many Indian people enjoy teasing, joking, telling stories, and discussing people and events. Talking freely usually means that people are at ease with family or friends. Silence may mean caution or dislike, or it may mean acceptance.

Indian cultures have strong oral traditions. While this does not necessarily mean a lot of talking, it does mean that talking can be of great importance. Knowledge, history, legends and traditions were maintained and passed down orally. Legends and stories used metaphor and powerful images to convey social lessons. Often, traditional stories held different meanings for each age group and individual.

In many Indian cultures, people with the ability to tell stories well or to express themselves eloquently are highly respected. Public speaking is often considered a special gift, and skillful orators are widely honored. Speakers often develop personal styles of story telling and dramatization. Indian people believe that great speakers are guided by the spirit. They 'speak from the heart' rather than from the head, and often do not pre-plan what they say. Gesture, movement and sound effects can add greatly to the impact of a skillfully told story.

As a general rule, conversation has a somewhat different rhythm in Indian cultures than in non-Indian society. Perhaps because most information was traditionally conveyed by word of mouth, it was, and still is, considered extremely important to listen and pay close attention when someone is speaking. Especially when teachers, elders or other people with knowledge or authority speak, other people are expected to be quiet and listen respectfully.

This pattern is still prevalent in many Indian communities today. *People tend to take turns talking, rather than to engage in the kind of back and forth 'conversation' typical of mainstream Americans. It is considered quite impolite to interrupt others, especially those who are older than oneself.* Some Indian people may talk longer at a time than is typical for non-Indians. Silences between sentences may also be longer, and silences may occur between speakers. At least in some traditional Indian societies, people may talk with each other for quite long periods without feeling that it is necessary to 'get to the point' or accomplish something specific. Many Indian people accept that time will be spent establishing rapport or understanding before trying to decide something, discuss something important or make a request.

Although many Indian people spend quite a bit of time talking with one another, the non-verbal aspects of conversation are often regarded as more important than the words exchanged. Often, much is left unsaid. Many Indian people are highly skilled at 'reading between the lines': they pick up on nuances of tone, gesture and glance. Often, Indian people can exchange a great deal of information in a very few words.

Problems can arise, however, in cross-cultural communication. Non-Indians or Indians from different cultural groups may misinterpret or totally miss non-verbal signals given by Indians. Similarly, Indians may draw mistaken conclusions from the body language of non-Indians.

The discussions which follow of eye contact, handshaking and thank-you gestures illustrate the dangers of cross-cultural misinterpretations. Since many cross-cultural differences are non-verbal, it may be quite difficult to pinpoint the exact nature of a misunderstanding or trace it to its origin. However, much can be gained if non-Indians working with Indian people develop an awareness of the importance of non-verbal communication and become familiar with the particular forms this communication takes. As one member of our team puts it, "you have to *watch* what I'm saying!".

Eye Contact

In some Indian cultures, direct eye contact is avoided. It may be considered disrespectful, intrusive or intimidating. People who traditionally lived in close physical quarters may have developed social norms for protecting one another's privacy, such as not trying to guess about other people's thoughts and feelings. Not looking directly into another's eyes may be a way of respecting the others right to privacy.

Staring may be interpreted as intimidating, unfriendly or at least impolite. Direct eye contact, especially on the part of younger people or people of less social standing, may be seen as bold or brash. To stare at other people may also be seen as a way of trying to gain power or control.

Some Indian people feel quite ill at ease with non-Indians who look directly into their eyes while talking. Some Indians may look down or look at something other than the speaker. Far from being disinterested or rude, this may be a way of showing respect and attentiveness, and should not be misinterpreted as rudeness. Many Indian children are taught not to stare, but instead to look down when they are addressed by their elders. This way of showing respect is sometimes misinterpreted by non-Indian teachers either as extreme shyness and withdrawal or as not paying attention.

Handshakes

Indian ways of shaking hands tend to be much gentler than non-Indian American handshakes. Non-Indian Americans tend to prefer a firm, outgoing sort of handgrip which is intended to convey self assurance, openness and trust, as well as to let one 'take the measure' of the other person. In contrast, most Indians offer their hand in a gentle touch designed to allow a respectful meeting, and sensitive exchange of energy.

Indian handshakes are usually more of a touching of hands than a 'grasp' or 'shake'. It is aimed at receiving impressions about the other person's spirit and personality, as well as allowing the other person to receive impressions about oneself. It is not intended to determine dominance, demonstrate self confidence, or (necessarily) to indicate a wish for friendship.

These different purposes and styles for the meeting of hands can lead to negative impressions and misunderstandings between Indians and non-Indians. Non-Indians may mistakenly consider the Indian handshake to be 'limp' and draw the conclusion that the Indian person is weak, meek, frightened or not willing to be friends. On the other hand, the Indian person may find the non-Indian hand shake to be aggressive, domineering, disrespectful and crude. In both cases, these judgments are liable to be inaccurate and may be damaging to any future relationship.

One interesting sidelight is that handshake style may reveal the degree of knowledge and exposure a person has had to the other culture. Thus, when a non-Indian shakes hands in the usual non-Indian manner with an Indian, the Indian person knows that this non-Indian is probably not very familiar with Indian culture. However, if the non-Indian gives a more Indian-style handshake, the Indian person is liable to conclude that this non- Indian has been around Indian people and is willing to learn and adapt to Indian ways. Similarly, many Indian people who have spent time in the non-Indian social world adapt their handshake style to match non-Indian expectations. This does not mean that the Indian person is 'acculturated', only that he or she understands what is expected in the non-Indian context and chooses to adjust.

Although both Indian and non-Indian styles of handshake may be used as greetings, when meeting people for the first time, and or when taking leave of one another, their purposes are not identical. In fact, they are to some degree mutually incompatible. *The Indian handshake is aimed at receiving information about the other person. The non-Indian handshake is intended to convey information about oneself, as well as to establish either equality between partners or the dominance of one person.* It may be impossible to receive subtle information about another person while trying to convey a message of ones own self assurance. It is probably even more difficult to show respect if one is trying to establish dominance.

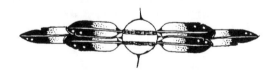

Thank-you and Give Honor Gesture

Aspects of social exchange which are culturally important tend to have both verbal and non-verbal expressions. Non-Indian American and European societies have developed gestures which indicate approval, agreement, recognition and submission (such as head nodding, bowing, victory or peace signs, hand kissing and even kneeling). Although some of these gestures may be used upon occasion to show gratitude, there is no specific European-American gesture which demonstrates thanks and giving honor.

In Coast Salish society, there is a specific and eloquent gesture which conveys a message of honor, recognition and thanks. When someone has said or done something which is particularly impressive, to the point, or helpful, other people may demonstrate their appreciation and gratitude by extending both arms forward, palms open and upward-facing and hands held in a natural and receptive position. Both arms are moved up and down several times in a coordinated and graceful gesture. The gesture seems to speak louder than words: 'thank-you'; 'your deeds (or speech) have brought up your status in my eyes'.

Often the person making this 'Honor/Thank-you' gesture may be a member of the family. In this case, the gesture signifies 'I (we) respect you, claim you as our own, and want everyone else to see that we value you for upholding our family honor.'

At other times the person making the gesture may be a respected or leading member of another family group. In this case, the gesture signifies recognition of the honored status of the other, of their service in upholding culturally valued traditions, and gratitude for their help or advice.

In both cases, the gesture signifies public recognition of a strengthened relationship between the two persons or families and their mutual participation in the traditional Coast Salish culture system.

This particular gesture is so expressive that it is not liable to be seriously misunderstood by anyone. If a non-Indian newcomer asks a Coast Salish person what it means, he/she is liable to be told that "She is thanking him." However, no one is likely to explain that the gesture condenses in it messages of approval, respect, claiming, gratitude, family honor and recognition of high social status.

Expression of Emotion

Although many Indian people are not emotionally demonstrative, the stereotype of Indians as 'stoic' and 'unresponsive' is largely due to a misunderstanding of Indian ways of showing feelings, as well as to Indian mistrust of whites. In some Indian cultures, expressions of feelings are more subtle than in mainstream American culture, which tends to encourage a high degree of extroversion and self expression. Many Indian people are circumspect and self contained. In some (but not all) Indian groups, strong outward expressions of feelings are seen as self indulgent, both in the sense of weak and of self centered.

Indian people have varied and strong feelings, just like all other people. However, they may feel strongly about somewhat different things than do non-Indians, and may also express feelings in different ways or at different times. For instance, Indian parents may show their love of a child by including the child in important family activities, rather than by playing games with the child. Some Indian people are careful not to show too much pleasure at their own achievements, for fear of being seen as boasting. Indian people may show anger by withdrawing or by ignoring another person, rather than by raising their voice. Some Indian people express sadness only in private.

These examples illustrate the tendency toward greater subtlety in Indian ways of expressing feelings. Non-Indians may miss or misinterpret Indian facial and other signs of emotions. This is frequently complicated by Indian distrust of non-Indians. Indian people may withhold expressions of feelings around people whom they do not know, do not like or do not trust. The same Indian person who seems remote and expressionless to a non-Indian social worker or teacher may show intense feelings when with family and friends.

Negative feelings in particular may be expressed more subtly by Indian people. This may be both because of social norms which discourage confrontation, and because of the history of accumulated losses and griefs. People who have experienced a great deal of trauma or deprivation may be less likely to demonstrate grief at a new loss than are those who have rarely faced a severe blow. People who grew up in families which were dysfunctional due to alcoholism or violence may have learned to protect themselves by shutting down their feelings.

Non-Indians are sometimes surprised and upset by the matter-of-fact way in which Indian people sometimes describe extreme tragedies. Those not familiar with Indian people may mistake courage, acceptance, or numbness stemming from emotional overload for insensitivity or lack of caring.

It is important to allow the Indian person to tell their story fully without expecting a demonstration of emotion. When great tragedies have been experienced, it can be very upsetting to re-examine these events and feelings. Sensitive mental health workers can help such clients to *gradually* identify and express a wide range of emotions.

Indian cultures often provide specific occasions for catharsis or

emotional cleansing. In some Indian groups, specific times are set aside for showing grief or other feelings. People may be explicitly told to put aside all negative feelings in certain places (such as in the Smokehouse) or at certain times (after a funeral or Burning or during a spiritual event). It is much more appropriate for mental health workers to help Indian clients express feelings in accordance with cultural norms than to attempt to bring about a changed style of emotional expression.

Humor

Humor is of great importance in all cultures for communication, entertainment and as a way of releasing social tensions. Many Indian people joke a great deal. Joking and teasing can be elevated to a true art form by the most accomplished masters.

As a general rule, Indian humor tends to be rather dry, subtle and deadpan. Understatement is skillfully used. Ambiguous or slightly painful aspects of human experience are sometimes commented upon through humor.

Indian people value humor as a way of enjoying themselves around friends. Poking fun at oneself, ones friends and non-Indians is a common and enjoyable pastime which unites joker and listeners in a bond of shared understanding.

Being kidded by Indian people is generally a sign of being accepted and liked. It may also be a way of testing new acquaintances, to see whether they are able to relax, play and take a little teasing. Indian friends tease one another a great deal. Certain men seem to specialize in teasing others. When women get together in groups, they often joke and tell funny stories about themselves and each other.

Some Indians are experts at diffusing social tension with the well placed use of jokes. The joke often acknowledges a social tension while at the same time rising above it and refusing to take it seriously. Although some jokes contain an element of criticism or of poking fun at vulnerabilities, they are generally offered and taken in good humor. *Sometimes a note of truth or seriousness in Indian jokes gives them rich double meanings. In Coast Salish communities, jokes are often followed by the comment 'oh well' or 'aay'. This lets the listeners know that the preceeding statement was in fact a joke and should be taken in that light.*

Non-Indians sometimes have difficulty telling whether or not Indians are being serious. The rather dry, straight-faced Indian joke, often commenting in a subtle way on social or cross-cultural tensions, may leave non-Indians feeling uneasy and unsure of how to respond. Sometimes Indians think that non-Indians have no sense of humor because they fail to 'get' Indian jokes.

Cultural differences in humor provide a promising field for research. Experiential workshops on Indian and non-Indian humor styles might promote cross cultural understanding of personality styles, communication, social tensions and world views.

Story Telling

Indian people often tell stories to teach children. Traditionally, grandparents told stories to children, especially on winter evenings. These "teaching stories" impart vital cultural knowledge and values. Several well-known Coast Salish elders, spiritual leaders and mental health specialists (including Vi Hilbert, Bruce Miller, Terry Tafoya and Johnny Moses) are making efforts to record and revive these stories, so that they will not be lost and can be brought back into use for teaching children.

Stories are also told to other, usually younger, adults. This allows moral and other messages to be conveyed indirectly in ways that avoid direct confrontation or rudeness. Listeners get the point without feeling put on the spot.

Traditional stories rely on familiar cultural symbols and metaphor. Cultural symbols "speak to" Indian people who have grown up learning a particular tribal world view. *Metaphors speak to the unconscious as well as the unconscious mind. The story may be heard on several levels, thus encouraging creative thinking and the likelihood of new insights.*

Traditional stories are designed to convey important ideas about how to live right. However, they do not provide simplistic answers or "the moral of the story." Instead, *Indian stories engage the imagination of the listener and encourage them to think about their behavior, assumptions, and problems in new ways. They point the way toward insights without spelling them out.*

Chapter Ten

Native American Worldview:
Spirituality Healing

Most Native American people believe strongly that a spiritual attitude is central to psychological and social well being. Spirituality is understood to be inseparable from all aspects of Indian private and public life.

Mental health workers, physicians, nurses and other professional workers in Indian communities must develop an understanding of the spiritual beliefs and practices found in the communities they serve. Because traditions and practices differ widely between tribes, some of the specifics discussed below may not apply to Indians of cultural groups other than the Coast Salish.

We hope that offering these examples of the deep cultural and psychological value of spiritual and religious practices will help workers in all Indian communities to develop an appreciation of the core importance of spiritual practices to Indian people.

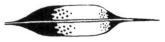

Due to cultural sensitivities, certain Indian spiritual experiences and aspects of traditional healing cannot be described in detail. Many Indian people regard these experiences as intensely personal, private and sacred. They are reluctant to share information about spiritual matters with non-Indians, especially in written form. Therefore, some important aspects of Indian life and Indian mental health work cannot be fully described here.

Readers wishing more information may want to consult anthropological descriptions (Amoss, 1978; Collins, 1974, Jilek-Aall, 1973).

SPIRITUAL WORLD VIEW

Spirituality pervades every aspect of Indian life in ways difficult to grasp by most non-Indian Americans. It effects world view, family relations, health and illness, ways of healing, and ways of dealing with grief.

Many Indian people see the world in fundamentally different ways than do most non-Indian Americans. The world is seen as less mechanistic, matter of fact, or ruled by scientific laws. Indian people are less likely to perceive the world as falling into discrete categories (e.g. physical, social, mental), and more likely to perceive an underlying unity or interaction between all aspects of life. Thus, Indians may be more likely to accept that things are not always what they seem to be on the surface, and may be more likely to look behind the appearance for influences which are not readily visible or apparent. This is particularly true in the realm of spiritual influences.

Spirituality is not treated as a separate or discrete part of life; it is not restricted to religious beliefs, ideals or ways of explaining the meaning of life. It is not confined to abstractions. It is not restricted to prayer, rituals or ceremonies conducted at special times and places. It is not seen as a separate realm of experience from the physical, bodily life, nor from the social, interpersonal life, nor is spirituality seen as affecting only certain people with strong spiritual beliefs. Instead, *spirituality is understood to be a fundamental reality of all life and all people, inseparable, connected to physical reality, bodily events, interpersonal relations, individual destiny, mental processes and emotional well-being.*

Every culture has ways of conceptualizing the relations between the physical, social, emotional and spiritual aspects of life. Non-Indian Americans tend to separate these aspects of life and treat them as distinct realms having little to do with one another. We might draw this view of life something like this:

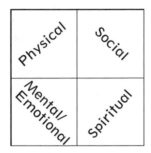

In contrast, **Indian people tend to see the spiritual, mental, physical and social aspects of life as inseparably connected and continuously interacting,** even though it may not be possible or important to pinpoint exactly how one thing has affected another. This world view might be drawn something like this:

Indian spirituality is broader than what most non-Indian Americans think of as 'religion'. It encompasses ones relation to ones family, living, dead and as yet unborn, since family members are bound by deep spiritual ties. It encompasses ones relation to the entire world of living beings, all of which posses a spiritual nature. It includes ones relation to the unseen world of spirits, of which there are many types.

Spirituality therefore has to do not only with beliefs, but also with how one conducts ones life, and with what happens to oneself and ones family. In the Indian view, it is a spiritual necessity to live in harmony with all other beings, not only because it is 'nice' or generally desirable to do so, but because it is distinctly dangerous not to. To be in a state of conflict, or to offend other people or spiritual forces, is to be in a dangerous and vulnerable state.

Some non-Indian Americans, especially younger, middle class Caucasians from progressive Protestant backgrounds, have become quite interested in Indian spirituality, or rather, in their notion of Indian spirituality. Many of these people tend to think of Indian spiritual beliefs as mainly related to living in harmony with nature, honoring and respecting all living things, etc. In other words, they tend to conceive of Indian spirituality in a rather one-sided and simplistic way as a peaceful, wise and orderly sort of nature worship. In general, they are ignorant of the complexity, ambiguity, power and dangerousness of many Indian spiritual experiences and beliefs. While they often are aware of certain aspects of Indian spiritual beliefs, there is a tendency to oversimplify and 'white wash' Indian spirituality in a manner which strikes many Indian people as naive, if not foolhardy.

In general, Indian people do not take spiritual things lightly. They recognize that in dealing with the spiritual realms of life, that one is dealing with powerful and largely unknowable forces. While these forces, or spiritual powers, often have a beneficial effect on human beings, they can also have destructive effects. Not all spiritual forces are seen as being "good": Some are good, some bad, and some neutral.

The relation between the individual person and a particular spiritual force is the critical factor in determining the effect of that force on a given individual. In this sense, Indian spirituality tends to be an intensely personal sort of experience. Specific beliefs, practices and relationships with the spiritual world differ not only from tribe to tribe and family to family, but even from person to person. This fact makes it quite difficult to generalize about Indian spiritual beliefs and practices.

Most Indian people approach spiritual matters with great care and respect. Respect is not merely a matter of giving honor, praise or positive recognition to the spiritual world; it is also a way of maintaining a safe and circumspect distance from unpredictable powers. *Respect implies a degree of caution toward potentially dangerous powers.*

It can easily be understood how Indian people with this sort of respectful and cautious attitude toward spiritual matters may often feel alarmed or annoyed by extroverted non-Indians who express an enthusiastic wish to join in Indian spiritual events.

Many Indian people find the eagerness of non-Indians to discuss and join in Indian spiritual practices to be intrusive or rude. The past history of religious persecution by white society has given Indian people just cause for caution and skepticism. Indian people may wonder why a non-Indian wants to learn about or participate in Indian spiritual doings. They may wonder if the non-Indian may be making fun of them or may be surreptitiously gathering information in order to write a book about them.

Indians may also feel, with some justification, that most non-Indians do not truly understand Indian spiritual ways. While this is due in part to a widespread feeling that non-Indians tend to be shallow, insensitive or 'not spiritual people', it is also due in part to the sense that *many non-Indians are disrespectful of spiritual things in the sense of taking them too lightly.* Since many non-Indians only perceive and relate to the positive aspects of the spiritual world, they are liable to expose themselves and others to dangers from the negative aspects. *It may be that the failure of most non-Indians to appreciate the complexity and potentially dangerous aspects of spirituality has as much to do with Indian reluctance to share spiritual knowledge with them as does the history of religious oppression.*

Non-Indian attempts to reduce Indian culture, especially spirituality, to simple explanations is also vexing to many Indian people. Indians wonder "why do they ask so many questions?" or "why do they always want to explain everything?" Whereas non-Indian Americans tend to take it for granted that everything can be understood if one has enough information, and, furthermore, that it is generally important to understand things, Indian people do not necessarily share this view.

In fact, many Indian people do not assume that all things are understandable; they do not assume that all things have a predictable, consistent nature which can be rationally explained. The questioning of non-Indians may strike Indians either as idle prying or as rather silly attempts to force the world to conform to rationalistic expectations. The potential for mis-communication and mutual frustration is thus enormous. It is particularly great in the area of spirituality, where the expectations are profoundly divergent and where Indian people may feel that the consequences of misconduct or disrespect are potentially dangerous or at times even fatal.

Because of the quality of danger involved in some spiritual matters, there are often prohibitions which Indian people observe when involved in spiritual practices, including both ceremonial activities and spiritual healing. These may have to do with avoiding certain actions (such as going near a cemetery, looking a person in the eyes, having sexual relations, cooking, etc.) or avoiding certain persons (such as mother-in-laws, pregnant women, children or individuals with strong or very new spiritual powers). These prohibitions vary considerably from one Indian culture to another, but are generally intended to protect oneself or others from harm.

Indians often believe that if a person treats spiritual matters lightly, that harm will result. It is seen as especially dangerous to play with spiritual powers without proper commitment or guidance. Proper spiritual training carries responsibility and builds character.

Spiritual Privacy

It is very important for mental health workers, as for anyone having close interactions with Indian people, to understand and respect the private nature of many Indian spiritual beliefs and practices. Not to do so risks offending Indian clients, colleagues and friends, and may seriously interfere with providing mental health services to Indian people.

Since the need to respect the privacy of some spiritual matters may seem to conflict with the need to support and utilize traditional spiritual healing resources, it is important to explore the meaning of this sense of privacy.

Spiritual knowledge and practices may be kept private for a variety of reasons, including the desire to:
   • preserve ones special relationship to a spiritual being

- *avoid loss of spiritual power*
- *avoid potential misuse of spiritual knowledge*
- *avoid ridicule or persecution from non-Indians*
- *demonstrate respect*

There is an enormous range in the degree of 'openness' of Indian spiritual beliefs and practices. Some are more or less public and are open to all interested persons, whereas others are strictly the personal property of certain individuals and are never shared, even with other Indian people who have the same spiritual beliefs.

Indian people also differ from one another in their feelings about non-Indian involvement or interest in Indian spiritual ways. Certain tribal groups are far more concerned about privacy than are others, who may be quite open. Some Indians feel that it is a positive thing to share their beliefs with other people in the hope of promoting understanding. Other Indian people feel that no aspect of Indian spiritual ways should ever be shared with non-Indians. They may fear that non-Indians will mock their ways, ridicule them, publish or record sacred songs or rituals, or may actually damage spiritual powers and practices.

Many Indians feel that spirituality is the core of being Indian, a core which has remained intact partly because it has been kept private and sometimes hidden. These people often feel that non-Indians have stolen 'everything else' from Indians, such as land, resources, language and even children. They may feel that the expression of spirituality is 'all we have left', and that this can only be protected by keeping it private. In other words, some Indian people feel that non-Indian contact with or even knowledge of Indian spiritual ways is inherently damaging to themselves and to their sacred ways. Of course, people who feel this way will generally refuse to discuss spiritual matters or may pretend to have no knowledge of such things. *For this reason, it is not uncommon for non-Indians to misjudge the extent of an Indian person's involvement with or belief in Indian spiritual ways.*

As a broad generalization, urban Indians are liable to be somewhat more open with non-Indians about Indian spirituality than are reservation Indians. Also, urban Indians are more liable to follow broad spiritual traditions drawn from several different Indian tribes, whereas reservation Indians are more liable to be involved with the spiritual practices traditional to their particular tribe.

Non-Indians should take the cue from Indian friends and co-workers as to how to best learn about and support Indian spiritual ways. Often, it is best to ask few questions. Instead, it is wise to demonstrate a quiet and non-intrusive interest, then wait to be told about beliefs and practices or invited to attend a ceremony or healing event. This will of course take time.

Spiritual Healing Tradition

All Indian cultures had traditional ways of healing physical and spiritual disturbances. Generally, there is considerable overlap between spiritual, emotional and medical forms of help, since these realms of human experience are not seen as separate. In many Indian communities these spiritual ways are still widely practiced.

While there is variety from region to region, tribe to tribe and even from family to family in traditional spiritual beliefs and practices, most Indian groups have ceremonial practices for such purposes as:
- healing the sick
- teaching proper conduct to young people
- acknowledging a new spiritual power or song
- showing respect for spiritual forces
- keeping in the proper balance with the seasons and with the forces of nature
- honoring the dead
- helping the family of the deceased to safely and successfully complete a period of mourning

Many Indian people feel that their personal and cultural strength is based in their spirituality. The survival of Indian people through generations of trials is seen as the direct result of being a very spiritual people who have special gifts and knowledge which have sustained and protected them.

Most Indian groups acknowledge certain persons as having special knowledge, power or spiritual gifts. Traditional spiritual healers and leaders of several types continue to be highly respected and important healers in many, if not in most Indian communities. Herbalists, diagnosticians, ritualists and healers are called by many different names and are found in great variety. Despite religious oppression, the availability of medical doctors and the scorn of mainstream educators, traditional spiritual healers not only exist, but often exercise considerable influence. Their gifts may include the gift of diagnosing the nature or cause of an illness, of knowing what must be done to heal the sick, of helping to return a soul to its owner, of removing negative or dangerous forces from a person or from a house, of healing through laying on of hands, of healing through song, or of communication with spiritual presences.

Different families within a tribe are liable to have somewhat different spiritual orientations. *Many spiritual beliefs, practices and gifts are special family possessions: only members of a particular family may have a certain type of knowledge or the right to perform a particular spiritual activity.* For instance, only certain people can conduct a Burning for the dead or use particular herbs. Only certain individuals are entitled to sing particular songs or use particular power objects.

Family participation is often central to spiritual healing. In some cases, permission of elders is required before undertaking spiritual activities. The presence and active involvement of family members is often needed in order to help heal the sick. In some Indian traditions, this is because the spirits of family members are so closely connected that one family member cannot be healed without the others.

Healing involves bringing the parts of the sick person back together; i.e. the physical, emotional, spiritual, mental and social. It also involves bringing people together. To be cut off or separate is to be sick. To be well is to be whole, balanced and connected.

In Indian tradition, the spirit must be healed in order to heal the mind. This fundamental assumption must be understood and respected in order help Indian people who are in distress. The client's own spiritual beliefs must be discovered and utilized in treatment. Moreover, we believe that it is imperative for mental health providers to openly declare support for traditional Indian spiritual and healing practices.

Prayer, Music and Song

Across all spiritual and religious traditions, most Indian people feel strongly that prayer is necessary for personal and social harmony. Prayer opens a connection to the power of the Creator and keeps the self and community in harmony with spiritual forces.

Prayer in Indian tradition is a way of putting oneself in tune with the greater cosmic realities, not merely of asking for divine assistance. ***When in tune with the spiritual side of life, the helper is better able to perceive the client's trouble and to discover the proper response.*** Silent times for reflection and meditation are frequently a part of Indian tradition. Silence may allow communication to take place on a spiritual level before people begin to talk or act.

Prayer is seen by most Indian people as an important aspect of healing, either as a way of directly effecting change or of putting oneself in tune with spiritual forces. Prayer can be reassuring to Indian clients in times of distress, helping them gain spiritual perspective on their troubles as well as reinforcing their trust in the helper. ***Often, it can be helpful to encourage clients to pray about their problems in whatever manner is most comfortable for them.***

Prayer can bring client and helper closer together by lowering personal barriers and acknowledging the greater power of the spiritual world. When helper and client share in this experience, a working alliance can more easily be developed. Helpers may themselves feel more confident and able to find the right approach to helping a client through prayer.

In Indian country, prayers involve a wider range of activities than is typical in mainstream American society. While spoken prayer is almost an art form in Coast Salish tribal communities, many other forms of prayer are equally recognized, including prayer songs, drumming as prayer, dances which are understood to be prayers and burning of candles and ringing of bells. In some other Indian cultures prayerful acts include burning of sage and sweet grass, smoking tobacco in a ritual manner and scattering sacred cornmeal. All are ways to worship the sacred. ***Prayer may be silent or aloud, alone or in groups, or embodied in actions which set the tone for prayerful contemplation.***

In Indian communities, prayer often takes a public form which is not common in mainstream America. Indian people often pray outloud during family, group and community gatherings. Prayer is a common and expected part of otherwise "secular" activities. ***Important public events, such as meetings, conferences, dinner gatherings, dedications of new facilities, funerals, etc. are usually opened and closed with prayer. There is no "separation of church and state" in the tribal community, in that both governmental and business meetings are bounded by prayer.***

Private prayer is a daily practice for many Indian people. In some tribal traditions, people retreat from society for periods of contemplation and prayer. This may take the form of a vision quest or preparation for acquiring new spiritual power. Time spent in sweat lodges is a prayerful retreat set apart from the rest of life. Other people simply practice daily quiet prayer.

Group prayer can align the minds and spirits of all participants in an activity in order to bring about harmony of purpose and understanding.

Music, drumming and songs have particular significance for most Indian people as a form of prayer. Drums bring people together and set the time and place apart from everyday life. Songs express deep feelings, often spiritual feelings. *Indian people have songs for many purposes: there are social songs, prayer songs, honor songs and power songs. Most songs are the property of either individuals or families; they can only be sung by those having the inherited or earned right to sing that particular song.*

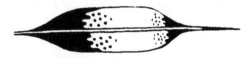

Spiritual Tolerance and Variety

Indian people tend to believe that spirituality is not confined to only one church. A number of Indian people actively participate in both a formal religious and a traditional spiritual system. For example, many Indian people are actively involved in a Catholic, Protestant or Pentecostal Christian Church. While for some, this is their primary or total spiritual pursuit, for others Christianity is combined in some manner with traditional Indian Spiritual traditions.

Indian spiritual open mindedness may be the result of a cultural tradition emphasizing personal spiritual experience and commitment, rather than of acceptance of an extensive body of religious belief and ritual.

The Swinomish Tribal Community in particular has achieved a broad tolerance for a range of religious beliefs and multiple ways of worship. It is common for leaders of differing spiritual traditions to collaborate in conducting spiritual and social events. Swinomish people are accustomed to having Catholic, Pentecostal, Shaker and Smokehouse prayers, songs and symbols mingled in a single "service" or other community function. Leaders of these groups tend to be supportive and respectful of one another.

Religious tolerance has not always been the norm. Early Christian ministries and United States governmental policies actually outlawed Indian traditional religious practices, as discussed in chapter I. This oppression and prejudice resulted in antagonism, anger and mutual suspicion between differing religious and spiritual groups, including the Smokehouse, Shakers and Catholics.

Happily, the strong Indian cultural emphasis on sharing and social tolerance has led over time to a re-thinking of these divisive attitudes. Forward-thinking elders, tribal governmental and spiritual leaders in the Swinomish community have encouraged a "live and let live" attitude and have taken courageous stands to demonstrate respect and promote tolerance.

The result is that at the time of this writing, **there is a remarkable degree of cooperation and openness in this tribal community between the various spiritual paths.** People who regularly attend either the Catholic or Shaker Churches may also be involved with the Winter Smokehouse ceremonials. Certainly all tribal community members expect to hear Shaker prayer songs at funerals during or following a Catholic funeral mass. At the dinner following a funeral, the "table manager" will consult with the family regarding their preference about who will offer the pre-meal prayer. Similarly, Catholic priests and Pentecostal pastors are often invited to "bless the table" or "witness" important spiritual work during Smokehouse gatherings.

In general, the attitude at Swinomish is that if a person feels happy and comfortable attending services beyond their primary affiliation, this is fine. Some people say directly that **at root "all the teachings are the same".** Others say **"If we all pray to the same God, we can pray in the same building".** It is clearly understood that if a person shows up at a given event, that they are lending their support for the "doings", even if they are not an active participant.

Treaty Day offers an interesting example of the blending of traditions at Swinomish. Treaty Day is celebrated on or near each Jan. 22 with a large winter Pow Wow, where dignitaries and leaders of both the tribal and mainstream communities are honored in the Smokehouse tradition. Treaty Day has a dual significance. First, **it honors the intergovernmental treaty enacted in 1855** which established the legal basis for the relationship between the governments of the Swinomish Tribal Community and the United

States of America, and therefore for the sovereignty of tribal government. Second, it also **celebrates the rights of Indian people to practice their own religions, and thus is a symbol of religious freedom.** Since Treaty Day takes place during the Smokehouse season, it especially affirms the legitimacy of this ancient spiritual path.

TRADITIONAL CONCEPTS OF HEALTH, ILLNESS AND MENTAL ILLNESS

Mental health and mental illness, more than almost any other aspect of life, are areas where cultural attitudes and world views must be considered. A peoples view of the causes of illness effects their symptom patterns as well as the kinds of treatments which will be effective.

Many Indian people have a holistic view of the world and of the person. This is tremendously significant for understanding health, illness and mental illness. Indian people tend not to focus on merely 'physical' or 'medical' causes of illness but also to examine the broader relation of the person to his or her total environment. Illness may have either physical, social or spiritual causes. 'Spiritual' is here meant in the broadest sense of the word, having to do not only with God, but with the mysterious spiritual nature of the world and of all things.

The idea of balance or of being in the right relation to the world, and especially to ones family, kin and significant others, is of central importance in most Indian cultures. This includes being in balance with the natural and spiritual world. To be 'well' means keeping the right balance in all things. Illness is due to some imbalance and in itself creates an imbalance. In the Indian worldview, illness may be caused by a mistake or misdeed on the part of the ill person, their family or some other person. Conflict with others, wrong or disrespectful actions or even unintentional mistakes may all cause dangerous imbalances and can lead to illness or other misfortune.

Because of the close connections between individuals and family members, the actions of ones family are often seen as having either positive or negative repercussions for the individual. Bad feelings, social conflict and unresolved tensions can make a person ill. Anger directed toward a person may make them ill, especially if the angry person has great personal power. Psychic or spiritual harm may be either intentional or unintentional, since negative thoughts or emotions can have a dangerous energy of their own.

Indian people do not always see eye to eye with medical doctors, mental health therapists and mainstream non-Indians about what makes people sick. Indian people do not necessarily believe that specific illnesses (e.g. flu, chicken pox, heart trouble, etc.) have a consistent and identifiable medical cause; (e.g. that the flu is 'caused' by a virus, heart trouble is caused by eating too many fatty foods, etc.). Instead, each individual case is examined to determine the particular nature of the imbalances in the person's life or environment which could have caused a particular illness. Accordingly, one person's flu might be 'caught' from some-one else (by transmission of a virus) whereas another person's flu might be due to social and emotional tensions on the job 'making her sick' and a third person's flu might be due to having come into contact with a spiritually dangerous force or situation.

In traditional Indian cultures there is generally less emphasis on rationality, consistency or mechanical causation than is typical in mainstream American 'scientific explanations'. Indian people do not assume that A always leads to B. Instead, many Indian people accept that A may lead either to B, C, or D. Similarly, B might be seen as caused either by A, by C or by D, depending on the specific circumstances. For example, many Indian people do not assume that the 'flu' is always caused by a virus. *This view of causality is in some sense more complex, since consistency of cause cannot be assumed between two occurrences of any given thing.*

While germs, viruses, bacteria and pollution may be accepted as contributing to illness, such things as anger, social tensions, sudden shocks or scares, soul loss, bad thoughts or wrong actions, ghosts, use of alcohol and drugs, dreaming of the dead, witchcraft or having

something 'put on you', failure to follow spiritual rules, eating the wrong food, coming into contact with a power which is too strong for you, being near dangerous things, or simply being too non-traditional are often thought to be the primary cause of imbalance, illness and disorder.

Indian interpretations of mental and emotional problems are also liable to differ from mainstream interpretations. Certain behaviors or conditions which are seen in non-Indian society as symptoms of 'mental illness' may not be interpreted in this way at all by many Indian people. Personal problems are more liable to be seen as externally caused than as due to psychological conflicts. The severity of stresses facing many Indian people makes this viewpoint very understandable. Most personal problems are attributed to physical illness, family conflict, drinking, misbehavior or spiritual forces.

Mental illness may be seen as shameful or unnatural and therefore tends not to be recognized or reported. Many Indian people show great acceptance and tolerance of personal peculiarities or social deviance. They may say that 'He's just that way' or 'Aunt Minnie has always been a little queer', without either rejecting that person or labeling them as mentally ill.

Another difference concerns experiences which might be called 'psychic'. *Many Indian people experience compelling intuition, visions and powerful dreams. These experiences are often valued as forms of special knowledge concerning psychic or spiritual realities.* People who have such experiences frequently or with unusual intensity are often thought to be blessed with a special gift for seeing, dreaming or otherwise receiving information. Unless these experiences are extremely disturbing and bizarre, they are generally not judged to be pathological. Unlike most non-Indian Americans, many Indian people are open to such experiences and greet them as special and valuable. It should be obvious that people with such a receptive attitude are likely to have a greater number of such experiences and to find them less frightening and more meaningful. *Mental health workers would do well to seek to understand the meaning of any such experiences for the client, as well as to be very hesitant to label them as symptoms of illness.*

In many traditional Indian cultures, severe emotional and psychological disturbance may be attributed to soul loss, spirit possession, loss of the breath of life, or to evil 'work' by an enemy. Each of these concepts is nearly universal in traditional North American Indian cultures, although the specific symptom patterns and beliefs differ.

Soul loss may be caused either by a sudden shock or fright or by the soul being drawn away by some stronger force. Symptoms may include loss of energy or appetite, difficulty sleeping, social withdrawal, etc. Treatment requires traditional experts who can diagnose the problem, locate the soul and restore it to the patient.

Spirit possession or spirit visitation may be caused by a spiritual force intruding on the person, either accidentally or purposefully. In certain cases it may be caused by a person failing to let the dead go, i.e. by emotionally calling them back or clinging to them. Symptoms may include restlessness, pains, sickness, crying, visions, unusual behavior, fearfulness, hearing songs, etc. In general, the cure either involves traditional specialists removing the outside influence, or helping the person to develop a productive relationship with it.

Evil 'work' can be accomplished in a number of ways, which have been amply described by anthropologists. Symptoms may include 'craziness', sudden illnesses, accidents, nightmares, etc. Such 'work' can only be undone by a person with special power to remove such negative influences. The evil may then be redirected back to the original sender.

Another category of disturbance might be called 'a disturbance of the breath of life'. This condition involves irregular breathing or perhaps hyperventilation. It may be caused by anxiety or by sudden shock. Such a weakened condition may leave a person vulnerable to negative spiritual influences.

Mental health workers need to be aware that Indian clients may have beliefs similar to these. Even people who do not believe in these types of influences or dangers sometimes become concerned about such possibilities when they are feeling ill, frightened or upset. If a non-Indian mental health worker has no knowledge of these matters, he/she may miss the true meaning of a client's comments or fears. Clients may not be willing to verbalize these concerns to non-Indian counselors who do not indicate some understanding, for fear of being ridiculed or labeled as crazy. In fact, non-Indians unfamiliar with Indian culture sometimes misinterpret such beliefs as delusional or paranoid and totally fail to understand either their cultural meaning or the opportunity which they present for culturally appropriate treatment.

Traditional Ways of Helping and Healing

Different views of the causes of illness require different forms of help. The type of help given must address the problem and its cause as seen by the client. If this basic principal is ignored many treatments will fail.

All traditional Indian cultures developed specific ways of responding to life crises, tragedies and emotional/psychological disturbances, including:

- Consultation with elders
- Bringing family groups together
- Giving immediate emotional support
- Prayer and song
- Certain individuals or families recognized as helpers
- Sharing meals
- Removing dangerous spiritual influences
- Dietary and herbal remedies
- Seeking to restore balance of spiritual forces both around and within the individual

Often, many of these elements can be productively combined with mental health approaches. Culture-specific consultation and expertise is needed to guide these efforts.

In general, Indian people know what type of help they need and go directly to the appropriate type of healer, e.g., medical, psychological or one of the several kinds of traditional spiritual healers.

Traditional clients who need spiritual help will generally find the right form of treatment without consultation from mental health workers. However, Indian clients who have less traditional beliefs or who are uncertain about their cultural identity may need the therapist or counselor to show some awareness and respect for traditional treatments. This is important because only the culturally 'right' treatment will work for these problems.

It can be very helpful for mental health workers to consult with tribal elders or spiritual leaders in order to determine when and how referrals should be made to traditional healers. In general, whenever an Indian client suspects that he/she may have lost their soul, been harmed by a spiritual force, or may have been the object of some malicious 'work', these concerns should be referred to an appropriate cultural specialist. If this is not done, the client may well get worse, and will probably lose faith in the mental health worker.

If the mental health worker does not fully understand what the client needs, it is best to say so directly and ask the client who he/she knows that would understand these matters and know the right way to deal with them. Even fairly 'acculturated' clients often know who could help, but may need the therapist's support and approval. When a client really does not know who to consult, it is best to call in an Indian colleague or elder who can provide the needed guidance.

It is important to point out that traditional beliefs about mental illness do not necessarily prohibit the client from benefiting from counseling, medication or other forms of mental health treatment, so long as the culture-specific aspects of their problems are also treated by culture-specific methods. If this is not done, this omission may prevent the success of other forms of treatment.

Just as a cardiac specialist would not try to treat asthma, but might suggest collaboration with a pulmonary specialist, a mental health specialist should not attempt to treat a condition he/she does not understand, such as soul loss or spirit illness. This is true *regardless of whether or not* the mental health specialist believes in the spiritual illness. What matters is that the client believes in it or at least fears that it might be the case. When a mental health specialist finds him/herself out of his/her depth, the thing to do is to suggest that the client talk to someone who will understand. When in doubt, refer!

Traditional Expectations of Helpers

Indian culture tends to define the helping role rather differently than does non-Indian society. Helpers are expected to be members of the same tribal-cultural system, that is, to be "one of us". People are accepted as helpers not primarily on the basis of their training, experience or job role, but on the basis of their personal connections in the tribal community. Helpers and the helper's ancestry must be known to the client and the client's family and they must be felt to have an understanding of Indian ways. Some Indian people think that mental health counselors only work with people who are "crazy." They may be more willing to seek help from a traditional Indian helper.

Helpers are expected to be available when needed, either on a drop in basis or after usual work hours. They are expected to come to the home of the person in need, and to remain as long as needed.

Helpers are further expected to lead exemplary lives and to have some special personal qualities, including caring, understanding and spiritual power. Often helpers are either spiritual healers or are religious people who integrate prayer with help. Certain individuals are recognized in every community as especially qualified to help. These include elders, spiritual leaders, and others who are seen as especially caring and knowledgeable. People in tribal communities know who to ask for a specific type of help. Helping roles are often openly acknowledged by both helpers and by the community as a whole.

In summary, helpers are expected to be:
- **Personally known**
- **Highly available**
- **Caring**
- **Good examples**
- **Spiritually gifted**

Collaboration Between Mental Health and Traditional Healing

Traditional expectations of helpers have implications for mental health workers and for the acceptance of mental health services in tribal communities. Mental health workers need to understand client expectations and to adapt their role behavior as much as possible to meet culturally specific expectations.

Mental health workers need to establish connections to a variety of 'natural helpers', for referrals, consultation and collaboration. When possible, it is desirable to hire natural helpers as mental health workers or consultants. This tends to increase the mental health program's credibility. It further ensures the cultural relevance of services, and joins traditional and modern mental health approaches in a manner likely to be effective for Indian clients.

Spiritual traditions alive at Swinomish will next be presented as specific examples of Indian spiritual healing ways: the Smokehouse, Indian Catholicism, Shakerism, Pentecostalism and Talking Circle.

THE SMOKEHOUSE WAY

The Smokehouse is a native spiritual and healing tradition with ancient roots in Coast Salish cultures. The word "Smokehouse" may refer either to the organization, to the actual building where spiritual activities take place or to the set of beliefs and practices stemming from the centuries old Coast Salish traditions. Although current Smokehouse practices differ in a number of ways from pre-Western contact days, they are none the less directly derived from those ancient traditional spiritual practices.

This tradition became known as "the Smokehouse" because of the intensely smoky atmosphere generated by the huge open fires in the interior of the traditional Big House or Longhouse where winter ceremonials were and are traditionally held. An event of great importance in the Swinomish Tribal Community was the completion of a traditional style smokehouse in 1992.

There is a considerable body of anthropological work documenting traditional smokehouse and related Coast Salish healing and religious practices, including: Pamela Amoss' *Coast Salish Spirit Dancing*; June Collins' *Valley of the Spirits* and Jay Miller's *Lushootseed Culture and the Shamanic Odyssey*. These and other works (e.g. Jillek) include discussions about how these practices relate to societal stress, and present native concepts of illness and healing. Unfortunately, little attention has been given to the need for mental health and other workers in tribal communities to understand and cooperate with traditional healing.

In order to provide culturally appropriate services to Indian people, mental health workers, physicians and other professionals in Indian communities must develop a basic appreciation for the connections between mental health, emotional wellness and traditional healing practices. Even though most non Indian workers have only limited exposure to the Smokehouse (and especially to the healing practices which occur outside of the large public dances), *it is of great importance that mental health workers and doctors understand the Indian concepts of psychological, emotional*

and spiritual disturbance and its culturally appropriate treatment which underlie the Smokehouse winter ceremonials. The following sections attempt to meet this need.

Spiritual Disturbance

Spiritual Disturbance or "Indian **sickness" is a form of distress which re-** ***quires specific cultural 'treatment'. Even more*** **importantly, it offers a way for the Indian indi-** ***vidual to reconnect with the meaningfulness of Indian culture.***

In Coast Salish Tribal communities there is a culturally specific pattern of acute psycho-social-spiritual disturbance sometimes referred to as "Indian sickness" or "being bothered" (by a spirit). This pattern is unique in that it is both a "culture bound" reactive disturbance (Yap, 1965; Kiev, 1964) and is at the same time a powerful expression of cultural values.

"Indian sickness" is centrally connected to the winter healing ceremonials known as "Indian dancing", "Smokehouse", "Spiritual dancing", "winter dancing", "Seowyn" or just "winter pow-wows". It is a fairly common syndrome which is recognizable to most Coast Salish people, and diagnosable by Indian spiritual experts. Although many Indian people believe that all Indians may have the potential to develop spiritual disturbance, only a (substantial) minority of Coast Salish people actually have this experience.

The onset is usually sudden, although often this follows a period of increased stress, emotional upset or social problems. Indian people understand fully that this acute "breakdown" of social and psychological functioning is related to unsatisfactory aspects of the person's health, behavior or social-psychological adjustment. ***As discussed previously, the Indian worldview, there is*** **no contradiction between psychological and spiritual disturbance** ***and healing, because all of life is seen as interconnected.***

Initial symptoms range from restlessness, visionary dreams, intense anxiety or irritability to a state of acutely altered perception, with fear, agitation, and sometimes uncontrollable cries known as "trying to sing". Physical symptoms, social withdrawal and apparent medical problems are common. A person in this state may be unable to sleep, eat or carry on usual activities.

Traditional people understand this condition to be due to the power of a Spirit Song which, having become attached to a person, makes the unprepared and impure recipient "sick" until they can be helped through traditional treatments to "bring out the song". The affected individual may be acutely frightened and confused and may be resistant to the Spirit's call. This situation is understood by all to be a crisis and a threat to the stricken person's health and safety. Family and community respond with an immediate rally of support, consultation and planning for the person's proper care.

If seen by a non-Indian psychiatrist or mental health worker who is not knowledgeable about Indian sickness, the affected person might be misdiagnosed as experiencing an acute anxiety state or even a psychotic reaction. Such misdiagnoses can lead to treatment that is ineffective or even damaging. Luckily, most Indian families prevent psychiatric interference at such times.

Indian Sickness develops only during the winter months, and generally strikes only individuals whose family members or ancestors have previously become "Indian dancers", although there are exceptions to this general rule. This condition is understood to be caused by a spirit attaching itself to a person and "bothering" him, partly in order to inspire or demand the performance of the Spirit's song and accompanying dance. This is not the individual's soul or personal spirit, nor is it an ancestral spirit. However, the spirit does have a deep personal relationship to the affected person, and often has been passed down from an ancestor who previously "carried" this particular Spirit's song.

Spirits and Songs

Spirits arrive from the East at the beginning of winter and remain until early Spring, thus defining the Smokehouse season which lasts from after Thanksgiving until early Spring, depending upon the geographical location. The word "Skalalitut" is often used to refer to these spirits, as is the word "Seowyn", though there is some reason to believe that the latter previously referred only the spirit's song. Many people refer to these spirits indirectly as "my Indian", or "what I've got". These rather oblique references may be seen as more respectful and safer than directly naming the spirit. Coast Salish people never name their spirit partners directly.

These spirits are somewhat ambiguous, in that they are neither "good" nor "evil". Such spirits are simultaneously seen as foreign entities attempting to establish a sort of control of the person, and at the same time as a personal Guardian Spirit coming to the aid of its distressed or erring human partner.

The Spirit's primary goal is to manifest itself through its personal "song" which it does by causing the chosen person to sing and dance in the exactly "right" and unique manner. *The Spirit song, and the accompanying dance, express the essence of the Spirit. The song is therefore not an invention of the singer: it is an urgent spiritual cry which overwhelms his/her defenses, making him/her "sick" until it is sung properly.* The new dancer, or "baby" does not automatically know how to sing or dance the Spirit's song, and must be "helped" by "workers" skilled in interpreting the proper song and dance movements.

The Spirit which "bothers" a person becomes his/her personal guiding power through the process of becoming a singer-dancer. There is a special, intimate and lifelong bond between the Singer and the Spirit whose song he/ she sings. While the singer serves the Spirit by allowing it to manifest itself in song and by honoring it in various ways, the Spirit in turn bestows specific and private gifts of power and fortune on the singer.

Resistance to Spiritual Call

Resistance to this spiritual-psychological demand is considered to be very dangerous, in that it could lead to serious physical or mental illness or even to death. As is true in many cultures, power and danger go hand in hand.

While the connection to a spiritual guide may bring a person considerable gifts of wisdom, personal strength and spiritual power, it must be handled carefully and respectfully, so as not to give offense. Careless or disrespectful treatment of the Spirit may result in severe harm, either to the Singer or to family members.

Nevertheless, in certain circumstances it may be inadvisable for a person to be initiated into the Smokehouse. Conflicting religious beliefs, a non-traditional or unsupportive family, lack of adequate financial resources, excessive youth or age, poor health, inflexible time commitments, or disrespectfulness may all be reasons why a person or their family might want to avoid an initiation into the Smokehouse. Furthermore, these reasons might prevent a given individual being accepted into the Smokehouse society.

In such cases Indian spiritual healers may be able to postpone the spirit's demands through use of prayer, songs or protective rituals. This is not always successful and may give only temporary relief. Success depends on many factors, such as the strength of the spirit, the persons's opposing (often Christian or Shaker) faith, or the strength of the spiritual assistance given by an "Indian Doctor", Shaker, or Christian minister. In many cases, such protective treatments will be only partially successful, requiring repetition, precautions in living or an eventual decision to become a Smokehouse dancer.

Entering the Smokehouse

Entering the Smokehouse is a serious decision involving personal, family and "worker" commitment. This process, which leads to becoming an "Indian Dancer/ Singer" is a lifelong spiritual and lifestyle commitment which must not be taken lightly. Older family members, such as parents, grandparents, aunts and uncles must agree to "put him/her into the Smokehouse" or "give him/her up".

Often the new dancer comes to the Smokehouse out of years of personal and social difficulties. This frequently includes alcohol or drug use, depression or other problems which have led family and tribal elders to be deeply concerned for the welfare of the individual. Entering the Smokehouse is often seen as a direct form of treatment or intervention into an unhealthy lifestyle.

There is a second route to becoming an Indian Dancer/ Smokehouse member. In some cases individuals are "given up" by family even without the individual having shown signs of "Indian sickness". Instead, the person's unhealthy or rebellious behaviors may have led to anxious concern for his/her well being. In such instances, the family may give permission to a specific group of Smokehouse workers to take their family member into the Smokehouse. Such a decision is never made lightly, and is probably only reached when family believe that a younger relative's life is in serious danger from his/her own poor choices. In this situation, "giving the person up" to the Smokehouse is in effect a last resort effort to save their loved one.

While the new dancer's agreement is certainly desirable, it is not always required and is never in itself sufficient. ***No individual*** *may enter the Smokehouse without the consent of family elders, who have spiritual authority, and are the guardians of family spiritual property such as Indian names, "teachings" and ceremonial privileges. In addition, families must make a considerable commitment of time and money when a family member enters the Smokehouse.*

Extended family are expected to be present at nightly dances to encourage the new dancer, to learn their song, and also to provide food for the workers for a period of weeks to months. In addition, the family must contribute substantially to the meals prepared at large public gatherings, as well as accumulate many gifts to give away to those who serve as formal witnesses of the new dancer's song, as well as other guests. The financial expenditures can indeed be considerable, and generally require the active contribution of the entire extended family.

Once the family has decided that a family member should enter the Smokehouse, "workers" must be found willing to take on the new dancer. This involves the willingness to provide 24 hour supervision for some weeks, to personally oversee a highly sensitive spiritual training process, and to remain partially responsible for and involved with the new dancer for a lifetime.

Initiation

Initiation into the Smokehouse is a rigorous process involving total removal from one's usual life and associations for a period ranging from ten especially intense days and continuing for three months. The new dancer is seen as embarking on a totally new phase of life. He or she is a "baby", reborn into Seowyn. This is seen as a total renewal of life not unlike the Christian concept of being reborn in Christ. It is a watershed between the old life and the new, in which values are embraced which are expected to result in both a more responsible social life and a more powerful and mysterious spiritual connection

The new dancer is given into the care of a team of selected Smokehouse "workers". These "workers" are people with special gifts related to teaching and training new dancers, and this team has total control of the new dancer's life for a period of time. The "baby's" activities are carefully monitored and severely restricted. The person is watched at all times, and must adhere to a strict regimen, including prohibitions on talking, eating, restrictions of sleeping and all bodily processes.

Rigorous daily cleansing and exercise, and demanding sessions dedicated to learning and practicing the newly acquired song and dance are central. Not only the new dancer, but the workers as well, must learn the new song and dance. The workers "help (him) sing" by drumming on their personal drums and singing along. It is extremely important that the song and dance be learned and performed perfectly in accordance with the wishes of the particular Spirit. In addition, *workers talk to the new dancers at length, in order to impart vital "teachings" necessary for the new life to be followed.*

Relief from the symptoms of acute anxiety is generally achieved within the first few days, and is associated with the cathartic outpouring of emotion, tension relief and status change which occurs upon acquiring and publicly singing one's Spirit song. The discipline, heightened emotional context, social expectations, physical exertion, ritual dress and rhythmic singing and drumming all contribute to the Indian dancer experiencing an intense, trance-like state of higher consciousness. *This altered experiential state is crucial in effecting a "cure" or improvement in the individual's psycho-spiritual condition.*

After the first four days of training, the new dancer is presented to the tribal community in a ceremony in which they are "stood up" and allowed to sing and dance for the first time in public. The following night the new dancer receives his/her hair hat, which is a key part of Smokehouse regalia.

For the new dancer, strict training continues throughout the first winter. The length of time a new dancer remains in isolation depends partly on how early in the season they entered the Smokehouse, as well as practical factors such as family and vocational responsibilities.

New dancers travel with their workers to a number of large Smokehouse gatherings which take place throughout the entire Coast Salish region each winter. This is a sort of "coming out" as a Spirit Dancer and as such is of great social importance.

Smokehouse Gatherings are quite demanding for the new dancers. Long hours of travel are followed by hours of sitting quietly on benches, not being able to speak, to see or to interact with others as everyone else does. Finally the moment of release comes when they are able to dance, and the preceding sensory deprivation heightens the alteration of consciousness which is intrinsic to the dance state.

This entire process is in effect a culturally specific form of psychotherapy. It is at once a re-education, a re-birth and a healing. It is expected that this treatment process will not only relieve the immediate symptoms of distress or illness, but will have a lasting impact on the personality, social conduct, health and spiritual life of the new dancer.

Smokehouse Gatherings

Every weekend night during the winter season there are large gatherings of Smokehouse dancers and community members throughout the Coast Salish cultural region. Invitations are generally given up to a year ahead, by announcement at large gatherings, and are open to all community members. These events often are sponsored by particular families in honor of a deceased family member (a "Memorial") or to recognize the "giving" of an Indian name.

New dancers, or "babies", dance nightly throughout their first winter training period. Especially important are the big winter Smokehouse gatherings which occur up and down the Coast Salish communities from Tulalip north into British Columbia, with a strong representation on Vancouver Island. These gatherings are very large, with between 200 and 500 people in attendance. Family groups travel long distances to attend, often structuring much of their winter schedule around these culturally central events.

Winter Smokehouse gatherings serve multiple cultural purposes beyond the obvious one of the Spirit Dancing which is the focus of the event. These gatherings provide opportunities for renewal of old friendships and acquaintances, for public demonstrations of changes in social status and for young people to meet prospective partners.

Perhaps more than any other activity, the Smokehouse gatherings reaffirm the cultural unity of the entire Coast Salish region and thus help to ensure the survival of Coast Salish culture as a living system.

Smokehouse dancing and singing create an aura of antiquity and awe, evoking a powerful awareness of the connection to one's ancestors and a sense of geographical place that is so central to most Indian cultures.

Participating in these events is a non verbal way of demonstrating one's loyalty to one's culture and Tribal community, and everybody understands this. Many non-dancers attend, and their presence is felt as a strong message of support for the dancers, the Smokehouse tradition and the culture.

However, it should be noted that not all Tribal members attend Smokehouse gatherings. Family and religious affiliations tend to determine who does and does not attend, at least on a regular basis. Some families are heavily involved with the Smokehouse and others are not.

Smokehouse gatherings are demanding for both dancers and non dancers, often lasting from perhaps 3 PM until 2 AM or even later. While people do socialize and eat, most of the time is spent listening to speeches from respected elders and watching the dancing.

The Work: Memorials and Namings

Larger Smokehouse dances generally accompany other special events. Memorials for deceased family members are one important type of event. Here, a family will honor one or more relation, often on the fourth year following the loss, as this signals the end of the formal period of mourning. Memorials feature speeches which review the merits of the deceased and exhort young people to respect their elders and ancestors and uphold tribal values. Often there is a formal presentation of photographs of the deceased. There may also be "work" done related to the spiritual possessions of the deceased.

Naming ceremonies may also take place during large Smokehouse gatherings. Indian names are family property which must be bestowed upon individuals by family elders. Indian names are given in a formal presentation to the community. This is an extremely important event in the life of a tribal member, signaling family support and a link to those ancestors who have carried this name before them. With the name come increased respect and social standing, as well as increased responsibility to a live a life worthy of the name.

Whatever the specific type of "work" being done, these occasions always require "witnesses." Witnesses are highly respected individuals chosen by the family to perform this function. *In an oral tradition, it is vital that there be people who remember what has happened in order to ensure that the work done will be acknowledged within the tribal society. Witnesses are expected to observe the work done, such as the names bestowed, and remember these and repeat the information as needed in the future. Witnesses are "paid" quarters by a lineup of younger family members to seal the agreement.*

Large Smokehouse events may require years of planning and saving by the sponsoring family due to the great expenses involved. Since one may not work on members of one's own family, respected elders and Smokehouse leaders must be enlisted to conduct the "work". Gifts of blankets must be accumulated to "thank" them for their help. Witnesses are also thanked with blankets, and cooks and other helpers are also given gifts. Food must be provided for hundreds of people. Finally, small gifts such as dish towels, scarves, oranges or canned salmon are often distributed to guests.

All of this is done in public, with appropriate speeches. Witnesses, workers and other respected helpers are usually asked to come forward onto the floor to receive their gifts. Especially respected individuals may receive Pendelton blankets to which younger family members pin bills of one dollar or more.

Needless to say, this all takes a good deal of time. The actual dancing often does not begin in earnest until several hours after the beginning of the gathering. *Activities in Indian country do not proceed by the clock, but instead according to a sort of organic time, unfolding as everything is ready and in place. Participants and attendees know how to be patient and receptive rather than demanding: they do not expect things to occur on a particular schedule and are not disturbed by long waits.*

There is a rhythmic pace to most Indian events which is best experienced by surrendering oneself to the rhythm; one must give up expectations of timeliness and simply relax into the events of the moment.

Singing, Drumming and Dancing

After the conclusion of the "work", the dancing begins. The drumming which is integral to smokehouse dancing sets the tone for the event, and is a powerful stimulus for alterations of consciousness, tending to produce a sort of mild trance state in non dancer witnesses as well as dancers.

The drums themselves are small, personal drums, unlike the "Big Drum" of plains origin. Coast Salish drums are hide stretched over wooden hoops about 14 inches in diameter, and are held and beaten by their owners in a powerful cadence accompanying personal songs. The drum is a highly valued spiritual object which must be treated with care and respect, as are all ceremonial objects and regalia employed in the Smokehouse.

The songs themselves are indescribable, both because of the private nature of these sacred possessions, and because of the raw power and cultural uniqueness which make them impossible to convey in words. They begin with the dancer becoming agitated as the song wells up inside and takes control of his/her mind and will. The dance is preceded by crying aloud as well as shaking, and often the workers must protect the dancer until the time comes to spring to the floor and begin the counter clockwise dance around the large rectangular hall. Workers stand by to prevent harm to the dancer or others, and workers and family follow closely behind drumming, singing and lifting their hands in the palm upward Coast Salish gesture of honor.

These songs are unlike anything else: they are powerful, gut wrenching expressions of ancient feeling. They are joyous, frightening, full of grief and rage, fulfillment and victory. Hearing them changes a person forever. After hours of sitting and filling one's heart and ears with this singing, the drums and songs reverberate in one's mind for many hours. Henceforth the Spirit world seems closer.

Living the Smokehouse Way

Smokehouse dancer-singers are not only expected to regularly attend winter ceremonials as active participants, but also to follow healthy and

respectful practices throughout the entire year for the rest of their lives.

Although the most rigorous training is during the first year when the new dancer is a "baby" and therefore the most vulnerable to spiritual dangers, they are considered to be "young" and in a period of extended training and supervision for the first four years.

The dancer owes a lasting obligation of respect and loyalty to his/her workers, who become a sort of new Smokehouse "family". The dancer is expected to turn to these individuals for personal guidance and instruction, and to offer them time, loyalty and material support when needed. ***The ties formed in the Smokehouse are considered as deep and binding as are blood ties.***

The ties are reciprocal: the workers acquire a life long obligation to provide support and "teaching" to the new dancers. The workers' reputations are impacted by how well the new dancer upholds his/her ceremonial obligations, as well as how they follow proper standards of behavior throughout the year. If a Smokehouse dancer is seen to be misbehaving, for instance by drinking heavily, his workers may try to talk to him and help set him back on the right path. Workers become concerned with a dancer does not attend Smokehouse ceremonies, because of the dangers of neglecting the Spirit's needs. There is a deep sense of mutual responsibility.

As the new dancer gains in spiritual maturity and ability to properly "carry" his Spirit powers, he or she will generally take on responsibilities in the training of new dancers. Certainly, he or she is seen as setting an example for all "younger" dancers in how to attain psychological balance, maturity, peace and personal spiritual power.

The dancer may become a "worker" and may also become recognized in the community as a spiritual authority, whose advice or "help" may be sought by others, not only from his own tribe, but perhaps by others from culturally inter-related Coast Salish tribes.

When a dancer is known to be a dedicated Smokehouse participant who upholds the rules of spiritual living, he or she acquires considerable social standing and respect throughout the entire Coast Salish culture area.

Risks of Smokehouse Participation

The consequences of not following the Smokehouse way, or of not "respecting" the "Seowyn", can be serious. The dangers are both social and spiritual and are especially acute during the "baby's" first year. Failure to "listen" and show respect to one's workers, learn and follow the ritual requirements, sing and dance in accord with the Spirit's requirements, can all lead to increased hardship and ordeals, to ridicule, shame or, in extreme cases, to a degree of social ostracism.

One's own family is apt to apply considerable pressure for conformity with these "ways", perhaps because they too are subject to both social pressures and spiritual dangers when a family member enters the Smokehouse. As noted elsewhere, status and respect tend to be family matters to an extent unusual in mainstream American society.

The Spirits themselves are 'ambivalent powers', not inherently either good or evil. They are dangerous by virtue of their power and 'otherness', and therefore require a respectful attitude on the part of humans who interact with them. Traditional teachings guide living people in how to approach dealings with Spiritual Beings in a cautious, ritualized manner aimed both at demonstrating respect and carefully preserving the boundaries which protect humans from the Spirit world.

The new dancer, as well as the individual who is "bothered" by a Spirit's song, are in especially vulnerable positions, unusually open to the Spirit world. At this stage, failure to acknowledge the spiritual roots of the disturbance, or refusal to accept appropriate "help", can be extremely dangerous. Without proper help, the Spirit might make the person increasingly sick or even "crazy".

If not treated with honor and respect, the spirit may also cause a variety of misfortunes to occur to the affected person or to members of their family. This may be especially true of people who turn away from or deny their Spirit songs without getting the proper help to "lift it off' them. There are many reports of physical illness, accidents, death and other misfortunes resulting from such abuses of one's relation to the Spirit.

These dangers affect close family members almost equally with the persons themselves. This view reflects the deep sense of mutual responsibility, vulnerability and shared fate of family members. It is also related to the fact that Spirit songs are passed along in families. A person may receive the song that a grandparent or great grandparent "carried", even if they had ever heard their relative sing the song or had not even known that relative. The connection of these songs and spirits to the person and their family is vital and unseverable.

One other risk of Smokehouse participation is that of having a distressing, painful or dangerous experience during the initiation. On rare occasions, unfortunate incidents have occurred. To prevent problems, some Smokehouse leaders first try to talk applicants out of joining, in order to weed out those who are not really serious or able to commit. Sometimes a medical examination is recommended. Other times tribal Community Health Representatives (CHRs) visit the new dancers during their seclusion to check on their health status. If needed, "babies" are taken to see the physician who works at the tribal clinic. Of course, this is possible only when the physician is knowledgeable about and supportive of the Smokehouse tradition.

Misuse of Smokehouse

Some Indian people express concerns over what they feel is a misuse of the Smokehouse and its traditions. They feel that at times the true purpose of spiritual renewal has been twisted into a method of forcing change on a person who is not ready for this. Some people point out that the crucial step of having a proper diagnosis of spirit illness made by a spiritual expert is too often skipped. They voice the concern that families sometimes "give up" younger relations to the Smokehouse who are in fact too young to learn from the experience or take it seriously.

In the past, individuals had to earn the right to become a Smokehouse dancer though proper conduct and service to the community. Over time, Smokehouse initiation has evolved into a way of trying to heal personal dysfunction, especially related to alcohol and drug abuse. When a dancer proves unable or unwilling to lead a respectful, constructive life without use of alcohol or drugs, some people point to the loss of strict criteria for entering the Smokehouse as the reason for this failure. These people would prefer that entering the Smokehouse be a privilege which must be earned by responsible behavior, rather than a correction for dysfunctional behavior.

Benefits of Smokehouse Life

There are many benefits to participation in the Smokehouse. For many Coast Salish people, the Smokehouse has enriched their spiritual lives, strengthened their personal cultural identity, and given them a secure family and social standing. The Smokehouse has also helped many Indian people achieve drug and alcohol free lifestyles.

Smokehouse tradition opposes the use of alcohol and drugs and provides culturally appropriate models for a positive lifestyle. Traditional methods for personal change make more sense to tribal members than do mainstream chemical dependency approaches. The network of close social supports provided in Smokehouse society is more effective than are non-tribal social and professional supports.

Some tribal members who have been unsuccessful in inpatient alcohol or drug treatment programs have been able to remain clean and sober following initiation into the Smokehouse. Although this is not always successful, clinical impression suggests that the Smokehouse may be a more effective "treatment" for Indian people with alcohol and drug problems than are mainstream inpatient programs or participation in conventional 12 step programs.

Membership in the Smokehouse society offers a secure place in tribal society, with clear roles and relationships. This is vitally important in helping individuals combat self-destructive lifestyles.

Tribal members who have been legally ordered into drug or alcohol treatment sometimes petition the court to allow them to enter the Smokehouse instead of a mainstream program. Smokehouse leaders have met with judges to explain the purposes of this form of "treatment". Upon occasion individuals with substance abuse problems have been placed in the "custody" of the Smokehouse and ordered to complete the period of initiation. There is some debate in the Tribal Community about this use of the Smokehouse, but it has been successful at times. This is one example of mutual support and collaboration between mainstream and traditional services.

SUMMARY

The Smokehouse has a powerfully beneficial impact on many Indian people. It is often, though not always, a "corrective emotional experience" which allows a person to overcome negative attitudes and behaviors and identify with positive Indian cultural values. The intense physical, social and spiritual stimuli create optimal conditions for personal change. Many Smokehouse members experience profound changes in psychological and spiritual functioning, and emerge from this process with a more balanced and mature adaptation to tribal society.

"Indian sickness" cannot be separated from its culturally dictated treatment of becoming a Smokehouse dancer. This is not only the preferred treatment for this culture-bound syndrome, it is the only treatment. Non-Indian diagnostic labels and treatment approaches would be both ineffective and harmful. *It is essential that therapists and medical professionals working in Coast Salish Tribal communities be aware of this syndrome, be respectful to the Smokehouse system of traditional healing, and be able to support the client's commitment to this therapeutic process by working collaboratively with elders and spiritual healers.*

Seen from a Western psychiatric viewpoint, "Indian sickness" is an acute reactive disturbance of the psyche, which like those rare instances of "creative illness" found in Western culture (William James, 1902; Ellenberger, 1970, Perry, 1976), requires an enormous outpouring of psychic energy and hopefully leads to a positive reconstruction of the personality.

Seen from the Indian standpoint, "Indian sickness" is a dangerous yet powerful and potentially uplifting experience of exposure to the ambiguous spirit world, which, if successfully 'treated', leads to spiritual revitalization, personal strength and cultural validation.

INDIAN CHRISTIANITY

Large numbers of Indian people were converted to Christianity by missionaries in the latter part of the 1800's. Indians today belong to a variety of Christian Churches, their denomination often depending upon which missionary group became established in their area. In general, Catholic and Pentecostal Churches seem to have been somewhat more successful in gaining and keeping Indian recruits than have non-evangelical Protestant Churches. This may be due both to the well-known Catholic flexibility in incorporating elements of Indian belief and spiritual practices into church activities and to the preference of many Indian people for emotionally powerful symbols and experiences over more abstract religious beliefs.

CATHOLICISM AT SWINOMISH

Catholicism was the Christian religion introduced to the Swinomish people in the 1840's. Some authorities have argued that Catholicism has had more success with Indian people than Protestantism due to its flexibility and adaptability to local customs. People at Swinomish have indicated that perhaps a deep Indian love of ceremony could have contributed to the acceptance of Catholic religion at Swinomish.

Nevertheless, there is a sad history to the advent of Catholicism in this tribal community, as perhaps in all or most others. The early priests, commonly known as "black robes", did everything they could to destroy the traditional spiritual beliefs and practices, especially the winter dances or Smokehouse ceremonies.

This led to considerable confusion and misunderstanding as well as deep emotional pain.

It has taken the dedicated work of open minded priests, nuns and traditional Indian healers to recover from this split. Jesuits in particular have led the way toward gaining forgiveness from Indian people for the harm done by their Catholic forbears.

Priests now acknowledge the unique value of Indian culture and strive to integrate Indian symbols and values with Catholic services.

For instance, Indian carvings and drumming are brought into the Swinomish Catholic church on a regular basis, and Catholics at Swinomish are now permitted to wear the traditional Coast Salish paddle shirts.

Recently, a young Swinomish Tribal Community Member and Jesuit seminary student chose, with the blessing of his supervisors, to go through the process of initiation into the Smokehouse. He has been allowed by his seminary to follow where his heart has taken him, toward expressing and integrating both of these sacred ways within his inmost being. Some people interpret this as a demonstration that the Smokehouse tradition is compatible with Catholicism in that it is an Indian cultural form of worship of the divine spirit. This has been seen as a landmark event, as was that of a non Indian priest from Vancouver Island becoming a Smokehouse dancer some years ago.

INDIAN SHAKER CHURCH

One important example of Indian Christianity in the Northwest is the Indian Shaker Church. The Indian Shakers are a Christian Church which is uniquely Indian. There is no connection between the now-extinct New England Shakers and the Indian Shakers. The Indian Shakers were so named because of the trembling motion affecting members when under direct spiritual influence.

Healing has been central to the Shaker religion form its beginning in 1880. Its founders, Mary and John Slocum, of the Squatin Tribe, discovered the "Shake" as a medium of direct divine intervention. John had apparently died and Mary was able to revive him with her spontaneously shaking hands. The Shakers believe that John died but was sent back to earth with a new religion which God had created to meet the needs of Indian Christians. The trembling "shake" has been seen as a sign of the presence of the Holy Spirit and a healing gift. Thus, from the start of this tradition, the focus has been on healing and revival.

John and Mary Slocum taught that Indian people should embrace the Holy Spirit and leave behind all traditional practices that were not Christian. The Shaker Church was formally recognized in 1910. ***Many Indian people were converted to Shakerism, which is still a strong and growing religious force today among Indian people in Washington, Oregon and Northern California.***

While there are two or more distinct branches of the Shaker Church, each with somewhat different beliefs and practices, all Shaker Churches are Christian Churches with a strong healing tradition as well as strict religious and moral beliefs. Shaker membership is overwhelmingly Indian, though non-Indian people sometimes attend services or join the Church. The Shakers believe that the Shake is a gift given to the Indian people by God, in order that they may have a form of Christianity which is specifically suited to Indian people.

One important feature of the Shaker Church is the widespread organization and interaction between many Shaker groups. Shakers elect a Bishop and state Elders as well as having Church Ministers. Ministers and other active Shakers travel frequently to other Shaker Churches to attend and support the services. Thus, in a very real sense, *the Shaker Church, like many older Indian spiritual traditions, helps to maintain social and ceremonial ties between people of neighboring tribes.*

This religion was born at a time of great attack on the traditional Coast Salish Smokehouse or winter ceremonial by Christian ministers and priests, the government and in fact by many Indian people who were frightened by the "Indian Doctor wars". It was felt that some Indian doctors or medicine people had become competitive with one another and were using their knowledge in harmful ways.

The Shaker way provided a positive Indian cultural alternative to both mainstream Christianity (which many Indian people found to be too abstract and culturally foreign) and to the "dark side" of the Smokehouse, which some people saw as dangerous or malign.

From the beginning, the Shaker tradition has been a healing tradition, aimed at helping Indian people heal form emotional pain, loss and addictions. In this sense it is not unlike the Cargo Cults of the Pacific or the Native American Ghost Dance Religion. But it does have a clear Coast Salish cultural tone.

The healing function of the Shaker Church incorporates elements of pre-existing Indian spiritual practices. For instance, in addition to having a strong tradition of worship, prayer and moral guidance, Indian Shaker services often involve specific efforts to heal sick or troubled individuals and families. Shaker prayers, songs and movements, utilizing candles, bells and sometimes preaching, can be directed toward people who are experiencing physical illness or emotional distress. Some Shaker members have particular healing gifts, enabling them to perceive and diagnose the nature of a physical or spiritual illness, and to spiritually remove the danger, sickness or intrusive object. This may be done through prayer, laying on of hands or by brushing the person off to remove the sickness.

Dancing and chanting produce a sort of religious trance allowing direct access to the divine. Healing occurs in this state. Prayer and good living are antidotes to alcoholism and other threats to a positive community. Healing experiences occur during group gatherings.

Unlike Catholicism but similar to both Smokehouse and Pentecostal traditions, Shaker practice rests on personal experiences attained during inspired states of consciousness. The spiritual experience is a highly personal and direct one, not primarily mediated by a priest or minister. Shaker ministers may lead the singing, stomping and ringing of the bells, and may pray for healing of ill or erring church members, and may also bring their personal healing powers to bear upon the patient, but they never prevent the individual member from having a direct spiritual experience which is theirs alone.

Shakers cure in group ceremonies, and do not accept money for their services. Some people feel that calling for the assistance of Shaker healers is safer than risking contact with Shamanic powers.

PENTECOSTAL CHURCH

The Pentecostal Church, like the Shaker Church, is focused on a personal relationship with God. Worship, prayer and confession are made directly to the Lord without human intercession.

The Pentecostal Church on the Swinomish Reservation is not far from the main tribal village. Although only a few tribal members now attend the church, there was a period of spiritual revival in Native communities in the 1950-1960's when many Swinomish families attended the Pentecostal church. However, after the Pentecostal Pastor left, attendance dropped away.

Pentecostal members believe that Jesus is the Son of God, that he died on the cross in order to bear the brunt of human sins, and thus allow forgiveness. The Holy Spirit was sent to humankind as a comforter. Jesus is understood to sit at the right hand of God.

He will return to judge both living and dead. Praise, worship of the Lord, song and Bible stories are basic components of the Pentecostal religion.

The rhythmic Pentecostal preaching and singing are generally experienced as charismatic, helping the members achieve an intense spiritual experience.

Pentecostal religion is also a healing tradition, allowing for divine intervention to permit recovery from grief and loss.

Members of this faith generally do not attend Smokehouse dances, feeling that this tradition is contrary to their beliefs.

TALKING CIRCLE

The circle or wheel is held sacred in many Indian traditions, symbolizing wholeness, interconnectedness and the cycles of nature. The tradition originated with the Plains culture, where the typee, the Sun Dance and the Medicine Wheel all echo the importance of the circle.

The Talking Circle tradition has spread throughout Indian Country. Several variations have developed, but all share the core process of talking and listening in a respectful and structured way within the sacred context of the circle.

Sometimes sweet grass or sage is burned as a form of prayer and to "smudge" the participants in the smoke in order to remove bad influences and purify them for the sacred "work" to be done. Other times simple prayer opens the circle, perhaps with the participants holding hands to make the circle a physical reality.

The basic process is that *each participant is given the opportunity to talk about whatever they wish, as long as they wish, while the other members of the circle give them full attention.* No questions, responses or interruptions are permitted. This is not a discussion; it is a sharing of personal and often intimate and heartfelt thoughts, experiences and feelings.

A sacred object is usually held by each speaker as they talk. This may be a ceremonial stick, an eagle feather, or any other natural object felt to have spiritual meaning. *Holding a sacred object conveys authority upon the speaker and also helps him/her to focus on the sacredness and importance of the words spoken.* When the speaker has finished, he or she passes the sacred object to the person sitting next to them, usually clockwise.

The rhythm of a talking circle is very different from that of mainstream meetings, discussion groups, or therapy sessions. It is tightly structured in the sense that there are no interruptions, but is not structured at all in the sense that there are no rules about what topics may be discussed. This can be a lengthy process up to several hours, as no one is interrupted and the circle continues until all members have had an opportunity to speak. Of course, later speakers may choose to refer back to issues raised by earlier speakers. If the circle was formed in the wake of a vital community event, most talk may revolve around that theme, but members are free to introduce whatever topics they choose.

There are two intertwined themes in Talking Circles which are essential to Indian culture. First, **respect for the individual is evident in that each person is given an equal chance to bring forth their concerns and each is listened to with respect.** The second theme is that each individual is a vital part of a greater community. The whole weight of the talking circle affirms the inherent value of each individual to the group as a whole. There is no pressure to agree or reach a consensus: **the important thing is that each person be heard by their community and that no voice be lost.**

In a traditional Talking Circle, all participants stay until the last person has finished speaking. There is an explicit understanding that what has been heard will remain confidential within the Circle. All efforts are made to ensure that this will be a safe and nurturing experience. Talking Circles generally close with a prayer of thanks for the sharing and healing that has occurred.

Summary

It could be said that Indian cultures are basically oriented towards spirituality. In spite of differences in beliefs and practices most Indian people believe that:
1. Spiritual life is of great importance.
2. Spirituality is closely connected to physical, social and emotional well-being.
3. There is a spiritual side to all living things.
5. There is a potentially dangerous side to spiritual powers.
6. Spiritual matters should be approached in a respectful manner.
7. Spiritual activities bring family and friends together.
8. Spiritual well-being depends upon living in harmony with

all beings.
9.   Some aspects of spirituality are personal and private.
10. Spiritual knowledge and power usually require some personal risk or sacrifice.
11. Everyone has some type of personal spiritual gift.
12. It is desirable to learn about and use ones spiritual gift.
13. Some people have far more spiritual power than others.
14. Older people generally have more spiritual knowledge than younger people.
15. The Spirit has many manifestations and there are many legitimate ways to worship.

Indian people may be the most tolerant and broad minded in the world: What other community of perhaps 700 people embraces such divergent traditions as Catholicism, Pentecostalism and indigenous Traditional Spiritualism?

Chapter 11
Traditional Healing Around the World: A Cross-Cultural Perspective

Spiritual beliefs and healing practices among indigenous people around the world share a number of intriguing similarities. All traditional approaches to healing are rooted in oral traditions and require that practitioners learn and remember a great deal of detailed information. Around the world, traditional healers are respected and honored for their knowledge, skills and power. *We hope that this information will broaden the reader's perspective concerning the foregoing discussion of Native American worldviews and traditional spirituality and healing.*

Common attributes of traditional healing worldwide are:

- A shared value system between the healer and the patient
- A personal relationship between healer and patient
- Provision of direct advice and social support by the healer, even extending at times to bringing the patient

into the healer's home
- Involvement of family and community in the healing process
- Shamans (not found in all cultures: see below) are "called" to this work by an intense and private personal spiritual experience, sometimes referred to in anthropological literature as an "initiatory illness".

Healing approaches and methods employed around the world also bear striking similarities, including:

- Personal and family participation and investment
- Purification rituals and procedures
- Sophisticated use of metaphors and stories to "speak" to the patient's unconscious
- "Suggestive methods" such as instilling hope by predicting success, encouraging the patient and "building up" the person's self esteem
- Induction in both healer and patient of altered states of consciousness such as trance states or spiritual experiences
- Use of culturally significant power objects and other symbols such as special power words, spells or invocations which have a non-verbal therapeutic impact
- Healing activities take place in a public and ceremonial context
- Dramatization or enactment of ancient and revered stories, myth or history containing a therapeutic message
- Opportunities for outward demonstrations of emotion, leading to relief of tension

"Purification rituals" are a common aspect of traditional healing systems. These activities are aimed at cleansing oneself and the healing environment of "badness", spiritual "pollution", negative feelings or the influence of addictive substances. These procedures may be physical, moral or emotional in nature, and generally precede other aspects of the healing process. Examples include sweat lodge, ritual bathing, fumigation with incense (called "smudging" in some Native American traditions), use of herbal emetics to purify the body (used in Islamic and Chinese traditions to treat drug addiction), rituals aimed at exorcism or driving out evil spirits (found in Christianity as well as in many indigenous

cultures). *All these methods serve to release built up anxiety and to prepare the participants mentally and emotionally to focus on the healing work.*

Community participation is a universally crucial component of all traditional healing systems. The combined efforts of healer, patient, and community result in a reinforcement of community and family ties. The individual patient is figuratively "re-anchored" within his/her community by the experience of other significant people participating in the healing process with their time, money and emotional energy. This leads to the patient feeling some obligation to get well and to behave in accord with community norms.

When relatives make sacrifices for the well being of family members, personal anxiety and family tensions tend to be relieved. Giving time, money and personal effort often produces a feeling of having "paid for" any personal imperfections or transgressions. In some traditional societies, there is an actual ritual transference of guilt or "badness" into some sacrificial animal or object.

Altered states of awareness, including trance states, are a universal human capacity wired into our central nervous systems, although generally suppressed in Western societies, (perhaps by child rearing practices emphasizing rational control). These states, when experienced within the context of ritual and community support can facilitate healing. Both psychological and physical techniques help participants enter altered experiential states. For instance, rhythmic drumming, singing, sensory deprivation and physical ordeals may assist in this process. *Altered experiential states can "open" participants for personal change and growth by disrupting usual patterns of thought and behavior. Conditions of heightened arousal and suggestibility help to create both expectations of positive change and shifts in self perceptions.*

Intense expressions of pent up feelings, (sometimes called "abreactions"), are generally therapeutic only under special conditions. In many traditional healing rituals, intense emotional releases are expected and accepted, such that "patients" feel validated and supported in expressing pent up feelings. In some cultures (such as Bali), aggressive or otherwise unacceptable emotions may be released through enactments of possession by spiritual entities. In this way, the individual may be "purged" of socially unacceptable feelings without risking social rejection.

Across many cultures, there are several broad categories of traditional practitioners, including Diviners, Medicine People and Shamans. Of course they are known by a great variety of terms.

Diviners are diagnosticians who identify the cause and nature of illnesses or psychic disturbance. They name the problem, which then allows for identifying the proper treatment. Once a problem is named and understood, it becomes manageable and treatable. The patient is told what they must do to correct some imbalance or transgression against spiritual rules or beings. *This naming and prescription in itself relieves anxiety and brings about hope for a cure.*

In traditional cultures, all physical and mental difficulties are understood to be meaningful events, not due to mere chance, exposure to viruses etc. Physical, mental and interpersonal imbalances are understood to be due to the interference of ancestral or spiritual beings, to a misdeed, or to the malicious powers or harmful acts of other people. Once the cause has been identified, the proper remedy tends to become fairly obvious.

Many traditional people understand illness as due to the (hopefully) temporary loss of some aspect of a person, particularly the soul, spiritual essence or spiritual power. Bad behavior or the power of others to steal or attract the soul are possible causes. This is the common explanation for illness in much of central Asia, Siberia, and Southern China, as well as in the Americas.

In such situations, the patient is generally referred to a Shaman. *Shamanism is the most ancient form of healing known to humankind, predating even herbal treatments.*

Shamans have the unique ability to provide a link to the Otherworld, in a manner which deviners, herbalists and ritualists do not. The specific role of Shamans is to retrieve lost souls or spiritual possessions. The Shaman enters a trance state which facilitates contact with the spiritual plane. Shamans are usually known to "travel;" to the spirit world in order to retrieve souls or to communicate with spiritual beings concerning an illness and it's proper cure. The form of travel is culturally determined. It may be via spirit canoe, spirit horse or other vehicle.

Medicine People are skilled practitioners in a particular system of traditional healing. For instance, they may be experts in herbal remedies, in physiological treatments such as sweating, fasting or dietary treatments, or they may be masters of complex rituals, prayers, songs, dances or other culturally specific healing techniques, such as Navajo sand painting. They are less likely to enter into altered states or intervene directly in the spiritual plane, though in some cultures there is considerable overlap between the roles of Medicine People and Shamans.

SUMMARY

Traditional healing systems among indigenous people worldwide have not only survived modernization, but in many cases have undergone a remarkable revival in the past twenty years, no doubt because they provide a kind of help not available through Western medical approaches.

Around the world, efforts are increasing to recognize the value of traditional forms of health care. It is particularly encouraging that the World Health Organization has gone on record in encouraging indigenous healing practices and cooperative partnerships between traditional and Western style medicine.

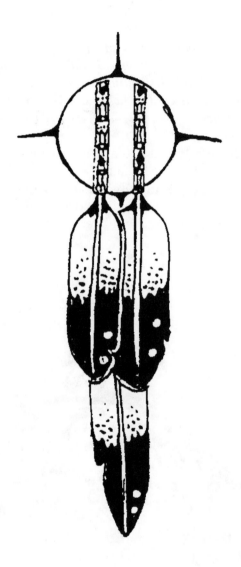

Chapter Twelve
Core Swinomish Tribal Values
Promote Mental Health

Gathering of Wisdoms Update Report

his chapter presents themes emphasized during the Swinomish Tribal Community dinners, forums and "Gathering of Wisdoms Update Process" Committee meetings. This chapter reflects the issues which community members feel are most relevant to mental health. Many other topics were discussed in this process, and are addressed throughout this book.

We are gratified that the GWUP process validated the insights we gained during the first seven years of the Tribal Mental Health Program. Many of the issues and concerns brought out by tribal members in the GWUP process were matters which had been addressed in the first edition of this book. This has let us know that we are "on track". Even though most of the material presented in this chapter is not new, it is of great importance in that it reflects the voice of the Swinomish people, as we hope is also true of the entire book.

Again and again in Swinomish and other Northwest Coast tribal gatherings, the same themes recur. The attentive listener soon becomes attuned to the deep concerns shared by members of these tribal communities.

While many of these ideas and values reverberate throughout this book, we felt it important to summarize them here in order to highlight the input of Swinomish Tribal community members. Because most readers read only one section at a time, considerable repetition of key ideas is unavoidable and perhaps even desirable.

Indian cultures contain intrinsic concepts of personal and psychological health. Core tribal values promote positive cultural identity and mental health. To elicit these core ideas, and "kick off" discussions, we asked community members questions such as:

"What is mental health at Swinomish"?

"What are healthy Indian life ways and behaviors"?

"What is mentally healthy about how this tribal community functions"?

"How is mental health different for Indian and non-Indian people"?

Tribal members identified spirituality, kinship, gathering together, sharing, interdependence and participation in traditional activities as the core of what is considered culturally healthy and healing in Swinomish, Lushootseed and Northwest Coast Indian cultures.

SPIRITUALITY

Participants in Swinomish GWUP dinners and forums universally emphasized the central importance of spirituality in a healthy Indian lifestyle. Because this is so vital, an entire chapter in this new edition of this book has been devoted to this topic, discussing the overall Native American spiritual worldview, concepts of spiritual healing and their relation to mental health, as well as four specific spiritual pathways at Swinomish. (see Chapter 10).

Tribal members expressed the importance of spirituality in many ways, including:

"Prayer is our strength".

"Participating in traditional ceremonies helps."

"We all need spiritual balance."

"Going to Pow Wows is healthy."

"We have to pray together."

THE CENTRAL VALUE OF KINSHIP

Psychologically, Indian people experience themselves fundamentally as family and tribal members. While individual personality differences and preferences are accepted and sometimes highly valued, Indian people seldom see themselves or others as primarily separate individuals. Instead, they relate to one another as representatives of a family, a church, and a tribe.

The Indian person's self concept does not revolve around their personal traits, accomplishments or goals. Instead ***the Indian person is constantly aware of the subtle social context, including the expectations and needs of family members*** for them to maintain proper behavior and uphold the family name.

Family togetherness is of enormous importance. Most Indian people spend the majority of their time with family. Northwest Coast Indian people form basic lifelong bonds, especially with siblings and cousins, who in many Northwest tribes are raised together by the same group of adults, including parents, grandparents, aunts and uncles.

Special teachings and proprietary family knowledge is shared only within families. The social standing of a family depends largely on having such special family wisdom. In order to maintain high social standing, families must not only have children to whom their teachings can be passed, but must also maintain ties with more distant relations. ***Family bonds are the most important thing!***

Close friends can become kin for all practical purposes. When friends are especially close, the may be "claimed" as a brother or sister, and can assume all of the responsibilities and privileges that go along with close kinship.

It is often remarked that all people in the Swinomish Tribal Community are related or "all family". This is probably true literally as well as psychologically. There is a keen awareness of the

historical and ancestral connections which bind certain families to other families.

The following are a few of the specific ways that these ideas were expressed during tribal community forums. In response to the topic of "What does it take to achieve a good, healthy, happy Indian family?," community members said:

"We should respect, care and love our family."
"Honoring one another, being respectful."
"Happy, bonded parents can support their kids."
"Being forgiving, helpful, sacrificing."
"Family unity."
"A healthy balance among all family members."
"Helping with household chores."
"Getting along with brothers and sisters."
"Remind kids of family "lines" (e.g. geneology)."
"Good family role models."
"Being "raised right"."
"Learn who we are related to."
"Learn to be a good husband, wife and parent."

GATHERING TOGETHER

"The MAIN THING is to build a strong, loving community. It is hard work. Our elders always pull us back to the MAIN THING." (Father Pat Twohy, during Swinomish GWUP forum)

All valued life in Coast Salish culture is communal life. Large gatherings in particular are of fundamental cultural and psychological importance as opportunities for socialization, sharing, distribution of food and goods, demonstration of cultural strengths and spiritual powers, and reaffirmation of kinship ties. This value runs deeper and is more complex in its cultural significance than is typical of social events or "get togethers" in mainstream American culture.

Large Indian gatherings in the Pacific Northwest generally involve one family or tribe hosting guests from other tribal communities. *The more important the event, the larger the number of guests and the greater the distance they are liable to have traveled to attend.* These events offer the hosting family a critical opportunity to display their material and spiritual wealth and to gain prestige through demonstrations of generosity. Hosting such an event reaffirms the family's standing in the greater Northwest Coast inter tribal network as well as within the tribe itself.

Giving of gifts helps to maintain and strengthen bonds of friendship and reciprocal support. Speeches highlight the roles of important elders, allow for teaching of the young and for reinforcement of traditional beliefs and values. Laughter eases social tensions and creates a sense of warmth and safety.

Eating together is probably important in all human cultures, in that it symbolizes that relationships are on a friendly, trusting basis. People who eat together are presumably not enemies. Offering food is an almost universal way to indicate the host's good will. Accepting food is a way of demonstrating trust in that good will.

In Indian communities in the Northwest, the importance of sharing food is paramount: no important event fails to include a meal. Meals are prepared by extended family who draw together to contribute both time and resources. Certain tribal members known to be good cooks may be asked to help and later publicly "thanked" with gifts.

Younger people are often recruited to help serve the tables. Their willingness to work, respectful attitudes, (or lack thereof), are noted by their elders. In fact, how one behaves in public gatherings helps determine a person's standing in the community. Respect, generosity, dignity, self control and cultural knowledge bring high social standing.

These ideas were expressed during forums by such statements as:

"We need to spend time together, more togetherness."

"It is good to have meals together."

"Celebrating together heals us."

"We need more community gatherings."

"Traveling together is good."

"Being with one another helps build a strong community."

SHARING AND INTERDEPENDENCE
PROMOTE COMMUNITY WELLNESS

There is a core idea in Swinomish, Lushootseed and indeed all Northwest Indian cultures that sharing is positive and honorable, whereas hoarding of resources is selfish and dishonorable. This is related to the idea that individuals are most valuable as a particular and unique part of the greater family and tribal network rather than for themselves separately.

Respect does not come from wealth or from personal or professional accomplishments. Tribal people earn respect through a life well lived within the cultural norms of serving the community, upholding family traditions and demonstrating a willingness to share with others.

Sharing and interdependence are crucial values in Indian culture: what one earns belongs to the extended family and what one does reflects on one's elders. Neither disgrace nor honor belong only to the actor: they impact the family almost equally.

The Swinomish, Lushootseed and Northwest Coast cultures generally are communal societies: the goal of most individual and community activities is to promote interdependent community connections.

A key cultural value is that individuals have a responsibility to serve others and to promote the well being of the whole community. This is seen as central to mental health.

Some ways that community members expressed these ideas during GWUP forums included:

"We share each other's strengths and hardships."

"We help the whole community."

"Being with one another builds a strong community."

"We should always give a helping hand."

"We are always there for each other."

"We bring food donations to gatherings."

"Helping with money problems is a family responsibility"

"You give even when you don't have nothing to give."

"Share all you have."

PARTICIPATION IN TRADITIONAL ACTIVITIES

 Participating in traditional cultural activities, skills and crafts are highly valued in tribal cultures. These activities strengthen Indian identity and community integrity. Examples of traditional activities, roles and crafts are discussed below.

Traditional Uses and Significance of Cedar: Historical Background

The cedar tree was fundamental to Northwest Coast traditional Indian cultures at least as much as was the salmon. Both Western Red Cedar and Yellow Cedar had specific uses. All parts of the tree were used, including the fibrous inner and soft outer bark, the aromatic and rot resistant wood, the roots, branches and fronds. Cedar was the primary building, tool making, clothing and artistic material. Posts and beams for long-houses were made from enormous logs, then planks were split for siding and roofs. Dugout Canoes were made from single logs. Clothing, rope, baskets, steam bent wood boxes, woven mats, cooking pots, carved totem poles, dance masks, head dresses and other ceremonial objects were all made from cedar.

The Resurgence of the Canoe Culture

The renewal of the Northwest Coast canoe culture has had a powerful impact on the mental health of Indian youth at Swinomish and elsewhere over the past decade. Up and down the Northwest Coast from Quileute and Quinalt to Bella Bella in the north there has been a stunning renaissance of the canoe culture.

It is impossible to understand Northwest Coast Indian cultures without understanding the role and importance of the canoe. Canoes, cedar and salmon are closely related cultural symbols as well as key components of traditional material culture.

Canoes were the primary means of transportation in pre-contact Northwest Coast Indian cultures. Canoes allowed fishing and hunting, as well as social travel. Both ocean-side dwelling tribes, and river dwellers relied on water transportation. It was far easier to travel by water than overland, due to the dense forestation of most of the North Pacific Coast. Therefore, almost all out-of-village activities depended on the canoe.

Bertha Dan, our Cultural Consultant, and now 91 year old Swinomish Elder, tells of a week-long canoe journey she made with her family at about age 10, around 1920. The family left Snee-oosh Beach near LaConner, and traveled to Vancouver Island through Deception Pass and the San Juan Islands. They camped at night on islands and paddled by day. This was a social trip, possibly to attend a large gathering. Bertha recalls that a school of sea lions swam near the canoe and that she and another child were made to lie in the bottom of the boat, covered with blankets, for fear that the sea lions would want them. Seeing traditional canoes arrive at Swinomish revived this memory of a long-ago sea voyage.

In Northwest Coast Indian cultures, canoes have always been considered spiritual beings. Every aspect of the creation and use of a canoe was and still is approached in a spiritually mindful, if not ceremonial manner. The carver must behave in a spiritually in-formed and responsible manner from the initial vision of the canoe, through the selection of the tree, and asking its permission to be transformed. Through the hollowing out, burning, steam-ing, painting and carving, there is an ever present awareness that this is a sacred undertaking. No bad language, bad thoughts, smoking or drinking are allowed to come into contact with the canoe.

In 1989 at the "Paddle to Seattle", a Bella Bella leader saw the potential for a rebirth of the native canoe tradition. He challenged other tribes to come by canoe to Bella Bella in four years' time, for the 1993 Qatuwas festival

A number of tribes took up the challenge and began not only practicing ocean going canoeing, but building their own traditional canoes. In preparation for this trip, people of many Indian nations had canoes made, formed canoe pulling teams and learned about traditional canoe making and the spiritual beliefs related to cedar and to canoes

The extent of the commitment may be understood when one considers that the journey from Quileute to Bella Bella and back took two months. Some people paddled as much as 1200 miles. Indian adults working with the youth sometimes had to quit their jobs in order to take this time. Families made great sacrifices of time and money to support their youth in this wonderful and revitalizing project. This has been a life changing experience for many: all who are involved have been emotionally touched.

The benefits have been stunning. Young people who have become involved with the canoes have learned discipline from the long hours of practice. They have learned to work together as a team in which every member is important. They have developed intimate knowledge of the water, tides, water fowl, islands and weather. They now have a deep and very personal understanding of the importance of the cedar tree.

The canoe revival has become a tool of healing for tribal youth. Attitudes and behaviors change as youth become invested in bringing back old ways. They learn about themselves, others and teamwork. Singing, dancing, drumming and feasting, traditional crafts of paddle making, and fashioning of traditional clothing are learned.

Canoe pulling offers a constructive alternative to drinking and drugging. Young people who pull canoe have come to value their health, physical strength and endurance in a new way. They have an incentive to remain healthy.

The canoe renaissance has helped many Indian people regain pride in their culture and therefore has improved cultural identity. For some young people, exposure to the way of the canoe has made their culture come alive in their hearts. They have begun to understand traditional concepts and values which may have been just words to them before.

The canoe journey is a spiritual journey. The young person has long hours to seek new understanding of him/herself and place in the world. Spiritual insights may be gained.

The canoe is far more than a boat; it is a metaphor for the tribal way of life. Water is the life that we travel through. In the canoe, like the tribe, what one person does affects everyone else. All must work together in sync if the canoe is to move smoothly through the water. The canoe members, like tribal members, must learn to put aside individual differences in the interests of the welfare of the whole.

The making of the canoe is a spiritual process. When someone decides to have a canoe made, they must approach this in a traditional way. They must have someone older go to visit a master carver to "speak for" them. A gift is offered to show respect and demonstrate the seriousness of their intentions. They tell what they plan to do, and ask for help.

The canoe is made of a single old growth Western Red Cedar. These trees may be 400 or even 1000 years old. It is understood that the tree is a living being, with a spirit. ***The canoe continues the life of the tree in a new form, with the same spirit guiding the process.***

The canoe "follows the log": it's size and exact lines emerge naturally from the particular tree chosen. The log must be hollowed out to the exactly right thickness, though a process of burning and scraping. Steaming is used to widen the central part of the canoe and shape it to the canoe maker's satisfaction. Older carvers teach younger carvers, thus allowing the continuance of this art as well as fostering a traditional way of learning through apprenticeship.

Once the canoe is finished, it is blessed with cedar boughs and songs and is given a name.

When the resurgence of interest in canoes began, there were very few carvers alive who knew the craft of canoe making. Some carvers studied traditional canoes in anthropological museums.

Certain canoe styles are "owned" by specific tribes or families, and no one would consider "stealing" this spiritual and intellectual property. There are several broad types of canoes, including slim 12 person racing canoes such have long been seen during Makah Days or at the Lummi "Stommish". There are war canoes, whaling and sealing canoes and ocean going canoes.

Canoo pullers sometimes make their own personal paddles. Paddles are brightly painted with Northwest Coast designs and may be pointed, a style deriving from a time when paddles were sometimes used as weapons.

Canoe pullers learn special paddling songs used to teach proper breathing and to set a strong and steady rhythm. Long hours of practice and the respect of other tribal members build a sense of pride and accomplishment. ***Canoe pullers become bonded to one another through their common experience.*** Ocean-going canoes may travel together in groups of up to a dozen or more canoes, which is an exilerating experience for those directly involved and an unforgettable sight for those who witness it.

When a canoe nears the shore of another tribe, masked dancers perform and sing in the prow of the boats to announce who the visitor is, the purpose of the visit, and to request permission to land. The host tribe welcomes the visitors with special welcome songs, followed by a feast. Intertribal social ties have been built and renewed on these occasions.

The gathering of canoes from several tribes for a given journey

helps to bridge gaps between the tribes. Disagreements fade as those from differing tribes jointly experience their common cultural roots. A new understanding of the life ways of tribal ancestors and especially of the central importance of the waterways and canoe travel reinforces a felt connection to other culturally similar tribes and to the culture as a whole.

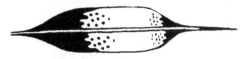

Drum Making and Drumming

Drum making and drumming are traditional activities with spiritual importance. Swinomish drums are small, personally owned drums made of hide stretched over a hoop frame. Like all ceremonial objects, drums are made with prayer and respect.

There are two types of drumming in Northwest Coast tribal communities. In traditional drumming one or many people together use their personal drums to accompany singing. While all singing has a spiritual meaning, some songs are more private and powerful, such as Smokehouse Spirit songs, whereas other songs are family songs for welcoming, for blessing, for thanking or for healing. As discussed elsewhere, songs are important personal or family property and cannot be used by others.

The second type of drumming is really an import from the Plains cultures, via the central Salish and Plateau peoples. This is the tradition of the "Big Drum". The drum is several feet across and sits flat on the ground surrounded by a circle of several drummers. Drummers are a team who "belong to the drum" in that they are spiritually connected and dedicated to the drum, both as an art form and as a spiritual path. The Big Drum is used on a variety of occasions, but is not generally involved in the Smokehouse or Shaker ceremonies. Instead, a particular drumming group may be invited to drum and sing for a wedding, funeral, large dinner, conference or other gathering. *Songs may be for healing, celebrations, thanking, blessing food or other purpose. They always have a meaning and always have a spiritual aspect.*

However, unlike the small personal Coast Salish Drum, Big Drum teams often perform at gatherings which are primarily social events. In fact, many drum groups participate in drumming competitions. Most Big Drum groups have no objection to being recorded, whereas this is often forbidden with the small drum songs, especially Smokehouse and personal spiritual songs.

The dances which accompany the Big Drum are of a Plains style, including "Fancy Dancing" and "War Dancing". One or several skilled performers dance with rapid and often very elaborate footwork. Some dances commemorate warriors, others welcome guests or convey honor. Costumes may be quite elaborate, with ribbon shirts, leggings, moccasins, feathers and head dresses.

Although the Big Drum and its style of singing and dancing is not a tradition native to the Northwest Coast, it has been adopted increasingly over several decades, such that many young adults have experienced this "pan-Indian" tradition throughout their lives.

Bone Games or Slahal

Summer "bone", "slahal" or "stick" games are traditional throughout Pacific Northwest Indian communities. These are part gambling/ part social activities derived from ancient divination traditions. People in teams compete to win sums of money based on proper guessing.

Although on the surface these are games of skill/ and or chance, the awareness of spiritual powers which is ever present in this culture permeates these games. Competitors are aware that the spiritual powers of each player are liable to influence outcomes: cautious boasting combines with watchful caution as players size each other up.

Summer bone games reinforce cultural integrity and inter-tribal relationships. People who meet over these games in their teens or twenties are likely to interact socially as long as they live. Tales will be told and remembered.

Traditional Occupations and Roles

Certain people are recognized as having special skills, knowledge and responsibilities. These are not just "jobs"; they are ways of providing culturally meaningful service to the community. Fulfilling these roles brings respect and social standing. These individuals are honored not only for their own accomplishments, but for the strength they add to tribal life.

Sometimes these roles are chosen. More often the person acquires the role either through inheritance, spiritual calling or by being chosen to "step up" to a particular job by tribal elders.

The following are examples of such special traditional roles. There are no doubt others, and these roles will differ between tribal groups.

Diagnosticians, Indian Doctors and Spiritual leaders *are discussed elsewhere in this book.* All tribal cultures have specialized roles for healers and spiritual leaders of a variety of kinds.

Speakers, or those whose role it is to speak in public, have special roles in some tribal societies. *They speak "from the heart", with great passion. It is a cultural norm in Coast Salish communities that public speakers have a sort of social permission to be frank and to "bring out" the deeper concerns of the whole community.* In fact, there is often more frankness in public than in private.

It is a great responsibility to have the job of identifying and naming the underlying issues facing the community. The speakers have to "hit it right" in order to bring about increased awareness of often sensitive topics, such as alcohol abuse, feuding between families, sexual misbehaviors, suicide or child abuse. Speakers try to guide and influence community members to make healthy life choices.

Cooks *are called upon to make food for large gatherings.* In Indian country, all important events require that a meal be served, as this is a basic component of hospitality and "togetherness". Certain people gain expertise in cooking for great numbers of people and coordinating the presentation of the feast.

Fishermen (and fisherwomen) are extremely important in Northwest Coast cultures. The special relationship with the Salmon and the water is their province. Many special skills are needed, including net making and maintainance, ability to run a boat, knowledge of tides, fish and waterways. Fishermen supply the tribe with the most basic food: Salmon. They are often called upon to contribute large amounts of fish to be barbecued for tribal gatherings.

Helpers at the Time of Death *are individuals whose "job" it is to help families who have lost a loved one throughout the time of grief and mourning.* They give both practical and traditional support. (see p.)

Coffin Makers *are respected for providing simple cedar boxes at the time of a death.* Their work allows the family to put away their loved one in dignity, and without impossibly expense. Coffin makers who acquire a good reputation may supply Indian families from distant tribes.

Artists and crafts people, *including carvers, drum makers, canoe makers, beaders, painters and basket makers, among others, all receive respect for helping to keep the traditional culture healthy. They speak to the community through the use of culturally meaningful symbols.*

For instance, carving of masks, totem poles, and canoes continues in Northwest Coast Tribal Communities. Men were and still are the traditional carvers in Northwest Coast societies, though some women have taken up the carver's tools. Skilled carvers with artistic talent have always been highly respected. Young people learn by watching master carvers. ***Personal mentorship is the teaching method used by traditional Indian people.***

This chapter has been placed at the end of Book One because it captures and summarizes many of the core views of community members about what is mentally healthy in this particular community, and also because it represents input received from Tribal Community members a decade or so after the publication of the first edition.

Book Two (chapters 13-29) presents our particular program's attempt to forge these insights and information into a cultural-specific mental health program that "works".

Book Two

Practical Information and Models for Tribal Mental Health Programs

Part Three

A Tribal Mental Health Program: The Skagit County Experience

Introduction
Book II, Part Three

T*his section presents one approach to providing culturally appropriate mental health services, as it has been developed in serving two small reservation communities, the Swinomish and the Upper Skagit.*

The main portion of this section (ch. 13-19) describes our program in order to give the reader a clear understanding of the nature of its philosophy, goals and services. Program goals and accomplishments are presented, as is an overview of the therapeutic orientation, treatment techniques, and cultural considerations. The viewpoints of each member of the Tribal Mental Health Team are presented. Problems encountered in program operation are discussed. Three case examples are presented which illustrate the services of the Tribal Mental Health Program.

Chapters 20- include a variety of practical program materials which we hope may be helpful to people developing tribal mental health programs, including:

- Tribal Mental Health Program policies. (These policies focus on differences between this culturally oriented tribal program and mainstream mental health programs. Support Counselor roles and responsibilities, criteria for service eligibility, and referral and intake policies are discussed.)

PART THREE A Tribal Mental Health Program

- Practical suggestions for tribal mental health program development and service delivery

- Program "start-up" ideas, regarding funding, staffing, budgeting, cooperative service agreements, job descriptions, etc.

- Information/suggestions related to service delivery

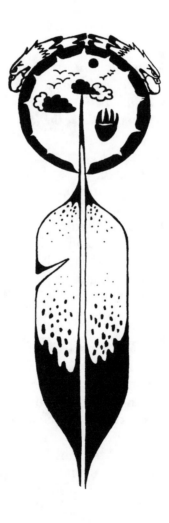

Contents
Book II, Part Three

Introduction 301

Contents, Part 3 303

Chapter Thirteen
*Overview of The Skagit /Swinomish Tribal
Mental Health Program*   307

Profile of the Swinomish and the Upper Skagit
Tribal Communities 307

Profile of Skagit Community
Mental Health Center 309

Overview of the Skagit Tribes'
Mental Health Program 310

Program Goals and Accomplishments 311

Developments in Swinomish Tribal Mental Health
Program and Tribal Social Services 313

Current Program Challenges 313

Chapter Fourteen
*Therapeutic Framework: Cultural Congruence
in a Tribal Mental Health Program*   319

Tribal Community Orientation of Program 320

Positive Cultural Identity Supported by
Services Which Reflect Tribal Values 323

Respect for Spiritual Values and Practices 324

Chapter Fifteen
Important Early Steps in Program Development   327

Initiating Linkages Between Tribes and
Mental Health Agencies 328

Tribal Mental Health Advisory Board 328

Recruiting Indian Mental Health Workers
and Consultants 329

Making Mental Health Services Visible and
Easily Accessible to Tribal Communities 330

Developing Working Relationships with
Other Community Services 331

Chapter Sixteen
Culturally Appropriate Service Approaches   333

Culturally Oriented Assessment of
Client Problems 335

Supportive Counseling 336

Home Visits 337

Services in the Context of Community
Functions and Gatherings 337

Working with the Extended Family 337

Cooperation with Traditional Healing Systems 338

Case Management 340

Crisis and As Needed Services 340

Play Therapy 341

Chapter Seventeen
Personal Perspectives of Tribal Mental Health Team Members   343

Mental Health Center Administrator's Perspective 343

Comments of Cultural Consultant/Swinomish Elder . 346

Comments of (Former) First Upper Skagit
Tribal Support Counselor 348

Comments of (Former) Second
Upper Skagit Tribal Support Counselor 349

Swinomish Tribal Support Counselor/
Program Coordinator's Perspective 349
Psychiatric Consultant's Perspective 351
Perspective of Original Program
Director/Implementor 354

Chapter Eighteen
Problems and Challenges
Encountered in the Program Operation   357

Unusual level of Effort Required for
Culturally Effective Service Delivery 358
Difficulties in Adapting the Mainstream
Mental Health System to Meet Tribal
Community Needs 358
    Record Keeping Difficulties 359
    Problems with State Priority Categories 359
    Problems using Conventional
    Diagnostic Systems 360
Role Conflicts and the Dangers of Staff "Burnout" 361
Confidentiality Challenges 362
Staff Changes 365
Barriers to Developing Written Descriptions
of Cultural Approaches... 366
Challenges Facing Non-Indian Providers
Working on Reservations 367

Chapter Nineteen
Three Case Examples   369

Three Case Examples 369

Chapter Twenty
Tribal Mental Health Program Policies   383

Introduction 383
Confidentiality and Service Agreement........................ 385
Agreement with Tribal Mental Health Supervisors 388
Tribal Support Counselor Personnel Policies 389

PART THREE   A Tribal Mental Health Program

Client Eligibility for Program Services............................390

Client Referral and Intake Procedures 392

Location and Timing of Client Services 395

Crisis Intervention Policies...398

Transportation Policy..399

Cooperation with Traditional Healers
and Spiritual Organizations 400

Confidentiality Guidelines for Tribal
Support Counselors 401

Chapter Twenty-One
Program "Start-up" Ideas and Materials   403

Practical Suggestions for Tribal Mental Health
Program Development and Service Delivery 403

Funding, Staffing and Administrative Options
for Tribally Based Mental Health Services...................407

Budget Considerations for
Tribal Mental Health Programs 409

Sample Service Agreement for
Mental Health Services to a Tribal Community 411

Tribal Support Counselor Job Description...................413

Tribal Mental Health Program
Supervisor Job Description...414

Sample Interview Questions for
Tribal Support Counselors 416

Chapter Twenty-Two
Information and Suggestions
for Direct Service Providers   417

Tribal and Non-Tribal Social Service
Resources Generally Available to Indian People 417

Therapeutic Techniques Adaptable to
Tribal Mental Health Programs 420

Practical Suggestions for Non-Indian
Mental Health Workers and New Comers
to Tribal Communities 422

Chapter Thirteen
Overview of The Skagit/Swimonish Tribal Mental Health Program

PROFILE OF THE SWINOMISH AND UPPER SKAGIT TRIBAL COMMUNITIES

Both the Swinomish and the Upper Skagit Indian Tribes belong to the Coast Salish culture group, which includes a number of Indian tribes living near the coasts of Washington and British Columbia. Historically, Coast Salish people lived in large extended family groups, linked by complex kinship, ceremonial and trade relations. Their economic life was centered on the salmon and cedar. Salmon supplied both food and a desirable resource for trade. Cedar supplied the primary material for building, clothing, utensils, and art objects. Canoes allowed travel for hunting, fishing, raiding and socializing. Rich ceremonial and religious systems have been central to Coast Salish culture for thousands of years.

Swinomish Tribal Community

Today, the Swinomish Tribal Community is made up of four aboriginal groups: the Aboriginal Swinomish, the Samish, the Kikialus and the Lower Skagit. Roughly 725 Indian people live on or near a reservation of 10 square miles adjacent to the town of La Conner, Washington. The native language is "Lushootseed."

Following the Point Elliot Treaty of 1855, people who had lived over a large area (including much of the Skagit Valley and Whidbey Island) were moved together onto a small portion of land. The reservation boundaries were formally established in the 1870's. Most tribal members have lived for several generations in a close knit community.

The Swinomish Tribal Community has been quite successful in developing programs for social services and resource development.

Despite serious financial and social problems facing most Swinomish families, this tribe has tended to be progressive in its policies and programs.

The Upper Skagit Tribe

The Upper Skagit Tribe consists of about 550 members, most of whom live near the town of Sedro Woolley on a reservation created in 1983. Despite the fact that the Upper Skagit have maintained a distinct cultural identity for hundreds of years, they were not federally recognized as an Indian tribe until 1972. Perhaps for this reason, many Upper Skagit people remained relatively isolated along the middle reaches of the Skagit River without a central congregation point or political focus. In relatively recent times many Upper Skagits left their homelands to become lost in mainstream society or to other reservations.

When the Upper Skagits were awarded a small reservation in 1983, a new community was built: A tribal center and a new housing development have brought families together into a small area.

This sudden change in lifestyle and recent reunification of their people has caused the Upper Skagit Tribal Community many growing pains. The Tribal organization has had to develop the expertise to administer a wide variety of programs. This has been an exciting and challenging time to be a part of the Upper Skagit Community.

PROFILE OF SKAGIT COMMUNITY MENTAL HEALTH CENTER

Skagit County is located in a rural area of Northwest Washington State approximately one hour north of Seattle. Its economy depends on lumber, fishing, farming, and tourism. The Skagit Community Mental Health Center is the primary mental health agency for the County, with the main office in Mount Vernon. The Center provides a wide range of mental health, substance abuse and child abuse treatment services, including:

- Individual outpatient, family and group therapy
- Medication evaluation and monitoring
- Case management
- A tribally-based Indian mental health program
- Special groups including: anger management, an adolescent group, a women's group, a group for families of Alzeimers patients, and a parenting-skills class
- Support to clients living in "adult family" homes or group homes
- Outreach to the isolated elderly
- Crisis services on a 24-hour-a-day-basis
- Voluntary and involuntary psychiatric hospitalizations
- Services for physically and sexually abused children
- A Vietnam veterans counseling program
- Services for clients with substance abuse problems

Skagit Community Mental Health Center has been unusual in its extensive cooperation with other local agencies. Close relationships exist with the local Community College, the Department of Social and Health Services, (D.S.H.S.), and the Community Alcohol Center.

Several unique situations increase the service demands on this mental health agency, including the location of several special, state-institutional programs in Skagit County, including Portal (a residential, intermediate care psychiatric facility which was on the grounds of the former Northern State Mental Hospital from 1978–1990), Pioneer Center North (an inpatient, involuntary commitment alcohol treatment facility), and the state's largest Job Corps facility, serving youth ages 17 to 23. Residents of these programs often choose to remain in Skagit County after discharge. Special cooperative programs have been developed to meet the needs of the particular client groups served by these agencies.

Besides three Coast Salish Indian tribes, several distinct ethnic and cultural groups exist in Skagit County. In particular, there are a substantial number of Spanish speaking people of Mexican descent, many of whom came as migrant farmworkers, but have stayed to live and raise families here. Historically, these groups have underutilized mental health services. Meeting the unique needs of these ethnic groups is a major goal of Skagit Community Mental Health Center. The Skagit Tribes' Mental Health Program was designed specifically in response to this kind of challenge.

OVERVIEW OF THE SKAGIT TRIBES MENTAL HEALTH PROGRAM

The Skagit Tribes' Mental Health Program began in July of 1984, is a cooperative effort between Skagit Community Mental Health Center and the Swinomish and Upper Skagit Tribes. Since 1994 the program has continued as a cooperative effort between the Swinomish Tribal Community and Skagit Community Mental Health Center. All program services have been provided at two tribal sites and are closely coordinated with tribal social services programs.

For the first seven years, two Indian "Tribal Support Counselors" at each tribe provided direct mental health services under the supervision of the Project Director, a half time psychologist with ten years of experience working with Indian people. Unfortunately, reductions in funding resulted in fewer support counselor positions. When the original Project Director left in 1993, the position was restructured in order that one of the Swinomish Support Counselors could assume the lead position. *The program combines direct client services with ongoing staff training. Key aspects of this program include:*

- The employment and training of tribal members who are seen in the tribal community as natural helpers
- Cooperation with traditional Indian healing systems
- Developing a culture - specific model of service delivery
- Serving traditionally oriented and "hard to reach" Indian clients
- Increasing linkages with other mental health and social services programs available in both tribal and mainstream communities

Program Goals and Accomplishments

Original program objectives were extremely broad, specifying only that culturally "enhanced" mental health services would be provided to 55 Indian clients who met the Washington State Division of Mental Health definition of "seriously disturbed", "acutely mentally ill", or "chronically mentally ill". These goals were met. In year one 63 Indian clients received culturally enhanced mental health services and in year two 67 Indian clients were served. In subsequent years, from 70 to 80 clients have been served. The program became a recognized and accessible resource to Indian people.

In addition, during the first program year four Support Counselors completed 63 college credits, and obtained certificates in "Tribal Mental Health" from Skagit Valley College. During the second and third year each Support Counselor pursued an individual educational program. (See Ch. 28 for a description of this training program.)

In early 1986 five program goals and measurable objectives were identified. Goals included:

- **Goal I** Provide culturally oriented mental health services to 50 Indian clients on the Swinomish and Upper Skagit Reservations yearly.
- **Goal II** Make mainstream mental health and social services more accessible and culturally sensitive to the needs of Indian people through referral, support, advocacy and consultation and education.
- **Goal III** Develop a theoretically coherent, specific and replicable model for culturally effective mental health services on Indian reservations.
- **Goal IV** Increase cooperation between traditional Indian healing and mental health systems in order to meet the unique psycho-social-spiritual needs of Indian clients.
- **Goal V** Provide ongoing and accredited training to four Tribal Support Counselors to increase their skills as mental health providers and to more effectively serve Indian clients.

Early Program Accomplishments

Over 165 unduplicated Indian clients received culturally oriented mental health services over the first four Program years. Client problems included:

- suicide attempts
- domestic violence
- social withdrawal
- spiritual problems
- family crisis related to substance abuse
- child abuse

- runaway teens
- unresolved grief
- conduct disorders
- somatoform disorders

Services were provided on a flexible schedule by Indian Tribal Support Counselors. Services included:

- home visits
- crisis intervention
- individual and family counseling
- referral and consultation to other needed services (see Ch. 16)

- case management
- traditional spiritual "work"

Additional services were provided which were not recorded in client charts. Twenty-six clients were served in preventive educational groups, including an alcohol support group, a teen group, and a group for young children of alcoholics. Approximately 40 Indian people received traditional spiritual or religious services which had the direct support of program staff. The Skagit Tribes' Mental Health program also developed a training program for tribal mental health workers and has sponsored four Support Counselors in their education (see Part V).

This program has been fundamentally committed to adapting mental health services to Indian ways, rather than vise versa. A discussion of how cultural factors affect Indian mental health work has been presented in Part II, including:

- **The importance of cultural identity for mental health**
- **The significance of the Indian extended family**
- **The therapeutic value of Indian healing practices**
- **Variations in the English language as used in Coast Salish Indian communities**
- **Indian patterns of alcohol use and their significance for mental health work**
- **The therapeutic advantages of traditional funerals and grieving processes**

DEVELOPMENTS IN SWINOMISH TRIBAL MENTAL HEALTH PROGRAM AND TRIBAL SOCIAL SERVICES

Over the past decade, there have been many changes in both the Tribal Mental Health Program and in the services available through other Swinomish Tribal social services programs. Despite the fact that program-specific funding from the Washington State Division of Mental Health and Skagit Community Mental Health Services has dwindled, innovative collaboration between the tribe and other funding sources has allowed the continuation of tribally controlled mental health services.

Appreciation for the fundamental importance of cultural identity for mental health has spread throughout the tribe, the Washington State Department of Social and Health Services and Federal funding agencies.

One key reason for this increased awareness is the nationwide movement toward Tribal Self Governance discussed in Book I, chapter 1. As discussed there, *tribes have acquired much increased ability to control and "reprogram" Federal (especially Indian Health Service) funds, including mental health funds, such that the services are under direct tribal control.* This has allowed tribes, including Swinomish, to hire staff and identify culturally appropriate service models and priorities. This has also been the case for state funds, such as Crime Victims Funds, Department of Alcohol and Substance Abuse funds, and Juvenile Justice Funds.

Not only tribes, but Federal and state agencies have begun to recognize the necessity for all mental health and social services for Indian people to be culturally oriented. In fact, *many granting agencies now require that tribal grantees design programs emphasizing cultural identity.* We would like to believe that this Tribal Mental Health Program and this book have made a small contribution toward these developments.

In effect, what has occurred is a melding of our Tribal Mental Health Program with other tribally based social and educational services, funded by a variety of sources. This includes Federal funds redirected from the Indian Health Service, and Washington State chemical dependency funds, preventive programs for high risk youth, Crime Victims-sponsored counseling for child abuse victims, and cultural education programs for both children and adults.

The following information on the specific ways this has developed in the Swinomish Tribal Community offers only one example of such collaborative efforts occurring across Indian Country. Perhaps the distinction between "mental health" and other health promoting activities and services has blurred, no doubt for the betterment of the community. This blurring will hopefully decrease the stigma attached to "mental health" services, make community members aware of the strong support for cultural values offered by mental health programs, and allow tribes to truly take control of the nature and priorities of mental health services in their communities.

Swinomish Tribal Community Developments

Health and social services offered through the auspices of the Swinomish Tribal Community have expanded considerably over the past decade, due largely to the increased availability of tribally controlled funding, related to legal mandates for tribal self governance.

The Swinomish Tribal Community has entered into "compacts" with the Federal government to "reprogram" Indian Health Service funds for a range of health care services. This has allowed direct tribal employment of medical and dental professionals, as well as mental health specialists. Community Health Representatives (CHR's) provide preventative and community outreach health services, especially for tribal elders. The tribe combines federal and state funds to provide substance abuse counseling and referral. The Swinomish Tribe also has a special model diabetes project.

The tribe was able to build a new Tribal Health Clinic as well as a dental services building. Increased service capacity has allowed Swinomish to serve Indian people from other tribes. In fact, some Indians from urban areas such as Everett and Seattle have sought services at Swinomish, due to shorter waiting times than may be the case in the city. This has broadened the awareness of tribal health care providers to issues facing urban Indians.

Tribal members have been deeply concerned about the risk of HIV infection as well as the high rate of teen pregnancies. Condoms have been made easily and freely available in tribal bathrooms. Treatment providers talk openly with tribal youth about safe sex and the range of options available. The result has been a sharp drop in teen pregnancies, with no births to mothers under the age of 18 over the past four years.

Prevention activities have become prominent at Swinomish. Washington State Juvenile Justice and Department of Alcohol and Substance Abuse funds have allowed the development of culturally oriented programs to prevent youth drug and alcohol abuse and other problem activities.

The tribe now runs an after school cultural program for school aged children. They make fry bread, dream catchers, learn to drum and learn about the canoes. There is also a weekly teen group for 13 to 18 year olds. The focus is leadership training, planning for weekend activities and attendance at conferences for tribal youth.

A culturally oriented Canoe Club has been funded by a Department of Alcohol and Substance Abuse "incentive" grant. Ever since Swinomish youth witnessed canoe races a few years ago there has been a tremendous upsurge of interest (see Book I, chapter12). Swinomish now has three tribal canoes, two of which were made locally. Swinomish youth are involved with canoe races as well as with training for canoe sea journeys.

Perhaps most exciting is the preschool class in Lushootseed language. There is a regular "family night" which has become popular. In fact, interest in learning the native language has become multigenerational.

Developments in Tribal Mental Health Services

Skagit Mental Health continues to pay the salary of the Swinomish Tribal Support Counselor/ Program Coordinator. However, other positions previously funded by State community mental health funds have been gradually discontinued over the past 7 years. However, the Swinomish tribe has succeeded in continuing culturally relevant mental health services through a combination of federal, state and tribal funds.

Diane Vendiola continues as the Swinomish Support Counselor and Tribal Mental Health Program Coordinator. Diane has been with our program since 1988. In 1994 she took over the lead position as program supervisor and coordinator. She continues to provide direct services to adults and teens with Post Traumatic Stress Disorder, anxiety, disturbances in adjustment to life circumstances, and relationship and family difficulties.

She actively supports many tribal community functions. For instance, she writes a monthly mental health information column for the tribal newsletter, Kee Yoks, is involved in the planning for the annual Native American Day (In collaboration with the town of La Conner), she sits on the tribal Health, Education and Social Services committee, and she attends monthly mental health planning and oversight meetings with the North Sound Regional Support Network and representatives of 7 other Northwestern Washington tribes. She also offers parenting skills training and provides cultural consultation to other tribal and non-tribal social services providers.

Recently, a grassroots Suicide Prevention Initiative has begun at Swinomish. Community members and spiritual leaders concerned over the loss of young men, have come together to share their fears, personal histories and hopes for a better future for the youth of this community. Basic suicide prevention training will be followed by Talking Circles to help bring the community together in feeling and spirit.

Many tribal members have expressed concerns about tribal youth who seem "lost" or drifting away from culture and community supports. One of the Gathering of Wisdoms Update Process team members, Beverly Peters, had the wonderful idea of using the Gathering of Wisdoms as a spring board for a class, perhaps offered at the tribe and taught by a tribal member, with either high school credit or credit through the Northwest Indian College. The goal would be to teach young people about tribal heritage, cultural values and positive mental health. Using this book could bring pride and a sense of "ownership".

Currently , Swinomish utilizes Indian Health Service funds to employ a licensed psychologist one day a week to provide assessment and treatment services to adult Indian clients. She sees adults with a range of difficulties, including depression, anxiety disorders, Post Traumatic Stress Disorder, anger problems, childhood sexual abuse, learning disorders, marital problems and bipolar disorder. She has also supervised psychology interns working toward graduate degrees in psychology. She consults with DSHS staff as needed and prepares reports for tribal and state court.

Funds diverted from the Indian Health Service also allow for the direct tribal employment of an experienced master's level native Indian mental health professional who has long ties to the Swinomish community. He provides one day a week of direct services as well as case consultation to the Tribal Mental Health Program Coordinator. He sees Indian adults with a variety of problems, including relationship, family and parenting difficulties, depression, and Post Traumatic Stress Disorder.

Washington State Crime Victims funds, which are channeled through Skagit Community Mental Health Center, permit the hiring of a master's level specialist in child abuse treatment. She treats clients under 18 years old for depression, physical and sexual abuse, grieving, Post Traumatic Stress Disorder, family violence and conflict, and school problems. She also provides consultation to tribal and state case workers.

Skagit Mental Health continues to provide psychiatric consultation one afternoon a month, primarily due to the loyal perseverance of Dr. Mark Backlund, who has refused to allow funding crunches to sever his ties to our program.

Current Program Challenges

When the second Swinomish Tribal Support Counselor left the program in 2001, Skagit Mental Health made the decision not to refill his position. This was a blow to our program, since it has decreased our capacity for community outreach. However, as described above, we are finding ways to ensure that continued mental health services are available to tribal members.

We have continuously felt the burden of state mandated requirements for documentation in the form of client charts and reports. As discussed elsewhere in this book, paperwork and written documents are particularly offensive to many Indian people.

Through the years, we have had a number of interns in both masters and doctoral psychology programs serve practicum assignments with out program. Supervision has sometimes proven difficult, as our staff time does not allow for much of this. However, each of these interns has contributed to our program, both through direct services provided and through their personal perspectives and shared cross-cultural journeys.

The Tribal Mental Health Program changes as the community changes. Progress is a two edged sword, bringing opportunities as well as new challenges. For instance, when public buss transportation came to Skagit County, it alleviated the severe transportation difficulties of many Indian people. However, it also allowed tribal youth the means to go into town to the malls and other places where they interact with youth of other cultures, sometimes with unhappy results such as increased drug use and gang activity.

The basic cultural orientation of this program remains unchanged. The remaining chapters in this book share the ideas and experiences we have gained through the years spent providing culturally congruent tribal mental health services.

Chapter Fourteen

Therapeutic Framework: Cultural Congruence in a Tribal Mental Health Program

The theory of Cultural Congruence provides a conceptual framework for our Tribal Mental Health Program. This theory states that effective mental health treatment must be based on cultural values. Therapeutic elements must be culturally integrated. On a practical level, this viewpoint requires that services be located at the tribe, be integrated with tribal programs, and that services be developed from within the tribal cultural context, rather than being superimposed from the outside, mainstream culture (see Book I, Chapter 6).

Our therapeutic orientation is based on three closely related concepts:
- **First, the tribal community as a whole is the true "client"**
- **Second, a positive cultural identity is necessary for good mental health and must be supported by service approaches which reflect tribal cultural values.**
- **Third, spiritual practices and values must be recognized and respected.**

TRIBAL COMMUNITY ORIENTATION OF PROGRAM

The underlying goal of this program is to meet tribal community needs. Thus, the true "client" is the tribal community, not only the individual. Like community mental health philosophy in general, this approach assumes that:

1. services should be located in the community to be served
2. services should be designed to meet the most pressing needs existing in that community
3. services should be aimed at helping individuals to live in, rather than be removed from their communities.

Our approach goes one step further: in asserting that the tribal community as a whole is the true "client", we believe that the mental health of individual tribal members is very closely tied to the mental health of the whole community. *The ultimate aim of all program services is to improve the mental health of the tribal community as a whole, rather than only that of individual tribal members.*

This philosophical approach reflects Indian tradition and psychological realities. Most Indian people are very closely identified with their tribal group, and strongly believe in caring for the welfare of all tribal members.

Being "an Indian" usually means that one is a member of a specific tribe. Tribal ties are the basis for both legal and cultural definitions of who is an Indian, as well as for personal cultural identity. Individuals who are not enrolled or eligible for enrollment in a tribe are generally not considered " Indian" for legal purposes, even when they are of entirely Indian descent. Individuals who are not closely socially involved with a tribe may not be considered culturally Indian, regardless of either enrollment or blood quantum. Most Indians see themselves (and are seen by others) as "tribal people", regardless of whether they live on a reservation or in an urban area.

This identification of the individual with the tribe results in important psychological differences between Indian people and most non-Indian people. *Many Indian mental health professionals have stressed that Indian methods of child rearing result in early emotional bonding for Indian children being not only to their mothers, but also to their extended family and ultimately to their tribal group.*

Independence is seldom encouraged or desired to the same extent as in mainstream American society. A psychologically healthy Indian person is not liable to be "out for #1" or a "social climber". Indian people do not usually describe themselves as primarily competitive, independent, career minded, or success oriented. The psychologically healthy Indian child is generally secure in his/her relationship to a somewhat fluid but nurturing and consistent group of adult relatives. He/she forms his/her identity as one who belongs to the family group.

The Indian child is ideally taught a complex network of family relationships, degrees of "closeness" and social relationships based on mutual respect and cooperation. The psychologically mature Indian adult is one who has achieved a balanced and adapted relationship to his/her family and tribe: he/she functions smoothly in the tribal system of shared responsibility and mutual exchanges; he/she is responsive to community opinion and deeply concerned for the overall welfare of the extended family and tribal group.

Thus, the psychological relation of the Indian individual to the tribe is considerably different from the mainstream American ideal or norm of adjustment to society. In general, Indian people perceive themselves as more closely tied to their families and tribal groups than do non-Indian Americans, who are more liable to emphasize individual choice, goals and independence.

In order for a mental health program to be responsive to the needs of the tribal community, it must be based at the tribe. This means not only that offices and services should be located on the reservation, but also that the program should have organizational ties to tribal social services.

It is crucial that tribal members perceive the program as "ours", rather than as a service brought in by an outside agency. In order accomplish this, tribal government must give initial approval for the program and tribal administration must maintain some control over program development and services.

In the Skagit Tribes' Mental Health Program, an Advisory Board made up of Tribal Council members, tribal staff and community members provides program guidance and chooses program staff. Program staff participate in tribal meetings, committees and functions along with tribally employed social services staff. This ensures that program staff feel connected to the tribal organization and that tribal employees and community members perceive the program as "ours".

One important aspect of our tribal community approach is that direct mental health services are provided by staff who are also members of the tribal communities in which they work. *Not only are these providers Indian, but they also belong to the particular tribal group served. They know their clients, their clients' extended families, their history and social situation in the tribe. This allows them to provide services within the ongoing context of tribal lifestyles and values.* For example, the Tribal Support Counselors generally know who in the community is depressed, suicidal, alcoholic or a victim of domestic violence. Likewise, they know what family and social resources are available to individual clients. They can often predict which treatment approaches are most likely to be successful with given individuals or family groups.

The Tribal Support Counselors' intimate knowledge of the tribal community is a source of strength for our program. It also leads to a variety of complex problems. (See Chapter 18). The strength derives from the awareness of community resources and access to distressed individuals in times of crisis. Problems arise from the extremely complicated role and confidentiality challenges.

POSITIVE CULTURAL IDENTITY SUPPORTED BY SERVICES WHICH REFLECT TRIBAL VALUES

A strong and positive cultural identity, involving acceptance, knowledge and appreciation of ones cultural group, is necessary for mental health. (See also Book I, Ch. 6)

A positive cultural identity is crucial for all people: we must know who we are, where we come from, and we must basically like and accept ourselves, including our culture. This does not mean that a person must glorify their culture, only that they must feel at ease with who they are.

Positive cultural identity is particularly crucial for Indian people precisely because it has often been lost or threatened. Loss of cultural knowledge, attacks on Indian ways, value conflicts and multiple social and economic problems have too often disrupted cultural knowledge and the sense of personal belonging with Indian culture. Ambivalence about Indian culture and about oneself as an Indian can lead to unhappiness, difficulty making decisions and to varying degrees of self destructive behavior. *In effect, lack of a positive cultural identity can create and complicate mental health problems for many Indian people.*

Mental health treatment must take cultural issues into account. In particular, treatment must consider the client's personal cultural identity, including cultural affiliation, closeness to Indian culture, and feelings about oneself as an Indian. *Until a person can accept and appreciate his culture, he is not free to explore his individuality, to appreciate other cultures or to make constructive life decisions. He is stuck fighting old battles against others or even against his own people. A positive cultural identity is a step toward maturity, mental health and psychological freedom.*

In order to support cultural identity, *mental health approaches must be more than "sensitive" to Indian values: services must be perceived by Indian clients as actively reinforcing their cultural beliefs and tribal unity.* Indian lifestyles, values and personality norms must guide the choice of service methods.

The success of a tribal mental health program is to a large degree dependent upon the program's ability to incorporate cultural values, beliefs and expectations into the delivery of mental

health services. Important cultural variables to consider include:
- tribal sovereignty
- extended family relationships
- Indian spirituality
- the role of elders
- different attitudes toward time
- unspoken rules of social etiquette
- a widespread distrust of mainstream society

(See Part 2)

Too strong an emphasis on the typical mainstream goals of individual autonomy, moving away from home or forming an independent nuclear family may be unrealistic, undesirable and unhealthy for many Indian people. In contrast, **culturally appropriate therapeutic goals include:**
- **building a strong and positive Indian identity**
- **working out problems in ones family and community**
- **developing a deep commitment of service to ones people**
- **learning to truly respect the insights and experience of ones elders**
- **learning to accept responsibility and leadership**
- **developing a mature ability to give and take**

RESPECT FOR SPIRITUAL VALUES AND PRACTICES

A third important aspect of our therapeutic approach is an emphasis upon spirituality. Indian people, by and large, are deeply concerned about their spiritual lives, and often recognize that their physical or mental health and their spiritual health are closely connected.

Traditional spiritual leaders are often healers who provide help for physical and emotional as well as spiritual problems. *Traditional treatments are often extremely effective and are an important resource for many Indian people.*

Unfortunately, the mainstream view that mental health counseling should be separate from spiritual guidance, that self examination should be distinguished from prayer, and that treatment should not include spiritual exercises has created significant and well-founded distrust among Indian people towards mainstream mental health approaches.

The separation of mental health services from traditional Indian spirituality has been a very serious barrier to the acceptance of mental health services by Indian people. Non- Indian therapists are generally ignorant of and sometimes suspicious, condescending or hostile towards Indian spiritual practices. They often make the mistake of interpreting Indian spiritual experiences as "only" psychological.

In addition, many Indian spiritual leaders have formed a mistrust of "mental health" work. Traditional Indian people may not accept mental health services because of a feeling that mainstream "mental health" is incompatible with spiritual beliefs and might damage their access to Indian spiritual experiences.

Our program responds to this problem by openly recognizing the therapeutic value of traditional Indian spiritual beliefs and practices. The Tribal Support Counselors are familiar with the various facets of Indian spirituality. They are themselves, in varying degrees believers and participants in this ceremonial-therapeutic system. The program attempts to cooperate with and support traditional spiritual practices. ***Through referrals, consultations, spiritual support and direct participation in healing ceremonies, Tribal Support counselors bring mental health work and traditional Indian spirituality closer together.*** (see also Book 1, Ch. 10)

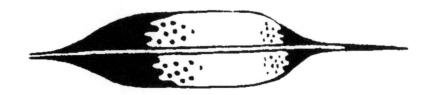

Chapter Fifteen
Important Early Steps in Program Development

In developing this special tribal Mental Health Program it was necessary to make special efforts to develop cooperation between the Community Mental Health Center and the two Indian tribes involved in the program. In addition, special steps were taken to ensure that services and treatment approaches were appropriate to the tribal culture. Important early program development steps included:

- Developing links between the tribes and the Mental Health Center.
- Developing a Tribal Mental Health Advisory Board.
- Recruiting Indian 'natural helpers' as mental health workers and consultants.
- Making Program services visible in the Tribal Community.
- Developing working relationships with other Tribal and non-tribal services.

Each step will be discussed in turn.

INITIATING LINKAGES BETWEEN TRIBES AND MENTAL HEALTH AGENCIES, INDIAN HEALTH SERVICE AND OTHER AGENCIES

State and Federal mental health funds should support services to tribal people. Our way to accomplish this has been to develop a Tribal Mental Health Program cooperatively between Tribal representatives and representatives of our local mental health agency.

In order for a mental health agency to initiate cooperation with a tribe, it is crucial to first identify an "inside" sponsor at the tribe to help recruit support for the proposed program.

In the case of our program a mental health specialist already employed by the Tribe half-time was simultaneously employed by the Mental Health Center to develop and supervise the new program. We found that it was critical to identify appropriate Tribal staff to work with the Mental Health Center Director, the Program Supervisor and other mental health staff. Thus, Tribal representatives had extensive input into the development of service approaches. Tribal social service directors, planners, business managers, social service committee members and social service staff people as well as members of the Tribal Government may all be helpful contact persons.

Special attention was paid to service needs identified by Tribal representatives. A Tribal Advisory Board was developed to ensure that Tribal needs would be met.

TRIBAL MENTAL HEALTH ADVISORY BOARD

When the Tribal Mental Health Program began, an Advisory Board was formed to to ensure responsiveness to the unique mental health needs of each tribal community.

The Advisory Board advised the Mental Health Center Director and Program Supervisor about program direction, training and service needs. The Board also helped identify, recruit and interview Tribal Support Counselor applicants. Over the first several years, the Board periodically reviewed program goals, service accomplishments, training priorities and developments in funding opportunities.

The Tribal Mental Health Advisory Board consisted of representatives from each tribe served. Board members were appointed by Tribal Government or Social Service Administrators. Tribal Council Members, Tribal Social Services Staff and members of the two Tribal Communities were represented on the Advisory Board.

RECRUITING INDIAN MENTAL HEALTH WORKERS AND CONSULTANTS

Positions for tribal mental health workers and cultural consultants were designed to allow flexibility and responsiveness to tribal social realities. Tribal mental health workers were hired who were "natural helpers", i.e. people who have the traditional knowledge, interpersonal skills and wide social acceptance in the tribal community which enable them to be seen by community members as helpers.

These tribal mental health workers are individuals who had been frequently sought out by community members in times of need. Tribal Social Service staff and Advisory Board Members were helpful in identifying and recruiting these individuals.

For instance, Advisory Board Members recruited a 74 yr. old Elder and another quite traditional woman, both of whom had long been seen as "helpers". It is unlikely that either of these individuals would have applied for these positions without being asked to do so. We have found that in a program of this kind the specific job responsibilities must be adapted to fit the skills and special interests of the particular individuals who are chosen to fill these unique positions. *In our program, one younger worker concentrated on problems of youth. Another served as a link to spiritual healers. Their roles envolved to fit their unique abilities.*

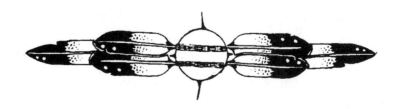

MAKING MENTAL HEALTH SERVICES VISIBLE, AND EASILY ACCESSIBLE TO TRIBAL COMMUNITY MEMBERS

The fact that there is a great need for mental health services in tribal communities does not necessarily mean that these services will be readily used when offered. Indian people do not necessarily recongize the need for or the potential benefits of mental health services. In general, new services offered in tribal communities will not be automatically used just because they are offered.

Indian people may not accept someone as a "helper" just because they have the job, training or educational background to provide a service. Many Indian people prefer to seek services from someone whom they know personally. It often takes some time before a new program or service will be accepted and utilized in a tribal community. Particularly when the service provider is an outsider, it is generally necessary for them to become somewhat 'assimilated' into the tribal social structure before their services will be fully utilized.

Steps that were taken in order to make our Tribal Mental Health services visible and accessible have included:

- locating mental health program offices at tribal sites
- hiring tribal members to provide direct counseling services
- attending tribal community functions
- making presentations to the Tribal Council, elders groups, parents committees, etc.
- spending considerable time developing communication and service networks with other tribal social services staff
- developing and distributing program brochures to tribal community households
- spending time in casual social exchanges with tribal community members
- tribal support counselors personally explaining and offering services to tribal members

Becoming personally known as a helper in the tribal community and making program services visible can be time consuming.

However, this step cannot be overlooked if program services are to be integrated with tribal community life.

DEVELOPING WORKING RELATIONSHIPS WITH OTHER COMMUNITY SERVICES

Early in the Program, it was necessary to develop cooperative working relationships with other social service programs within both the tribal and the mainstream communities. Staff contacted other providers to discuss program plans, mental health needs and mutual referrals.

Tribal mental health workers had to become familiar with the range of services available to Indian clients. They became familiar with the services offered by various programs, and their client eligibility criteria; they further developed working relationships with key providers. In addition to making resources more easily accessible to clients, program staff also encouraged providers in other social services programs to make referrals to the Tribal Mental Program and to seek case or cultural consultation as needed. These activities paved the way for smoother case management services to program clients (see Chapter 16).

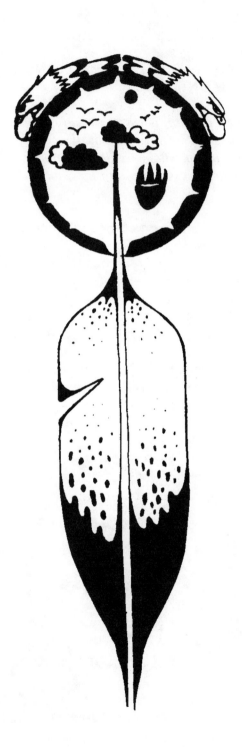

Chapter Sixteen
Culturally Appropriate
Services Approaches

Mental health services should be congruent with tribal values. Since standard approaches are often inappropriate for Indian people, their effectiveness should not be taken for granted. Approaches must be reexained for their applicability to the tribal situation. Culturally oriented mental health services require unusual flexibility, commitment and creativity.

Tribal mental health services must make sense in Indian terms:
- they must meet the immediate needs of Indian people for practical help in emergencies
- they must recognize the extended family as the actual and appropriate "unit of treatment"
- they must be flexible about the time and place of meetings
- they must fit into everyday tribal community life

Services in the Tribal Mental Health Program are culturally based: they are provided by Indian staff, in an Indian manner and in the overall context of tribal community life.

The therapeutic style of the program is informal, and highly flexible. Many services are provided in client homes or in the context of naturally occurring tribal community functions, such as community dinners, funerals and other "doings". Referrals are accepted from either the client or family members. Tribal Support Counselors are available for crisis work.

Intake procedures are more informal and more gradual than is typical in mainstream programs. Charting and record keeping are kept at a minimum, because of the strong cultural bias against labeling or putting things in writing. (See Part IV.)

We emphasize holistic approaches to both assessments and treatment.

Tribal Mental Health staff attempt to ensure that clients receive all needed services, through referrals, case management and active advocacy in dealing with other tribal and non-tribal services. Each person's physical, social and spiritual needs are seen as related to their mental health.

The tribal communities we serve are in many ways communities in trouble; most individuals in the tribal community are affected either directly or indirectly by serious social, psychological and economic problems. For this reason, it is crucial that services not be limited to individual clients only, must but encompass the entire family and tribal system. In fact, services to one person often effect other family members. In this sense, some of our services are "indirect".

In our experience, most clients seek services on and off as the need arises. For this reason, and because of the tribal expectation of open availability of services, "cases", are generally kept open even when a client has not been seen for a long period of time.

Specific Services include:
- culturally oriented assessment of client problems
- supportive counseling
- home visits
- services in the context of community functions and gatherings
- working with the extended family
- problem solving case management, referrals and advocacy
- immediate support in crisis situations
- play therapy

A brief discussion of the nature of service approaches follows.

CULTURALLY ORIENTED ASSESSMENT OF CLIENT PROBLEMS

Assessment of clients in the Tribal Mental Health program is somewhat different than in mainstream mental health programs. Assessment generally takes place over a longer period of time and requires a knowledge of Indian culture. If assessment is not conducted in a culturally sensitive manner, treatment is likely to fail.

Evaluation of Indian clients often requires a team approach. It is necessary that Indian workers be involved in the assessment process in order to provide important background information, facilitate communication and interpret cultural differences.

Indian clients may not express their difficulties in terms familiar to non-Indians. For example, Indians may understate the intensity of their feelings or have difficulty finding words to describe their feelings. When asked how they have been doing many Indian clients answer "O.K.", even when they have been feeling anxious, confused or suicidal. Indians may be reluctant to discuss personal and family problems or to express cultural beliefs about spiritual problems with non-Indians. Without consultation from cultural insiders, the severity of the client's problems can easily be either under or over-estimated. Tribal Support Counselors can ensure that normal cultural behavior patterns and cultural beliefs are not mistaken for pathological symptoms.

Different symptom patterns among Indian clients may also complicate assessments. Whereas the underlying causes and basic symptoms of major mental illnesses such as schizophrenia or manic depressive illness are universal across cultures, the content of delusions, hallucinations and abnormal conduct differ between cultures. **When client and evaluator are from different cultures, there is considerable risk of misdiagnosis.**

Certain diagnostic categories are particularly problematic. For instance, 'depression,' although widespread among Indian clients, is often masked by other problems such as domestic violence, substance abuse or job problems. Diagnoses of 'personality disorders' are based on patterns of deviation from socio-cultural norms, and are therefore liable to be culture-specific.

In addition to having evaluators who are familiar with Indian culture, it is also important to access somewhat different content areas when evaluating Indian clients. These include:
- **the value the client places on cultural identity**
- **tribal and family resources**
- **degree of traditional orientation**
- **familiarity and comfort in dealing with mainstream resources**
- **the client's status, role and obligations in the extended family**
- **appropriateness of involving family members in treatment**
- **the client's health, educational, vocational, financial and spiritual needs**

SUPPORTIVE COUNSELING

Supportive counseling consists of providing the client with understanding, empathetic clarification of his/her problems, encouragement, reassurance, practical suggestions and caring but realistic feedback. The helper listens, reflects, expresses concerns and asks clarifying questions. Silent support, casual conversation and practical help may be offered as well as verbal interactions.

Decreasing anxiety and building the client's sense of self esteem and competence are emphasized over developing insight or cathartic release of feelings. While the helper may be somewhat directive in pointing out resources or even giving advice, he/she generally does not prescribe behavioral programs or give homework assignments.

HOMEVISITS

Homevisits are an essential component of Tribal mental health services because they:
- demonstrate caring and acceptance of the client and his/her lifestyle
- allow the helper to become integrated into the client's natural support system
- help the counselor understand the client's home situation
- facilitate involvement of other family members
- make services more accessible for clients who are homebound, have young children or who are not comfortable with formal office appointments
- facilitate the development of a warm and personal relation between helper and client

SERVICES IN THE CONTEXT OF COMMUNITY FUNCTIONS AND GATHERINGS

Tribal-wide or large family gatherings often provide opportunities for contact with tribal members who are uncomfortable with formal professional relationships. By participating in such events, counselors become visible and easily accessible. They demonstrate their understanding and acceptance of tribal life and maintain their social standing the in Tribal community. Sometimes large gatherings offer an opportunity for considerable social exchange, including discussion of client concerns. Some gatherings have an explicit healing function, either for a family or for the tribal community as a whole. It is extremely important for tribal mental health workers to participate in such events.

WORKING WITH THE EXTENDED FAMILY

The importance of the Indian person's extended family cannot be over-estimated. An Indian person is carefully trained in family relationships and traditions, and his/her social place is largely determined by family connections. Fulfillment of family obligations and a comfortable adaptation to family interactions is crucial for Indian mental health.

Our Tribal Mental Health services rely heavily on family involvement. Even when "family therapy" is not specifically used, extended family are often involved as consultants and helpers in the treatment process.

Tribal Support Counselors know the client's extended family and are often able to gain their support. *In Indian culture, important decisions generally require the approval of spouses and of senior relatives, particularly grandparents.* Without the support of key extended family members, mental health treatment is likely to be ineffective or even sabotaged. Client problems often involve family members. For all these reasons, it is important to gain the cooperation of the client's family.

Extended family approval and involvement is particularly essential when traditional spiritual help is being considered. For practical (e.g. monetary and ritual) reasons, as well as for spiritual reasons, Indian spiritual treatments cannot be successfully administered without family cooperation. In general, *it would be culturally inappropriate for mental health staff to arrange spiritual treatments without the involvement of the client's family.*

The process of gaining family support is a sensitive task, which must be approached in the culturally "right" way. Utilizing "inside" family connections is a key in this process. *Our program's employment of a 78 year old tribal elder as our Cultural Consultant has been a significant element in our ability to mobilize family involvement.*

COOPERATION WITH TRADITIONAL HEALING SYSTEMS

It is important for mental health practitioners to recognize the healing value of traditional spiritual practices. This program attempts to make mental health services respectful of and cooperative with traditional spiritual healing. This is done in several ways:

- **employing tribal mental health workers who have natural access to traditional healing systems**
- **respecting each client's right to choose a personal religious or spiritual path**
- **recognizing the religious/spiritual dimension of life and**

its importance for balanced mental health
- assisting clients who are experiencing spiritual difficulties to contact appropriate traditional practitioners
- consulting with traditional healers concerning the client's mental health and spiritual needs, when culturally appropriate
- attending traditional healing services on behalf of clients as a participant observer
- assisting clients with songs, prayers, drumming, etc. when requested by the client

In order to cooperate with traditional healing practices, a tribal mental health program must employ mental health workers who are not only Indian, but are themselves respected participants in traditional spiritual activities.

Only such knowledgeable and respected individuals can facilitate cooperation and understanding between mental health and traditional practitioners. Indian mental health staff must exercise considerable judgment as to when it is appropriate to make a referral to a traditional practitioner. They must consult with the family to decide which of the several systems of traditional healing is most appropriate for the particular client and how active they personally should be in the particular spiritual activity.

Some of the Tribal Mental Health Program's Support Counselors have pre-existing traditional spiritual roles in the tribal community. It is sometimes necessary for them to make fine distinctions between their traditional helping roles and their tribal mental health worker roles.

This is not a simple matter: *traditional spiritual beliefs and practices are often culturally sensitive areas which must be handled with proper respect and discretion.* The overlap in spiritual and mental health worker roles can create delicate situations.

Nevertheless, *forging links between these two forms of help and healing is absolutely crucial in improving mental health services to Indian people.* Despite the fact that this is a difficult task, open to misunderstanding by both Indian and non-Indian people alike, tribal mental health staff must make a clear philosophical and behavioral commitment to developing cooperation between these two systems.

CASE MANAGEMENT

Clients in the tribal community often have multiple and interacting health, financial, vocational, and family needs, all of which effect their mental health. However, cultural barriers, pride, fear of rejection, transportation problems, limited verbal and written skills, conflicting family responsibilities, etc., may all interfere with the Indian clients receiving needed services. (See Book 1, Chapter 4.)

When clients have mental health problems, they may experience low energy, low self-esteem, confused thinking, self destructive patterns etc. Such individuals are liable to find the state and county social services bureaucracy truly overwhelming. Therefore, it is necessary for tribal mental health workers to assist these clients in locating and dealing with other services as needed.

Tribal mental health staff must examine each client's needs in the areas of health, vocation, education, finances, family situation, etc. *Mental health staff must assist clients to find appropriate resources and must act as advocates for the client with other social services agencies*. In addition, it is important to check back with other services to ensure that the client's needs have been successfully met.

Services available to clients in tribal communities vary considerably from one area to another. Tribal mental health workers must become familiar with the particular local resources. (See Chapter 22.)

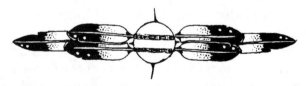

CRISIS AND AS-NEEDED SERVICES

Another important service for tribal mental health programs is the availability of crisis or "as needed" help. This is true because:
* Indian people tend to expect immediate help when needed.
* Many Indian clients are not oriented towards keeping weekly appointments.

- Crisis situations requiring immediate intervention are fairly common in the tribal community.
- Clients are often more receptive to mental health services during times of crisis.

The Tribal Mental Health Program makes services available on an as needed basis whenever possible. Although appointments are made, Support Counselors do not insist that clients be seen only when appointments have been made. Services are often provided in a spontaneous and informal manner. Such contacts may be initiated either by the provider or by the client.

Often Support Counselors are called in time of crisis. At times of family crisis, such as a death, Support Counselors often go to the client's home.

Outreach and crisis services are not restricted to hourly units; Support Counselors frequently spend several hours with clients, as needed. (See Chapter 20.)

PLAY THERAPY

"Play Therapy" is a subtle and complex therapeutic method which a trained therapist can readily adapt to the tribal situation. It is particularly helpful for Indian children because it places less emphasis on talking, explaining and analyzing than do many western "therapies".

Since children generally do not express their feelings and problems in words, it is difficult for them to benefit from "talk therapy". Instead, they act out their concerns in their play by expressing emotions and trying to gain control of problems through repeated dramatization and rehearsing possible solutions. Play does more than give children an outlet for feelings; it helps them develop understanding, social competence and problem solving skills. In fact, many childhood problems are resolved by the child himself during free play.

In play therapy the child's play becomes a mode of communication with the therapist. The child's approach to the unstructured new situation, choice of play materials, play themes and ways of resolving them all tell the therapist about the child's inner experience of himself and the world. *The therapist has three roles:*

1. To provide a safe and consistent play environment with firm outside boundaries.

2. To be fully present with the child, attentive, accepting, non-interfering.

3. To carefully adapt and time comments or 'interpretations' to the child's changing relation to the situation and readiness to accept a new perspective.

The therapeutic features of play therapy include:

1. A consistent time and place where the child can safely explore and express all feelings, including those which are not safe or acceptable to express in other times and places.

2. A reliable, warm and accepting relationship with an adult who gives the child his or her complete attention.

3. Carefully designed and timed therapeutic actions and comments aimed at helping the child build healthy responses and resolve conflicts.

Many Indian children come from homes where verbal skills are less emphasized than are practical, physical and artistic skills. Talking about feelings and problems may not be encouraged. Play therapy can help 'break the ice,' develop a strong therapeutic relationship, and provide the child with symbolic tools for resolving difficulties.

It is especially helpful if play therapy can take place in familiar, culturally congruent tribal facilities, using culturally familiar play materials. It is also very helpful if the therapist is Indian, since it makes it easier for the child to identify with him or her. Play therapy lends itself naturally to the exploration of cultural identity and cultural conflict, as well as other issues.

Story telling is a culture-spoecific technique often interwoven into counseling by Indian mental health workers. (See Ch. 9 for a discussion of the cultural value of story telling.)

Chapter Seventeen
Personal Perspectives of Tribal Mental Health Team Members

THE MENTAL HEALTH CENTER ADMINISTRATOR'S PERSPECTIVE ON THE TRIBAL MENTAL HEALTH PROGRAM
—Jere LaFollette

For a number of years before beginning the Tribal Mental Health Program, Skagit Community Mental Health Center had made special efforts to serve local Indian communities. A member of the Agency's professional staff went to Swinomish one day per week for several years. Few clients presented themselves for treatment. Later we hired an Indian "home-visitor" who would, under the supervision of mental health staff, make outreach visits and provide supportive services to members of the tribe. This helped to create goodwill between the Mental Health Center and the Tribe. However, due to the lack of specialized training and enough Mental Health Center support at the tribal location itself, this effort was only moderately successful.

While not fully successful, these two experiences helped establish critical linkages and relationships between members of the Mental Health Center staff and the tribal community. However, it was not until we began the current Tribal Mental Health program that our Agency was able to deliver the type of extended services called for in terms of the needs of these two tribal communities.

A number of factors have come together to make this program a success. Most important has been the high quality of the staff that has been attracted to this program. We have been exceptionally fortunate in the selection of a Project Director, Jennifer Clarke, Ph.D., who has a combination of experience in working with tribal communities, in-depth clinical skills, and direct practical experience in the area of mental health. Likewise, the Support Counselors who have worked with this program have been not only dedicated, but willing to try new roles and new approaches in providing service to other members of their communities.

From the standpoint of the Mental Health Center administrator, several factors seem critical in initiating joint programs between mental health centers and Indian tribes. These include:

Prioritization and Commitment

There is no question that the need for community mental health care far exceeds the ability of community mental health programs to meet these needs. Whether it is serving the chronically or acutely mentally ill, the elderly, or children, there continue to be much greater demands for service than can be provided. Thus, it is easy for mental health centers to take the position that services are available to all and fail to make the extensive commitment necessary to reach difficult to serve populations.

We have been fortunate to have the support of the Division of Mental Health to undertake this special program. We feel it has been quite successful. This program has demonstrated that *if a community mental health agency makes a commitment to extend its services to an under-served population, those services will be used if they are presented in a culturally appropriate manner. In order to do this, a high priority must be placed on working closely with the tribe and in committing resources beyond those normally available.*

The Need for the Mental Health Agency to Reach Out at All Levels of the Organization

If a community mental health agency is to initiate services in conjunction with tribal communities, a variety of levels and supports must be in place to work with members of the tribe and direct service staff. This certainly begins with the agency administrator. He or she must be willing to spend time at tribal locations, meet with representatives of tribal government, social service programs, and community elders. He/she must whenever possible attend functions on the reservations, as well as spend time with direct service staff working within the tribal community.

In that services are generally most effective if provided at the tribal site, other members of the Agency staff should be prepared, willing, and enthusiastic about offering their support to tribal mental health providers and project staff. Agency psychiatric staff, geriatric outreach personnel, children's specialists and others must be willing to lend their support to the project in delivering specialized services when appropriate. *If such a program is to be successful, the mental health center must take the initiative in reaching out to the tribal community.*

The Importance of Education and Training

In setting standards for the delivery of direct care, it must be expected that considerable time will need to be expended in training Indian Support Counselors. In that services will be greatly enhanced through the delivery of service by members of the tribal community, it is often necessary to ensure that the opportunity for extensive education will be available. This may include attending courses through local colleges, workshops in specialized treatment techniques, and through staff training endeavors. As the skill and expertise of direct service personnel increase, the effectiveness of the program and its ability to work closely with other mental health personnel also increases.

The Need for Flexibility

In the operation of programs in conjunction with tribal communities it is important to remain flexible concerning standards and procedures. Due to cultural and community differences, an Agency cannot simply overlay the standard community mental health structure within Indian communities in terms of expectations for the delivery of service. Again, the issue of prioritization should be considered.

For example, in that tribally employed social service providers are paid twice a month, we have gone to a twice monthly paycheck for Support Counselors rather than insist they be paid only once a month as continues to be the standard for other members of the mental health center staff. We have also allowed Indian Support Counselors to take not only the standard holidays available to other mental health personnel, but have respected the importance of other significant dates such as Treaty Day or the closure of tribal offices for funerals or other significant occasions related to the tribe. Once again, *we have made these decisions, even though it means making exceptions from standard procedures.*

We have found our Support Counselor staff extremely dedicated, hardworking, and concerned about other members of their tribes. In order to help them achieve the goals of the delivery of direct mental health care in conjunction with the Agency to members of their community, we have had to employ flexibility in standards and procedures. We feel the success we have achieved has been well worth this effort.

Over the years in which we have been extensively involved in the provision of mental health care to the Swinomish and Upper Skagit tribes, we have learned a great deal about the delivery of tribal metal health care, as well as about the culture and priorities of these tribal communities. This has enriched the Community Mental Health Program. We hope it has been of equal value and use to members of these two tribes.

COMMENTS OF CULTURAL CONSULTANT/ SWINOMISH ELDER –Bertha Dan

The Tribal Mental Health Program here on this reservation is just like it opened the door to let us see the needs of our people, which maybe they didn't even understand. With our training and with our advisors and supervisors, we've been able to put it in perspective so that we could in turn recognize what sort of help is needed.

We are caught between two cultures, and this causes emotional upsets. I see the needs of the Indian community as kind of falling into two categories:

- *younger people need to learn more about themselves, their cultural traditions and spiritual life.* Sometimes this knowledge is lost. Elders need to pass on their knowledge so it won't be lost to the youth.

- **elders generally understand their culture but need reinforcement of their beliefs.** Some experiences can be frightening to them and so they need culturally sensitive support.

In the process of trying to be helpful to our people we have had to use the medical doctors, nurses, nutritionists, psychologists and all sorts of other helpers to try and sort out what's best. Sometimes it's a combination of all. We have also had to use Indian Spiritual doctors. At Swinomish, and at some other tribes, we have the 'Skwedilic' and also the 'Tusted' poles. These are used in certain selected cases when this is advised by people with the appropriate cultural knowledge.

It takes all of us to accomplish something in the line of help. My role as Cultural Consultant is to give advice, support and reinforcement. My role is often to help decide which type of help is needed, traditional or modern day. I also consult with our Program Director and Mental Health Center Psychiatrist about these decisions.

Another thing we do is give comfort to families at the time of death and dying, whether this is from natural causes or from accidents. Families may go into a state of shock and need lots of support. We help the family take steps to overcome their grief. They need to do something to make a final break, so they won't be thinking all the time of their loss. *We often recommend a traditional Burning of the deceased's favorite clothing and possessions. This is our traditional way of giving a final touch to the separation. A Burning lets the family know that that's the end of the mourning period, and that no matter how much it hurts, that life has to go on. And that's part of our work too.*

I personally have tended to specialize in working with elders and older adults. The other worker at Swinomish concentrated on work with young people and children. My knowledge of our Indian dialect has been helpful in working with our older people. When it comes down to it, *I don't think our upsets are too different from any other race, we just handle it in different ways.*

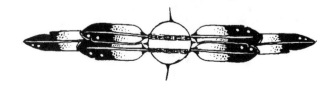

COMMENTS OF FORMER UPPER SKAGIT TRIBAL SUPPORT COUNSELOR –Pearl Rodriguez

One thing this program has done is that I found myself in myself: I found out who I was. It's a deeper thing, that you never have known was there before.

I have a lot of concern over the young people and teens. A lot of people dismiss them and think they're just a nuisance. ***We don't really see the inside of what a child goes through in life.*** We usually focus on the needs of either very young kids or elders and miss the needs of the in-between ones who are going through a lot of crisis in their lives.

I've learned that our elders do know the future of a person. They pick certain ones out and talk to them about our cultural ways and what they are supposed to do in life. The elders have a dream of this young person's future. They talked and talked to me, and I thought I'd never be what they wanted me to be, but here I am! ***The teachings from my elders are guiding me in my work now. Their teachings are to me like a permission to go ahead and do my work now.***

There's no easy way to please all people. Sometimes you have to go one day at a time. Sometimes your family suffers until you meet your work goals. When I was going through classes and studying all the time, I couldn't be as available to them as I used to be.

My personal goal when I started this job was to last five years, and I'm almost there now. Then I'll feel that I've done something in my life to talk about.

I think this program has opened the eyes of many of our tribal members to the idea that mental health is O.K. in a tribal setting. They come to us now when they're in crisis.

COMMENTS OF UPPER SKAGIT TRIBAL SUPPORT COUNSELOR –June Boome

One of the first things I thought about this job was that it would be easy, because I counsel and help people anyway. People are always coming and asking me things, maybe because of my nursing background.

When I got into this work I realized how deep it was. I saw that most of my reasons were selfish for being here, because I was learning to understand many things from our courses and seminars. This has helped me personally: I found that by helping my people I was also helping myself.

After I began to understand myself, why I did things and why I expected either too much or too little from others, I was able to understand more clearly what our program was all about. I learned ways to help others, including members of my own family who have had so many problems.

I could see the needs of my people better and could see new ways to help them. I also found that people would respect the things that I said as an elder.

As time goes by, I am learning to cope with all the sadness and helplessness that our people have. I have learned to shield myself and cope with all the things that make us sad.

This program has given me increased confidence in myself and that I can help my people, if only by listening to them and letting them talk and self-disclose.

As our program goes on I think our people will gain more confidence in the Tribal Support Counselors and will learn to trust us more.

SWINOMISH SUPPORT COUNSELOR/PROGRAM COORDINATOR'S PERSPECTIVE –Diane Vendiola

The remarks I wrote for the first edition of 'A Gathering of Wisdoms' 11 years ago, marked my being the newest Tribal Support Counselor of two and a half years. Many changes have occurred. *Today, I am the longest employed and sole Tribal Mental Health (TMH) Program Support Counselor and also Program Coordinator.* Our faithful and dedicated psychiatrist, Dr. Backlund, continues his vital involvement with the program. I now staff my cases weekly with Jay Samson, therapist for Indian Health Services (IHS). Diana Lowry, therapist is employed in collaboration with a grant from the Washington State Crime Victims Program and the Swinomish Tribal Community (STC). Two STC Alcohol Program counselors have joined Diana and myself in our weekly seminars, broadening our program to include co-occurring disorders. The STC has assumed financial responsibility for contracting with two additional therapists to provide mental health services, as community mental health funding for the TMH program has dwindled. The program continues to operate under the auspices of Community Mental Health Services (CMHS) of Skagit County. And both the STC Social Services director and the CMHS representative supervise the program.

The opportunities offered to the individual willing to serve his/her own community remain 1) on-the-job training, 2) in-depth awareness and enhancement of one's own mental health, 3) formal recognition for being a natural helper, as was true 11 years ago.

In addition, the program provides the opportunity for the TMH Support counselor to help promote, encourage and facilitate sound life-management practices for clients and their families. *Being in a position to contribute to one's community in this manner brings a great sense of personal satisfaction.*

During the thirteen years in which I have served as Support Counselor for my people, I have seen a gradual change in community attitudes toward the seeking of mental health services. The generation following me recognizes now, I think, that mental health, although originating from the white man's system, is an important component in the pursuit of balance and harmony. Seeking balance and harmony is a traditional Indian value, considered to be a worthwhile endeavor. When "mental health" services facilitate achieving that endeavour, I believe that clients recognize that seeking of services needs to be done when necessary. More importantly, *the younger generations recognize mental health is connected to overall health in general, and thus may perceive mental health service provision as a treaty promise to all Indians.*

The stigma attached to mental illness and sometimes even to the seeking of mental health services is a phenomenon that appears to coincide with the degree of awareness regarding this seeking of balance and harmony and the belief about Indian health being a treaty promise.

Along with the problems common to all communities, Indian people face the issues of loss of culture and religious practices, cultural assimilation, past major dissemination of Indian populations, poverty, unemployment and racism. There is an underlying, ongoing struggle to maintain cultural identity in a time of unrest and change in the world at large.

Even as I write this, community people have enlisted the support and services of the TMH program to assess the mental health needs of our community and to collaborate with traditional healers, spiritual helpers and tribal leaders to address the issue of suicide. *Indian people assuming responsibility for the well-being of the total community is one of our traditional Indian values. It is in the spirit of this value that the tribal mental health program endeavors to operate.*

PSYCHIATRIC CONSULTANT'S PERSPECTIVE
–Mark Backlund

Overview

As a healing profession, psychiatry has often had the responsibility of bridging such "opposites" as mind/body, emotions and thoughts, and male and female. The differences between Coast Salish and mainstream white culture, while perhaps not "opposite", certainly provide enough of a gulf to challenge the best of bridge-builders.

One-and-a-half years after the start of the Tribal Mental Health Program, it was determined that consultation by a Community Mental Health Psychiatrist could be useful in several ways:

(a) By increasing the linkages between the clinic and the tribal program, it would enhance the flow of information back and forth, increasing awareness of the needs, problems and resources of each. It was thought perhaps other clinic programs might become more accessible to Indian clients as well.

(b) The Tribal Support Counselors could receive training on a variety of psychiatric issues which they were having to deal with on a daily basis, including group dynamics, bodily reactions to stress, when to use psychotropic medications, how to recognize certain common physical illnesses, and so on.

(c) Case consultation could also be provided to expand on that already being provided by the Program Director.

(d) Direct services to Tribal clients could be provided in a safe setting and with the benefit of Tribal Support Counselor input

(e) Finally, it provided a major learning opportunity for the Medical Director of the Mental Health Clinic, who has an ongoing interest in Indian people and gladly volunteered for the task.

The Consultant's Role

Consultation has provided a number of remarkable challenges. The role of psychiatrist itself carried with it many powerful images. Since this psychiatrist is also a white male, the images are multiplied: healer, representative of the invading white culture and of our society's current white-male power structure.

In representing the white power structure, the psychiatrist must deal with the resentment and mistrust this naturally creates. How those feelings are handled by the consultant plays a critical role in the success of the consultation. *By sharing power with the counselors rather than holding it over them, the counselors are encouraged in their efforts to deal successfully with that power structure.* This can be done indirectly through encouragement and affirmation or directly by discussing how to affect the mainstream bureaucratic system. The primary goals are:

• to increase the Tribal Support Counselors' senses of positive cultural identity

• to increase their personal feelings of competence in dealing with the mainstream culture

• to increase their ability to successfully advocate for their clients.

It is essential that the psychiatrist not be afraid to be a student as well as a teacher. While the psychiatrist is an expert on a specific body of medical knowledge, the Support Counselors are experts on their tribal history, traditions and values. Information is shared both ways in order to support the core basis of the Tribal Mental Health model: positive cultural identity.

The psychiatrist is also called upon to provide direct clinical service to tribal members. This may occur in a variety of settings, including the client's home. *Flexibility is critical to the provision of client services.*

Finally, the psychiatrist provides case consultation on prob-

lems with individual, family, and large group dynamics. ***Understanding the intricate family and tribal ties and major cultural
differences while applying mental health concepts truly requires a
team effort between the consultant and the Support Counselors.***

***Attending tribal functions, such as special dinners, funerals, or
pow-wows enriches the experience for the psychiatrist as well as
increasing his/her credibility and therefore effectiveness with tribal
members.*** These activities add dimensions of experience seldom
found in mainstream psychiatric work.

Thus, one is required to play a number of roles to work
effectively within tribal systems. Blurring of roles is accepted by
most Indian people and is consistent with the multiple expectations daily faced by the Support Counselors.

Phases of the Consulting Relationship

In retrospect, consultation with the Tribal Mental Health Program went through three stages:

1. ***Proving Ground: Establishing the Psychiatrist's qualifications to
   work with the counselors was the first step.*** Formal presentations, question and answer sessions on topics such as physical
   illness, depression, medications, etc. all were a part of this
   initial phase. The consultant's style and attitude as well as his
   psychiatric knowledge were closely examined for trustworthi-
   ness.
2. ***Learning: A period of quiet absorption followed*** in which the
   consultant felt less compelled to answer and more inclined to
   listen, ask questions, and seek advice on aspects of Salish native culture.
3. ***Interactive: A sense of mutual trust and respect was established***
   which allowed a freer exchange of ideas and perceptions in
   both directions. This stage seemed to combine the previous
   two in a more natural, spontaneous fashion.

Stumbling Blocks

Consultation has presented the following challenges:

1. ***Cultural style differences:*** This could cover a book itself. Different verbal styles (white culture-talkative, analytical, explana-
   tory vs. Salish culture-reserved, accepting or passive, waiting),
   sex role expectations, time boundaries, etc. all create opportunities for confusion and misunderstanding.
2. ***Alcoholism:*** I list this as a separate item simply because it is so

complexly embedded in current native American life. Dealing with the causes and impacts of alcohol abuse is a frustrating and dominant fact of our consultation and treatment efforts.

3. *A bitterly learned mistrust of written work* (treaties, contracts, state required paperwork, progress notes, intakes, releases of information, etc.) has required significant efforts in negotiating with state and local agencies to evolve a system more likely to succeed with our Native American clients.

4. *White mental health workers may have difficulty in appreciating the extent to which Native Americans feel themselves involuntarily held hostage by the white culture.* Understanding this, along with their incredibly long range sense of time is critical to grasping the problems faced by Indian people.

The sense that "we didn't really want you here in the first place, and we intend to just wait until you go away again", along with a fatalism or perhaps a respect for forces larger than oneself, account in part for the 'passive resistance' which seems to characterize Native American relations with the white subculture.

Summary

Psychiatric consultation committed to strengthening positive Indian cultural identity provides an unparalleled opportunity for professional enrichment and growth. A sincere and long term commitment, along with professional knowledge and flexibility, create the conditions in which a successful working relationship can take root and flourish.

PERSPECTIVE OF ORIGINAL ROGRAM DIRECTOR/ IMPLEMENTOR –Jennifer Clarke

Challenges in the Role of Program Director

Developing a new and innovative program is always full of challenges. Differences in communication styles and cultural perspectives among team members made this position both difficult and stimulating.

A major part of my role as Program Director was to balance the needs and values of the Tribal Support Counselors with the requirements of the Mental Health System. I have found that this required both determination and flexibility.

Value of the Tribal Mental Health Program

For three years before the beginning of this program I had worked as a mental health therapist in tribal communities. During this time *I had concluded that there was a need for increased cultural orientation of services and that in order to accomplish this, more Indian direct service providers were needed.* This program gave me an opportunity to work closely with Indian people to change existing mental health approaches and encourage Indian people to develop careers in mental health work.

This program is based on shared authority, experiences and communication. Our team developed the ability to give and receive feedback in an increasingly frank manner. We learned about ourselves and one another through close interaction. The dynamics within our Tribal Mental Health team taught us about culture and about culturally appropriate ways of delivering services.

This program allowed us to serve a more traditional and "hard to reach" segment of the tribal population than can usually be reached by mainstream approaches. Indian workers who are themselves from traditional backgrounds can work with other traditional people in a natural and comfortable manner.

It has always seemed to me natural and important for mental health workers to learn about and cooperate with traditional spiritual healers. However, as a non-Indian working alone in a tribal community, it was difficult to find the right channels for communication and building trust. *The Tribal Support Counselors, because of their existing family and spiritual ties, were able to make a significant start toward real interchange of ideas and healing approaches between traditional Indian medicine and western mental health.*

The Personal Impact of the Program

Being a non-Indian working in a tribal setting was an important although not always easy personal experience. There was a long period of testing and building mutual trust. Repeated surprises about how Indian people perceive events, personalities and the things people say led to a deepening process of personal and cultural self discovery.

Working for a tribe requires a greater personal commitment than is the case in most jobs. As a non-Indian, it is necessary to spend quite a lot of time in a tribal community before one begins to "belong." Over time I found myself becoming more and more emotionally involved with the tribal community. I think that *non-Indians must become to some degree "absorbed" into the Indian world before they can be effective helpers*. Going through this process inevitably changes one's own cultural perspective.

I have found it necessary to repeatedly renew my personal commitment to stick with this program and this process. Part of my role as Program Director was to encourage each Support Counselor to also stick with it. In order to do this I had to develop and repeatedly demonstrate the attitude that whatever the problem, (personal, political, administrative or communication), we WILL solve it!

I have found it important to be emotionally receptive without being "thin skinned" or easily hurt. It is important to be resilient, determined and not to take set-backs personally. As a non-Indian Program Director, it was also crucial to try to understand and respect Indian standards of tact. This job required modeling helping behaviors by being personally available and as flexible as possible while also being able to define program limits and remain responsive to the overall context of the Mental Health Center and State funding system. Despite the fact that the Mental Health Center has been exceptionally supportive, I have sometimes found it difficult to balance these two sets of demands.

The overwhelmingly serious client problems we deal with often seem to be piled on one another with little relief. These circumstances effect each of us personally as members of the Tribal Mental Health Team. The dangers of depression, numbness or giving up must be directly confronted time and again. As Program Director I found it necessary to find within myself sources of hope and the ability to move from a negative situation to a positive response.

Conclusions

The Tribal Mental Health Program has made enormous differences in the lives of all involved. It has changed our perspectives and taught us much about each other, about the nature of culture, about commitment, stamina and courage to face very difficult situations day after day while maintaining hope. This program has allowed us to provide services to otherwise unreachable clients and has changed the tribal community's perspective on "mental health."

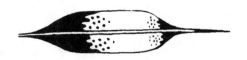

Chapter Eighteen
Problems and Challenges Encountered in Program Operation

O ver the 18 years of operating the Tribal Mental Health Program, a variety of challenges have been encountered, including:
- The unusually high level of effort for service delivery
- Difficulties adapting mainstream mental health system requirements to meet tribal needs
  —Record keeping difficulties
  —Problems with state priority categories
  —Problems with conventional diagnostic systems
- Role conflicts and the danger of staff "burnout"
- Confidentiality challenges
- Staff changes
- Barriers to developing written descriptions
- Challenges facing non-Indians working on reservations

This section describes these situations and how they have been met.

UNUSUAL LEVEL OF EFFORT REQUIRED FOR SERVICE DELIVERY

Tribal mental health services require more "indirect " staff activity to produce an hour of "direct" client service than is typical of mainstream mental health services. This is true for a variety of reasons, including:

- The need to develop new approaches and procedures appropriate to tribal culture.
- The need to familiarize Tribal community members with the purpose and benefits of mental health services.
- The need to train para-professional Indian mental health workers in counseling and mental health approaches.
- The complexity of the social, health, vocational, environmental and spiritual problems confronting Indian people.
- The need to provide services in client homes and tribal community settings.
- The frequency of missed appointments.
- The cultural expectation that the helper be immediately available, especially during times of crisis.
- The amount of time that must generally be spent before program services will be accepted and fully utilized by tribal community clients.
- The need for service providers to interact socially as well as professionally in the tribal community.
- The great variation in the length of time spent in client contacts.

Therefore, staff must spend unusual amounts of time in "indirect" service activities in order to make services accessible and effective. Funding sources and administrators should recognize and plan for this need. (see Chapter 21.)

DIFFICULTIES IN ADAPTING THE MAINSTREAM MENTAL HEALTH SYSTEM TO MEET TRIBAL COMMUNITY NEEDS

Services which reflect Indian values do not easily blend with mainstream mental health expectations and requirements. This is a particular problem in the areas of record keeping, staff roles and diagnosis. Also, Indian ideas regard-

ing appropriate behavior, the significance of symptoms and about appropriate treatments are often very different from those of the mainstream mental health system. For these reasons, it is necessary for tribal mental health workers to:
1. identify and describe cultural factors which call for exceptions to mainstream policies, and
2. negotiate creative compromises with funding sources.

Direct service providers cannot be solely responsible for making services "culturally appropriate"; funding authorities also must recognize the need for innovation and flexibility. Without creative collaboration, bureaucratic requirements may unintentionally stifle innovative minority programs.

Record Keeping Difficulties

Record keeping and reporting systems are an area of particular cultural incongruity between Indian and mainstream approaches. These difficulties, as well as the ways we deal with them in our particular program, are discussed in Part IV, "Record Keeping for a Tribal Mental Health Program".

Problems with State Priority Categories

Mental health services supported by state funds are generally restricted to clients meeting the state "priority population" definition: clients must be "acutely mentally ill", "chronically mentally ill", or "seriously disturbed". These "priority" definitions can pose serious problems for programs serving Indian people.

Although Indian clients often experience severe life stresses and emotional-behavioral problems, they do not always meet the state "priority population" definitions. This is because:
1. *Indian people often show different symptom patterns than do non-Indian clients.*
2. *Indian clients often have no history of utilizing mainstream services, and therefore may not be considered "chronic" by state definitions.*

Lack of utilization of mainstream services is due to:
- The Indian cultural value placed on families caring for disabled family members without outside interference,
- The widespread mistrust of mainstream services.

Even severely mentally ill Indian clients may have never used mainstream mental health services. For these reasons tribal mental health programs may tend to have more clients fitting into the "acute" and "seriously disturbed" categories than into the "chronic" category.

The purpose of the state "priority" classifications is to ensure that the most needy clients have priority in receiving mental health services. It is important that these "priority" definitions do not unintentionally eliminate severely disturbed Indian clients from eligibility for services. *State priority definitions should be re-evaluated and modified so that Indian and other minority clients will not be denied needed services.*

Problems Using Conventional Diagnostic Systems

Most state-funded programs are required to give all clients a diagnosis from the standard Statistical Manual of Mental Disorders, Fourth Edition, (DSM IV). Both the accuracy and the cultural appropriateness of conventional DSM IV diagnosis for Indian clients must be carefully examined. Differences in family structure, values, child rearing patterns and social circumstances result in different symptom patterns as well as different prevalence rates for particular disorders. Culturally distinct patterns of disturbance may not fit in the DSM IV classification system.

In using the diagnostic system of one culture to label psychological conditions experienced by individuals belonging to another culture, we risk a form of "cultural imperialism". Applying DSM IV diagnosis to Indian people implies several assumptions which may or may not be warranted, and which should at any rate be made explicit.

First, the use of DSM IV diagnosis assumes that mainstream mental health professionals are qualified to judge the condition of Indian persons in distress. We question this assumption. The Skagit Tribe's Mental Health Program has attempted to deal with this particular problem through teamwork: diagnostic decisions are generally made only after consultation between para- professional Indian providers and (non-Indian) mental health professionals. Diagnoses are selected to reflect Indian views of the client's problems as much as possible.

A second assumption implied by the use of DSM IV labels to describe Indian clients is that the psychiatric conditions and 'diagnostic entities' present in Indian culture are essentially the same as those found in western culture. A review of the literature in cross-cultural psychiatry, cultural anthropology or 'psychiatric anthropology', shows that this is by no means a settled issue. In fact, a hot debate over the question of "cultural uniqueness" as opposed to universality of mental illnesses has continued for many years. So long as this question remains unresolved, the accuracy and ethical appropriateness of cross cultural diagnosis will remain dubious.

Although a program such as ours cannot resolve these questions, we must consider them because they are relevant to service delivery. Diagnostic categories which seem particularly 'culturally loaded' (such as the "personality disorders"), are best avoided. Less negative and judgmental labels (such as "adjustment disorder" or "anxiety disorders") seem preferable whenever a diagnostic choice is possible.

Diagnostic labels may be confusing to both clients and mental health providers because diagnostic terms may suggest a symptom picture quite different from that actually presented by the Indian client. Tribal mental health providers should be particularly aware of cultural variations in the symptoms of anxiety, somatoform and personality disorders. ***Forcing the problems of Indian clients into majority culture categories can distort the nature of the problems, fail to accurately describe the client's symptom picture and can confuse and alienate the client.***

Another serious problem with the use of DSM IV diagnosis in a tribal mental health program is that such labeling can stigmatize clients and set them apart from family and society.

The terms "mental illness" and "mental health" themselves tend to have a very negative connotation in Indian communities. Indian mental health staff often feel a profound reluctance to apply such impersonal and seemingly demeaning diagnostic labels to individuals whom they know well. Paraprofessional staff are liable to feel especially uncomfortable with diagnostic responsibilities, because they have not received extensive diagnostic training.

DSM IV diagnosis may be perceived by both client and provider as an intrusion from the outside, mainstream system which is incompatible with a culturally oriented approach. For instance, clients may feel frightened, confused or angry if told that they have been diagnosed as having "schizophrenia", "a personality disorder" or a "somatoform disorder". Such terms may not be at all consistent with the way the clients and their family members understand their problems.

Funding requirements and the need for some system which describes client problems have made it impossible to avoid diagnoses entirely. However, we have attempted to deal with the difficulties of diagnosis by:

- having diagnoses selected jointly by Tribal Support Counselors and Supervisors
- selecting the least negative diagnostic labels possible
- selecting diagnoses which correspond as closely as possible to the client's own understanding of his/her problem
- noting down Indian terms for the problem on the intake form along with the DSM IV diagnosis whenever

Ideally, an Indian culture-specific diagnostic system would give culturally appropriate names to client conditions. Until this can be accomplished, caution in diagnosis is extremely important.

ROLE CONFLICTS AND THE DANGERS OF STAFF "BURNOUT"

Perhaps the most difficult challenge facing the Tribal Mental Health Program has been the enormously complex and difficult demands placed on Tribal Support Counselors. Due to the tight knit nature of the tribal community, Tribal Support Counselors must often work with friends, enemies and relatives. They inevitably have a great deal of personal and historical information about their clients and may learn things about clients which the clients themselves do not tell them. The Support Counselors are equally well known to clients and other tribal community members. Thus, they are as vulnerable to community social pressures (such as gossip, family pressure or shaming), as are their clients.

The complex role demands on Tribal Support Counselors make the positions extremely stressful. Support counselors must be able to maintain client confidentiality, must be able to withstand subtle family pressures and must be able to make sophisticated decisions concerning appropriate relationships with clients. Support Counselors live in the tribal community and often provide services after regular working hours. They may be visited by clients at home or may informally consult with them at social events. Thus, there is a danger of the Support Counselors feeling always "on duty".

Because of these unique role challenges, it is crucial for tribal mental health programs to recruit staff who:
- **are able to be flexible**
- **who are able to set limits and be firm**
- **who are socially placed so as to have access to a broad range of subgroups in the tribal community.**
- **who have good common sense**

Tribal mental health programs must maintain flexibility in role expectations and must ensure that Support Counselors have access to adequate supervision and support.

CONFIDENTIALITY CHALLENGES

Maintaining confidentiality in a tribal community is more complicated than in most mainstream mental health agencies. In small tribal communities everyone knows a great deal about every one else and their family. There is considerable curiosity and gossip which reflect both genuine concerns for other tribal members and act as a form of social control.

The confidentiality dilemmas faced in a tribal community are heightened when working with the extended family of clients. Members of the extended family generally have extensive knowledge about the client's difficulties. Their cooperation is also often necessary for treatment success. Workers must find the appropriate balance between maintaining strict individual confidentiality and involving family members. This is a delicate matter calling for clinical judgment and evaluation of each particular client's needs.

Another reality facing Tribal Support Counselors is that they are likely to know their clients and their clients' families for ten, twenty or thirty years. Therefore, they must realize that their commitment to confidentiality is forever, even if they stop working as a Support Counselor. As one of our Tribal Social Service Directors has pointed out, this lifelong commitment to confidentiality is rather like that demanded of CIA employees!

The types of confidentiality situations which arise in tribal mental health programs differ considerably from those faced in mainstream programs. Tribal community members often see a client go into a mental health worker's office or may see the worker at the client's house and later ask questions about the client's difficulties. At times, clients will not speak to workers in public for fear that others would identify them as a client and therefore as possibly "crazy". Other clients may begin discussing personal matters in public, leaving the counselor uncertain as to how to respond.

The following situations illustrate the types of confidentiality challenges which arise in tribal communities:

• While you are meeting in your office with a client, there is a persistent knock at the door. When you open the door the teenager outside leans his head in to see who is with you.

• A family member of your client gives you important information about your client but insists that you not tell the client.

• A community member expresses concern about a friend, asks you to see that person and later asks you how their friend is doing.

• A member of the tribal counsel or tribal administrative staff asks you about a case or tells you what to do in a particular case.

• After a group meeting you learn that one client has been spreading information shared by another person in the group.

• You make a home visit to your client. Other family members or friends do not leave the room or come and go during your meeting.

• Your third cousin's daughter is your client. Relatives expect you to discuss her with them as you have done in the past.

• A friend of yours is falling in love with a man whom you know, (from information given you by a former client), to be physically abusive and unfaithful in love.

• During a tribal dinner a client begins to discuss his personal problems with you in such a manner that you fear others may overhear.

Preparing paraprofessional mental health workers to cope with the above types of situations requires thorough training in the laws regarding confidentiality of client information. Supervision, discussion between mental health and tribal social services staff and role-playing of these types of delicate situations can be helpful.

Because tribal community life presents many situations which may not be foreseen, it is not a simple matter to devise clear and all encompassing confidentiality rules. Workers must realize that keeping confidentiality is crucial in gaining client trust. Mental Health Center staff must recognize that keeping confidentiality in the tribal community is difficult and that Support Counselors must often make decisions which are more subtle and complex than is typical in mainstream programs. (See Chapter 20.)

STAFF CHANGES

People in the tribal community prefer continuity and stability; changes in program staff can lead to disruption of client services. This is particularly true because of the strong preference for seeking help from persons who are well known in the community and because of the relatively long time required for a new helper to become accepted.

Some turnover in tribal mental health workers is to be expected. Although turnover in the Skagit Tribe's Mental Health Program has been minimal (for example, over the course of the first six and a half years there was a change in only two of five positions and our remaining support counselor has now been with the program for 14 years), these changes have posed some challenge to the program.

New workers are generally at different points in their academic and professional preparation. Staff changes therefore necessitate restructuring of training plans and staff schedules. It has sometimes been necessary to review material which has previously been covered in staff meetings or training groups. *Staff turnover necessitates special efforts in order to maintain group cohesiveness and provide ongoing staff education.*

Flexibility regarding staff roles and percentage of time worked is also necessary in order to meet program goals and accommodate the unique personal circumstances and skills of tribal mental health staff.

For example, the Tribal Mental Health Program has employed a tribal elder since the beginning of the program. For the first year she worked 3/4 time as a Support Counselor. Later, she chose to reduce to half time to better accommodate her energy level. At that time, she and the Program Director agreed to change her title and job description to "Cultural Consultant" in order to more accurately reflect her particular role and responsibilities. At the age of 77, she chose to further reduce her time. At the age of 80 she continued to function as our Consultant on an 'as needed' basis rather than on a fixed schedule. At the age of 90 she is still a strong support to our program.The flexibility to make these changes prevented our losing this very valuable member of our team. (See also Ch. 13, Developments in Swinomish Tribal Mental Health Program.)

BARRIERS TO DEVELOPING WRITTEN DESCRIPTIONS OF CULTURAL APPROACHES

In order to be culturally appropriate, tribal mental health programs must first identify just how Indian culture and belief systems pertain to the delivery of mental health services. It is necessary to show funding sources, administrators and evaluators how and why program services must be adapted to tribal culture.

This is not always easy: it is difficult to explain complex cultural differences in terms which can be easily understood by people lacking familiarity with tribal life. Written descriptions can be especially difficult, because many Indian people feel uncomfortable or mistrustful of written documents. Attempts, such as this book, to present Indian viewpoints in writing are important steps, but can never give a complete picture of Indian culture.

The cultural orientation of our program has become increasingly clear over the years. Many discussions among our team members and with consultants have helped us to define our model. Putting our approaches in writing forced us to think through many problems.

Describing the cultural knowledge upon which our therapeutic approaches has been difficult, due to:
* time constraints
* the subtlety of cultural perspectives

• the cultural sensitivity of certain matters.

In particular, there is a strong feeling that certain Indian spiritual beliefs and practices should not be recorded or analyzed. This has sometimes made it difficult to describe, justify and further develop models of culturally congruent mental health service for Indian communities, especially since cooperation with traditional healing is an important aspect of our approach. We have responded to these challenges by:

1. *Limiting written descriptions of culturally sensitive material, especially in client charts*
2. *Discussing all cultural matters in the staff seminar and with Cultural Consultants before writing about them*
3. *Having Tribal Support Counselors and our Cultural Consultant review written materials to be sure that they reflect Indian views.*

CHALLENGES FACING NON-INDIAN PROVIDERS WORKING ON RESERVATIONS

It is no simple matter for a newcomer or non-Indian to acquire the necessary cultural knowledge and social acceptance needed in order to function effectively as a mental health worker in a tribal community. Newcomers often underestimate cultural differences between tribal and mainstream communities and mistakenly assume that mainstream mental health approaches can be easily modified to fit the tribal situation.

Too often, newcomers take it upon themselves to try to change established ways of doing things in the tribal community. Non-Indians especially need to spend time learning about the Indian point of view and must realize that it is up to them to adjust their role, services and expectations to fit into the Indian world, rather than vice versa.

Professionals coming into Indian communities often mistakenly assume that their expertise will be automatically recognized and valued. The typical mainstream expectation that a professional should take charge and move quickly to get things done is liable to be interpreted as presumptuous and disrespectful in

Indian communities. Non-Indian professionals must be careful to avoid the trap, so common in the history of Indian/ White relationships, of attempting to "save" or "educate" the Indians. *It is important for outsiders to avoid being either 'pushy' or judgmental.*

Some tribal members feel resentful when non-Indians are hired to work at the tribe. *A newcomer to the tribal community, particularly a non-Indian, should expect to be observed and tested over a period of time.* In general, it is necessary to be seen and met personally before being accepted as a helper. Simply waiting for clients to make office appointments is generally ineffective.

Mainstream mental health professionals may unintentionally and unknowingly offend people in the tribal community. A formal interview and intake style is liable to offend clients. Professional "jargon", rapid speech, and long words may be perceived by some Indian clients as intentional put-downs. Newcomers to the tribal community need to re-examine their style of communication from the Indian viewpoint. In order to do this, they should ask for feedback from tribal members concerning how they are being perceived.

Hiring and training Indian tribal mental health workers avoids many of these difficulties. However, when Indian mental health professionals are not available or do not have a particular kind of expertise, it may be necessary to hire non-Indian specialists. Also, *in certain cases clients from the tribal community prefer to seek mental health services from non-tribal members or even non-Indians due to concerns about confidentiality or social pressures.*

It is difficult, but not impossible for non-Indians to be effective mental health workers in the tribal context. The sensitive non-Indian mental health worker can bring a fresh perspective to the difficulties experienced by Indian clients. The non-Indian worker who does not take things for granted, has taken the time to become accepted in the tribal community and who is sincere in his/her support of Indian cultural identity can be a valuable asset to a tribal mental health program.

(See Chapter 22 for suggestions to newcomers and non-Indians working in tribal communities.)

Chapter Nineteen
Case Examples

T the following three cases illustrate the kinds of clients seen and services provided through the Tribal Mental Health Program. They have been generalized from many experiences of our Tribal Mental Health Team members and do not represent any specific situations or persons. The names are not those of any known persons.

CASE #1 – MARCUS TOMMY

Acute hallucinatory and conversion state in a chronically anxious elderly man.
(DSM IV diagnosis: Somatization Disorder; Priority: Acute exacerbation of chronic illness).

Initial Problems

Marcus Tommy is an elderly, traditional Indian man with a long history of physical and emotional problems, including alcohol abuse. He has difficulty hearing, heart problems, and complains of fluctuating pains. He describes himself as "nervous" and has a history of going from one physician to another when displeased with the treatment. Marcus has experienced a great deal of tragedy and hardship, including the death of several children.

Recently Marcus has experienced a number of severe stresses. The death of his wife resulted in sadness, guilt, anger and loneliness. A recent hospitalization due to sudden and intense heart palpitations was both frightening and socially isolating to this traditional Indian elder. Marcus' children report that he has become forgetful, accusing and dependent. He has crying spells, alternating with angry outbursts. He also complains of head pains and sudden weakness.

Over the past year, Marcus' children and grandchildren have spent less time with him. He resents their attempts to stop him from drinking alcohol and has accused them both of neglecting him and of bossing him around. Marcus' dependency and anger frustrate family members and tend to drive them away.

When Marcus' doctor told his family that his problems were due to his being "thin-skinned" and "over-wrought", his daughter contacted one of the Tribal Support Counselors for advice. The daughter feared that the doctor meant literally that Marcus' skin was too thin and that he might be 'rotting' physically, but she had not felt comfortable asking the doctor for clarification. The Support Counselor reassured her that the doctor's use of the terms "thin-skinned" and "over-wrought" probably meant that Marcus was nervous, emotionally sensitive and liable to over-react to stress.

Soon after, Marcus became acutely disturbed and mildly disoriented. He began to experience crying spells, agitation, sleeplessness and to complain of seeing threatening visions. He was excitable, fearful and afraid of the dark. He also developed a sudden stiffness in his legs and had difficulty in standing. He appeared to experience brief periods of deafness. His daughter again contacted the Support Counselor, asking for assistance in a spiritual healing effort to take place at Marcus' home that evening led by an Indian Spiritual Healer, usually referred to as an "Indian Doctor".

Treatment Goals

Treatment goals (as developed by the Tribal Support Counselor in consultation with Marcus, family members, The Spiritual Healer and the Program Supervisor) included:
1. To obtain a thorough evaluation of Marcus' mental status
2. To obtain symptom relief and decrease in his anxiety
3. To identify possible spiritual disturbance
4. To assist Marcus' family to meet to his realistic needs

Services Provided

The Tribal Support Counselor assisted the Indian Spiritual Healer in a healing session at Marcus' home, lasting several hours. While it would not be appropriate to discuss here the details of this healing effort, several features can be mentioned without betraying spiritual trust:

- First, **the treatment used symbols, objects, songs, and prayers familiar to and trusted by the client.**
- Second, **the treatment was designed to alleviate the problem as understood and perceived by the client;** the spiritual work focused upon removing spiritual dangers, recognizing and respecting his spiritual/emotional turmoil and helping him to gain control of his experience.
- **Third, the treatment brought together extended family members in a nurturing and supportive way, with Marcus as the center of attention.** He was told that his spiritual life was all "mixed up", that he needed to concentrate on traditional cultural activities, and to follow the orders of his doctor.

Attention was also given to the needs of Marcus' family. Family disagreements, responsibilities and feelings of guilt were aired. It became apparent that some relatives were spending less time with Marcus since his daughter had accused them of visiting him only in order to "mooch" food, whereas they had meant to help care for him. Several family members felt frustrated and guilty at not being able to relieve Marcus' anxiety and pain and had fallen into the pattern of trying to meet all of his demands even when these were unreasonable.

The Tribal Support Counselor and the Spiritual Healer both "talked to the family", and tried to "build up their thinking", to encourage cooperation and to relieve the feelings of undue responsibility.

Although Marcus felt better after this session, he insisted soon after that the family call in a different Indian Spiritual Healer. When this traditional specialist learned of the previous treatment, he told Marcus and his family that they needed to "straighten up their thinking", "stick with one thing" and that "there is no one magic cure".

The next step taken was to arrange for a staff person from the Mental Health Center's Geriatric Outreach Program to make a home visit accompanied by the Tribal Support Counselor, in order to evaluate Marcus' condition and needs. The Tribal Support Counselor explained the purpose of this meeting to Marcus and his family. They felt that this meeting was helpful in further clarifying Marcus' needs. Marcus agreed to see the psychiatrist at the Mental Health Center for an evaluation of his medication needs. An agreement was also made for the Geriatric Outreach staff person to make bi-monthly home visits along with the Tribal Support Counselor.

The Support Counselor took Marcus to see the Community Mental Health Center Psychiatrist shortly after the session described above. The Psychiatrist felt that improvement had been significant following the previous interventions, such that medication was not needed.

Outcome

Marcus responded well to the treatment. His acute symptoms disappeared immediately following the intervention with the Spiritual Healer: he regained full mobility, ceased to see threatening visions, ceased having crying spells and seemed less anxious. The treatment resulted in decreased family tensions and increased support of Marcus. Family expressed more hope and appeared more willing to communicate with Marcus and with one another. The family rallied around him not only during the traditional service, but continued to show concern over a longer period.

Comment on Outcome

This case illustrates cooperation between the Tribal Mental Health Program, Spiritual Practitioners and other community mental health staff. All three types of services were needed to meet this client's needs.

The Tribal Support Counselor made initial contact with this traditional client and family. She assessed needs and arranged other needed services. Traditional spiritual help was needed to satisfy the spiritual needs of both the client and family. Both Spiritual Healers involved in this case developed sophisticated psychological evaluations and provided effective family therapy. Additional services from the Mental Health Center included both Geriatric Outreach and Psychiatric consultation. These services were helpful in ruling out neurological problems, in reassuring the family and in developing a workable ongoing treatment team.

The role of the Tribal Support Counselor deserves emphasis:
- *First, she was contacted at a time of crisis primarily because she was known and trusted by the family and because she was culturally qualified to assist in a traditional healing session.*
- *Second, she was able to communicate with the client and family in the local Indian style of speaking, something non- Indians could not do.*
- *Third, her training enabled her to recognize the need for additional mental health services.*
- *Fourth, she was an active facilitator and participant in all sessions with non-Indian helpers, in order to ensure communication.*

The involvement of family members in treatment is characteristic of many Tribal Mental Health cases. In Indian culture almost all matters are family matters. Medical or mental health treatments must take this into account in order to be effective.

Cooperation of the family is essential to successful treatment and follow-through. In addition to care of the 'identified patient', it is important to assess and meet family needs. Individual treatment is often unsuccessful whereas family treatment is effective. This is both because individual distress may be symptomatic of family dysfunction and because family participation is culturally defined as necessary for cure.

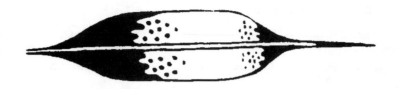

CASE #2 – EMMY DAVID

Conduct Disorder in a ten year old girl undergoing accultura-
tion trauma (DSM IV diagnosis: Conduct Disorder. Priority: Serious).

Presenting Problem

Emmy David is a ten year old Indian girl referred to the Tribal Mental Health Program by her school counselor. Emmy, one of few Indian children in her school, had become a behavior problem to teachers and school administration. She had been involved in repeated fights at school and was achieving well below her grade level despite normal ability. She was described as " hostile" and "withdrawn", with poor communication and social skills.

School attempts to work with Emmy's parents had been unsuccessful. Her father, a recovering alcoholic, was very angry about the school's treatment of his daughter. Although he often found his daughter's behavior to be a problem at home, he blamed school prejudice for her problems and supported her anger.

When the Tribal Support Counselor met with Emmy and her parents, she learned that Emmy felt misunderstood and picked on by other kids at school. Emmy saw the teacher as unsupportive and had decided that she needed to protect herself by being tough and not showing feelings. According to the school, Emmy was the problem. According to her parents, "school" was the problem. According to Emmy, she had "no problem." According to Emmy she had "no problem". According to her parents, "school" was the problem.

Treatment Goals

The following treatment goals were cooperatively established between Emmy, her parents and the Tribal Support Counselor. Goals included:

1. Assist Emmy in identifying and expressing feelings, including but not limited to anger.

2. Help her to learn constructive ways of expressing anger without fighting.
3. Explore Emmy's identity issues, particularly her Indian identity and her feelings about being an Indian student in a predominately white school.
4. Explore possible difficulties related to parent-child relationships, including possible history of alcohol related abuse or neglect.
5. Assist school staff to develop a better understanding of Indian culture and needs.

Services Provided

The Tribal Support Counselor met with the school counselor and teacher in order to get a clear understanding of their concerns, and to attempt to educate them about the possible conflicts facing an Indian child in this situation. Out of this meeting came a general realization that Emmy may not have been the only child picking fights and that the school needed to take steps not only to protect her, but also to deal with the school wide problem of aggression.

Next, the Support Counselor met with Emmy and her parents in order to obtain the views of each. Thereafter, the Support Counselor met each week with Emmy, picking her up at school or at home and going for walks or drives. During these meetings they discussed feelings and ways of expressing them, and practiced writing down feelings and expressing them. Emmy's relationship with her alcoholic father and younger brother became increasingly the focus of concern. Emmy and the Support Counselor explored what it was like for her as a young Indian child in a predominately non-Indian school.

Weekly sessions continued for three months. At that time Emmy and the Support Counselor decided to meet only monthly unless Emmy requested more frequent contact.

Outcome

Emmy and the Tribal Support Counselor developed a good rapport, which allowed her to begin expressing her feelings. Her increased self acceptance resulted in her learning new ways to relate to others.

By the end of the counseling sessions, Emmy had stopped

fighting with other children. However, she still seemed to be generally 'angry' at the world. It had become apparent that her anger and frustration were not confined to the school but included both family and tribal targets as well. Some tribal members considered Emmy to be disrespectful of her elders and of traditional activities. They also expressed disapproval of Emmy's father's failing to take responsibility for her behavior.

Discussion

There have been many gains through the services provided to Emmy and it is reasonable to expect that further contact may result in further improvement. However, treatment has not resolved all of Emmy's difficulties.

The gains are in three main areas:

First, school authorities seem to have broadened their perspective on Emmy's problems. Instead of seeing her as the main source of the problem, they now realize that the prejudice of other students and the lack of adequate school response have contributed to her difficulties.

Second, Emmy developed a trusting relationship with a young Indian woman Support Counselor who provided a positive role model. This was especially important to this girl who is living in an environment where she frequently faces prejudice toward Indians. Emmy had become quite isolated from Indians other than her family. Her angry and distrustful attitude had also made it difficult for her to form friendships.

The Support Counselor was a good role model because she is Indian, has succeeded in a non-Indian environment, and is deeply sensitive to issues of cultural conflict and identity. Her ability to deal with school authorities helped win Emmy's confidence.

Third, Emmy made great strides in being able to express her feelings. This was made possible by the rapport established and by the casual and non-threatening approach to treatment.

Unresolved problems remain. Emmy's great difficulty with trust has made it necessary to proceed slowly. Her father's unwillingness to take responsibility has been a barrier to treatment and also suggests underlying family problems.

There are also cultural reasons why this type of treatment poses problems. Indian people are frequently not oriented towards keeping regular weekly appointments and may see verbalization of feelings as a "white man's" approach. Emmy's father has had difficulty accepting help and is very sensitive to any implied criticism of his parenting. It is particularly difficult for this middle aged Indian man to accept help from a young woman who at age 25, might not be considered to be fully adult in traditional Indian society.

Despite these drawbacks, this approach was chosen because it seemed to best fit Emmy's needs. It was imperative for Emmy to change aggressive behaviors which were leading to school failure. It was also critical for Emmy to have regular contact in order to allow trust to develop. The on-going goal is for the Support Counselor to meet at least monthly with Emmy and to seek to establish a deeper trust with both Emmy and with her parents. The Support Counselor functions as a role model and emotional support, not as a directive, analytical or questioning therapist.

CASE #3 – CHARLEY BEN
Suicide attempt in a young man (DSM IV diagnosis: Major Depression, Priority: Acute)

Presenting Problems

This young Indian man came to the attention of program staff following a serious suicide attempt. Charley Ben had been socially withdrawn, moody, periodically violent and preoccupied with death for approximately one year, since the tragic death of his six-year old son and subsequent divorce. He had begun frequent drinking to the point of intoxication, during which he became impulsively self destructive. The suicide of a close friend had led to further disillusionment, alienation and self blame. He had also become quite dependent on his girlfriend, towards whom he was periodically physically abusive.

Following an intoxicated fight during which she threatened to leave him, Charley shot himself in the chest. Emergency medical procedures were necessary to save his life.

Services Provided

The hospital physician contacted the Program Supervisor to arrange a post-discharge appointment for Charley. The same day Charley's mother came to see the Program Supervisor and a Support Counselor. (Being contacted at this time of crisis probably occurred only because of a pre-existing relationship between the Counselor and Charley's mother). She was given emotional support and specific suggestions about what to do in the event of a second suicide attempt. She requested services for Charley and also asked the Support Counselor to come immediately to the home of Charley's great-aunt, who was extremely upset.

The counselor arrived to find Charley's parents, great-aunt sisters and girlfriend in the living room. Charley himself lay on the couch with his face to the wall holding his girlfriend's hand and not speaking. Other relatives came and went during the two-and-a-half-hour session which followed.

During this meeting the counselor focused on pointing out and reinforcing family strengths, including the mother's devotion, the great-aunt's role as respected elder, the emotional bond between Charley and his girlfriend and the community support. The counselor tried to support the roles of all family members by expressing empathy for the mother's pain, telling the great-aunt that she was not at fault and was loved and respected by all, and stating that although Charley should not be pressured to talk that night, that he would be able to discuss his experiences the following day in his appointment with the therapist.

When the great-aunt raised concerns about possible spiritual dangers effecting the whole family, the therapist supported their seeking traditional spiritual help. Family members decided to call in the help of a nearby Indian Shaker healer that night.

The next day, Charley and his girlfriend met with the counselor. Problems in their relationship were discussed, including Charley's jealousy and resentment of family interference. They discussed her father's wish to have her enter a spiritual group and Charley's concerns about this. Charley discussed his fear that she would leave him, as well as his depression, and thoughts of death. Although Charley refused to make a "no-suicide contract", he thanked the counselor and shook hands over an agreement for regular, twice-weekly therapy sessions.

Soon after, Charley's girlfriend entered a spiritual organization at her tribe. Charley was upset because this meant that she would be away from him for several weeks. He reacted by getting drunk and threatening to shoot himself. His mother contacted the Support Counselor who phoned the police. Charley was taken to the hospital where he was held for several days. The Tribal Support Counselor spent several hours comforting the upset family.

After the Program Supervisor had spoken with a psychiatrist from the hospital, Charley was discharged with follow-up counseling to be provided through the Tribal Mental Health Program. The night before Charley's discharge, his mother, brother and great aunt went to the home of the Support Counselor to discuss plans for his care, including spiritual treatments. A plan for collaboration was confirmed.

During the next month, Charley received three kinds of help. First, he was seen eight times in individual counseling. Despite initial guardedness, he kept his appointments and discussed a variety of personal problems, including his fear that all women would leave him, his preoccupation with death and guilt, his sense of personal doom, his resentment of family pressures, his inability to control his drinking, his difficulty sorting out his heritage from two very different Indian tribes, and his related indecision as to which of two Indian spiritual paths he would follow.

It soon became clear that Charley's suicidal thoughts, social withdrawal, chronic worry and difficulty making decisions were connected to his fears about growing up, having to make decisions and accepting adult realities, including death. The series of traumatic events which he had experienced had undermined his self confidence and left him, feeling angry, dependent and helpless.

Therapeutic goals were:

(1) *to help Charley develop an understanding of how his self destructive feelings were related to the impasse in his development,*

(2) *to help Charley commit himself to constructive adult roles, such as family responsibilities, a career choice, a non-abusive love relationship, an integration of his cultural heritage, and a commitment to a spiritual tradition.*

The second kind of help Charley received was spiritual help provided by a powerful Indian doctor at the family's request. The Support Counselor helped to arrange this treatment, which took place at the family home. The traditional healer performed spiritual 'work' to remove dangerous influences, to strengthen the spirits of all family members, and to heal Charley's strained family relationships.

The third kind of help came through Charley's attendance at traditional ceremonies to support his girlfriend. Although not allowed to talk to her, he was expected to be present, to help bring in firewood, serve coffee, participate in drumming, and otherwise give his support. Charley was at first unsure of his appropriate role. Since another of the program's Support Counselors was a worker in the girlfriend's spiritual group, she was able to provide guidance and emotional support to Charley.

Services through the Tribal Mental Health Program ended when Charley himself entered a spiritual group at another tribe with similar spiritual values. This was a crucial step for Charley in resolving his deep psychological ambivalence and developmental impasse.

Outcome

Charley completed his spiritual training. This re-established the balance in his relationship with his girlfriend, improved his social status in traditional Indian society, and represented both a long-term spiritual commitment and a partial resolution of his cultural identity conflict.

Charley made no further suicide attempts or threats over the next ten years. He appeared more cheerful, less troubled and less withdrawn. He was better able to communicate with his family and formed new social relationships. He began classes at the local community college and has gone for long periods without drinking. However, ups and downs continued in his relationship with his girlfriend. Both of them continued to participate in spiritual activities.

Comments on Outcome:

The key features of this case are:

1. *The client's multiple presenting problems, including suicide attempts, grief, alcohol abuse, violence, spiritual distress, cultural identity confusion, dysphoria and social withdrawal.*
2. *The crisis oriented nature of some of the problems and services offered,* including immediate response to family distress, after hours and weekend services and intervention into a suicide attempt.
3. *The teamwork between the program supervisor/ a mainstream psychiatrist, two Tribal Support Counselors at two tribes, an Indian doctor, a Shaker healer, spiritual experts, and extended family members.* Complex interpersonal relationships with multiple roles were involved.
4. *The involvement in treatment of several members of the extended family, at least three of whom also received some service.*
5. *The interface at four points of traditional Indian spiritual treatment with mental health service, including: a Shaker healing, participation in the girlfriend's spiritual activities, the work of an Indian doctor, and the client himself becoming a member of another spiritual group.*

Although not all program cases involve all of the above features, this case is not unique and exemplifies the complexity of client problems, family and work roles, and services offered. Although it is impossible to determine which services were most helpful, it seems clear that the pre-established personal relationships, the involvement of extended family, the availability of services in the tribal community, home visits and support for spiritual services were crucial components. It seems likely that the Support Counselor's intervention prevented a second suicide attempt. Individual therapy may have helped Charley to clarify the sources of his distress, identify his options and integrate aspects of his personal and cultural identity. Traditional spiritual services were critical in roviding reassurance and cementing culturally meaningful roles.

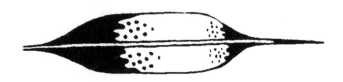

Chapter Twenty
Tribal Mental Health
Program Policies

E xcept as described below all policies of Skagit
Community Mental Health Center, apply to
the tribal Mental Health Program. Differences
reflect the cultural and practical demands of this
tribally-based program.

These policies resulted from our experiences
over the first seven years in providing culturally-
oriented mental health services to two specific
tribal communities. Changes have been made in
these policies as our program has evolved. Thus,
they are not seen as final.

While some of our policies may not fit the
needs of other tribal communities or mental
health agencies, we hope that sharing these
examples may be helpful to other tribal and
mental health programs as they develop practical
guidelines suited to their unique situations.

Tribal Mental Health Program Policies included in this Chapter are:

- Confidentiality and Service Agreement between Skagit Community Mental Health Center, the Swinomish Tribal Community and the Upper Skagit Tribe.
- Agreement with Tribal Mental Health Supervisor, not employed by Skagit Community Mental Health Center.
- Tribal Support Counselor Personnel Policies.
  1. Work hours and schedules
  2. Benefits
- Client Eligibility for Program Services
- Client Referral and Intake Procedures
  1. Referral Procedures
  2. Intake Procedures
  3. Obtaining the Client's Consent to Receive Services
- Location and Timing of Client Services
- Crisis Intervention Policies
- Transportation Policy
- Cooperation with Traditional healers and Spiritual Organizations
- Confidentiality Guidelines for Tribal Support Counselors

CONFIDENTIALITY AND SERVICE AGREEMENT BETWEEN SKAGIT COMMUNITY MENTAL HEALTH CENTER, THE SWINOMISH TRIBAL COMMUNITY AND THE UPPER SKAGIT TRIBE

This agreement outlines the conditions for Skagit Community Mental Health Center's provision of mental health services within the Swinomish and Upper Skagit Tribal Communities, with particular reference to the "Skagit Tribes' Mental Health Program."

Tribal Social Services

The Swinomish Tribal Community and the Upper Skagit Tribe each provide social, educational and health services for Indian clients on their respective reservations. These programs operate under the direction of the tribal governments. Each Tribal social and health program is therefore a branch of the Swinomish or Upper Skagit Tribal service organization, even though programs are funded by a variety of sources. Day to day operation of tribal programs is coordinated at the tribal level, with each program providing its specialized service in the context of a continuum of care to clients. Thus, each program operates under Tribal service policies and procedures, (which for Swinomish are outlined in the "Swinomish Social and Health Services Policies". Specifically, each tribal provider makes and receives referrals, provides and seeks case and program consultation, and exchanges information concerning clients with other Tribal providers who have a need for such information in order to ensure quality services.

Both tribes provide basic medical care through the services of a nurse practitioner and/or physician, and through community health representatives (CHR's) who provide outreach and follow-up. Both tribes also provide dental services, an elders' program, and certain educational and vocational services.

Some mental health services are provided by Tribal staff. Tribal Child Welfare and Alcoholism services are also available.

Skagit Tribes' Mental Health Program

Skagit Community Mental Health Center provides a variety of mental health services to Skagit County residents, including a special Tribal Mental Health Program in cooperation with the Upper Skagit and Swinomish Tribes. This program is designed to increase the quality and extent of mental health services to Indian clients in Skagit County by providing trained Tribal Support Counselors to work in the two reservation communities. Support Counselors, though Community Mental Health Center employees, are based in the Tribal community and form a component of the Tribal social service teams. The Program is directed and coordinated by the Community Mental Health Center, with input from an Advisory Board made up of tribal representatives.

Support Counselors receive supervision from mental health professionals for their counseling, case management, preventive and outreach work. Support Counselors work cooperatively with both Tribal and Mental Health Center staff in helping Indian clients gain access to and understanding of all appropriate services.

Agreement

Skagit Community Mental Health Center, the Upper Skagit Tribe and the Swinomish Tribal Community agree that:

1. Four Support Counselors will be employed by Skagit Community Mental Health Center, two of who will be based at Swinomish and two at Upper Skagit.

2. The Support Counselors will form a component of the social services team of the tribe at which they work. They will: (a.) follow Tribal social service and office policies, (b.) participate in tribal case conferences, (c.) seek consultation from tribal staff as needed, (d.) make and receive referrals among tribal staff.

3. Support Counselors will also form a component of Skagit Community Mental Health Center's services: they may participate in staff meetings and case conferences, seek consultation and make and receive referrals among Mental Health Center staff.

4. The Tribal Mental Health Program will be administered and monitored by the Mental Health Center, with planning and evaluation from an Advisory Board made up of tribal representatives.

5. Overall program supervision and coordination of training and work assignments will be the responsibility of the Program Director.

6. Day to day administration of work schedules, office space, use of equipment, secretarial support, etc., will be provided by a Tribal Coordinator/Administrator assigned by the Tribe.

7. Clinical supervision of Support Counselors' client cases will be provided at the tribe by mental health professionals employed as detailed in the "Field Placement Plan". (See Part V.)

8. Program staff, other Mental Health Center staff, and Tribal staff will be mutually bound to keep confidential all client information exchanged in the course of program operation.

9. Support Counselors will maintain client files at tribal sites. Record keeping will conform to customary tribal procedures, as well as to the reporting requirements of the Mental Health Center. Client service statistics will be submitted to the Mental Health Center on a monthly basis.

10. Office space, desks, utilities and secretarial support will be provided by the Tribes.

11. All other program expenses, including salaries, mileage, xeroxing, supplies, long distance calls, tuition and training materials, will be provided by the Mental Health Center.

Skagit Community Mental Health Center Director   Date

Upper Skagit Tribal Chairman   Date

Swinomish Tribal Senate Chairman   Date

Tribal Mental Health Project
P.O. Box 388 • La Conner, Washington 98257 • Phone (360) 466-3163

AGREEMENT WITH TRIBAL MENTAL HEALTH SUPERVISORS NOT EMPLOYED BY SKAGIT COMMUNITY MENTAL HEALTH CENTER

I_____agree to provide professional supervision and case consultation to Support Counselors of Skagit Community Mental Health Center's Tribal Mental Health Program who provide direct client services at the _____tribe. I will support program policies and will consult periodically with the Program Director. I agree to be bound by Skagit Community Mental Health Center's confidentiality policy and not to disclose information concerning agency clients to any other party, except as may be required by law.

Signed_____

Date_____

A Cooperative Effort

Swinomish Tribal Community	*Skagit Community Mental Health Center*	*Upper Skagit Indian Tribe*
P.O. Box 388	*208 Kincaid*	*2284 Community Plaza*
La Conner, WA 98257	*Mt. Vernon, WA 98273*	*Sedro-Woolley, WA 98284*

TRIBAL SUPPORT COUNSELOR PERSONNEL POLICIES

These personnel policies have been developed in order to:

- Clarify the work responsibilities of the Tribal Support Counselors
- Clarify differences between Tribal Mental Health Policies and other Community Mental Health Center Program policies.

Work Hours and Schedules

Tribal Support Counselors generally work 75% time, with roughly 35% time devoted to training and supervision and 40% to direct service provision. Schedules are arranged with the program supervisor, and may vary from time to time. Support Counselors work their full hours each week unless other arrangements have been made ahead of time. However, the program allows for considerable flexibility in scheduling, such that Support Counselors can respond to emergency and after hours client needs. It is the responsibility of each Support Counselor to keep the Program Director informed about his/her after hours work, so that arrangements can be made for schedule changes as needed. If it is necessary for Support Counselors to be more than half an hour late for work or classes, they are asked to call the Program Supervisor or Tribal Coordinator. Repeated lateness results in a review by the Supervisor and may lead to the Support Counselor being placed on probation.

Benefits

Tribal Support Counselors have the same benefits as other Mental Health Center employees, including vacation, sick leave, medical insurance and retirement. These benefits differ in some ways from those of employees of the Tribes.

It is the Mental Health Center policy that vacation cannot be taken in the first 6 months of employment. After that, vacation may be taken with pre-approval by the Program Supervisor. Sick leave may be taken as needed up to the amount earned. When ill, the Support Counselor must let the Program Supervisor or Tribal Coordinator know within the first hour of the day. If the period of illness exceeds accrued sick leave, this time must be taken without pay, unless special approval is given for an emergency medical leave, as outlined in the agency policies. Tribal Support Counselors receive all holidays granted to other Community Mental Health Center Staff. In addition, administrative leave is granted for other holidays or closures observed by the Tribe at which the Support Counselor works. This includes Tribal closures for Treaty Day, funerals and other closures declared by Tribal government or administration. All such leave must be cleared ahead of time by the Program Supervisor.

CLIENT ELIGIBILITY FOR PROGRAM SERVICES

The Skagit Tribes' Mental Health Program serves Indian people who fall into one of the three "priority population" categories defined by the Washington State Division of Mental Health. Program services are available to members of the Upper Skagit and Swinomish Tribal Communities, including enrolled tribal members, and other Indian people living in or closely affiliated with one of these two tribal communities. **Tribal and cultural definitions of community membership and Indian status form the basis for determining eligibility.**

Skagit Community Mental Health Center has a service agreement with the Swinomish and Upper Skagit Tribal Communities. It is therefore necessary that the program primarily focus on service to these communities. It is important to protect our valuable working relationship with these tribal organizations, as well as to maintain clear program purposes and achievable objectives. It is also important not to intrude upon the sovereignty of other tribes by providing services in their communities without the approval of appropriate tribal authorities.

It was the original intent of this program to serve only Indian clients residing in the Swinomish or Upper Skagit Tribal Communities. *However, it has been necessary to somewhat expand and clarify our service eligibility guidelines.* Upon occasion Indian clients from tribes outside of Skagit County or even outside of Washington State, have requested services from Tribal Support Counselors. *These situations have fallen into four general categories:*

- Indian people living in Skagit County but not on either the Upper Skagit or Swinomish reservation.

- clients from other tribes who are temporarily residing at Swinomish or Upper Skagit.
- clients from other tribes who come to Swinomish or Upper Skagit to ask help from one of the Tribal Support Counselors.
- Indian people from outside of Skagit County who ask Support Counselors to travel to their homes to provide services.

Because of the closely interwoven nature of Indian family, social and Tribal networks, it is often appropriate to provide services in the four situations noted above. In most cases, clients from outside of the Swinomish and Upper Skagit Communities who seek program services are extended family members of other clients. **Coast Salish Indian People recognize large extended family systems with complex family ties linking people belonging from many different Tribes in Washington, Oregon and in British Columbia.** It is a goal of the Tribal Mental Health Program to serve not only chronically, acutely and seriously disturbed Indian individuals but also to serve their extended families. Therefore it is often necessary to serve people who are not themselves members of the Swinomish or Upper Skagit Tribal Communities.

Historically, Coast Salish Indian People have often moved from one tribal community to another, and frequently back and forth across the Washington-British Columbia border. Because of this traditional mobility and the fact that many Indian people have close family members living on either side of this border, *it has been the policy of the Washington State Department of Social and Health Services (D.S.H.S.) to recognize all Canadian born Indian people as eligible for state funded social services. Thus, both tribal cultural traditions and established state policy have encouraged flexibility in interpretations of program service eligibility criteria.*

It is not uncommon for Coast Salish Indian People to seek help from healers of other tribes, particularly for spiritual problems. Some of the Support Counselors have traditional spiritual helping roles in the Indian Community. This has at times increased the likelihood of their services being requested by Indians from other tribal groups. Role conflicts have been avoided by the Support Counselors often providing such spiritual services on their "own time". However, it is inevitable in this type of program that some overlap of traditional services and mental health services will occur.

Because of the above considerations, **it is the policy of the Skagit Tribes' Mental Health Program that all Indian people who meet State Division of Mental Health priority population criteria are eligible for services,** *provided that they are either:*

1. Members of the Swinomish or Upper Skagit Tribal Communities regardless of whether or not they are enrolled tribal members.
2. Enrolled members of the Upper Skagit or Swinomish Tribes regardless of whether or not they live on the reservation.
3. Temporarily residing in the Swinomish or Upper Skagit Tribal Communities.
4. Residing in Skagit County.
5. Extended family members of clients, regardless of their residence.

Services provided outside of Skagit County are generally not recorded in the MIS reporting system or in client charts; these services are instead documented in the "Alternative Community Services Tracking System" (see Part IV).

CLIENT REFERRAL AND INTAKE PROCEDURES

Client referrals and intake procedures are more flexible and informal in the Tribal Mental Health Program than is the norm in mainstream mental health programs. This is necessary for the following reasons:

1. **The two tribal communities we serve are small and close-knit:** most community members know one another well and often are familiar with each others' personal and family problems.
2. **Tribal Support Counselors often have pre-existing relationships with potential clients** and clients' families.
3. **Many Indian people are reluctant to request services for themselves;** in this culture it is more typical for family members to request help for a troubled relative.
4. **Many potential clients are unfamiliar with mental health services,** and their possible benefits: therefore they are unlikely to initiate a request for services.
5. **Indian people often expect a personal relationship with a helper,** and prefer to seek help from known individuals rather than from agencies. For this reason, clients are usually seen by the worker whom they first approach, rather than being reassigned to a different service provider.

6. *Many Indian people expect that help will be given immediately upon request;* some people feel puzzled, irritated or insulted if forced to go through a formal intake and evaluation process before being given service.
7. *Services are generally initiated and provided in the tribal community rather than at the Mental Health Center.* Clients make contact directly with Support Counselors rather than going through a receptionist. There is no clerical support for intake, consents and setting up charts.
8. *Many Indian people dislike formal and business-like procedures* which interfere with the personal relationship between client and helper.
9. *Many Indian people have a mistrust of written forms* and documents based upon negative past experiences and lack of familiarity with the purpose of such documents.

Referral Procedures

Referrals are accepted from a variety of tribal community sources as well as from non-tribal agencies. Family and friends are a frequent source of referrals. Referrals are often made by other social service providers working in the tribal community, such as alcoholism counselors, headstart teachers, nurses, nutritionists, early childhood educators or child welfare workers. Referrals are also accepted from school personnel, DSHS staff or other social service providers in the larger community. Any written referral is kept in the client's chart.

Intake Procedures

It is not required that clients of the tribal mental health program make a formal application for services prior to meeting with Tribal Support Counselors. Upon occasion Tribal Support Counselors approach clients to offer their services. This must be done in a sensitive manner, and frequently in a casual manner. Typically, the Tribal Support Counselor expresses concern for the potential client and may mention that family or tribal staff have expressed concern on that person's behalf. Clients may indicate their willingness to receive services simply by beginning to discuss personal problems with the Support Counselor. Typically, the relationship is gradually clarified and formalized over the first several sessions.

The Tribal Support Counselors discuss new cases with their Supervisors. The client's problems are discussed and decisions are made about what further information may be needed in order to form a diagnosis and treatment plan. Diagnosis and initial treatment plans are made jointly between Support Counselor and Supervisor.

Obtaining the Client's Consent to Receive Services

As mentioned above, many Indian people are distrustful of written forms and may be reluctant to sign consents for treatment. In traditional Indian communities agreements are sealed with a handshake or exchange of gifts. Some Indian clients may feel offended if asked to sign a consent for services which they have already agreed to verbally. Asking for written consent is particularly awkward with clients whom the Support Counselors already know well. Insisting that clients sign formal consents for service can put Support Counselors in an awkward and unproductive position. Even with clients whom they do not already know, the introduction of written forms can cause a break in the development of rapport.

The Tribal Mental Health Program's consent procedures and forms are as simple and non-intrusive as is possible within the State required limits. A brief disclosure statement and consent form have been developed, the "Tribal Support Counselor's Client Service Policy," and "Client's Consent to Receive Services." (See Part IV). These forms are written in clear and simple language, and minimize lengthy explanations. The Tribal Support Counselor explains the program's purpose, the client's rights, grievance procedures, confidentiality and conditions for mandated reporting. The client is given a copy of these procedures to read and keep. The client is then asked to sign a brief statement indicating an understanding of these policies and a willingness to receive program services. When handled in an informal yet matter of fact way, Tribal Support Counselors have been successful in getting signed consents from most clients.

However, at times a client is unwilling to sign a consent for treatment. In other instances cultural etiquette forbids the Support Counselor asking the client to sign (such as because of the client's age, relationship or crisis state). In such cases, the Support Counse-

lor signs a statement indicating the date when the client gave informed verbal consent. This Procedure is in compliance with WACS 275-56-260 and 275-56-265 as has been verified by the Washington State Division of Mental Health Minority Program Coordinator.

Due to the sensitive nature of many client-staff relationships and to the cultural distrust of written material, it has at times been necessary to delay obtaining formal consents for a considerable period after the beginning of services and until a therapeutic rapport has been developed. In some cases, it has not been possible to obtain signed or clearly informed verbal consent. In these cases client services are recorded as an "Alternate Community Services" without client names or diagnoses and no individual client chart is opened.

Individual Service Plans (ISP's) are verbally discussed between client and Support Counselor. In most cases the client is not required to sign the treatment plan, since it is felt that the signed consent for treatment is sufficient. Instead, the Tribal Support Counselor signs the treatment plan and enters the date when the client verbally agreed to the plan of service (See Part IV).

LOCATION AND TIMING OF CLIENT SERVICES

It is the policy of the Skagit Tribal Mental Health Program that client services be provided at times and places accessible and acceptable to Indian clients. Therefore, services must be provided at Tribal sites rather than at Community Mental Health Center offices. This ensures that program services are not only physically accessible to Tribal members, but are also perceived as being a part of the Tribal organization and social services. Ease of physical access and psychological accessibility are of equal importance in providing mental health services to Indian clients.

In mainstream mental health practice it is assumed that fixed times and settings are necessary to ensure good service to clients. It is also assumed that the client and therapist relationships should be restricted to counseling hours, in order to protect confidentiality and avoid role conflicts.

In the Tribal Mental Health Program, good service is ensured by operating within the physical setting and traditional social standards of the tribal community. Instead of having the client therapist relationship set off from the rest of social life, it is integrated into the overall functioning of the tribal community. This makes our services acceptable and comprehensible to our clients.

The "boundary" and "structural" guidelines observed in our program reflect the psychological boundaries and social norms of the tribal community, just as those in mainstream programs reflect mainstream expectations and norms. Whereas in mainstream culture, social life, work life, health and mental health care tend to be kept separate from one another, in tribal life they often blend into each other. In tribal life, important social boundaries are sometimes drawn between extended family groups or religious groups, and the roles of youth are more clearly differentiated from those of elders than is typical in mainstream society. *Perhaps the most important social "boundary" in tribal life is that between the tribal and non-tribal communities.*

It is our policy that the location and timing of tribal mental health services, as well as the client-therapist roles, should reflect tribal norms, expectations and social realities. While it may appear that the "boundary" and "structural" guidelines observed in our program are far more fluid than in mainstream programs, they are in fact simply different.

Client services are provided as frequently in client homes or other tribal sites as in staff offices. Services may be provided in tribal meeting rooms, at funerals, social functions or in the context of traditional Indian healing services. In short, *location of services is not restricted to offices or other prearranged sites: services are provided at locations convenient for clients.*

Appointments and Walk-in services

Appointments for client services are made whenever this seems consistent with client needs. However, appointments are frequently not kept and we do not consider missed appointments to be a cause for termination of services. Conversely, client services are quite frequently provided without appointments having been made.

Many Indian people operate on a more fluid and less structured time schedule. Clients frequently drop in to see mental health staff. It is a cultural expectation that providers of helping services will respond immediately to the client's need whenever possible. Therefore, tribal mental health staff generally do not know exactly which clients they will work with on a given day. Whenever possible, staff respond to the needs of clients when and where they occur. Although this can result in a crisis-oriented mode of service, it is also true that *clients in the tribal community return repeatedly to seek services from program staff.*

After Hours Service

Tribal Support Counselors are often asked for help after "normal" working hours. *This sort of 'immersion' in the tribal community is traditionally understood, honored and expected of people in helping roles.* Therefore, Tribal Support Counselors work flexible hours. Although Support Counselors are not formally "on call" and are not required to provide services outside of regular work hours, they are encouraged to do so when this does not interfere with personal or family plans.

Length of Client Sessions

The amount of time spent in a client session can also vary greatly. It is not unusual for Support Counselors to see some clients briefly on a daily basis. They are thus in a position to maintain close contact with the clients life and to provide frequent supportive feedback.

Conversely, it also occurs that clients may receive services of up to several hours at a time. This is particularly true in crisis situations or when Support Counselors assist clients in receiving Traditional Spiritual Healing Services, which can last several hours and may be repeated on consecutive days. A culturally oriented mental health program must also allow sufficient flexibility in the timing and duration of services to enable coordination with traditional healers.

CRISIS INTERVENTION PROCEDURES

General Crisis/Emergency Service Policy

Although, Support Counselors are encouraged to respond to emergency situations, "walk-ins" and after-hour client needs when possible, the Tribal Mental Health Program does not attempt to provide 24 hour emergency coverage and cannot guarantee staff availability to respond to crisis situations. If Support Counselors need consultation in crisis situations, they may call the Program Supervisor at home.

Suicide Intervention Policy

Tribal Support Counselors receive periodic training in assessing suicide potential and in procedures for intervening in high risk situations. *In the event of an acutely suicidal client, Support Counselors contact the Tribal Police* (or the County Sheriff if the Tribal Police are unavailable or if the client is not on the reservation) *and/or contact the local Crisis Line in order to reach an on-call mental health professional.* Support Counselors will attempt to get the client to speak with the on-call provider. In the event that the on-call professional needs to meet with a client in person, the Support Counselor may assist the client in getting to the emergency room of Skagit Valley Hospital where this meeting can take place.

Involuntary Hospitalization

In the event that Tribal Support Counselors encounter clients whom they judge to be in need of immediate detention in order to protect the client or others from harm, the Support Counselor will follow the procedure outlined above. When deemed appropriate by either the police or the on-call emergency service provider, the County Designated Mental Health Professional (CDMHP) will be called to evaluate the client for possible involuntary detention and hospitalization. *Tribal Support Counselors will cooperate with both the police and the CDMHP, but will in no case be responsible for deciding whether or not a client should be involuntarily detained.*

When a client is hospitalized (on either a voluntary or involuntary basis), Tribal Support Counselors may provide supportive services to the client and the client's family, as appropriate. For example, Support Counselors may explain the process of hospitalization or involuntary detention to family members, may provide transportation and emotional support, or may assist police and tribal child welfare staff in locating appropriate family resources for the emergency care of the client's children.

TRANSPORTATION POLICIES

The scarcity of cars available to some Indian families make it very natural that Indian clients frequently request transportation from Tribal Support Counselors. This transportation policy has been developed in order to clarify when it is and when it is not appropriate for Tribal Support Counselors to transport clients.

At times Tribal Support Counselors accompany clients to appointments with non-tribal mental health or social services providers. When the role of the Tribal Support Counselor is to encourage and assist the client in receiving a needed service, or to facilitate communication in a cross-cultural exchange, they may transport the client to the appointment.

Support Counselors may not transport clients to appointments, meetings or on other errands which are not directly related to the client's mental health treatment plan and for which the Support Counselor's presence is not required. Support Counselors consult with their supervisor to determine when transportation of clients is appropriate. Support Counselors and supervisors work together to maintain reasonable flexibility and a helpful attitude toward clients while avoiding the Support Counselors becoming seen as responsible for client transportation.

COOPERATION WITH TRADITIONAL INDIAN HEALERS AND SPIRITUAL ORGANIZATIONS

Traditional Indian people see both physical and emotional health as closely connected to spiritual balance. For most Indian people, a healthy spiritual adjustment is critical to good mental health. Even when spiritual practices are not specifically aimed at improving mental health per se, they often have con- siderable therapeutic benefits. *Physical and emotional problems are sometimes thought to have spiritual causes and may therefore be treated by spiritual methods. Although traditional treatments vary from tribe to tribe and from one traditional practitioner to another, in general they are aimed at correcting imbalances between the person and the social and spiritual world.*

It is the policy of the Skagit Tribe's Mental Health Program to support each client's right to choose their own spiritual identity and to make commitments to spiritual practices with which he/she is comfortable. Program staff do not attempt to influence the client's choice of spiritual activity. Instead, staff express respect for traditional spirituality by:

- encouraging clients to consult with elders and spiritual leaders whom they trust
- discussing the client's spiritual concerns with them without attempting to reframe the problems as only "psychological"
- upon request, assisting clients to contact appropriate traditional spiritual providers
- accompanying clients to spiritual services, upon request, and participating if culturally appropriate

Clients retain full responsibility for deciding whether or not to participate in spiritual activities. The Tribal Mental Health Program does not assume responsibility for any therapeutic benefits or risks involved in spiritual or religious activities.

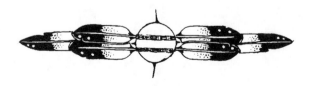

CONFIDENTIALITY GUIDELINES FOR TRIBAL SUPPORT COUNSELORS

Ensuring the confidentiality of all client information is both extremely important and extremely difficult for mental health workers in small tribal communities. These guidelines have been developed to assist Support Counselors with complex and delicate situations often encountered in working within their own communities.

1. *Each client is a person who has a right to privacy.*
2. *Never repeat things you are told by clients,* even to members of your family or of the client's family.
3. *Do not discuss a client's problems with anyone who doesn't have a job-related "need to know".* Don't allow yourself to get drawn into community gossip, no matter how interesting or harmless it may seem.
4. *Explain to clients that your services are confidential, but be very careful not to promise more confidentiality than you can legally keep.* Be sure you understand the limits of confidentiality: Learn what things you must tell someone else about---(child abuse, suicide threats, and other situations where clients are a danger to themselves or someone else.) Also learn who you should tell in these situations---(usually your supervisor and/or the police, child protective services or the county designated Mental Health Commitment Officer.) Fortunately situations like these where the law requires you to report information in order to protect your client or someone else are rare. However, it is very important that you understand and explain these confidentiality limits to your clients. *Don't promise to keep "secrets",* especially before you know what they are.
5. *Learn Tribal and Mental Health Center policies about information sharing among staff.* Know when you need to talk to other workers, and when not to. It is often appropriate to share some but not all information about a client with other staff. It is important to explain these policies to clients so that they will feel comfortable that their privacy is protected.
6. *Become familiar with the Privacy Act of 1974.* You will be given training in confidentiality. You should also discuss questions or difficult situations with your supervisor.

7. **When you want to discuss a case with an "outside" person, (such as a worker at another agency, an attorney or a family member), you must first get written permission from your client.** This is true even if the client has asked you to talk to the other person. The permission form must spell out who you will talk to, the agency involved, why and what information you can share. *Without this written permission, you must not share anything about a client, even whether or not a certain person is your client.* The signed release form is kept in the client's chart and must be dated as to when it was signed and the date permission to share information expires.

Chapter Twenty-One
Program "Start-up"
Ideas and Materials

PRACTICAL SUGGESTIONS
FOR TRIBAL MENTAL HEALTH PROGRAM
DEVELOPMENT AND SERVICE DELIVERY

Our experience in operating a Tribal mental health program have led to the following suggestions:

1. *Involve Tribal Council and Tribal social services staff in initial planning,* grant proposal (if appropriate),and hiring of all program staff.
2. *Hire a program director experienced in working with both Tribal communities and with local agencies.* Preferably, this person should have an established relation to the Tribal community to be served. Ideally, this person should be an Indian mental health professional.
3. *Create a program Advisory Board made of Tribal Council members,* tribal staff and other interested tribal members to help define mental health worker roles, plan training curriculum and provide ongoing direction and feedback quarterly concerning program approaches and services.
4. *The core program services should be provided by Indian staff.* Preferably, these people will be members of the Tribal communities to be served. These individuals should be respected in

their tribe, and be culturally defined "helpers". Ideally, one or more of these individuals should be active in traditional spiritual healing practices and be "socially placed" so as to have natural access to spiritual leaders.

5. ***Provide services within a "Tribal Community" model which takes into account prevailing lifestyle, customs, values and beliefs. Specifically:***

   a. "The Tribe", not the individual, must be understood to be "the client".

   b. Primary stationing of program services must be in the tribal community, and must be made as "visible" as possible.

   c. Program services must be integrated into existing tribal social services programs, in order to encourage teamwork with tribal programs and to allow tribal members to perceive the program as "theirs", rather than as an "outside" agency service. In order to do this, confidentiality and information sharing agreements must be entered into by the tribe and the mental health center. (see Chapter 20) Tribal social services administration must have some day-to-day oversight of program services, and tribal mental health staff must participate in tribal social services meetings, committees and other functions.

   d. Methods of receiving referrals, processing "intakes" and diagnosing client problems must be maximally flexible and minimally intrusive. This means that procedures for opening cases will be relaxed and informal, and paperwork, especially such things as client service "applications" will be restricted to an absolute minimum.

   e. Client diagnoses and service plans will be cooperatively developed between Indian paraprofessionals and professional supervisors. Diagnoses will reflect Indian views of the "problem" whenever possible. "Dual diagnoses" (Indian and DSM IV) will be given when appropriate.

   f. Conventional client and provider role definitions will be modified to reflect tribal realities.

   g. Confidentiality guidelines will be developed which reflect tribal realities.

   h. Work schedules of tribal providers must be highly flexible, with provision for after hours crisis work, "walk-ins", schedule changes, and attendance at important tribal functions. The program must also adjust to seasonal fluctuation in client loads.

 i. Tribal providers should attend functions such as funerals, dinners and spiritual events whenever possible in order to increase their perceived availability and tribal involvement, and to provide direct services to individuals and families in crisis.

 j. Mental health services must be offered in client homes on a flexible basis.

 k. Whenever possible services must include extended family members of the identified client, especially spouses, parents, grandparents and adult children. Service plans must emphasize family resources and helping clients adjust to family realities. Traditional family decision-making processes must be recognized and respected, e.g., consulting with a grandmother or calling a family meeting may be necessary and appropriate.

6. ***Providers must respect and support various cultural and spiritual beliefs and practices, such as traditional treatment of spiritual disturbances, the work of Indian Doctors, Shaker healing, etc. This must be more than a neutral "sensitivity" to these cultural practices: it must involve active support, with participation and advocacy as appropriate on a case by case basis.*** In order to accomplish this, the following factors are necessary:

 a. Identification and hiring of tribal members who are knowledgeable of and sensitive to this area of concern.

 b. Program staff must openly affirm the psychological value of cultural beliefs and the therapeutic value of cultural healing practices.

 c. Tribal providers must attend spiritual functions and, when appropriate, assist in the spiritual treatment of individual clients.

 d. Referrals should be made to Traditional Indian Healers when either the client or the tribal provider thinks appropriate.

 e. Referrals from Traditional Healers must be responded to promptly and with professional courtesy.

 f. Teamwork relationships with these providers should be developed.

 g. Above all, client spiritual beliefs must not be undermined, challenged or ignored. The client must perceive the provider and program as respectful and supportive of his/her particular belief system.

7. ***Tribal mental health providers must receive ongoing and comprehensive training geared to their individual educational backgrounds, work experience, and vocational goals. Training should:***
   a. Begin at the educational level of the provider and proceed at an individually geared pace.
   b. Contain a major component of courses and workshops specific to Indian mental health issues and the day to day practicalities and stresses of tribally based services.
   c. Familiarize the provider with the mainstream mental health delivery system, including its language, concepts, provider roles, theories and service modalities.
   d. Be accredited and lead toward a recognized degree. Training should enhance employability and be specifically related to vocational goals as well as to immediate job priorities.
   e. Be fully paid for by the program and occur during working hours.
8. ***Paraprofessional tribal providers should receive weekly individual professional supervision of their direct service efforts.*** This supervision should attempt to develop the trainee's therapeutic effectiveness and self confidence as well as to oversee client services. Supervisor should provide emotional support and problem solving help as needed to assist the trainee to cope with personal problems, stresses and role conflicts aggravated by the job. Supervisory staff - whether Indian or not - must share an appreciation and understanding of culturally approved/recognized treatment approaches and be able to support paraprofessional staff in culturally oriented treatment techniques.
9. ***Build close working relationships between tribal and nontribal programs,*** so as to increase cultural accessibility and sensitivity of all available mental health and social services. This should be approached by:
   a. Tribal providers becoming educated about mainstream mental health services.
   b. Tribal providers informing non-Indian providers about tribal mental health services and about Indian cultural values.
   c. Regular contact should be maintained between tribal staff and community mental health staff to facilitate cross referrals and case consultation.
   d. Tribal providers may provide co-therapy with non-Indian providers, or may accompany Indian clients to appointments with non-Indian providers, as appropriate.

FUNDING, STAFFING AND ADMINISTRATIVE OPTIONS FOR TRIBALLY BASED MENTAL HEALTH SERVICES

Finding adequate funds for a tribal mental health program can be a challenge. Tribes vary enormously in the level of existing services and in the level of available funds. The particular needs of each tribe as well as the local options for funding should be explored in cooperation with tribal authorities.

Because of current policies favoring Indian self-determination, a variety of creative funding possibilities exist. Cooperation between tribes, community mental health centers and the Indian Health Service can lead to the design of innovative funding packages to meet tribal mental health needs. When a commitment to provide services to Indian people is present, a way to fund the program can be found. Possible funding sources include:

- Community Mental Health Funds (from State, Federal or County Sources) either contracted directly or in cooperation with a community mental health center.
- Indian Health Service Funds (With services either provided directly by the Indian Health Service or through a contract to the tribe under Public Law 638)
- Funds generated by tribal enterprises
- Special grants from private foundations.

Community Mental Health Funds

Washington State law requires that Regional Support Networks and community mental health centers serve Indian people, and do so in a culturally appropriate manner. However, mental health centers are also required to give first priority to serving the "acutely" mentally ill, second priority to serving the "chronically" mentally ill, and third priority to serving the "seriously disturbed". This requirement can hinder services to Indian clients in two ways: first, the large number of "priority" mentally ill clients in the general population combined with the limited funds may result in mental health centers not addressing the special needs of Indian people; second, many needy Indian clients either do not come to the attention of mainstream mental health centers or do not fit the state priority definitions (as discussed in Chapter 18). Therefore, *special efforts must be made to ensure that Indian clients will actually receive services.*

The state requires that all licensed mental health centers employ or have on contract a "Minority Mental Health Specialist" for each minority group in their service area. However, this may only result in minimal services to minority people, and is rarely sufficient to ensure that the needs of Indian people are met. ***Therefore, Tribal government, community mental health boards and county mental health administrators must urge Regional Support Networks and Community Mental Health Centers to make a substantial commitment to provide culturally appropriate services to tribal communities. Tribal council people and administrators should develop mechanisms for ongoing input into Regional Support Network planning and budget allocation processes to ensure that the needs of Native American people are given appropriate attention.***

Community mental health centers may serve tribal communities by:
- hiring professional or paraprofessional Indian staff
- stationing existing staff directly in the tribal community

Even before staffing assignments are made, mental health centers and tribes may work together to:
- identify contact persons to help coordinate services for tribal members
- train mental health staff regarding important cultural variables
- inform tribal social services staff about the services available through the community mental health center

In order to develop a more comprehensive tribal mental health program, ***tribes and mental health centers may want to explore a combination of state, federal and tribal resources.***

Indian Health Service

The Indian Health Service is the agency designated by the federal government to provide mental health services to federally recognized Indian tribes, either directly or through contracts with tribes.

Larger tribes often have Indian Health Service mental health workers assigned to tribal locations. Members of smaller tribes may receive services from "field" mental health staff who come to the tribe one or more days per week. In other cases clients must travel to a nearby Indian Health Service clinic.

As a general rule, larger tribes are liable to have more control over the nature of the services provided by IHS, especially when providers are stationed at tribal sites. Smaller tribes which share the services of mental health staff with other tribes tend to have less control over the nature of the services provided. In addition, when mental health workers are placed only one or two days a week at a tribe, they are less likely to become integrated into the tribal community. It may be more difficult for these workers to become adequately familiar with the culture, lifestyle and family networks of the tribes to which they provide services.

The Indian Self Determination Act (public law 638), allows tribes to contract directly with I.H.S. to operate their own mental health programs. Funding allocations are based upon the tribe's population: in practice this means that large tribes may be allotted funds sufficient for several full time positions, whereas small tribes may only be allotted funds to pay for a fraction of a position. In such cases tribes must develop additional funding sources to meet their mental health needs. Two or more small tribes may form a consortium, the tribe itself may be able to contribute funds, it may be possible to combine a part time 'mental health' with a part time 'social service' position, or it may be possible to combine Indian Health Service funds with state or county funds.

It is important that mental health services for tribal people be tribally based and under the direction of tribal government and administration. However, interagency cooperation can greatly increase financial, staff and program resources available to tribal communities.

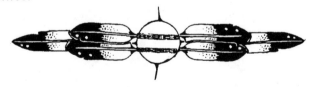

BUDGET CONSIDERATIONS FOR TRIBAL MENTAL HEALTH PROGRAMS

Like other outreach programs designed to serve 'hard to reach' clients, tribal mental health programs require a strong commitment on the part of participating agencies. Funding authorities and program administrators must recognize that providing culturally appropriate services in tribal communities may require more effort per unit of service and per client served than in other mental health programs. Funding sources must earmark special funds for mental health services to Indian clients. Without such a commitment, Indian clients will remain unserved, and their mental health needs will continue to mount.

In addition to the need to allocate funds for Indian mental health programs, program planners should be aware of the following specific budgetary needs:

Training expenses, including college tuition, books and transportation to training opportunities should be provided. Training should be provided on work time.

Cultural consultation from elders, tribal leaders and traditional spiritual leaders is needed to ensure that services remain culturally congruent. These consultants should be fairly reimbursed for their time and expertise.

Travel expenses are liable to be greater in tribal than in mainstream mental health programs. Home visits are necessary and in some cases clients live in rural areas at a considerable distance from program offices. Upon occasion, tribal mental health staff may need to transport clients to meetings with other mental health or social services providers. Therefore, mileage costs are liable to be considerably greater than in most programs.

SAMPLE AGREEMENT FOR MENTAL HEALTH AGENCY SERVICE TO A TRIBAL COMMUNITY

This agreement outlines conditions for cooperation between _____Mental Health Center and the _____Tribe in providing mental health services to Indian clients.

Tribal Programs and Services

The _____ Tribe provides the following social, educational and health services for Indian people living on or near the reservation:

_____

_____

_____

_____

Community Mental Health Services

The _____ Mental Health Center provides the following services:

_____

_____

_____

Tribal Mental Health Service Agreement

Both the _____ Tribe and the _____Mental Health Center want to increase the quantity and quality of mental health services available to Indian people in _____County. In order to do this, service must be easily accessible to Indian people and must be delivered in a manner which is compatible with Tribal values. Therefore, the Tribe and the Mental Health Center have made a commitment to work together in the following ways:

    1. The Mental Health Center will employ specific staff who are either Indian or will be trained to work with Indian people.

    2. Staff offices will be located at _____

    3. Services will be offered at _____

4. Services will include:_____

_____

5. Mental Health staff will work closely with tribal administration and social services staff.

6. The _____ Tribe will guide Program development and staff selection in the following ways:

_____

_____

7. Services will be coordinated by

_____

8. Supervision will be provided by_____

9. Training will focus on

_____

_____

10. Client files will be kept at_____

11. Mental Health Center staff and Tribal staff will be mutually bound to keep confidential all client information exchanged in the course of program operation.

12. The program will be funded in the following way (s):

_____

_____

13. Program expenses and accounting will be handled by:

_____

_____

14. Reporting requirements will include:

_____

_____

15. This agreement may be ended or amended in the follow ing way:

_____

_____

Signed:_____ Date:_____
Tribal Chairman
Signed:_____ Date:_____
Mental Health Center Director

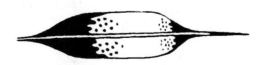

Tribal Mental Health Project
P.O. Box 388 • La Conner, Washington 98257 • Phone (360) 466-3163

SAMPLE TRIBAL SUPPORT COUNSELOR JOB DESCRIPTION

General Position Description

This is a 3/4 time counselor training and direct service position at the Swinomish Tribe through Skagit Community Mental Health Center.

The position requires attending college in Human Services and involves on-going training in mental health.

The person hired for the position will provide counseling, crisis support, and information and referral.

Some out of town travel will be required.

Qualifications
- Familiarity with Swinomish Tribal Community
- Demonstrated interest in helping members of Tribal community
- Interest in obtaining additional training/education in Human Services/Mental Health
- Ability to cooperate with traditional/spiritual workers
- Maturity and ability to handle delicate role issues and to respond to crises
- Valid driver's license and reliable transportation
- Experience and education in Human Services/ Mental Health desirable

Duties
1. Attend college classes/ participate in training
2. Provide counseling, advocacy and crisis support for those most in need in the Tribal community
3. Work with supervisor to develop case plans
4. Maintain client records and other required reports
5. Coordinate service delivery efforts with Skagit Community Mental Health Center and with other agencies serving Indian clients

Tribal Mental Health Project

P.O. Box 388 • La Conner, Washington 98257 • Phone (360) 466-3163

SAMPLE TRIBAL MENTAL HEALTH PROGRAM SUPERVISOR JOB DESCRIPTION

(.5 F.T.E. position)

General Position Description

The Tribal Mental Health Program Supervisor will be responsible for the supervision and training of the Tribal Support Counselors working with the Swinomish and Upper Skagit Tribes. This program is sponsored by Skagit Community Mental Health Center.

Qualifications

- A masters or doctoral degree in Human Services, Social or Behavioral Science.
- Two years instructional or related experience demonstrating the applicant's ability to develop curriculum, coordinate training services and supervise paraprofessional mental health workers.
- Direct experience providing mental health services to Indian clients demonstrating the applicant's ability to relate to the special needs of this cultural group.
- Experience working with and coordinating service with other health and human service agencies, community colleges and other community organizations.

Duties

1. In conjunction with the Tribal Mental Health Advisory Board, develop course curriculum for intensive initial training and for on-going training for Tribal Support Counselors.
2. Coordinate field placements for Tribal Support Counselors in tribal community settings.
3. Provide consultation, training and supervision to Tribal Support Counselors.
4. Assist Tribal Support Counselors in providing consultation and liaison to other Community Mental Health Center programs as well as other community agencies serving tribal clients.

5. Work closely with the social service programs of both Tribes to integrate mental health services with tribal social services.
6. Work closely with Tribal Support Counselors and cultural consultants to develop a culture-specific model of mental health service delivery for Tribal Communities.

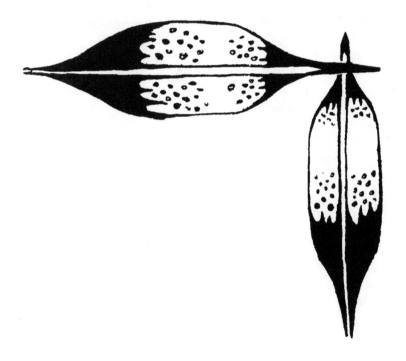

Tribal Mental Health Project
P.O. Box 388 • La Conner, Washington 98257 • Phone (360) 466-3163

SAMPLE INTERVIEW QUESTIONS FOR TRIBAL SUPPORT COUNSELOR APPLICANTS

1. What interests you about this job?

2. What experiences have you had which have prepared you for mental health work?

3. What types of personal or family problems do you see in your tribal community?

4. What types of help would you like to see provided?

5. How do you feel about attending classes, studying, reading and doing homework assignments?

6. How are your reading and writing skills?

7. Do you have reliable transportation?

8. Do you feel comfortable talking and sharing in a small group?

9. Would you like to help lead a parenting class or support group for clients?

10. How do you think you would feel about discussing your work and your cases with your supervisor?

11. What problems would you expect to have in doing this type of work in your own community?

12. How do you think it would be to work with people you know?

13. How do you think you would be at keeping good notes in client charts and other record keeping?

14. How comfortable would you be serving as a "link" or "translator" between mental health therapists and Indian spiritual leaders?

15. How do you see spiritual and mental health systems working together?

16. How would you feel about working with people with alcohol problems? With battered women? With sexual abuse victims? With suicidal people? With mentally ill people?

17. Do you think that keeping confidential what you learn from clients could be a problem in a small tribal community? How would you deal with this?

Chapter Twenty-Two
Information and Suggestions
for Direct Service Providers

TRIBAL AND NON-TRIBAL SOCIAL SERVICES
GENERALLY AVAILABLE TO INDIAN PEOPLE

Direct service providers in tribal Communities should be familiar with the range of tribal and non-tribal social, educational and health services available to tribal members.

Tribal Services

It is usually desirable to refer Indian clients to tribally based social services whenever possible. These services tend to be easily accessible, understood and accepted by Indian people and are more liable to be culturally appropriate.

Most tribal communities offer a range of social, health, education and general support services. These programs may be funded by a variety of agencies, including the Indian Health Service, The Bureau of Indian Affairs, Housing and Urban Development, church organizations, schools or colleges, state and county contracts or by tribal funds. Most programs located on reservations are coordinated and administered by tribal government. It is important to understand both the funding source and the administrative lines of authority.

Client eligibility criteria may differ from one program to another depending on the regulations of the funding authority. Some services may only be available to enrolled members of the particular tribe. Other services are open to any Indian person living in the tribal community, whereas certain other services may be open to the general public.

The following services are found in many tribal communities:

Alcohol programs, *(usually funded by I.H.S.) including:*
- referral to Indian-oriented residential treatment
- out-patient counseling
- antabuse monitoring
- support groups

Indian Child Welfare Programs (usually funded by the BIA) focusing on implementation of the 1978 I.C.W. Act, *including:*
- Investigation of Child Abuse and Neglect or Coordination with State Child Protective Services
- Family Reconciliation
- Child Welfare Casework
- Foster Home Recruitment and Licensing
- Tribal Representation in Court Proceedings

Services for elders, *including:*
- Hot Lunches
- Field Trips
- Special Cultural Events

Health programs, *(generally funded by the Indian Health Service):*
- Direct Medical Care
- Referral to Contract Providers
- Nutritional Services
- Services of Community Health Representatives (CHR's)

Educational services provided at or in close cooperation with the tribe including:
- Early childhood intervention programs
- Johnson O'Malley (JOM Federal funds for Indian education)
- Preschool or Headstart Programs
- Programs offering special services to Indian students in the public schools such as tutoring, counseling or school supplies

- Adult education services including tutoring, assistance in obtaining the G.E.D., and funding for college tuition
- BIA higher education grants for qualified Indian individuals

Youth activities
- Summer youth work programs
- Culturally-oriented youth clubs
- Youth Recreational activities and tournaments

Housing Services

Churches and Traditional Spiritual Organizations

Tribal community functions and special cultural events

Non-Tribal Services

When tribal programs cannot meet the needs of Indian clients, it may be appropriate to refer them to outside community services. In these cases tribal mental health workers can be particularly helpful in reducing miscommunications due to cultural differences.

Community Mental Health Center Programs *such as:*
- Day Treatment
- Medication Evaluation and Monitoring
- Crisis Services and Involuntary Treatment
- Outpatient Counseling
- Other Special Programs

Department of Social and Health Services (DSHS) *programs including:*
- Child Protective Services (CPS) (often including a specialized Indian caseload)
- Aid to Families with Dependent Children (AFDC)
- General Assistance (GAU)
- Vocational Rehabilitation Services
- Services for clients with developmental disabilities
- General Indian community workers are employed at some DSHS offices

Community Crisis and Referral Agencies, *including:*
• Suicide Prevention lines
• Battered Women's Services
• Rape Relief Programs
• Emergency Shelters
• Food Banks, etc.

Alcohol Services *including:*
• Community Alcohol Centers providing evaluation and outpatient services
• Alcoholic Anonymous
• Alanon groups
• Adult Children of alcoholics (ACOA), etc.
• Residential Alcoholism Treatment Programs

Educational Services, *such as:*
• School Counselors and School Psychologists
• Headstart Programs
• Minority Affairs Coordinators in local Community Colleges.

Large urban areas often have specialized Indian medical, educational or social services organizations. Although many tribes are not near to such organizations, tribal mental health workers should become familiar with Indian resources in nearby cities.

THERAPEUTIC TECHNIQUES ADAPTABLE TO TRIBAL MENTAL HEALTH PROGRAMS

Certain mental health techniques seem particularly suitable for tribal programs. In addition to outreach, supportive counseling, case management, crisis intervention, and traditional cultural approaches (such as prayer, drummings, teaching stories, songs, or in spiritual gatherings) the following approaches might also be helpful:
• *Art Therapy* using traditional Indian crafts and styles may encourage self esteem and cultural identity.
• *Music and Dance*, with consultation from Indian elders and cultural specialists may be useful for some clients.
• Treatment for Post Traumatic Stress, Child Abuse, battering or Violence

- *Play Therapy* can help Indian children through nonverbal exploration of feelings, interpersonal relations and conflicts. Indian dolls and play materials may increase the child's comfort, identification and ease of exploration of cultural conflicts.
- *Specific Theme Groups* adapted to the experiences of Indian people can be helpful in prevention or treatment. Parenting, stress, anger management, adult children of alcoholics (ACOA), and self-esteem groups are relevant to many Indian clients. Groups can encourage a positive Indian cultural identity.
- *Adlerian therapeutic approaches* can support tribal values by emphasizing the individual's relationship to family and community and by encouraging social responsibility.
- *Jungian approaches* which emphasize balanced personal development are consistent with many traditional Indian philosophies (such as the Medicine Wheel). Use of symbol, dream, artwork and active imagination may help clients integrate important Indian psychic and spiritual experiences.
- *Bettleheim's use of myth and fairly tales* in work with children might be usefully integrated with the therapeutic use of traditional Indian teaching stories.
- *Educational and preventive programs* can reduce social problems in a community. Helpful adjuncts to tribal mental health programs include:
  –Culturally-oriented children's, teen & adult activities, clubs & classes
  –Family Planning and Prenatal Care
  –Job Training and Employment Programs
  –Adult Education Programs
  –Nutrition and WIC (Women, Infants and Children) Programs
  –Alcohol and Drug Education
  –Support Groups for Teens, Young Women, Parents, Elders, etc.

Various other techniques may also be useful. Which therapeutic techniques are effective varies between programs and depends on the availability of therapists trained in specific approaches. Tribal mental health staff not having expertise in a given area may be able to arrange for Indian Health Service, a community mental health center or other agency to provide specific services at tribal facilities, perhaps with a co-therapist from the tribal program.

PRACTICAL SUGGESTIONS FOR NON-INDIAN MENTAL HEALTH WORKERS AND NEWCOMERS TO TRIBAL COMMUNITIES

1. Keep in mind that you are the "foreigner" in "Indian Country": it is up to you to adapt and learn about Indian ways.

2. Do not assume that you are 'needed', 'right', or should be in control; be respectful at all times.

3. Go slowly; be cautious about attempts to change Indian people and tribal systems.

4. Spend time in informal social exchanges with staff and tribal community members: talk, listen, be seen, help out.

5. Avoid professional jargon: remember that some clients may be unfamiliar with long words. Explain written forms.

6. Make yourself as available as possible; accept that clients will not always make or keep appointments.

7. Explain your role and services; do not assume that clients are familiar with mental health services.

8. Be flexible and adjustable about your role; and be prepared to change gears and pitch in during tribal events.

9. Develop team relationships with Indian social services staff who can help you learn about family resources, Indian values and culturally appropriate service approaches; ask for feedback; don't let yourself become isolated.

10. Learn who is related to whom and how this affects social roles.

11. Respect traditional beliefs and practices.

12. Remember that spiritual matters may be private; do not pry; watch, express respectful interest and wait to be told.

13. Be careful what you say about clients, staff and tribal members; remember that your attitudes and ability to keep confidentiality will be examined and that the person you are speaking with may be related to the person you are discussing.

14. Be willing to adjust your therapeutic expectations; understand that you are working with complicated and long term problems in a system which you do not completely understand.

Part Four

Record Keeping
for Tribal
Mental Health
Programs

Introduction
Part Four

Record keeping is an inherently sensitive area for tribal mental health programs, perhaps because it is the major point where culturally oriented services must mesh with state or federal standards for monitoring and accountability.

CONVENTIONAL MENTAL HEALTH RECORD KEEPING SYSTEMS MUST BE ADJUSTED TO MEET TRIBAL AND CULTURAL NEEDS BECAUSE:

1. *Formal written procedures tend to alienate Indian clients.*
2. *Some Indian people do not feel comfortable signing written documents such as consent forms.*
3. *Certain traditional and spiritual activities or treatments cannot be recorded or described in detail because they are sacred and culturally sensitive.*
4. *Confidentiality is an extremely delicate matter in small tribal communities where clients and mental health providers often know one another socially.*
5. *Paraprofessional Indian mental health workers may not have extensive training in writing and record keeping, and may feel uncomfortable with conventional charting procedures.*
6. *Content of client records should be somewhat different from those of mainstream programs to include culturally relevant information on tribal status, blood quantum, extended family, traditional orientation and involvement in tribal cultural activities.*

PART FOUR Record Keeping

Chapter 23 provides general guidelines for culturally sensitive record keeping and focuses on practical differences in how record keeping is handled in our Tribal Mental Health Program as opposed to other community mental health programs. Problems with state requirements, difficulties in obtaining written consents for service and differences in record content are discussed. Our approach will be best understood after reading Part III.

Chapter 24 includes instructions developed for the use of paraprofessional Tribal Support Counselors in how to use the record keeping forms in ch. 25.

Chapter 25 presents the actual record forms developed for this program. These are included in the hope that some of our ideas may be useful to other tribal mental health programs which are in the process of developing or revising record keeping systems.

Contents
Part Four

Introduction, Part Four 425

Contents, Part 4 427

Chapter Twenty-Three
General Guidelines for
Culturally Sensitive Record Keeping   429

Forms and Procedures 430

Ongoing Procedures 430

Culturally Sensitive Matters 431

90 Day Case Reviews 432

Termination of Services and Closing of Chart 432

Chapter Twenty-Four
Sample Record Keeping Instructions for
Tribal Mental Health Counselors   435

Record Keeping Instructions 436

Client Services 436

General Requirements for Client Charts 437

Referral Form 438

Client Intake 438

Example of a Treatment Plan 440

Consent For Exchange of Information 441

Client/Family Data 442
Description of Culturally Oriented Mental
Health Services and Codes 442
90-day Case Review 442
Tribal Support Counselor's Guide to M.I.S. System .. 443
Tribal Support Counselor's Checklist 446
Alternative tracking System 447
Monthly Status Reports 448

Chapter Twenty-Five
Sample Record Keeping Forms for
Tribal Mental Health Programs   449

Introduction 449
Client Information Sheet 451
Client Consent for Treatment 452
Referral Form 453
Client Intake Form 454
Client Family Data Sheet 460
Progress Note Form 461
Description of Culturally Oriented Mental Health
Services and Service Code List 462
Consent for Exchange of Information 465
90-Day Case Review/Case Summary Form 466
Quarterly Tracking Sheet
for Alternative Community Services 467
Monthly Statistical Report Form 468

Chapter Twenty-Three
General Guidelines for
Culturally Sensitive
Record Keeping

Record keeping for a culturally oriented mental
health program serving Indian clients in a
tribal community setting must be kept simple,
minimally intrusive and maximally congruent
with tribal community values. Record keeping is
an area of inherent difficulty. Tribal Mental
Health Programs must attempt to resolve this
difficulty by maximizing flexibility in record
keeping systems.

FORMS AND PROCEDURES FOR RECORD KEEPING WHEN A CASE IS OPENED

Intake Procedures in Tribal Mental Health Programs need to be more informal and flexible than is the norm in mainstream mental health programs (See Chapter 20.) No formal application for service is required prior to service, nor is an extensive history taken. Each client is given a short statement of program policies (Client's Service Policy) and asked to sign a consent for treatment which is written in clear and simple language. When a client is unwilling to sign but gives verbal consent, the Support Counselor signs a statement to that effect. This Procedure is in compliance with WAC 275-56-260 and 275-56-265.

When a signed or informed verbal consent for treatment can be obtained from the client, a chart is opened. The intake, diagnosis and treatment plans are discussed between Support Counselor and Supervisor. Treatment plans are jointly developed with clients. In contrast to mainstream records, *the intake, social history and treatment plan in Tribal Mental Health records specifically include an assessment of extended family resources, traditional spiritual orientation and cultural identity.*

For each client for whom a chart is opened, an "entry document" is also done, in order that statistical service data can be entered into the computerized Community Mental Health Center "MIS" System. "Entry documents" and "service tickets" are the only forms of record keeping maintained at the Community Mental Health Center; *all client charts and other confidential information are kept in locked file cabinets at the tribal site where the service is provided.* Thus, a separate set of charts, with its own numbering system is maintained at each Tribe.

ONGOING RECORD KEEPING PROCEDURES

Each client contact is recorded in a progress note kept in the client's chart. (See Chapter 25.) Progress notes are brief and simple. Data and time of contact is noted so that after hours or weekend services will be readily identified. Whether the service is a pre-set appointment, walk-in or emergency service is also noted.

In order to reduce the amount of writing required and to be sure that program records show the cultural sensitivity of services, a special Service Code system was developed by the Tribal Mental

Health Program. (See Chapter 25.) This Code System facilitates documentation of the cultural basis of the services provided without expecting the Tribal Support Counselors to enter into a lengthy explanation of the cultural orientation of services in each client's chart.

Each chart contains an information sheet describing the service categories and code system, and explaining the cultural basis of the various services provided by this program. Two letter "service codes" are entered in client charts at the end of progress notes or in other case record forms to indicate the category of culturally oriented services which have been provided.

For each client contact, "service tickets" are also filled out for use in the Community Mental Health Center's computerized client information (MIS) system. Service tickets are turned in to the Community Mental Health Center at the end of each month.

RECORDING CULTURALLY SENSITIVE MATTERS

Certain culturally orientated services (including religious or spiritual practices, ceremonies, and help provided in cooperation with Traditional Indian Doctors) are not described in client charts. *These matters are considered sacred and culturally sensitive and therefore cannot be recorded in detail.* For those clients having an open chart, a brief note may be made to the effect that spiritual services were performed or a referral made, but specific practices are not described. While this may pose something of a dilemma for state reviewers and auditors, it must be understood that some tribal people feel that it is inappropriate to mention traditional services at all. *Cultural standards of respect and tact require that caution and metaphor be used in any reference to the spiritual needs and treatment of individual people.*

90-DAY CASE REVIEWS

The Washington State Administrative Code (WAC) requires that a review of each client's progress and of the effectiveness of the services provided be made every ninety days. These "90 Day Reviews" are discussed between Support Counselors and Supervisors. Even when a client has received little or no service during the 90 day period, a brief note is made on the review form indicating no change of status or that no services were provided during this period. 90 day reviews are signed by Support Counselors and Supervisor.

TERMINATION OF SERVICES AND CLOSING OF CHARTS

The policy of the Tribal Mental Health Program concerning termination of services and closing of client charts differs from that of other programs of Skagit Community Mental Health Center. These differences are due to cultural variables and expectations in the Indian Community. For instance, it is a cultural expectation that helpers will maintain an "open door" policy for clients, and that they will respond at time of need or crisis. This expectation applies even when a client has not seen the provider for a long period of time.

Many clients in the Indian community are not oriented toward keeping regular weekly or biweekly appointments. Instead, they tend to return periodically seeking support, advocacy and therapeutic services.

While some Indian clients feel comfortable with regularly scheduled appointments, it is our experience that many perceive such scheduling as impersonal and unnatural. *Rather than trying to change the expectations and help-seeking behavior of Indian people, our program has tried to develop services which conform to existing Indian lifestyles and expectations of help.*

Because of the different patterns of service utilization in the Indian community, it would be artificial, confusing, and time consuming to close client files each time a client was absent from treatment and then later to have to reopen the case each time the client returned. At least in the small reservation communities we serve, *our staff have found it most practical to leave client charts open on an ongoing basis unless there is a clear reason to close the case.* Such clear reasons include:

- the death of a client,
- the client's moving away from the tribal community,
- the client's statement that he or she no longer wishes to receive mental health services,
- a judgment by the support counselor, in consultation with the supervisor, that the client no longer needs or is liable to be benefited by services.

Missing appointments or not receiving services within a certain arbitrary time period does not result in a termination of service or closing the client's chart. Only those charts falling into one of the specific categories outlined above are relegated to an "inactive" file. This policy results in a great variety in the frequency of services received by clients with "open" charts.

When a decision is made to close a chart, a "Client Summary" form is completed, describing the services provided, the progress made by the client and the client's mental health status at the time of termination. Any plans for referral or future services are noted on the client summary. An "exit document" is also done at this time and submitted to the Community Mental Health Center for entry into the computerized information system.

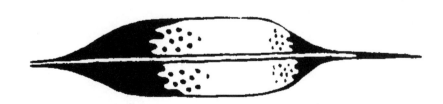

Chapter Twenty-Four
Sample Record Keeping Instructions for Tribal Mental Health Counselors

I n this chapter we share record keeping guide-lines/instructions developed as a training tool for our Tribal Support Counselors.

These instructions are for the record keeping forms in Chapter 25. These instructions were developed into a packet for easy reference.

While these forms and guidelines may not meet the precise needs of other programs, Tribal Mental Health Programs are free to use and/or amend these instructions.

RECORD KEEPING INSTRUCTIONS FOR TRIBAL SUPPORT COUNSELORS

Every mental health-social service activity which you do on behalf of a tribal community member, family, or the Tribe as a whole must be recorded in one of two ways:

1. When the person or persons served are your formal "clients", services are recorded in that individual's chart.
2. When the service falls into one of several "alternative community service" categories (see below), it will be recorded as an Alternative Community Service.

CLIENT SERVICES

In order for a person to become your client they must:

1. Be eligible for the program services (e.g. must meet state priority population definitions).
2. Need a service which you are able to give.
3. Consent to receive the service.

Every tribal community member who requests counseling, case management or advocacy services should be regarded as a possible "client". You should make sure that the person understands what services you can offer as part of your job. Briefly explain your job and services to the person when you first talk with them. This may seem somewhat awkward with people whom you already know well, especially if they approach you at home or in the community outside of usual work hours. With these individuals you will need to be particularly careful to explain your job and ask if they want your services.

Determining what services the client needs and whether you can provide this help is part of the "intake" process. Once you have decided that this person is an appropriate client for this program, he or she should be given a copy of the "Tribal Support Counselors' Client Information Sheet" and asked to sign the "Client's Consent to Receive Services". Tell the client that the first sheet explains your services and is for them to keep. The second sheet records their agreement to receive services through this program. Explain that we need their signature because:

1.) this protects their rights to only receive services which they understand and choose,

2.) it allows you to work with them as part of your job,

3.) it provides a record that you have served this person.

If the client feels uncomfortable signing this form even after you have explained it but does understand and want your services, then you may indicate that for cultural reasons the client did not sign, the date when he or she gave verbal consent and sign the form yourself. (This procedure is consistent with WAC275-56-260-265.)

The signed consent for service form must go into every client's chart. There should be only one chart for each client, and each client needs to give their consent only once.

(Before you open a new chart, check to see if one has already been opened for that person. If so, record your services to that client in the progress notes, but do not fill out another intake or entry document.

When you provide service to a client who already has an open chart, be sure to discuss this with the other Support Counselor involved. Sometimes two people may work together on one case as a team. This is especially likely when the client has several types of needs. Whenever this happens be sure to decide who, will do what, who will do 90-day reviews on the case and to keep each other well informed about the case. Each worker fills out service tickets for the services they give. If confusion arises about who should do what, consult with your supervisors.)

GENERAL REQUIREMENTS FOR CLIENT CHARTS

1. *Every client must have a chart which shows what the problem is, the type of service being given, and the plan. Every chart must have the client's signed consent for service* or the Support Counselor's signed verification of the client's informed verbal consent.

2. *Every contact and service provided to or on behalf of a client must be recorded in the client's chart.*

3. *Client charts should be kept up to date.*

4. *A summary of the case events and the client's progress should be done every 90 days.*

5. *The charts should clearly show how the services are culturally appropriate.*

6. Ongoing progress notes and case summaries are kept on the left side of the chart. Other forms, correspondence, etc. are kept on the right. This allows information to be found easily.

The Skagit Tribes' Mental Health Program has developed a set of forms which facilitate meeting state and program requirements. A complete packet of these forms is included in Chapter 25. Readers may wish to examine each form along with the explanations for its use given in this chapter. *Programs serving Indian people may duplicate and/or adapt for their own use any of these forms.*

REFERRAL FORM (Ch. 25, p. 453)

You may use this form either to record a referral you have received, or to make a referral to another provider. (If the client approached you his/herself, no referral form is needed.)

INSTRUCTIONS FOR CLIENT INTAKE (Ch. 25, p. 454)

An intake form is filled out for every client when the case is first opened. It should include information about the client's history and problems and about the plan for services.

Follow these guidelines in completing each section of the intake form:

Identifying Data - Record client's full name and the date when you first opened the case. A file # should be assigned to the case. The number will be either "SW" (for Swinomish) or "US" (for Upper Skagit) and a 3 digit number. (Later, separate client ID numbers will be assigned by Skagit Community Mental Health Center for their computerized data bank.)

Presenting Problem - List the main reasons why the client needs or wants service. Usually this will be the client's own view of the problem. Include as much detail as you can.

Relevant History - Here you put other important information about the client's general social situation and life history. What is the home situation? What supports does the client have in his/her life? Record any other information that would help give a broader understanding of the client and client's problem.

Previous Treatment - Here, check any type of treatment the client has had before your service. How has the client tried to solve the problem? What have been the results?

Physical/Sexual Abuse History - If you work with a client for any length of time, try to find out if he/she have ever been abused (as a child or as an adult). Check whether he/she has ever been neglected or abused. (If you don't have this information at the time of intake, leave this section blank and fill it in later, noting the date when you record the information.)

Developmental/Educational History - Here you record any information you have about the client's early life, such as health, growth, illnesses, learning problems, education, etc.

Work History - In this section you should note what type of work the client does, as well as his/her overall work history and habits. Has work been a problem for this person, and if so why? Does this person have special work strengths?

Spiritual Involvement - Is this person active in any church or spiritual group? How important is this in his/her life? Is this a source of support?

Medical Involvement - Note any physical problems, name of physician or nurse and any medications client takes.

Mental Status - Check all that apply to client and give examples when appropriate

Drug and Alcohol Use/Abuse - Note here the client's use of drugs or alcohol. Have drugs or alcohol caused the client any health, legal or social problems?

Support Counselor's Observations and Assessment - This is a very important section where you describe your own impressions of the client's situation, problems and needs. How serious are the problems? What kind of help does the client need?

Tentative Diagnosis - Write in your diagnosis of the problem. Discuss this with your supervisor. (Both Name and DSM IV Number of diagnosis must be listed. The number must be the same as that on the client's Entry Document.)

GAS Opening - Write in the Global Assessment Score which best reflects the client's level of functioning. (The number should be the same as the score on the "Entry Document".)

Priority Code - Record "100" for Acutely Mentally Ill, "200" for Chronically Mentally Ill, or "300" for Seriously Disturbed. (This should be the same as the priority code number shown on the Entry Document.)

Initial Service Plan (I.S.P.) - Here you outline the services you plan to provide the client in order to help him/her with his/her problems. Write down each problem, including such things as depression, family violence, social withdrawal, etc. then write what you hope to accomplish in regards to each problem. Finally, check the specific treatment modalities, frequency of contacts, and expected timeframe of treatment.

EXAMPLE OF A CLIENT TREATMENT PLAN (I.S.P.): (p. 6 of intake form)

1. Problem
    a. suicidal thoughts
    b. Indian spiritual disturbance

2. Expected Outcome
    a. prevent suicide attempts
    b. client will be less depressed
    c. client will gain healthy spiritual balance

3. Treatment Plan
    a. support counseling 2x/week for 2 months or as needed
    b. extended family networking 1x/week for 2 months
    c. traditional consultation weekly or as needed for 1 year

Referral To - Here you indicate if you are making a referral to another tribal provider, outside agency, or spiritual leader.

It is important that you discuss the service plans with your client and make sure that they understand and agree to the plan. Then you and the client sign the form and date it. You can fill out the service plan (p. 6 of Intake Form) with your client and have them sign it and the consent form at the same time if this seems comfortable. *If it is culturally inappropriate for the client to sign the I.S.P., the cultural reason and the date you obtained verbal consent must be documented on this form.*

Review Date - This should be done three months from the intake date. You must do a client review sheet every 90 days for each open chart.

CONSENT FOR EXCHANGE OF INFORMATION FORM
(See Chapter 25, p. 465)

Use this form to get the client's written permission for you to discuss them with an outside person or agency. You do not need this form in order to talk to your supervisor or to other staff of Skagit Community Mental Health Center. Generally, you do not need this form to talk to other service providers at your Tribe. (You should be guided by the Tribal Social Service Policies and Inter-Agency Service Agreements.)

Use the Consent for Exchange of Information when you either want to give or receive information from an outside agency or other party, such as an attorney, physician, DSHS caseworker, or probation officer. If the client has already signed such a form at the other agency, you do not need to have them sign this form, but you must get a copy of the consent for your file. The consent should be signed before you talk to the outside agency. If you receive a phone call or other inquiry about a client, you should not answer any questions (even whether or not a certain person is your client or is in the community) before getting the client's permission.

The consent should specify to what agency or person the information is to be given, what information may be shared, and the purpose of such sharing. It should be signed and dated and placed in the client's file. You may need to make a xerox copy and give this to the other provider.

CLIENT/FAMILY DATA SHEET
(See Chapter 25, p. 460)

This form records relevant identifying information about clients and family members. List all household members and other significant relations. Show tribe, enrollment status, and degree of Indian blood, if known. Keep this form on top, on the right side of the chart, where it can be easily found.

DESCRIPTION OF CULTURALLY ORIENTED MENTAL HEALTH SERVICES AND CODES
(See Chapter 25, p. 462)

This form was developed in order to:
1. *Describe the cultural basis of various program services.*
2. *Provide a simple code system for referring to these services in client records.*

Keep a copy of this code list in each chart, at the back on the left side. Use the Letter Codes, (e.g., S.C., H.V., E.F., etc.) on progress notes, 90 day reviews and other forms to show how services were culturally relevant.

90-DAY CASE REVIEW/SUMMARY
(See Chapter 25, p. 466)

The state mental health system requires that a case review be done for each client every 90 days to pull together case developments and to assess progress. Reviews should be signed by both Support Counselor and Supervisor.

You will also use this form as a Summary when closing a case. (This form may also be used to make a report to an outside agency or to prepare for a case conference.)

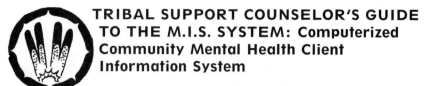

TRIBAL SUPPORT COUNSELOR'S GUIDE TO THE M.I.S. SYSTEM: Computerized Community Mental Health Client Information System

This is the State Mental Health System's official system for keeping track of the number of clients seen and units of service provided by each program. Standard State forms must be filled out and turned into the Mental Health Center each month. These are the only client records kept at the Mental Health Center office. (All client charts are kept in program offices at Tribal sites.) Tribal Programs not using state funds do not need to use these forms or read this section.

Instructions for filling out "Entry Documents"

You need to fill out one "Entry Document" for each client when you first open the case. The following instructions will help you to fill out each part of this two page form.

Instructions for Part 1 of Entry Document

Center Number: 048
Client ID Number: Leave this blank
Skagit Community Mental Health Center Secretarial Staff will assign a number to each case. This number allows them to enter the data on their computer.

1. Client's name should be full name. (Leave title blank.)
2. Enter the client's social security number.
3. Leave blank.
4. Date of entry is the date when you first saw the client.
5. Occupational Codes are on back of form Record under "client-current" if client is an adult.
6. Check only one main source of income.
7. Education - if you don't know, guess. (If less than high school graduate, leave blank.)
8. Legal status for our program is always "voluntary".
9. Census tract for Swinomish is "555"; Upper Skagit is "556".
10. Skagit County is 29.
11. Referral Codes are on back of the form.
12. Guess about monthly income if you do not know exact amount.
13. Number of people who depend on the family's income.

14. Number of years of the client's education.
15. Check "alcohol" or "drug" if the person's use of the substance has caused substantial problems.
16. Check whether or not the client has been hospitalized for a mental health problem. (If you don't know, leave blank.)
17. Check whether or not the client has had mental health treatment before. (Remember that seeing any mental health counselor is considered previous outpatient treatment.)
18. See "Global Assessment Scale" to decide what number best reflects the client's current level of social/psychological functioning.
19. 0 + your personal provider number, given to you by the Mental Health Center.
20. Leave blank.
21. Enter the code # for the client's diagnosis. (Discuss choice of diagnosis with your supervisor. Diagnosis should be the same as on the Intake Form.)
22. Check one. "Acute" refers to severe mental illness with a sudden onset. "Chronic" refers to longterm mental illness. "Serious" refers to serious mental health problems which do not involve psychosis.
23. Leave blank.
24. Leave A and B blank. In C, write 100 if Acutely mentally ill, 200 if Chronically mentally ill, 300 if Seriously disturbed.
25. Your name and date.

Instructions for Part 2 of Entry Document

1. Client's Name.
2. Tribe, Town.
3. Name or N/A.
4. Client's Birthdate.
5. State where born.
6. Handicap status. Check only one box.
7. Employment status. Check all applicable.
8. Ethnic Background. Check one.
9. Language. Check all applicable.
10. Sex. Check one.
11. Marital Status. Check one.
12. Residence. Check one.
13. Who client lives with. Check all applicable.
14. Number of times client has moved in past five years. (If you

don't know, guess.)

15. Phone. Leave blank if no phone.

Sign and date the form at the bottom of page 2.

Turn in all entry documents to the Program Director before the end of each month.

(If these are not turned in to the Mental Health Center by the first of the month, services for these new charts will not be included in computerized statistics for that month.)

Instructions for filling out Client Service Reports

Fill out one service report for each contact you have with a client or with someone else on behalf of the client. Therefore, you will have several of these for each client. Fill them out each day or week and turn in to the Program Director by the end of each week, at seminar time.

Center Number 048

Check "individual" if you saw the client alone.

Check "couple and family" if you saw more than one family member.

Check "group" if you met with clients in a group.

1. Leave client # blank. Write in client name or names. If client canceled, enter "C". If client didn't show up, write "N". Leave "cost center" and "other codes" blank.
2. Print your initials and provider number.
3. Check only one type service (Check "individual", "marital", "family", or "intake" if you saw the client directly; Check 50 or 51 if you saw other family members, friends, teacher, doctor, etc., on behalf of the client; Check "other service code" if your service to the client was a spiritual consultation)
4. Date you provided service
5. Time of service
6. Length of service
7. Place of service Usually this will be "Client's Residence" or "Other" if the service is provided in your office or somewhere else in the tribal community
8. Enter either number of collaterals (family, friends, other providers) seen or contacted on behalf of the client. If you did not meet with any collaterals, enter "0"
9. Check #50
10. The Tribal Mental Health "subprogram" number is 56

REMEMBER....

- *Set a specific time every day to fill out service tickets*
- *Do a service ticket for every client contact, consultation, or collateral contact*
- *Hand in the week's service tickets at each seminar.*

TRIBAL SUPPORT COUNSELOR'S CHECK LIST FOR CLIENT CHARTS

Please check that each client chart contains the following information:

1. Client's dated written or verbal consent for service, witnessed by you.
2. The age, sex and tribal status of the client (to be recorded on face sheet or intake form).
3. An Entry Document and an Intake, containing:
   - A history of the client's problems and immediate concerns (on p. 1 of Intake).
   - Client's social history (family, resources, and overview of the client's social adjustment).
   - A mental status exam.
   - Your initial diagnosis should be recorded on both Intake (p. 5) and Entry Documents), cosigned by your Supervisor.
   - The Global Assessment Score must be recorded on both Intake (p. 5) and Entry Document.
   - A Treatment Plan, (including the client's problems, overall goals of treatment and specific steps to be taken toward achieving each goal) should be recorded on page 6 of the Intake form.
4. A dated progress note for each client contact - with length of time spent, service code numbers and your signature.
5. The chart should contain documentation of the cultural basis of the services (in treatment plan, progress notes, or client summaries).
6. Ninety day summaries for all clients with open charts, signed by you and by your Supervisor.
7. For clients who are deceased, have moved away, refused service, or who are not expected to return to service, be sure that an "Exit Document" has been done and turned in to the Mental Health Center. Also do a Case Summary and have it cosigned by your Supervisor.

ALTERNATIVE TRACKING SYSTEM FOR COMMUNITY SERVICES (Ch. 25, p. 467)

Many services and activities performed by Tribal Support Counselors cannot be recorded in client charts. This can happen for any of the following reasons:

1. The person receiving services is unwilling to sign a consent form or give verbal consent, or does not see themselves as a 'client'.

2. It is inappropriate, (due to the cultural context, family ties or the expectations of the particular client) for the Support Counselor to ask for a formal consent for treatment.

3. The Support Counselor's role in the service being provided is essentially spiritual or religious in nature; therefore, it would be against his/her personal convictions to record this activity in client charts.

4. The client does not fall into any of the three state-defined priority populations; i.e. the client is neither "acutely" nor "chronically" mentally ill nor "seriously disturbed".

5. The service being provided is essentially an "educational" rather than therapeutic activity, aimed at community awareness, prevention or increasing the visibility and accessibility of mental health services, rather than at treatment of existing problems.

6. The activity is aimed at developing general inter-program or inter-agency cooperation, coordination and referral networks, rather than at serving a particular client or clients.

7. The activity is a "Tribal community service function," aimed at increasing community cohesiveness, self esteem, support, and thereby improving the overall mental health status of the Tribal community.

8. The service is provided at a Tribal community other than Swinomish or Upper Skagit.

9. The activity is a training/educational experience for the Support Counselor.

10. The activity is a general supervision experience for the Support Counselor, not focusing on the needs of a particular client.

Monthly Status Reports

Each month a single page statistical report is filled out by the Program Supervisor and turned in to the Skagit County Human Services Coordinator. This form summarizes the number of clients served and number of direct client service hours recorded in client charts and on service tickets for that month. In addition, alternative services (indirect and uncharted program activities) are summarized, including paraprofessional training hours, alternative client services and educational and preventative community service. (See Ch. 25, p. 468)

Chapter Twenty-Five
Sample Record Keeping Forms

INTRODUCTION

This chapter contains the record keeping forms developed by the Skagit Tribes' Mental Health Program. Instructions for their use are given in the previous chapter (Ch. 24)

O ur own experience has been that it is difficult to develop record keeping forms which are culturally acceptable and useful and can at the same time satisfy state or federal requirements. We have revised our forms several times and expect that it may be necessary to do so again.

Other tribal mental health providers should feel free to use or adapt any of these forms in whatever ways seem most practical for a specific program.

This chapter and the preceeding one may be most useful for program administrators struggling with how to meet funding and legal requirements in ways that are minimally invasive.

Tribal Mental Health Program forms included in this chapter are:

Client Service Policy and Consent for Treatment

Referral Form

Intake Form (6 pages, including Social History, Assessment, Mental Status Diagnosis and Initial Service Plan)

Client Family Data Sheet

Progress Note Form

Description of Culturally Oriented Service Types and Service Code List

Consent for Release of Information

90-Day Case Review/Case Summary Form

Quaterly Tracking Sheet for Alternative Community Services

Statistical Report for the month of _____

(Not included are the State Mental Health Management Information System (M.I.S.) forms, the "Entry Document", "Service Report" and "Exit Document" Forms. Programs receiving state funds will have these forms. Others will not need them.)

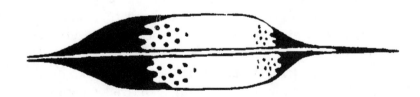

Tribal Mental Health Project
P.O. Box 388 • La Conner, Washington 98257 • Phone (360) 466-3163

TRIBAL SUPPORT COUNSELORS' CLIENT INFORMATION SHEET
(Support Counselors explain this sheet to each client. Client keeps a copy.)

The Tribal Support Counselors are part of a special "culturally oriented" program offered by Skagit Community Mental Health Center in cooperation with the Swinomish and Upper Skagit Tribes. This program is aimed at making counseling and social services for Indian people culturally acceptable and more available. The Support Counselors are tribal community members who have received paraprofessional training in counseling and community resources. They are supervised by mental health professionals working for the Tribe or for Skagit Community Mental Health Center.

THE SERVICES OFFERED BY THIS PROGRAM INCLUDE:

Supportive counseling for individuals and families

Referrals to tribal or county social services

Referrals and support for Traditional Services

Home Visits

Crisis Help

Advocacy for clients dealing with other programs or agencies

Consultation with other providers to ensure that the needs of Indian clients are met in a culturally appropriate way

Clients will discuss and help plan their services with their Support Counselor. Clients may request a meeting with the Program Supervisor if they have any problems or questions.

Personal information about clients will be kept confidential except as disclosure is required by law (as for suspected child abuse, when a client is thought to be a danger to self or others or when ordered by a court having jurisdiction), or as required by standard program policies to ensue the quality and coordination of services to Tribal clients (information may be shared with other Tribal mental health or social services staff who need the information in order to do their jobs). No information will be released to outside agencies or private persons without the client's written permission.

A Cooperative Effort

Swinomish Tribal Community	*Skagit Community Mental Health Center*	*Upper Skagit Indian Tribe*
P.O. Box 388	*208 Kincaid*	*2284 Community Plaza*
La Conner, WA 98257	*Mt. Vernon, WA 98273*	*Sedro-Woolley, WA 98284*

Tribal Mental Health Project

P.O. Box 388 • La Conner, Washington 98257 • Phone (360) 466-3163

CLIENT CONSENT FOR SERVICES

I have read and received a copy of the "Tribal Support Counselors' Client Information Sheet". I understand these policies. I wish to receive services through this program (or for services to be provided to my child or legal dependent). My consent will continue in force until such time as I give written notice withdrawing consent.

Person to receive service: _____

Signed: _____

Witness to client's informed

written consent: _____

Date:_____

****

For cultural reasons this client _____was not asked to sign _____ felt uncomfortable signing. Specific cultural reasons are:

_____client is an elder _____client does not read well _____client dislikes written documents _____client would be offended if asked to sign

Other: _____

I certify that I have explained the contents of the Client Information Sheet to this client, that he or she understands the conditions of service and has given fully informed and voluntary verbal consent to receive services.

_____

Support Counselor's Signature

_____

Date Consent Obtained

A Cooperative Effort

Swinomish Tribal Community	*Skagit Community Mental Health Center*	*Upper Skagit Indian Tribe*
P.O. Box 388	*208 Kincaid*	*2284 Community Plaza*
La Conner, WA 98257	*Mt. Vernon, WA 98273*	*Sedro-Woolley, WA 98284*

Tribal Mental Health Project

P.O. Box 388 • La Conner, Washington 98257 • Phone (360) 466-3163

Referral Form

(Use this form to make referrals or to record a verbal referral received)

Client's Name: _____ Date: _____

Age:_____

Client Address and Phone: _____

Person making referral: _____

Referral Made To: _____

Type of Service Referred For:

____Personal or Family Counseling   ____Evaluation

____Information/Referral to Outside Agency   ____Crisis Support

____ Case Management/Client Advocacy   _ _ _ _ T r a d i t i o n a l
____Other:_____   Service

CLIENT'S SITUATION, NEED AND BACKGROUND:

Problem or Need:

Current Situation:

Background:

Does client understand reason for referral:

____Yes ____No ____Needs more explanation

Plans:

Appointment made for ____/____/____, at ____a.m./____p.m.

Client to make contact _____

Provider to contact client _____

Other Plan: _____

A Cooperative Effort

Swinomish Tribal Community *P.O. Box 388* *La Conner, WA 98257*	*Skagit Community Mental Health Center* *208 Kincaid* *Mt. Vernon, WA 98273*	*Upper Skagit Indian Tribe* *2284 Community Plaza* *Sedro-Woolley, WA 98284*

Tribal Mental Health Project

P.O. Box 388 • La Conner, Washington 98257 • Phone (360) 466-3163

CLIENT INTAKE

Client Name: _____ Date: _____

File#: _____ Family Contact Person: _____

Address & Phone :_____ Birthdate: _____

Tribal Status: _____ Referred by: _____

PRESENTING PROBLEMS: (Include client's view of the problems and their causes)

RELEVANT HISTORY: (Family, marriage, support system, traditional orientation, etc.)

PREVIOUS TREATMENT: (Include counseling, self help, hospitalizations, spiritual help, etc.)

____ Mental health counseling, provided by: _____

____hospitalization for _____   ____ Smokehouse help

____A.A.   ____Indian Doctor

____Alanon   ____ACOA Group

____Indian Child Welfare help   ____Alcohol treatment

____Other:_____

Comments:_____

_____

_____

A Cooperative Effort

Swinomish Tribal Community *P.O. Box 388* *La Conner, WA 98257*	*Skagit Community Mental Health Center* *208 Kincaid* *Mt. Vernon, WA 98273*	*Upper Skagit Indian Tribe* *2284 Community Plaza* *Sedro-Woolley, WA 98284*

p.2 of Intake

Name(s):_____

PHYSICAL/SEXUAL ABUSE HISTORY:

____ Physically Abused as ____ Child, ____ as Adult, by _____

____ Neglected as child

____ Sexual Abuse ____ as Child, ____ as Adult, by _____

____ No History of Abuse   Comments: _____

_____

DEVELOPMENTAL/EDUCATIONAL HISTORY:

Education completed:_____

Childhood Learning Ability was ____ very low ____ low, ____ average,

____ high, ____ very high

Childhood problems in ____ reading, ____ writing, ____ getting along

with others, ____ difficulty concentrating or sitting still

Comments: _____

_____

WORK HISTORY:

Most recent job: _____

Usual job: _____

Training in: _____

Work Adjustment: _____

Comments: _____

_____

SPIRITUAL INVOLVEMENT:

____ Shaker   Other: _____

____ Smokehouse   Family Spiritual involvement_____

____ Catholic   Personal involvement _____

____ Pentecostal   Comments:_____

_____

MEDICAL/PHYSICAL PROBLEMS: _____

_____

PRIMARY HEALTH PROVIDER: _____

_____

MEDICATIONS:_____

p.3 of Intake

DRUG AND ALCOHOL USE/ABUSE:

____ Alcohol Abuse	____ No Substance Abuse
____ Drug Abuse	____ Alcohol/Drug Problem in Family

Comments:_____

MENTAL STATUS:

Appearance

____ Healthy Looking	____ Clean/Tidy
____ Unusual Physical Characteristics	____ Unusual Clothing

Comments/Examples: _____

_____

Movements (Motor Activity):

____ Normal Posture	____ Rigid/Tense
____ Normal Gait	____ Slumped
____ Unusual Gestures	____ Relaxed
____ Moves Fast	____ Restless or Fidgety
____ Moves Slowly	

Comments/Examples: _____

_____

Speech:

____Rapid	____Slurred
____Doesn't Talk	____Slowed
____Stammers	____Blocked
____Loud	____Not Understandable
____Soft	____Clear

Comments/Examples: _____

_____

Affect/Mood:

____Depressed/Sad	____Angry/Hostile	
____Negative or Gloomy	____Fearful	____Anxious/Tense
____Suspicious	____Changes Quickly	____Dulled or Bland
____Shows no Feeling	____Elated/Euphoric	
____Doesn't seem to fit thoughts or situation		

Comments/Examples: _____

_____

p.4 of Intake

Thought Content

____Disorganized   ____Hallucinations:_____
____Confused
____Obsessive (repeated,   ____Suicidal Thoughts
    uncontrollable thoughts)   ____Jumps from one thing to the
____Compulsive (cannot stop   next; ideas seem disconnected)
    doing something)   ____Phobias
____ Delusions _____   ____Feelings of unreality or of disas-
          sociation or depersonalization

Comments/Examples: _____

_____

Cognitive Functions

____Attention/Concentration Problem   ____Impaired Reasoning
____Disoriented (confused about when,   ____Difficulty Making
    where or who   Routine Decisions
____Memory Problem   ____Good Insight   ____Poor Insight

Comments/Examples: _____

_____

Reality Contact

____Good   ____Seems Out of Contact   ____Distorted

Comments/Examples: _____

_____

Other

____Difficulty Falling Asleep _____ ____Recent Weight Loss
____Wakes Early or Many Times _____ ____Recent Weight Gain
____Nightmares

Comments/Examples: _____

_____

p.5 of Intake

SUPPORT COUNSELORS' OBSERVATIONS AND ASSESSMENT
(Describe current level of functioning, strengths, problems and needs.)

TENTATIVE DSM IV DIAGNOSIS (Name of condition and Code #)

Global Assessment Score at   Intake:_____
PRIORITY CODE: ____Acute (#1)   ____Chronic (#2)
                        ____Serious (#3)   ____other

Supervisor:_____

p.6 of Intake

Name(s):_____

INITIAL SERVICE PLAN
1. Client Problems/Needs
  a.
  b.
  c.

2. Expected Outcome of Treatment (client's behavior, skills, attitude, etc.)
  a.
  b.
  c.

3. Medical Necessity Indicates the following treatment:

Modality	Frequency	Timeframe
Support Counseling	_____	_____
Home Visits	_____	_____
Traditional Consultation	_____	_____
Client Advocacy/Case Management	_____	_____
Extended Family Networking	_____	_____
Medical Evaluation	_____	_____
Play Therapy	_____	_____
Children's Group	_____	_____
Parenting Group	_____	_____
Other _____	_____	_____

Referral to:_____

The above individual service plan has been discussed between client and Support Counselor and the above goals have been agreed to.

Client's Signature_____ Date: _____

Support Counselor Signature_____ Date: _____

For cultural reasons this client ___was not asked ___ refused to sign this form, but the client did give verbal consent to above treatment plan.

Support Counselor Signature _____ Date: _____

Supervisor Signature_____ Date:_____

CLIENT/FAMILY DATA SHEET

Client_____ Birthdate _____ File #_____

Date Opened _____ Living With _____ At_____

_____ Phone _____ SS# _____

Messages With _____ Marital Status _____

Tribal Status _____

Primary Caseworker/Counselor _____

Name	Relationship	Birthdate	Tribal Status	Degree Indian Blood

Changes in Data: (Note Nature and Date of Change)

A Cooperative Effort

Swinomish Tribal Community   *Skagit Community Mental Health Center*   *Upper Skagit Indian Tribe*
P.O. Box 388   *208 Kincaid*   *2284 Community Plaza*
La Conner, WA 98257   *Mt. Vernon, WA 98273*   *Sedro-Woolley, WA 98284*

TRIBAL MENTAL HEALTH PROGRESS NOTES

Client_____ File#_____

Date: / / M-F ___Weekend___8 a.m-5___5 p.m.-8 p.m.___8 p.m.-8 a.m___
Pre-set appt.___ Walkin___ Emergency___

_____
_____
_____
_____
_____
_____
_____
_____

Service Codes: _____ Minutes: _____ Signed: _____

Date: / / M-F ___Weekend___8 a.m-5___5 p.m.-8 p.m.___ 8 p.m.-8 a.m.___
Pre-set appt.___ Walkin___ Emergency___

_____
_____
_____
_____
_____
_____
_____

Service Codes: _____ Minutes:_____ Signed: _____

Date: / / M-F ___Weekend___8 a.m-5___5 p.m.-8 p.m.___8 p.m.-8 a.m.___
Pre-set appt.___ Walkin___ Emergency___

_____
_____
_____
_____
_____
_____

Service Codes: _____ Minutes: _____ Signed: _____

Tribal Mental Health Project
P.O. Box 388 • La Conner, Washington 98257 • Phone (360) 466-3163

DESCRIPTION OF CULTURALLY ORIENTED MENTAL HEALTH SERVICES AND CODES

This sheet explains the cultural basis of the various services offered by this program as well as the simple two letter code for service categories used to simplify record keeping.

A copy of this two-page description should be included in every client's chart for easy reference by reviewers.

Type of Service	Service Codes
Tribal Support Counselor Provider	SC
Home Visit	HV
Tribal Community Contact	TC
Traditional Spiritual Consult	TS
Religious Work	RW
Extended Family Networking	EF
Tribal Function	TF
Cultural Education to Non-Tribal Agency	CE
Client Advocacy	CA
Consultation with Tribal Social Service Provider or Supervisor	CN

Definitions of Service Categories and Cultural Justification

Tribal Support Counselor Provider (SC): These are natural helpers in Tribal communities hired by the program and given specific mental health skill training to allow a unique blending of Indian and standard mental health approaches.

Home Visits (HV): Since Indian lifestyles tend to be family oriented, the Indian home is often the most effective to provide service directly in client homes, and for community members to visit those in crisis as a sign of respect, support, acceptance and concern. Therefore, the "Home Visit" has unique cultural meaning and is not merely a convenience or 'outreach' effort. It is a valuable component of mental health service to Indian clients.

A Cooperative Effort

Swinomish Tribal Community	*Skagit Community Mental Health Center*	*Upper Skagit Indian Tribe*
P.O. Box 388	*208 Kincaid*	*2284 Community Plaza*
La Conner, WA 98257	*Mt. Vernon, WA 98273*	*Sedro-Woolley, WA 98284*

Tribal Community Contact (TC): This project not only emphasizes providing mental health services within the Tribal Community, but also by members of this community. Many services are provided at unstructured "natural" times and places within the flow of community life. Support Counselors respond to clients as they encounter them throughout the daily cycle as well as at prearranged appointments. Likewise, Support Counselors respond to concerns, information, and referrals made by community members.

Traditional Spiritual Consults (TS): This refers to seeking evaluation, recommendations or service from a recognized Indian Spiritual Leader, Healer, or Indian doctor. These individuals may be either Indian Shaker Ministers, Smokehouse or Powwow leaders, or Medicine People who heal through personal powers. Such specialists may be called in either as advisors or as direct providers, when agreed upon between client and counselor.

Religious Work (RW): This refers to direct spiritually oriented activity engaged in by Support Counselor with the client. This includes such things as traditional or Shaker prayer, or direct participation by the Support Counselor in spiritual healing services for a client.

Extended Family Networking (EF): The basis of Indian life is often considered to be the large and complex extended family ties, which involve reciprocal responsibilities and deep emotional bonds. Indian people tend to define themselves by their unique place within their kinship networks, and to be very conscious of their special roles and responsibilities in respect to extended family members. "Family" usually includes many people beyond the typical non-Indian nuclear family, and in some cases may include over a hundred people recognized as "close" family members. The Indian person's mental health status is often greatly affected by the health and degree of harmony of these family relationships. Working with extended family is therefore critical in providing effective and acceptable service. Extended family may need to be called upon for support, discipline, teaching, or for spiritual activities. The permission, advice and endorsement of family elders is often needed in order to help clients accept and benefit from services.

464 Record Keeping for Tribal Mental Health Programs

Tribal Function (TF): This refers to mental health services offered during or in the context of a traditional tribal event, function or affair. Tribal life consists of a seasonal round of "doings" and "gatherings" to celebrate, honor, or mourn. Some are regular annual events, such as bone games, canoe races, powwows and holiday "dinners". Others are new functions started by tribal government or sponsored by community groups such as the Ladies Club, church groups, elders, parents' committee, etc. Still other functions are sponsored by particular families, generally to honor a family member. These may be either secular or religious functions. All are times when tribal community members gather and when help and support may be given to individuals and families in need. Funerals are particularly important times in tribal community life and are especially important for offering help to families in grief.

Cultural Education to Non-Tribal Agency (CE): One service performed by this program is the education of non-Indian mental health and social service providers concerning Tribal culture, values and practices. This service is vital to Indian clients, in order to reduce the misunderstandings and barriers they face in seeking needed services.

Client Advocacy (CA): This refers to active advocacy on behalf of an Indian client in dealing with external agencies. Support Counselors may seek and arrange needed services for clients. Clients may be accompanied to appointments by Support Counselors, who may also be asked by the client to "speak for them", i.e., to express their needs and viewpoints. In Indian culture where individuals are taught to rely on family and not to appear aggressive or self serving, an advocate who can understand and express the client's viewpoint is often needed.

Consultation with Tribal Social Service Providers or Supervisors (CN): Our holistic model of services requires that mental health be integrated with other health, education and social services, and that these services be tribally based. Cross-disciplinary coordination is important. Also, in order for Support Counselors to provide quality services, supervision by professional mental health specialists is required. Clients benefit from these consultative services in the enhanced quality and comprehensiveness of the services they receive.

Tribal Mental Health Project
P.O. Box 388 • La Conner, Washington 98257 • Phone (360) 466-3163

CONSENT FOR EXCHANGE OF INFORMATION

I, _____ give my permission for the Support Counselors of the Skagit Tribes' Mental Health Program to exchange confidential information about me with:

Name of Agency _____

Address _____

Type of Information to be released:

_____

_____

_____

Purpose for exchange of information:

_____

_____

_____

My permission to release information under the above conditions will continue in force until revoked in writing, or until 90 days after my last face to face service contact.

Authorizing Signature: Relationship to Client:

_____   _____

Witness: _____   Date: _____

To Recipient: <u>This information has been given to you from confidential records. Any further disclosure of it without specific written consent of the person to whom it pertains is prohibited by law.</u>

A Cooperative Effort

Swinomish Tribal Community	*Skagit Community Mental Health Center*	*Upper Skagit Indian Tribe*
P.O. Box 388	*208 Kincaid*	*2284 Community Plaza*
La Conner, WA 98257	*Mt. Vernon, WA 98273*	*Sedro-Woolley, WA 98284*

Tribal Mental Health Project
P.O. Box 388 • La Conner, Washington 98257 • Phone (360) 466-3163

90 DAY CASE REVIEW AND/OR FINAL CASE SUMMARY

Client's Name _____ Date _____

File # _____ Case Review _____ Case Summary _____

Date Case Opened _____ Date of Most Recent Entry _____

Type of Service Given: (Check all that apply)

____Personal Counseling   ____Client Advocacy

____Family Counseling   ____Case Management

____Home Visits   ____Referred to Tribal Provider

____Traditional Spiritual   ____Referred to Non-Tribal Service

____Extended Family Networking   ____Other: Specify

Course of Treatment: (Progress and Need for continued tx)

Current Status and/or Circumstances at Termination: (New problems, goals, tx)

Medical Necessity Indicates the following Treatment:

Modality   Frequency   Timeframe

Client Signature: _____

Closing Diagnosis:_____ Support Counselor: _____

Closing GAS:_____   Priority:_____

Supervisor:_____ Date:_____

A Cooperative Effort

Swinomish Tribal Community	*Skagit Community Mental Health Center*	*Upper Skagit Indian Tribe*
P.O. Box 388	*208 Kincaid*	*2284 Community Plaza*
La Conner, WA 98257	*Mt. Vernon, WA 98273*	*Sedro-Woolley, WA 98284*

Tribal Mental Health Project

QUARTERLY TRACKING SHEET
for ALTERNATIVE COMMUNITY SERVICES

NAME: _____ REPORTING PERIOD: _____ to _____

Instructions:
Record # of Hours of Activity in top half of weekly block.
Record # of Tribal Community Members served in bottom half. ⟶

Total number of hours of service in each category and unduplicated # of clients served during the quarter. Record in column at far right.

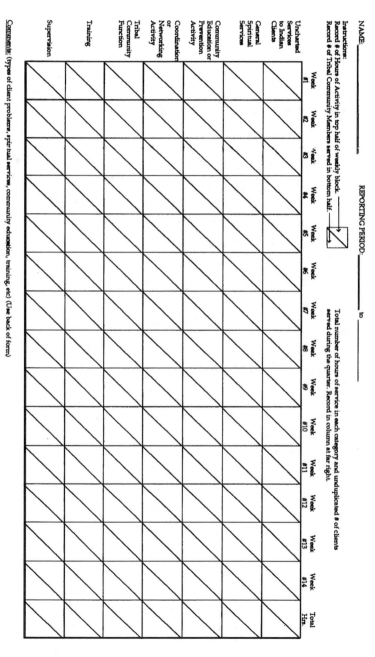

	Week #1	Week #2	Week #3	Week #4	Week #5	Week #6	Week #7	Week #8	Week #9	Week #10	Week #11	Week #12	Week #13	Week #14	Total Hrs.
Uncharted Services to Indian Clients															
General Spiritual Services															
Community Education or Prevention Activity															
Coordination or Networking Activity															
Tribal Community Function															
Training															
Supervision															

<u>Comments</u>: (types of client problems, spiritual services, community education, training, etc) (Use the back of form)

Tribal Mental Health Project
P.O. Box 388 • La Conner, Washington 98257 • Phone (360) 466-3163

STATISTICAL REPORT FOR THE MONTH OF _____, 200__

This report is submitted to the Skagit County Human Services Coordinator, in compliance with contract requirements for monthly statistical information concerning the operation of Skagit Community Mental Health Center's TRIBAL MENTAL HEALTH PROGRAM.

Number of clients served during this month _____
Unduplicated number of clients served this
                                    fiscal year _____
Number of units of direct service provided   _____
Number of hours of paraprofessional mental
                        health training provided _____
Number of units of alternative community
                            client services provided _____
Number of units of preventative/educational
                                services provided _____

Comments: _____
_____
_____
_____

A Cooperative Effort

Swinomish Tribal Community
P.O. Box 388
La Conner, WA 98257

Skagit Community Mental Health Center
208 Kincaid
Mt. Vernon, WA 98273

Upper Skagit Indian Tribe
2284 Community Plaza
Sedro-Woolley, WA 98284

Part Five

Training for Indian Mental Health Workers

Introduction
Part Five

This Fifth Part presents an approach to training tribal mental health workers which has been developed by the Skagit Tribes' Mental Health Program.

Included in this part are:
- A discussion of the need for training Indian Tribal Mental Health Staff.
- A description of a college-accredited training program developed for Tribal Support Counselors.
- Practical suggestions for the development of tribal training programs.

Practical training materials, including:
- A curriculum for a two year Associate Degree program in Human Services with a specialization in Tribal Mental Health
- Selected course outlines
- A plan for accredited tribal field placements
- Learning contracts
- Support Counselor Evaluation form
- Selected materials developed and distributed in 1989 for a series of Washington State Inter-Tribal, Inter-Agency Tribal Mental Health Conferences, including: flier, course description, sample agendas, sample exercises, selected handouts, and conference evaluation form.

PART FIVE Training for Indian Mental Health Workers

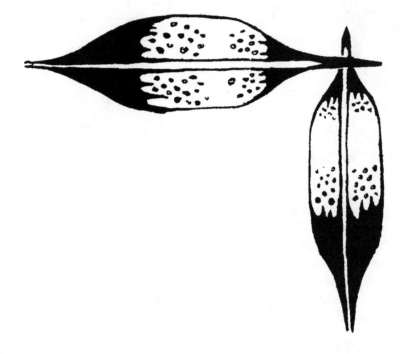

Contents
Part Five

Introduction to Part 5 471

Contents, Part 5 473

Chapter Twenty-Six
***The Need for Tribal Mental Health
Worker Training and The Skagit Tribes'
Mental Health Worker Training Program***   475

The Need for Tribal Mental Health
Worker Training 475

Startup Training Activities 477

Developing Linkages with
Local Community College 478

Tribal Practicum Seminar 480

Field Placements 481

Supervision 481

Individualized Training Plans 482

Chapter Twenty-Seven
***Practical Suggestions for
Tribal Mental Health Training***   485

Practical Suggestions for
Tribal Mental Health Training 486

Chapter Twenty-Eight
Sample Training Plans and Outlines   489

Survey of Training Priorities 489

First Year Tribal Mental Health
Training Program Leading Toward
One Year Certificate in Tribal Mental Health 493

Second Year Tribal Mental Health
Training Program 496

Additional Special Training and Workshops
attended by Tribal Support Counselors 498
Plan for Accredited Field Placements 500

Supervision of Field Placement and Direct
Client Services Individual Supervision 501

Group Supervision 501

Evaluation of Field Experiences 502

Quarterly Field Placement Learning Contract 503

Field Placement Evaluation 504

Tribal Practicum Seminar Outline 507

Introduction to Mental Health Counseling in the
Native American Community Course Outline 508

Sample Exam 508

Tribal Life Cycles Course Outline 509

Chapter Twenty-Nine
Healing Through Cooperation and Tradition
Conference Materials and Exercises   511

Letter of Invitation 513

Course Description:
Tribal Mental Health Approaches 514

Conference Flyer/Healing Through
Cooperation and Tradition 515

Sample Conference Agenda, Healing
Through Cooperation and Tradition 516

Cultural Mixer Exercise 521

Positive Cultural Identity - Poster 522

Panel - Inter-Related Aspects of Indian Culture 523

Stereotypes Exercise 524

Tribal Lifestyles Exercise 525

What Mental Health Workers Can Learn
From Indian Culture - Poster 526

Complementary Roles for Professionals
and Paraprofessionals in
Indian Mental Health Programs - Poster 527

Information Exchange 528
Information Exchange Sheet 529

Worksheet for Tribal/Mental Health
Agency Collaboration 530

Conference Evaluation Form 532

Chapter Twenty-Six
The Need for Tribal
Mental Health Worker Training
and
The Skagit Tribes' Mental Health
Worker Training Program

To be effective, tribal mental health workers must be knowledgeable and competent in both Indian and mainstream culture and treatment systems. They must be able to comfortably straddle the cultural gap, so as to be able to help Indian clients receive the most appropriate services.

Ideally, tribal mental health workers should be Indian people familiar with Indian culture. When non-tribal services are needed, Indian mental health workers must assist clients with the unfamiliar, impersonal and often frustrating "white" mental health and social services system.

Because of these complex needs, tribal mental health workers need specialized skills. Unfortunately, there are not enough Indians trained in mental health theory, practice and service delivery to meet existing needs for service.

Indian mental health specialists are often employed by Indian organizations in Urban areas and may not be available in small reservation communities. In addition, Indians from other tribes may not have intimate knowledge of local family resources and day to day tribal community life.

A great need exists for mental health training for Indian people for the following reasons:

1) *There are not enough Indian Mental Health Specialists to meet service needs.*

2) *There is an even greater shortage of trained mental health workers who are members of small reservation communities.*

3) *The training in mental health and social services provided by most colleges and universities does not adequately prepare mental health workers for the unique challenges of working in tribal communities.*

The approach of the Skagit Tribes' Mental Health Program is to hire and train members of the tribal community where services are delivered. Thus, *the Tribal Support Counselors are not only Indian people but are also fully participating members of the tribal communities in which they work.*

These tribal mental health workers were *selected by their Tribes* due to their familiarity with their community as well as their skills as "natural helpers". Our approach has been to identify individuals in the tribal community who were respected and trusted as "helpers", and then to provide them with intensive training in mental health concepts and treatment skills.

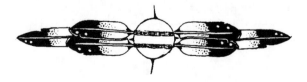

THE SKAGIT TRIBES' MENTAL HEALTH WORKER TRAINING PROGRAM

Training of Indian mental health workers has been a central aspect of the Skagit Tribes' Mental Health Program. Advisory Board members and program staff agreed that training needed to:

- **Prepare Indian mental health workers for the practical challenges of working in their own tribal communities.**
- **Be college accredited and lead toward a recognized degree.**
- **Include instruction by Indian professionals and other mental health specialists experienced in working in the Indian community**
- **Allow flexible and individualized training suited to the educational background and career goals of each Tribal Support Counselor.**
- **Provide on-going training as a regular and paid part of the job.**
- **Provide training which is responsive to cultural values.**
- **Encourage cross-cultural learning exchanges between Indian and non-Indian mental health providers.**

STARTUP TRAINING ACTIVITIES

The first step taken in designing the training program was to conduct a survey of Program Advisory Board members and Tribal Social Services Staff concerning:
1) mental health needs in the tribal community
2) areas of training considered most important for tribal mental health workers.

The priority areas identified in this survey (see Chapter 28) were compared with available training resources. It was decided that the needs could best be met by a combination of:
- Specialized workshops on Indian Mental Health Issues
- Formal coursework in Mental Health and Human Services
- Seminars on Tribal Mental Health Issues
- Supervised Field work

Because our original four Tribal Support Counselors were all new to the Human Service/Mental Health field, an initial period of intensive training was needed in order to orient these workers to the field and provide basic counseling skills. Therefore, the Support Counselors spent their first month in full-time training. Some training was provided by the Program Director and other staff of the Community Mental Health Center.

The Support Counselors also participated in a month-long series of Indian-oriented alcoholism and counseling courses offered at the Swinomish Tribe through Northwest Indian Community College. This was especially good introductory training because it focused on tribal realities and Indian values. The instructor was an Indian alcohol counselor.

DEVELOPING LINKAGES WITH THE LOCAL COMMUNITY COLLEGE

Meetings were held with representatives of the local Community College to discuss how college resources could be combined with program resources to meet the unique training needs of the Tribal Support Counselors. College administrators and Human Service Department instructors responded favorably to the idea of collaborating in providing a specialized training program which would give credit for tribal learning experiences as well as selected Human Services courses. The college was eager to attract Indian students and glad to arrange credit for new courses offered by Mental Health Center program staff, especially since this entailed no cost to the college for instructor fees.[1]

A one year accredited Tribal Mental Health Certificate Program was developed. (see First Year Training Plan, Chapter 25). All courses and field experiences for this one year certificate program were arranged so that they would also apply toward the two year Associate of Technical Arts Degree in Human Services. This was done by comparing our Program's training priorities with Human Services Department requirements: *A plan was developed whereby courses specific to Indian and tribal issues were substituted for regular Human Services degree requirements.*

Culturally oriented courses were provided in two ways:

1) Mental health and alcoholism classes offered through Northwest Indian Community College were incorporated into the Tribal Mental Health Certificate Program, and credits were transferred from Northwest Indian College to Skagit Valley College.

2) Courses specific to tribal mental health work were designed and added to the community college catalog, were taught by the Tribal Mental Health Program Director at tribal sites, and were open only to the tribal mental health Support Counselors. (See course descriptions in Chapter 25.)

Cooperative arrangements with the Community College helped Tribal Support Counselors feel at ease in the college setting and promoted cultural awareness on the part of all Human Service students and instructors. This was done by:

• Tribal Support Counselors taking courses at both the Community College at Tribal sites.

• The Program Director maintaining close communication with the chairperson of the Human Services Department at the Community College.

• The Program Director teaching the "Psychopathology" class at the college for all Human Services students, including the Tribal Support counselors.

• Arrangements were also made for an Indian alcoholism professional to teach two substance abuse courses at the college.

During the first year of this program the Tribal Support Counselors spent approximately ten hours each week in training and educational activities, as a regular part of their paid work hours. All tuition, book expenses and mileage to class were provided by the Community Mental Health Center, or by financial aide when available. Most training focused on the development of basic counseling and social services skills needed in the tribal setting.

In the first year of the Program, all four Tribal Support Counselors completed 65 college credits and obtained a one-year certificate in Human Services.

TRIBAL PRACTICUM SEMINAR

A particularly important training experience has been our "Tribal Practicum Seminar", offered three hours each week at Tribal settings (course description in Chapter 28). This seminar is coordinated by the Program Director and focuses upon practical service related issues and case plans.

Presentations are made by the Program Director, psychiatric and other staff of the Community Mental Health Center or by other Indian mental health professionals. *Discussions are interactive and focus upon exploring approaches which are appropriate for Indian culture. The seminar provides an opportunity to discuss client needs and also to explore staff interactions and the personal stress experienced by Support Counselors in working in their own communities.*

Seminar training topics have included:
- client service approaches
- treatment plans
- record keeping
- confidentiality
- reporting laws
- depression
- empowerment
- tribal environmental issues
- child abuse
- Indian child welfare laws
- Indian drinking patterns
- traditional Indian ways of coping with grief
- the therapeutic value of Indian spiritual practices
- age and sex roles in the Indian Community, etc.
- Post Traumatic Stress Disorder

An important training opportunity for the Tribal Support Counselors has been the regular involvement of a Community Mental Health Center Psychiatrist in the Tribal Practicum Seminar. This Psychiatrist meets with Program staff once a month for clinical training, case consultation and cross-cultural discussion. (See Part III, Chapter 17 for comments of psychiatrist). These contacts have:
1) strengthened the skills of tribal staff
2) increased the cultural sensitivity of the non-Indian mental health personnel

3) highlighted the importance placed on this program by the Mental Health Center.

FIELD PLACEMENTS

All 21 credits of field placement required for the two year Associate of Arts degree in Human Services were earned by Tribal Support Counselors as a regular part of their work schedules at Tribal sites. (See Field Placement Plan in Chapter 25) During the first Program year, the Tribal Support Counselors took 7 credits of field placement each quarter.

Each quarter an individual "Learning Contract" was developed cooperatively between each Support Counselor, the Community College Human Services Instructor and the Tribal Program Supervisor. Support Counselors selected areas of particular interest such as depression, working with isolated elderly, working with sexually abused children or working with clients with spiritual difficulties.

Goals and objectives for experiential learning through direct services to Indian clients were specified in Learning Contracts. Support Counselors and Supervisors worked together to meet these goals.

SUPERVISION

Professional supervision is important not only in maintaining the quality of client services but also in providing emotional support to the Tribal Support Counselors, whose jobs are inherently stressful. A combination of individual and group supervision has been found in this program to be the most helpful.

Group supervision allows exchange of experiences and ideas between the Tribal Support Counselors, provides a forum for discussion of practical challenges in tribal mental health work and builds group cohesion among Program staff. This is especially important since the Program served two Tribal Communities located approximately forty minutes apart. Weekly group supervision through the Tribal Practicum Seminar provided a much needed occasion for all Program staff to meet in one place. These seminars were a central means for building Program identity.

Individual supervision was equally important. Diagnoses, intakes and client service plans were discussed by Support Counselors and Supervisors. Individual meetings also provided an opportunity for Tribal Support Counselors to explore personal issues relevant to counseling and other mental health services. Individual supervision encouraged communication between Tribal Support Counselors and supervisory staff.

Individual supervision was also provided weekly, by the Program Director, other mental health professionals employed by the Tribes, the Indian Health Service or the Mental Health Center. Both the tribes and the Indian Health Service donated supervision time to the Tribal Mental Health Program. Supervisory assignments were changed periodically in order to ensure that Tribal Support Counselors had the opportunity to work with therapists of different backgrounds and orientations.

Changes in staff availability at the tribes on occasion produced problems in providing enough individual supervisory time. In that individual supervision is essential to providing Support Counselors with needed emotional and clinical support, other alternatives for supervision were developed. For example, a fourth-year psychiatric resident from the University of Washington was recruited to provide weekly supervision to two Support Counselors over a six month period. This resulted in a satisfactory learning experience both for the Support Counselors and for the psychiatric resident. On another occasion, a master's level psychology student serving an internship at the Community Mental Health Center provided case consultation and therapeutic assistance to Support Counselors.

INDIVIDUALIZED TRAINING PLANS

In the second and third program years training plans for each Support Counselor became individualized due to:
1. The unique interests of each Tribal Support Counselor
2. Differing levels of previous education
3. Individualized academic and career goals.

One Support Counselor completed a B.A. degree in Community Services. Two other Support Counselors pursued associate degrees in Human Services. Following completion of the one-year Tribal Mental Health Certificate, our Cultural Consultant chose to take specialized workshops. Both Tribal Practicum Seminar and supervised field work continued. Tribal Support Counselors also attended various specialized Indian mental health and social services workshops as these become available from time to time.

Notes and References

1. Skagit Valley College's willingness to collaborate in developing this innovative program may be partially due to their established cooperative relationship with Skagit Community Mental Health Center, as well as to the fact that the Tribal Mental Health Program Director had previously been an instructor in the Colleges' Human Services Program and so was familiar with that program and college requirements. Prior to this arrangement the college had had difficulty attracting Indian students. Since the program began, the number of Indian students at the college has greatly increased, with several individuals, in addition to the Support Counselors, taking Human Services courses.

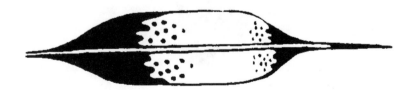

Chapter Twenty-Seven
Practical Suggestions for
Tribal Mental Health Training

T he following suggestions are based on the experiences of the Skagit Tribes' Mental health program. This training program was funded as part of a special grant administered by a community mental health center. The training was designed for paraprofessional Indian mental health staff. However, it is hoped that the following suggestions may be useful in a variety of funding situations and for tribal mental health workers with a wide range of experiential and academic backgrounds.

Practical Suggestions for Tribal Mental Health Training:

1) *The tribe and/or agency administrating the tribal mental health program must make a strong commitment to specialized training for all tribal mental health workers.*

2) *Tribal government, Advisory Board members and tribal social services staff should have early and ongoing input* into the development of the training program in order to ensure that the program will be responsive to the needs of the particular tribal community.

3) *All agencies involved in the tribal mental health program should collaborate* in developing a training program; in particular a tribe, a mental health agency and a community college or university can successfully cooperate in training. Other agencies such as the Indian Health Service or local social service agencies may offer supervision, field placements or workshops.

4) *Training activities should earn college credits* and arrangements should be made for both course work and field placements to apply toward a specific degree program. If local colleges cannot offer needed training, it maybe possible to arrange for training at local tribal sites under the auspices of another college. For instance, the Northwest Indian Community College, (formerly Lummi Community College) is offering a Human Services training program and may be able to work with other tribes to provide Human Services courses, college breadth requirements or special cultural classes. Often local community colleges may be able to add course offerings, especially if the tribe or mental health agency can provide an instructor.

5) *The training curriculum should include course work on Indian culture,* the natural resources and strengths of the Indian community, the therapeutic value of traditional healing, culturally oriented mental health approaches and practical preparation for working in tribal communities.

6) *Training should include courses and seminars offered at tribal locations as well as at regular college settings.*

7) *Whenever possible training should be provided by Indian instructors* and other mental health specialists experienced in working in tribal communities. This will provide positive

Indian role models and will ensure that training is in tune with tribal realities.

8) ***Considerable time should be allowed for building group cohesiveness, rapport and a strong program identity.*** This is especially important in the initial phase of a new program. Human potential techniques and experiential learning can be adapted to fit cultural values and communication styles. For example, care should be taken that less verbal staff not feel pressured to self-disclose or talk in a group setting until they chose to do so. Training exercises should be sensitive to Indian extended family experiences and values.

9) ***The educational background and reading level of each tribal mental health trainee should be assessed*** and training experiences should be selected which are appropriate to the existing skill level of the trainees. Opportunities for skill building in areas of educational weakness should be provided. This may take the form of tutoring in reading and writing or assisting the tribal mental health trainee to get his/her G.E.D.tribal situation. For instance, confidentiality laws should be reviewed in terms of the particular challenges faced in reservation communities; family dynamics theory should be discussed in terms of its applicability to Indian extended family patterns, andthe challenges of working with family members should be directly addressed.

10) ***Efforts should be made to relate general mental health concepts and practices to the realities of the tribal situation.*** For instance, confidentiality laws should be reviewed in terms of the particular challenges faced in reservation communities; family dynamics theory should be discussed in terms of its applicability to Indian extended family patterns, and the challenges of working with family members should be directly addressed.

11) ***Small group discussion may be more productive than a lecture format or extensive reading.*** A seminar or discussion groups involving all program staff can be helpful in maintaining program cohesiveness and keeping the program culturally "on track".

12) ***Indian-specific training materials should be used*** whenever possible, including articles, books and videos. (see Part VI)

13) ***It is important to expose tribal mental health trainees to a variety of viewpoints*** and approaches. Both Indian and non-

Indian mental health specialists can be invited to make presentations on a variety of topics. Field trips to visit other tribal programs and mainstream mental health agencies may also be helpful.

14) ***Training must be made financially accessible*** to tribal mental health workers. Training and course work should take place during regular paid work hours. Financial aide for college course work is often available through Tribal Adult Education programs, Bureau of Indian Affairs Scholarships or through the Financial Aide Programs at local colleges. Trainees should be assisted in locating and obtaining financial assistance.

15) ***Evaluations of the mental health trainees' progress toward educational goals should be made on a regular basis.*** Trainees should receive feedback concerning their performance. Training programs should be adjusted to meet the changing needs of each trainee. Recognition should be given for accomplishments.

16) ***Training should ideally be ongoing and adjusted to the training needs and career goals of each tribal mental health worker.*** Training should be tailored to the background and ability of each worker. This reduces job burnout, avoids trapping capable staff in entry level positions and avoids the frustration which results from a "one size fits all" approach. It also helps to increase the pool of qualified Indian mental health workers.

17) ***Recognition for increasing levels of staff competence should include:*** awards, dinners or other celebrations, increased job responsibilities and increased pay commensurate with education and skill development.

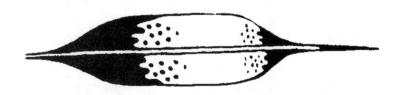

Chapter Twenty-Eight
Training Plans and Outlines

SURVEY OF INITIAL PROGRAM TRAINING PRIORITIES

Dear Advisory Board Member or
Tribal Social Services Staff Member,

In preparing the first year's training curriculum for the Tribal Support Counselors, we want to be sure to address the needs of the Tribes. Therefore, We are asking you to take a few minutes to rate the importance of different training areas.

On the attached form you will find descriptions of a number of classes/topics which are often included in mental health and human services training. Please circle the number that best reflects the importance that you would place on each topic, as follows:

1. This area is of little or no importance for Tribal Support Counselor training
2. This area might be useful if there is enough time
3. This area is somewhat important; training desirable but not necessary
4. It is quite important that some basic training happen in this area
5. This is a very important area and should be a central training requirement.

Please feel free to make comments or other suggestions.

Tribal Mental Health Project

P.O. Box 388 • La Conner, Washington 98257 • Phone (360) 466-3163

SURVEY OF TRIBAL MENTAL HEALTH PROJECT
TRAINING PRIORITIES

Subject Areas to be Covered	Importance Rating				
Overview of Mental Health Agencies' service delivery systems, funding, resources, professional ethics, roles, confidentiality	1	2	3	4	5
Training in Communications Skills: - including Listening, Feedback, "I statements", Assertiveness, "Fair Fight":	1	2	3	4	5
Counseling Skills- Basic introduction to helping relationships, role exploration, value clarification, interpersonal skills, problem solving, and counseling processes	1	2	3	4	5
Case Management- developing perspective and skills in working with other agencies, identifying resources, making referrals, coordinating efforts to ensure that clients receive needed services, record keeping, duty to report child abuse, etc.	1	2	3	4	5
Interviewing - Developing skills in information gathering, question asking, assessment, gaining client cooperation, "setting the stage" for treatment and change	1	2	3	4	5
Crisis Intervention - Skills in immediate response to a variety of crisis situations, including suicide threat, domestic violence, sexual assault, child abuse/ neglect, death	1	2	3	4	5
Tribal Mental Health Issues - Explore the realities of service delivery in tribal communities - special needs of Indian clients, cultural and spiritual issues, role of support counselors, confidentiality in tribal community	1	2	3	4	5

Child Development and Parenting Skills - Physical, psychological and social development of children birth through 18, children's needs and knowledge of parenting skills training	1	2	3	4	5
Adult Life Stages - Stages and crises in adult life; focus on self examination and development of tolerance for varied lifestyles and personal problems. Special emphasis on cultural issues including Indian family patterns, views of mental health and aging	1	2	3	4	5
Group Dynamics - Experience of participation in small training/ experiential group; development of skill in group leadership	1	2	3	4	5
Introduction to Mental Illness - Overview of the behavior and subjective experiences of clients from a variety of diagnostic groups, introduction to DSM III-R Diagnostic System	1	2	3	4	5
WorkingWith Families - Course designed to acquaint students with family systems theory and how to work with families	1	2	3	4	5
Indian Child Welfare - Child abuse and neglect, CPS and the state system, courts, child welfare programs,ICW Act	1	2	3	4	5
Alcohol and the Family - Alcoholism as a family disease. Role disturbance, inconsistency, communication problems. effects on children and spouse	1	2	3	4	5
Battered Women/Domestic Violence/ Rape Relief Training - Students learn about patterns of domestic violence, how to respond to crisis, how to effectively use local resources	1	2	3	4	5
Tribal Mental Health Seminar - Weekly group meetings to discuss the work experiences, problems, and personal learning associated with field placements	1	2	3	4	5

Tribal Field Placement - Supervised   1   2   3   4   5
experience working directly with Indian
clients in the tribal community

* * * * * * * * * * * * * * * * * * *

It may not be possible to provide training in all the above areas during the first program year. In making training decisions, how important do you feel it is that the training areas chosen be "transferable" for college credit? Specifically, how much weight do you think should be given to designing training experiences that will count toward a two year occupational degree in mental health/human services?

1   2   3   4   5

College credit should   Very Important that training
not be a factor in making   count toward degree
training decisions

We hope to orient our training program toward Indian culture and tribal realities. Often decisions will need to be made concerning the most efficient use of available training resources. How important do you feel that it is for Tribal Support Counselors to receive Training that is Indian oriented as opposed to training that will prepare them for dealing with the 'mainstream' mental health/social service system?

1   2   3   4   5

Indian trainees already   It is crucial that ALL
know about Indian culture;   TRAINING be specifically
they need most to learn   oriented toward Indian
to work well in the mainstream   culture, lifestyle and
mental health system   values

Tribal Mental Health Project

P.O. Box 388 • La Conner, Washington 98257 • Phone (360) 466-3163

FIRST YEAR TRIBAL MENTAL HEALTH TRAINING PLAN – Leading Toward One Year Certificate in Tribal Mental Health

The following courses, offered in cooperation between the Skagit Tribes' Mental Health Program and Skagit Valley College in 1984-85, met the requirements for a special one year Human Services Department CERTIFICATE OF TRAINING AND COMPETENCY IN TRIBAL MENTAL HEALTH. This first year's training program was intensive and largely oriented toward Indian issues. Special arrangements were made with the college for credits for tribally based courses, for substitutions of the usual 2 year degree requirements, and for 3 courses offered at the college for all Human Services students to be taught either by the Program Director or by an Indian alcoholism instructor.

I. Summer Quarter
August - September

The following courses were offered jointly through Northwest Indian College and Whatcom Community College to an intertribal group of alcoholism and social service staff. All four courses were taught by an Indian Alcoholism Instructor.

Interviewing and Diagnosis Skills, 3 credits
Introduction to Indian Alcoholism Counseling, 3 credits
Group Facilitation, 3 credits
Crisis Intervention, 3 credits

TOTAL CREDITS = 12

These 12 credits were transferable to Skagit Valley College for credit toward a TRIBAL MENTAL HEALTH CERTIFICATE in Human Services and were substituted for usual Associate degree requirements.

A Cooperative Effort

Swinomish Tribal Community	*Skagit Community Mental Health Center*	*Upper Skagit Indian Tribe*
P.O. Box 388	*208 Kincaid*	*2284 Community Plaza*
La Conner, WA 98257	*Mt. Vernon, WA 98273*	*Sedro-Woolley, WA 98284*

II. Fall Quarter
September - December

HS 106 Communication Skills, 4 credits, Skagit Valley College
*HS l99 Tribal Field Placement, 7 credits, 18 hours per week at Swinomish or Upper Skagit, Schedules to be arranged with Placement Supervisors
*HS 200 Tribal Practicum Seminar, 1 credit, Swinomish or Upper Skagit
*HS Introduction to Mental Health Counseling in the Native American community, 3 credits, Swinomish or Upper Skagit
TOTAL CREDITS = 15

III. Winter Quarter
January - March

HS 101 Introduction to Human Services, 4 credits, Skagit Valley College
*HS 131 Tribal Life Cycles, 4 credits, at Swinomish
*HS 141 Alcoholism, 4 credits, T.B.A., Skagit Valley College (substitutes for HS 201)
*HS 199 Tribal Field Placement, 7 credits, Schedules to be arranged with Placement Supervisors
*HS 200 Tribal Practicum Seminar, 1 credit, at Tribal site
TOTAL CREDITS = 20

IV. Spring Quarter
March - June

*HS l99 Tribal Field Placement, 7 credits
*HS 200 Tribal Practicum Seminar, 1 credit
HS 223 Psychopathology of Mental Illness, 4 credits, Skagit Valley College, (Taught at College by Tribal Mental Health Program Director, by special arrangement)
HS 232 Family Therapy, 4 credits, Skagit Valley College
HS 242 Alcohol and the Family, 3 day workshop, 2 credits, Skagit Valley College, (Taught at Community College by Indian Alcoholism Instructor)   TOTAL CREDITS = 18

*Taught by Tribal Mental Health Program Director at Tribal sites, credit through Skagit Valley College, open only to Program staff.

V. Total Credits Required for one year CERTIFICATE IN TRIBAL MENTAL HEALTH

July - September	= 12 credits
Fall Quarter	= 15 credits
Winter Quarter	= 20 credits
Spring Quarter	= 18 credits

TOTAL = 65 credits

NOTE: .All 65 credits for the Certificate in Tribal Mental Health Services may be applied toward the 107 credits needed for the Associate of Technical Arts Degree in Human Services at Skagit Valley College.

Students completing the year's Tribal Mental Health Certificate Program met all field placement requirements, and roughly half the academic requirements for the two year degree.

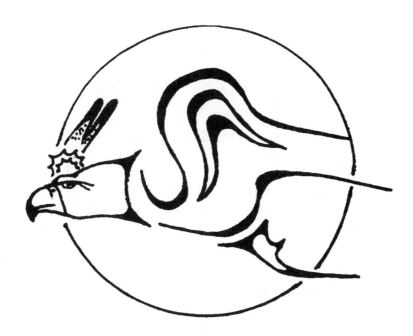

Tribal Mental Health Project

P.O. Box 388 • La Conner, Washington 98257 • Phone (360) 466-3163

SECOND YEAR TRIBAL MENTAL HEALTH TRAINING PLAN

Overall Goals:

1. Assist each Support Counselor to obtain specific needed job skills.
2. Assist each Support Counselor to pursue appropriate vocational or academic degree program.

Specific Training Objectives:

Each Support Counselor will receive basic training in the following areas:
1. Counseling Skills
2. Mental Health Treatments
3. Case Management
4. Child Abuse and Domestic Violence
5. Indian Child Welfare
6. Substance Abuse

These job related training priorities will be met in a manner which also promotes pursuit of an appropriate academic degree. Requirements for the two-year A.T.A. degree in Human Services incorporate all work done for the one year Tribal Mental Health Certificate. Training will continue to reflect an emphasis upon tribal mental health issues.

In addition to regular courses, staff may receive training in study skills, reading or may attend workshops of special interest. Some staff may choose to participate in selected training topics without pursuing an A.T.A. degree.

A Cooperative Effort

Swinomish Tribal Community *P.O. Box 388* *La Conner, WA 98257*	*Skagit Community Mental Health Center* *208 Kincaid* *Mt. Vernon, WA 98273*	*Upper Skagit Indian Tribe* *2284 Community Plaza* *Sedro-Woolley, WA 98284*

TENTATIVE SECOND YEAR COURSE SCHEDULE FOR TRIBAL SUPPORT COUNSELORS
Pursuing A.T.A. Degree in Human Services

(NOTE: Order of courses is subject to availability of courses, time, and student preference. Some courses may be taken through Northwest Indian College and transferred to Skagit Valley Community College).

Summer Quarter
June - August

HS 152 Indian Child Welfare Workshop, 2 credits, 2 1/2 day
  workshop, at Tribal Site
HS 200 Industrial Safety and Hygiene,(First Aid) 2 credits, Skagit
  Valley College
PE 160 Experimental Physical Education, 1 credit, Independent
  Activity at Tribal Site
English 100 or 101, Composition, 3 credits
$$TOTAL = 8 \text{ credits}$$

Fall Quarter

HS 202 Case Management, 3 credits, Skagit Valley College
HS 231 Therapeutic Interventions in Mental Health, 4 credits
  Elective (e.g. Assertiveness training, Ceramics, Indian Song
  and Dance), 3 credits
$$TOTAL = 10 \text{ credits}$$

Winter Quarter

HS 222 Advanced Counseling, 4 credits, Skagit Valley College
SP 123 Interpersonal Communications, 3 credits, Skagit Valley
  College
Elective 3 credits
$$TOTAL = 10 \text{ credits}$$

Spring Quarter

HS 142 Chemical Dependency, 4 credits, at College
HS 134 Special Project, 2 credits, offered at Tribal Site
Eng l02 or 270, 3 credits
Elective, 3 credits (e.g., Ethnic Studies, History of the Northwest
    Indians, or Contemporary Issues of the Native American)
TOTAL = 12 credits

YEAR'S CREDIT TOTAL = 40

*The above courses complete A.T.A. requirements in Human Services
for tribal support counselors having 1st year tribal mental health
certificates. Since most of these credits require classroom attendance, they may most practically be completed over a two year
period.*

ADDITIONAL SPECIAL TRAINING AND WORKSHOPS

*Support Counselors attended a wide variety of special work-
shops, lectures and training experiences. A number of these special
training opportunities were sponsored by local tribes and were
oriented toward the special needs of tribal clients. Included were:*
- A 30 hr. training by the local Battered Womens/Rape Relief
  Center on domestic violence, rape and crisis intervention.
- Presentations by Mental Health Center staff on:
  - substance abuse
  - child sexual abuse
  - depression
  - suicide prevention
  - geriatrics outreach and evaluation
- Fetal alcohol syndrome workshops
- Adult Children of Alcoholics workshops
- Self esteem for tribal social service providers
- Suicide prevention workshop at the University of Washington
- An inter-tribal workshop on death, loss and grief
- Alcoholism and alcohol prevention in tribal communities

Culturally Relevent Ethnic Minority Services Coalition

An unusual and exciting area of training received by Tribal Support Counselors was a series of workshops offered by each of seven ethnic mental health demonstration programs funded by the State of Washington from 1984–1990 (the "CREMS" programs). Two Native American programs (including our Tribal Mental health Program and that of the Seattle Indian Health Board), two Hispanic programs, one Black program and two Southeast Asian refugee programs were represented.

Trainings focused on the mental health needs, beliefs and values of each specific cultural group as well as on shared experiences in providing culturally oriented mental health services. These trainings were particularly important in helping to expand our understanding of the nature of culture and it's relationship to mental health. Examples of these training topics include:

- Southeast Asian spiritual beliefs and traditional healing
- Curanderismo (Mexican spiritual and herbal healing)
- Mental health issues in working with refugee clients
- The effects of rapid cultural change on the mental health status of minority groups
- The relation between religion and psychotherapy
- Culture-bound mental health syndromes and problems in diagnosis

As a part of these ethnic mental health training workshops, the Skagit Tribes' Mental Health Program sponsored two workshops in tribal mental health for a multi-ethnic group of mental health workers. Topics included:

- **Indian culture, philosophy and healing**
- **Mental health and Indian spirituality**
- **A psychiatric view of the value of traditional healers**
- **The therapeutic value of traditional ways of dealing with grief and loss**
- **The pros and cons of working for one's own tribe**

These early workshops helped prepare our tribal mental health team for the 1989 series of "Healing through Cooperation and Tradition" Conference described in Ch. 29.

The CREMS programs are jointly documented in <u>Multi-Ethnic Mental Health Services: Six Demonstration Programs in Wash-</u>

<u>ington State</u>, 1989. The section of that book describing the Skagit Tribes' Mental Health Program is the forerunner to this book.

PLAN FOR ACCREDITED TRIBAL FIELD PLACEMENTS

Field Placements in the tribal community setting are a core aspect of the Skagit Tribes' Mental Health Program. This is both a training and a direct service program, with the overall goal of increasing and improving the quality of mental health services to Indian people.

Tribal Support Counselors spent the majority of their time in activities related to direct client care. These activities were structured to provide supervised "practicum" experiences. Field placements were an integral and accredited part of the one year Tribal Mental Health Certificate Program and of the two year Associate of Technical Arts degree program in Human Services through Skagit Valley Community College.

Tribal Support Counselors completed all 21 credits of field placement required for the A.T.A. degree during their first year. Field placements were broken into quarter-long blocks, such that each trainee could complete the three quarters of tribal placement during their first program year.

Each placement had a specific focus on an area of service delivery of concern in the tribal community. For instance, a quarter's field placement might emphasize domestic violence, youth and family problems, child sexual abuse, spiritual problems and healing systems, or problems related to substance abuse. Each Support Counselor worked with a tribally-based mental health supervisor to design a field experience emphasizing direct work in one of these areas. Support Counselors and supervisors jointly developed specific learning and behavioral objectives which formed the basis of quarterly "Learning Contracts."

First year field placements began at 19 hours per week, and earn 7 credits per quarter, to a total of 21 credits for the year. Support Counselors arrange field placement schedules with supervisors. Schedules were flexible in order to allow Support Counselors to respond to client crises and to the natural rhythm of tribal life.

Supervision of Field Placement and Direct Client Services

Individual Supervision

Placement Supervisors were mental health professionals working in the tribal community in which the placement occured. Thus, they were individuals knowledgeable about Indian culture and tribal life. Ideally, they had direct clinical responsibilities in the tribal community, were a part of the tribal social service teams and were familiar with the clients and families with whom the Support Counselors were working.

Support Counselors received one hour of individual supervision each week and could also seek additional consultation when problems arose. Supervisors oversaw case loads and work experiences. They assigned clients referred from outside agencies and assisted Support Counselors in diagnosis, counseling and case management decisions. Supervisors could at times see clients jointly with Support Counselors.

Each Support Counselor worked with at least two different field placement supervisors each year. This ensured exposure to a variety of clinical skills and approaches. Usually two supervisors were available to rotate placements at each tribal site, including tribally funded mental health specialists, Indian Health Service mental health counselors, and the Tribal Mental Health Program Director.

Assignments of Supervisors were made by the Program Director, taking into account student wishes, training needs, service requirements and smooth program operation.

Field placements were monitored by the Program Director, who met frequently with Supervisors to assess the progress of Support Counselors and to help resolve problems.

Group Supervision

The Program Director led a weekly "Tribal Practicum Seminar", which was equivalent to Skagit Valley College's Human Services Practicum Seminar, (HS 200) and earned college credit each quarter. The seminar focused on exploring the realities of service delivery to Indian clients, cultural and spiritual issues, the roles of the Support Counselors, and professional issues such as confidentiality in the tribal community. This seminar also provided an opportunity for Support Counselors to discuss cases and to share experiences and personal reactions to their work, and thus was an important supportive experience and a form of group supervision.

Evaluation of Field Experiences

Evaluation of field placement experiences is an ongoing process throughout the year, with dialogue and feedback between Support Counselors, Supervisor, and Program Director. Objectives developed for each placement are used to evaluate Support Counselor progress at the end of each quarter by having both Support Counselors and Supervisors rate the accomplishment of learning objectives.

Narrative evaluations are also prepared. Evaluations are discussed between Support Counselors and Supervisors and are kept in personnel files.

The evaluation process is intended to be a constructive learning experience which gives feedback to the Support Counselor, improves the quality of supervision and helps to keep the program as a whole "on track" in responding to community and cultural needs.

Tribal Mental Health Project

P.O. Box 388 • La Conner, Washington 98257 • Phone (360) 466-3163

F. QUARTERLY FIELD PLACEMENT LEARNING CONTRACT

Each quarter Support Counselors identify new learning objectives for field work experiences (to be listed below). Objectives must be specific and measurable. At the end of the quarter both Support Counselors and Supervisors will be asked to rate the level of accomplishment of each objective by marking A, B or C to the right of each objective. Each should keep a copy of this contract.

What type of service or client population will be emphasized during this quarter's field experience? _____

_____

Quarter:_____

Number of hours per week: _____ Number of College Credits: _____

Work Schedule: _____

Tribal Community: _____

Time for weekly supervisory meetings:_____

Learning Objectives (stated in specific measurable terms)	Rating (A Accomplished Objective) (B Made Progress) (C Failed to make significant progress)
1._____	_____
2._____	_____
3._____	_____
4._____	_____
5._____	_____
Comments: _____	Rated by:
_____	_____

We approve the learning objectives listed above. The Placement Supervisor and Program Director agree to provide the necessary supervision to ensure that the Support Counselor received appropriate educational benefit.

Placement Supervisor	Support Counselor	Program Director

A Cooperative Effort

Swinomish Tribal Community
P.O. Box 388
La Conner, WA 98257

Skagit Community Mental Health Center
208 Kincaid
Mt. Vernon, WA 98273

Upper Skagit Indian Tribe
2284 Community Plaza
Sedro-Woolley, WA 98284

Tribal Mental Health Project

P.O. Box 388 • La Conner, Washington 98257 • Phone (360) 466-3163

G. FIELD PLACEMENT EVALUATION

Support Counselor _____ Tribal Community _____
Supervisor _____ Quarter _____

In order to encourage feedback to the Support Counselor, and Support Counselor participation in the evaluation, each Supervisor is being asked to: 1. Write a narrative evaluation of the Support Counselor. 2. Discuss it with the Support Counselor and have her/him sign it. 3. Then return it to the Program Director. The information you give will be used to help assess the Support Counselor's progress, as well as the quality of the training program. Therefore you are urged to be frank in pointing out both strengths and weaknesses.

Basic Job Responsibilities: (e.g., attendance, punctuality, responsibility, ethical standards, preparation for field work, etc.)

Interactions with Clients:

Human Quality: (e.g., warmth, empathy, tolerance, flexibility, etc.).

Communication Skills (accurate listening, feedback, honesty, clarity)

A Cooperative Effort

Swinomish Tribal Community
P.O. Box 388
La Conner, WA 98257

Skagit Community Mental Health Center
208 Kincaid
Mt. Vernon, WA 98273

Upper Skagit Indian Tribe
2284 Community Plaza
Sedro-Woolley, WA 98284

Tribal Mental Health Project
P.O. Box 388 • La Conner, Washington 98257 • Phone (360) 466-3163

Therapeutic Style/Approach (e.g., supportive, confrontative, non directive, etc.)

Understanding/Maintenance of Appropriate Roles

Responses to Stress and/or Crises

Understanding/Knowledge/Insight

Tribal Teamwork/Staff Relationships (How well does the Support Counselor trainee understand and contribute to tribal treatment plans, understand staff roles, initiate contact with other staff, contribute in case conferences, differentiate between personal and work relationships?)

Knowledge of Resources and Relationships with non-Tribal Agencies

A Cooperative Effort

Swinomish Tribal Community
P.O. Box 388
La Conner, WA 98257

Skagit Community Mental Health Center
208 Kincaid
Mt. Vernon, WA 98273

Upper Skagit Indian Tribe
2284 Community Plaza
Sedro-Woolley, WA 98284

Tribal Mental Health Project

P.O. Box 388 • La Conner, Washington 98257 • Phone (360) 466-3163

Charting/Documentation (Are required progress notes, forms and reports completed in a timely, clear and thoughtful fashion?)

Response to Supervision: (e.g., initiative, openness to new ideas and criticism, personal and therapeutic insight, working relationships, etc.).

Areas of Major Strengths:

Areas of Needing Greatest Improvement:

Additional comments about Support Counselor, Training Program, or _____?

A Cooperative Effort

Swinomish Tribal Community	*Skagit Community Mental Health Center*	*Upper Skagit Indian Tribe*
P.O. Box 388	*208 Kincaid*	*2284 Community Plaza*
La Conner, WA 98257	*Mt. Vernon, WA 98273*	*Sedro-Woolley, WA 98284*

Tribal Mental Health Project

P.O. Box 388 • La Conner, Washington 98257 • Phone (360) 466-3163

TRIBAL PRACTICUM SEMINAR OUTLINE

3 hrs. each week, schedule varies each quarter

Topics to be covered:

1. Support Counselor trainees' experiences in their field placements will be discussed and shared with each other. Problems they encounter will be discussed.
2. The roles and responsibilities of the Tribal Support Counselors will be discussed in detail.
3. Confidentiality and ethical issues in field placement will be discussed.
4. Support Counselor Trainees will learn the reporting system requirements of their job.
5. The mental health needs of the tribal communities will be discussed, as well as culturally oriented treatment approaches.
6. Interactions between the tribal and mainstream mental health programs will be discussed as well as between the tribal community and the non-Indian community.

Reading assignments for each placement will be made and reviewed. Each student will make at least one class presentation in their area of field placement focus.

Guest speakers will invited to make presentations to the seminar group and field trips may be arranged to other programs.

Students will be evaluated on participation, thoughtfulness and mastery of the reporting system. There will be no final exam. (Support Counselors pursuing an ATA degree in Human Services may receive one credit per quarter for this seminar.)

A Cooperative Effort

Swinomish Tribal Community *P.O. Box 388* *La Conner, WA 98257*	*Skagit Community Mental Health Center* *208 Kincaid* *Mt. Vernon, WA 98273*	*Upper Skagit Indian Tribe* *2284 Community Plaza* *Sedro-Woolley, WA 98284*

INTRODUCTION TO MENTAL HEALTH COUNSELING IN THE NATIVE AMERICAN COMMUNITY

Three hours per week

Course Outline

Topic areas to be covered:
1. Discuss and define concepts of "mental health", including cultural variables.
2. Discuss culturally appropriate methods of information gathering and interviewing.
3. Discuss vocabulary and word usage in mental health work.
4. Role play interviewing situations typical in tribal settings.
5. Orient counselor trainees to basic types of counseling, including "client centered", "directive", "behavioral", "family", and "dynamic" and "spiritual".
6. Discuss counseling approaches most effective in tribal community.
7. Review counseling approaches successful with Indian clients.
8. Inventory sub-groups in tribal community and discuss applicability of group dynamic theories to tribal life.
9. Discuss individual Support Counselor roles in tribal group life and how this effects their work.
10. Plan how existing tribal groups and social systems may be utilized to improve the overall mental health of the tribal community.

   Homework assigned most weeks. Students will keep a notebook of new words they encounter in readings and classes.

   There will be a final exam.

Sample Exam

Introduction to Mental Health Counseling in Indian Communities

On a separate piece of paper, please answer the following:
1. What is "Mental Health".
2. What are the goals of the Tribal Mental Health Program?
3. Briefly describe the roles of the tribes, of the Washington State Division of Mental Health, and of The Community Mental Health Center.

4. What is the "Battering Cycle"?
5. How and why do drinking patterns differ between Indians and non-Indians?
6. Explain the meanings of two new words you have learned that are related to mental health.

Describe briefly what you would do in the following situations:

7. A community member tells you about someone they know who is having serious emotional problems.
8. You go to see a client and find no one home except a two year old child.
9. Your client says that there is something he wants to tell you, but first he wants to know that you will keep it absolutely confidential.
10. A person from an outside agency calls you to ask about a client of yours.
11. A community person says to you "Who do you think you are to be telling other people how to live their lives?"
12. A client comes to your house with a black eye and says she's scared to go home tonight because her husband will beat her.
13. During an afternoon home visit to a client you notice that she has alcohol on her breath, that her hair isn't combed and that the house looks less orderly than usual. She meets you at the door and tells you that every thing is "fine", that she hasn't been drinking and is no longer fighting with her boyfriend. She keeps glancing toward the bedroom as you talk. You stay only a few minutes and then leave.

Please make a progress note of the above client contact:

14. Please write here anything else you have learned about Mental Health work from this course.

TRIBAL LIFE CYCLES - COURSE OUTLINE

4 credits - three hours per week

This course is designed to introduce you to the concepts of life cycle, stages of human development, and marker events, from an Indian tribal perspective. Much of the learning in this course will be personal and experiential, but you will also be expected to develop insights about the life cycles of Indians and of people in general.

This class meets every Thursday from 1-4 P.M. In addition, you will be expected to put in approximately one hour of homework (reading and writing) and one hour of assigned activity each week.

In class we will study the phases of individual and family life, through presentations, discussion and experiential exercises.

Topics to be Covered
- Overview of class and Basic Concepts
- Life Wheels
- Birth of a Tribal Member
- The Indian Childhood Experience
- Life Scripts
- Indian Extended Family as the context for Individual Development
- Indian Marriage and Parenting Patterns
- The Indian Experience of Aging
  The Role of Tribal Elders and Grandparents
- Death, the Final Stage of Growth
- Indian Concepts of Death
- Tribal Ways of Coping with Death

Readings will concern key aspects of human development and Indian life.

Major Assignments for Quarter:
1. You are to interview two tribal elders concerning important events in their lives. These interviews will follow an assigned structure, and will be taped. You will be given a more detailed explanation of this assignment and will have three weeks to complete it.
2. You will create a short personal autobiography, reflecting your learning about life stages and "marker events". Although you will be given guidelines for this project, you may feel free to use your own ideas about the format.
3. You will have a written test at the end of the quarter. The test will be an opportunity for you to show what you have learned from class discussions and readings.

Chapter Twenty-Nine
Tribal Mental Health Conference Materials and Exercises

I n addition to training for providers of direct mental health services in tribal communities, there is a great need for several other kinds of training, including:

• Cultural Awareness for Non-Indian Mental Health Workers and Agency Administrators
• General Mental Health Awareness Training for Tribal Social, Education and Health Service Staff, Law Enforcement, Judicial Personnel, Tribal Government and Tribal Members in General
• Opportunities for Exchange of Information and ideas among Tribal Mental Health Workers about successful program approaches, about how Indian culture effects the mental health of tribal members, and about culturally appropriate service approaches
• Opportunities for Inter-Agency, Inter-Tribal and Inter-system information exchange and discussion of possible consultation, referral systems or inter-agency collaboration

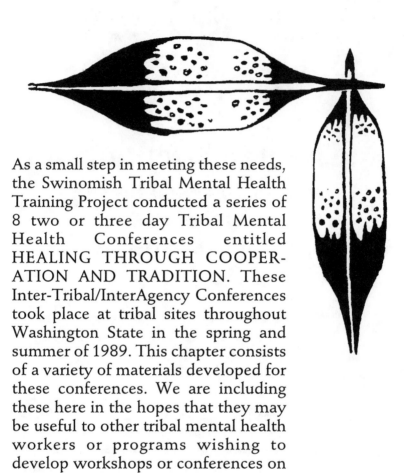

As a small step in meeting these needs, the Swinomish Tribal Mental Health Training Project conducted a series of 8 two or three day Tribal Mental Health Conferences entitled HEALING THROUGH COOPER-ATION AND TRADITION. These Inter-Tribal/InterAgency Conferences took place at tribal sites throughout Washington State in the spring and summer of 1989. This chapter consists of a variety of materials developed for these conferences. We are including these here in the hopes that they may be useful to other tribal mental health workers or programs wishing to develop workshops or conferences on cultural approaches to mental health.

Tribal Mental Health Project

P.O. Box 388 • La Conner, Washington 98257 • Phone (360) 466-3163

Dear_____

    You are invited to an Inter-Tribal/Inter-Agency TRIBAL MENTAL HEALTH CONFERENCE to take place at the _____TRIBE on _____.

    We hope that this will be an exciting event which will bring together key people from local tribes, Indian Health Services, community mental health agencies and other interested people, such as county coordinators, tribal government, planners and administrators, tribal alcohol program staff or school counselors from the _____ area.

    The goals of this conference are four-fold:

1. To Explore How Indian Culture Effects Mental Health.
2. To Present Information on Indian Mental Health Problems and Approaches for Culturally Oriented Service Delivery.
3. To Exchange Information about Local Tribal and Community Services.
4. To Explore Options for Funding, Staffing, Consultation, Contracting, Coordination and /or Collaboration for Tribally based Mental Health Services.

    Included with this packet you will find:

- a Flyer / Poster Announcing this Conference
- a Tentative Agenda
- a Map / or directions
- a List of Tribes and Agencies who have been Invited to Participate in This Conference

    In order for this conference to be a success, it is important that each agency send as many key decision makers and mental health/social services staff as possible. Please share this information with others in your tribe/ agency who may be interested, as well as with other agencies and providers in your area. Although there is no cost for this conference and pre-registration is not required, we would greatly appreciate your letting us know how many people to expect from your tribe or agency. If you have not previously done so, please phone _____ at the_____Tribe at _____with this information. Hoping to see you soon.

                                  Sincerely,
                                  Jennifer Clarke
                                  Director, Tribal Mental
                                  Health Program

A Cooperative Effort

Swinomish Tribal Community	*Skagit Community Mental Health Center*	*Upper Skagit Indian Tribe*
P.O. Box 388	*208 Kincaid*	*2284 Community Plaza*
La Conner, WA 98257	*Mt. Vernon, WA 98273*	*Sedro-Woolley, WA 98284*

Course Description:
Tribal Mental Health Program Approaches

A series of workshops of one to three days each will be given at tribal sites in Washington State. Workshops will focus on sharing Tribal Mental Health Program approaches and on facilitating an exchange of ideas and experiences concerning mental health services for tribal communities. The facilitators will be three to five mental health professionals, tribal support counselors and traditional consultants who work with the Skagit Tribe's Mental Health Program. Participants will be tribal social services staff, tribal government representatives, community mental health providers and administrators, Indian mental health specialists and other interested parties.

Workshop Goals:

1. Participants will develop a clear understanding of how cultural factors require differences between tribal and mainstream mental health programs.
2. Participants will learn about the experiences of one particular Tribal Mental Health Program.
3. Participants and facilitators will exchange information and ideas concerning mental health funding, staffing, cultural considerations, treatment approaches, therapy aids and challenges encountered by tribal programs around Washington State.
4. Participants and facilitators will explore possibilities for interagency cooperation to increase services to tribal communities.

Objectives:

1. Participants will be introduced to the Skagit Tribes' Mental Health Program through a video presentation.
2. Participants will become familiar with the series of Swinomish Tribal Mental Health Booklets.
3. Participants will identify cultural factors effecting mental health services to Indian people.
4. Funding, staffing and program design alternatives will be discussed.
5. Participants will identify problem areas facing their tribe in the areas of mental health service needs and program development.
6. Tribal participants will develop action plans for program development.

Credits: 1 or 2   Time: To be arranged

HEALING THROUGH COOPERATION & TRADITION :

INTER-TRIBAL / INTER-AGENCY

TRIBAL MENTAL HEALTH CONFERENCE

on _____ and _____

9:00 A.M. - 4:00 P.M.

at _____ TRIBE

OPEN TO: TRIBAL MEMBERS / TRIBAL STAFF,
TRIBAL GOVERNMENT, MENTAL HEALTH PROVIDERS,
SCHOOL COUNSELORS INDIAN HEALTH SERVICE
PERSONNEL, DSHS STAFF, COUNTY COORDINATORS

No Charge – But PLEASE contact _____
at _____ if you want to attend or for more information
* College Credit Available

HEALING THROUGH
COOPERATION AND TRADITION

SAMPLE CONFERENCE AGENDA _____

Hosted by the_____Tribe, in cooperation with
Swinomish Tribal Mental Health Project

At_____

1st Day   –   INDIAN CULTURE AND MENTAL HEALTH

9:00 A.M.   Coffee / Registration

9:15   Welcome
                Opening Prayer

9:20   Overview of Conference

9:30   Introductions and Sharing of Expectations

9:45   Cultural Awareness Experience

10:10   Cultural Identity as a Mental Health Issue

10:45   BREAK

11:00   <u>Panel Discussion of Aspects of Traditional</u>
<u>Indian Culture Which Effect Mental Health</u>

-Extended Family Relations
-Communication Styles and Conflict Resolution
-Attitudes Toward Time
-Age Roles in Tribal Social Life and the Special Role of Elders
-Beliefs About the Nature of Health, Illness and
 Mental Illness

12:00 Noon   NO HOST LUNCH

<u>AFTERNOON SESSION</u>

1:00   <u>Spirituality and Spiritual Healing</u>

1:30   <u>Traditional Ways of Dealing with Grief</u>

2:00   <u>Tribal Life Styles</u> - Importance of Tribal Location
and Control of Services (Small group exercise)

2:45   BREAK

3:00   <u>What Mental Health Workers Can Learn from</u>
<u>Indian Culture</u> (small groups)

3:30   Discussion Circle

4:00   CLOSING PRAYER

2nd Day   -   TREATMENT CONSIDERATIONS FOR TRIBAL
MENTAL HEALTH PROGRAMS

9:00   Coffee / Registration

9:15   Welcome and Prayer

9:20   Overview of the Day

9:30   OVERVIEW OF MENTAL HEALTH PROBLEMS
IN TRIBAL COMMUNITIES: The Cycle of Depression,
Alcohol Abuse, Violence, Self Destructive Behavior

10:15   Indian Adult Children of Alcoholics

10:45   BREAK

11:00   Provider Issues Small Groups
-Complimentary Roles of Professionals
and Paraprofessionals (Handout)
-Advantages and Disadvantages of Working for
One's Own Tribe
-Use of Natural Helpers / Elders / Traditional
Consultants and Healers
-Suggestions for Non-Indian Mental Health
Workers (Handout)

11:45   -Large Group

12:00 noon NO HOST LUNCH

AFTERNOON SESSION - CULTURALLY ORIENTED SERVICE
APPROACHES

1:00   Skagit Tribes' Mental Health Program Video and Approach
to Inter-Agency Collaboration

2:15   Service Issues Panel -
-Need for Flexibility in Roles, Setting, Timing
-Confidentiality Dilemmas
-Record Keeping Challenges for Tribal Programs

3:00   BREAK

3:15   Discussion Circle

4:00   CLOSING PRAYER

3rd DAY - WORKING TOGETHER

MORNING SESSION - INFORMATION EXCHANGE

9:00 A.M.   Coffee / Registration

9:15   Opening Prayer

9:20   Overview of Day's Events
           Distribute Evaluation Forms

9:25   Information Exchange: Each participating Tribal, Mental
           Health Agency and IHS Program will give a brief
           description of their funding, goals, staffing and services.

10:30   BREAK

10:45   Information Exchange: Priorities, Funding, "638" Contracts,
           Service Models, Staffing Patterns, Consultation to Tribes and
           Mental Health Agencies

11:15   Washington State Division of Mental Health Perspectives on
           Funding, Priorities, Licensing and Service Agreements

12:15   NO HOST LUNCH

AFTERNOON SESSION - INTERAGENCY COLLABORATION

1:15   Community Mental Health Centers - programs, services and
           relation to Tribal Communities

1:45   Establishing Linkages between Traditional and
           Modern Healers

2:15   Each Agency / Tribe Identifies what they would like to see
           happen in terms of Inter-Agency Relationships (Handout)

2:30   Challenges in Inter-Agency Collaboration: Funding, Control,
           Coordination and Communication, Record Keeping,
           Confidentiality, Cultural Barriers, etc.

2:45   BREAK

2:50   <u>Local Tribal / Mental Health Agency Teams Assess their Working Relationships:</u> Where we are <u>now</u> in terms of <u>Referrals / Consultation / Meeting Client Needs</u>

3:15   <u>Teams Set Goals and Priorities: where we want to be</u>
-identify inter-agency contact people
<u>-agree on one or more mutual goals</u> (e.g. meetings,
 consultation, staff assignments, service agreements,
 joint proposals, etc.)
-set local timetable for next step

3:45   <u>TALKING CIRCLE</u>
-Discuss Day's Events
-Identify Needs for Future Meetings and/or Conferences

4:00   CLOSING PRAYER

<u>*Please</u> hand in evaluation form before you leave.

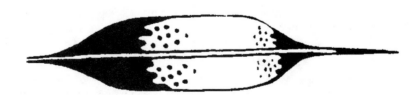

CULTURAL MIXER

INSTRUCTIONS: On each page of this booklet you will find a question. You and your first partner will have two minutes to exchange answers to the first question. You and your second partner will have two minutes to exchange answers to the second question and so on. You are now facing your first partner . . . Do Not turn page until told to Do So!

1. What is your own Cultural Background?

2. How does your cultural background effect you on your job?

3. How big is your family? Who is in your family?

4. What languages are in your family background?

5. What special events do you celebrate?

6. At what age are people in your family or social group considered "grown up"?

7. What do you do for fun? Who do you do it with?

8. What are two things that are important about your culture?

9. What are two things that are important about you?

10. What has this exercise taught you about your own culture?

11. What has this exercise taught you about cultural differences?

A POSITIVE

CULTURAL

IDENTITY

IS ONE KEY TO GOOD

MENTAL HEALTH

PANEL DISCUSSION

INTER-RELATED ASPECTS OF INDIAN CULTURE WHICH EFFECT MENTAL HEALTH

Introduction: *the entire cultural context effects mental health, mental illness and mental health care.* The aspects listed below are particularly important, but are certainly not the only important cultural variables. These aspects are inter-related and difficult to separate from one another, because they are only parts of a living cultural whole.

One member of the panel will be asked to take about five minutes to present basic information about each of the following aspects of Indian culture. Other panelists will be given a chance to respond. There will be time for questions at the end of the presentation.

• **The Indian extended family system as the basis for Indian social life** (e.g. the size and complexity of Indian families, the importance of ones family in determining social position and spiritual obligations, the need to know who ones clients are related to, relationships between different families, why mental health care must involve family systems).

• **Indian communication styles** (e.g. the use of silence, non-verbal signals, different ways of speaking, public speaking, eye contact, typical communication difficulties between Indians and non-Indians, etc.)

• **Different attitudes toward time between Indians and Non-Indians** (e.g. The reality of "Indian time", different priorities concerning appointments, punctuality, keeping on a schedule, how these differences can interfere with Indian people receiving mainstream services, etc.)

• **Age roles in Tribal social life** (e.g. role of children, youth, young parents, and elders in the family and tribal community, the relative value of youth and age, the special spiritual and social roles of elders.)

• **Beliefs about the nature of health, illness and mental illness** (e.g. Physical Illness, Spiritual Influences, Connections between Physical, social mental and spiritual life.)

STEREOTYPES EXERCISE

Ethno-centric or "Culturally Self-centered" attitudes come from assuming that our own life ways, beliefs and attitudes are "right", and that all others are "wrong", "primitive" or "stupid". Most people tend to make negative assumptions about what they do not understand, giving rise to negative stereotypes. Stereotypes are dangerous because they blind us to the truth and lead to discrimination.

This exercise is aimed at helping us to examine and question our own prejudices and stereotypes, by building our awareness that all people tend to have some stereotypes about those who are culturally different. This exercise requires openness to examining ones self.

INSTRUCTIONS

Please fill out the column for your own cultural group first. You may write in your own views or stereotypes which you think others have about your cultural group. Next, fill out the other column, about the other group. If you belong to a group other than "Indian" or "White", please make a list on a separate piece of paper. If you see yourself as both "Indian" and "White", please fill in both sets of stereotypes.

White People   Indian People
1.   1.
2.   2.
3.   3.
4.   4.
5.   5.
6.   6.
7.   7.

Now you will meet in a small group of 4 - 5 people, made up of persons from different cultural backgrounds. The group will nominate someone as "Recorder", who will write down all the stereotypes of the group. Each person will read their list. The task is to listen to each person without comment or debate. Remember that these "stereotypes" are not necessarily the views of the presenter. Once the group has a combined list, please spend 10 minutes discussing your reactions and feelings about the exercise.

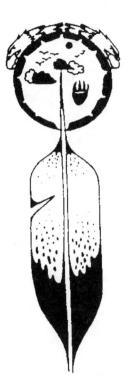

TRIBAL LIFESTYLES EXERCISE

Divide into groups of 5 by numbering off 1, 2, 3, etc .

One Facilitator will join each group.

Each group should choose a Recorder.

TASK OF GROUP - You will have 15 minutes to discuss the following questions:

1. What are 3 or 4 important aspects of tribal LIFESTYLES?

2. In what ways do tribal lifestyles make it important for mental health services to be located at tribal sites and under the control of tribal government or advisory boards?

Return to large group prepared to discuss your group's views.

—

What Mental   *Health Workers*
Can Learn   *From*

INDIAN   CULTURE

Show Respect to Others
Each Person Has a Special Gift

Share What You Have
Giving Makes You Richer

Know Who You Are
You Are a Reflection on Your Family

Accept What Life Brings
You Cannot Control Many Things

Have Patience
Some Things Cannot be Rushed

Live Carefully
What You Do Will Come Back to You

Take Care of Others
You Cannot Live Without Them

Honor Your Elders
They Show You the Way in Life

Pray for Guidance
Many Things are Not Known

See Connections
All Things are Related

COMPLEMENTRY ROLES FOR PARAPROFESSIONALS AND PROFESSIONALS IN TRIBAL MENTAL HEALTH PROGRAMS

Indian Paraprofessionals

- Cultural and Community Knowledge

- Knowledge of Extended Family Resources

- Access to Traditional Healing Systems

- More Likely to Understand and to be Understood by Indian Clients

- Crisis Availability

- Outreach in Community

- Provide Links to Other Resources

- Consult with Non-Tribal Providers about Cultural Factors

Professionals

- Diagnostic Skills

- Evaluate Severity of Client Problems

- Medical / Psychological Knowledge

- May Prescribe and Monitor Medications

- Trained in Specific Therapeutic Approaches

- Write Grants and Reports

- Program Development

- Provide Supervision, Training and Support to Tribal Workers

- May be less Vulnerable to Community Pressures

TOGETHER WE CAN HELP!

INFORMATION EXCHANGE ON EACH TRIBAL MENTAL HEALTH AGENCY OR INDIAN HEALTH SERVICE PROGRAM

One goal of this conference is to familiarize each participating agency with the services available through all other local agencies. We will therefore spend a block of time presenting the key aspects of each program. Please come prepared to make a brief (5 minutes) presentation concerning your agency or program's:

1. Funding sources, and funding level

2. Major Goals

3. Staffing Patterns

4. Services for Indian Clients

5. Major Concerns regarding Mental Health and Related Services to Indian Clients

The enclosed Information Sheet may be useful to you in gathering and presenting this information. If possible please bring copies to be shared with other participants. You may also want to bring handouts on your program:

Agency brochures, goal statements, statistical reports, job descriptions, questions, etc. would all be very helpful.

INFORMATION EXCHANGE FOR TRIBAL MENTAL HEALTH WORKSHOP

Name of Tribe or Agency _____

Address _____

Phone _____

Major Goals of Agency/Program _____

_____

Funding Source (s) _____

_____

Services/Programs _____

_____

Description of Mental Health Service for Indian Clients _____

_____

_____

_____

Number of Staff in Agency/Tribe _____

Number and Type of Mental Health Positions_____

_____

_____

Name (s) and Position (s) of Tribal or Agency Contact Person (s)

_____

_____

_____

Major Concerns/Needs/Questions about Mental Health Services for Indian
Clients _____

_____

_____

Worksheet for

TRIBAL/MENTAL HEALTH AGENCY COLLABORATION

Ideas and Hopes

Please take ten minutes to fill in the following:

1. What are the needs of your agency or service population which are not currently being met?

   _____

2. What services do you think might be provided to you, your agency or your people by another agency?

   _____

   _____

3. What tribe(s) or agency(s) would you possibly like to work with?

   _____

4. Would you like to see an inter-tribal/inter-agency relationship in the area(s) of

   _____ contact people

   _____ referrals

   _____ consultation

   _____ regular meetings

   _____ staff placement or position sharing

   _____ collaborative program

5. What I (We) would ideally like to see happen would be

   _____

   _____

   _____

BARRIERS/CHALLENGES TO INTER-AGENCY COLLABORATION

Worksheet

I.   Attitudes

    _____

    _____

    _____

II.   Funding

    _____

    _____

III. Agency Structure/Reporting Requirements, Priorities, etc.

    _____

    _____

    _____

IV.   Geographical

    _____

    _____

V.   Other

    _____

    _____

VI.   Ideas for Overcoming Barriers

    _____

    _____

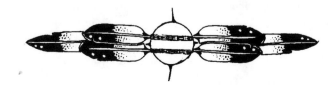

EVALUATION
(for feedback to Swinomish Mental Health Project Team)

Inter-Tribal/Interagency Tribal Mental Health Conference

held at _____ on _____

I represent: ____a tribe   ____state agency
                   ____a mental health agency   ____county
                   ____Indian Health Service   ____private agency
                   ____other (please specify: _____)

1. Staff of my tribe or agency had approximately ____ 1-2, ____ 3-5, ____ 5-10
   contacts with staff of the Swinomish Mental Health Project before this
   conference, including ____ written information, ____ phone contact,
   ____ personal meeting.

2. Our tribe or agency was consulted about the conference agenda.
   ____ yes, ____ no

3. Staff of our tribe or agency contributed to a presentation made during this
   conference. ____ yes, ____ no

4. How many members of your tribe or agency attended this conference? ____

5. This conference presented information about:

____Cultural Identity   ____A Model for Culturally
____Indian Family Systems   Oriented Tribal Mental Health
____Spiritual Beliefs and   ____Roles/Challenges of Tribal
    Practices   Paraprofessionals
____ Communication Styles   ____Community Mental Health System
____Traditional Ways of   ____Indian Health Service Mental
    Dealing with Grief   Health System
                                   ____Local Tribal or Community
____   Programs
                                   ____Funding Options
____Mental Health Problems   ____Alternative Models for Inter-
    Found in the Tribal   Agency Collaboration
    Community   ____Suggestions for Non-Indian
                                       Mental Health Workers

6. What I liked about the conference was:

7. The conference's weakest point(s) was:

8. This conference was useful to me and/or my tribe or agency in the following ways:

9. What I _____ to see included in this conference which was not was:

10. A video presentation was made which was
    ____interesting,   ____boring,   ____no video shown.

11. Handouts were distributed during the conference which were
    ____useful,   ____possibly of some use,   ____a waste of paper and time.

12. I would____, would not____ like a followup meeting to be held in our local area.

13. I would____, would not____ attend a Statewide Tribal Mental Health Conference to be held either at Swinomish or in Seattle.

14. A set of Tribal Mental Health Booklets were presented which will be useful to:

____Our Program
____Tribal Government/Administrators
____Tribal Social Services
____Tribal Mental Health Workers
____Community Mental Health Clinics
____County Coordinators
____State Representatives
____Indian Health Services
____Other: _____
____Do not seem very useful

15. What I like about these Booklets is:

16. What I do not like about these Booklets is:

17. What I would have liked to see which is not included in these Booklets is:

18. Please make any other comments or suggestions which you feel would help us evaluate this conference and/or the entire Tribal Mental Health Project.

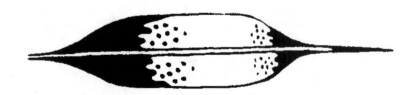

Part Six

Resource List for Tribal Mental Health

Introduction
Part Six

P **art Six** consists of a much revised and reduced list of written references and other resources related to Indian mental health. It was felt that the extensive resource listed included in the first edition was too large and academic to be truly useful. We hope that this shorter list will help familiarize mental health workers with the range of existing references and organizations.

This list is neither comprehensive nor up to date. There are many valuable publications not included. We have chosen references of particular interest to us and relevance to this program.

Many people have contributed information for this resource list. We particularly wish to acknowledge the generous help of Julia Putnam, Linda Anderson and the Seattle Indian Health Board. Julia Putnam pointed out that an extensive library of Native American mental health material had been compiled at the Seattle Indian Health Board as part of a National Institute of Mental Health Project conducted from 1977 through 1982. Linda Anderson, then Mental Health Administrator for the Health Board, opened the library and catalog for our review.

Another helpful source was the Native American Research Information Service (NARIS), operated by the University of Oklahoma. NARIS periodically updates their information bank.

Bruce Miller, anthropology professor at the University of British Columbia, brought several useful references to our attention.

Mary Ellen Cayou of the Swinomish Tribe combined and organized selections from many reference lists, bibliographies, books and articles to make these resources available in a systematic fashion.

Appendix One consists of an alphabetized list of books, monographs, unpublished papers and articles from books. Particularly comprehensive and useful references listed in this section are Attneave and Kelso's American Indian Annotated Bibliography of Mental Health, Manson's New Directions in Prevention Among American Indian and Alaska Native Communities, the Seattle Indian Health Board's Indian and Alaska Native Mental Health Seminars: Summarized Proceedings of 1978-1981, and Triandis and Dragun's six volume Handbook of Cross-Cultural Psychology.

Appendix Two is a brief list of Journals, Newsletters and periodicals of interest for Indian mental health work, as well as a list of journal articles.

Indian organizations and other resources which may be useful to tribal mental health workers are listed in Appendix Three. Resources in Washington State are emphasized, though a number of national resource groups and other miscellaneous resources are also included.

Appendix Four presents a list of Indian Tribes both within and outside of Washington State. Although this information is readily obtainable elsewhere, it may be helpful particularly to mainstream mental health agencies which would not otherwise be liable to have this list on hand. It may be helpful to mental health and social services workers trying to locate family members of clients, explore client enrollment, etc.

We hope that this resource list, however incomplete, will help to acquaint readers with the wide range of work available in the field.

Contents
Part Six

*Resource List
for Tribal
Mental Health*

Appendix One

Books, Papers, Monographs
and Articles from Books 541

Appendix Two

Journals, Newsletters, and Journal Articles 549

Appendix Three

Indian Organizations and Other Resources 551

Appendix Four

Native American Tribes
Washington State Indian Tribes 557
Tribes Outside of Washington State 559

Appendix One
Books, Papers, Monographs
and
Articles from Books

Ackerknecht, Erwin H. *Medicine and Ethnology: Selected Essays*. Baltimore: The Johns Hopkins Press, 1971.

Amoss, Pamela. *Coast Salish Spirit Dancing: The Survival of an Ancestral Religion*. Seattle: University of Washington Press, 1978.

Amoss, Pamela. "The Power of Secrecy Among the Coast Salish." In *The Anthropology of Power*, Fogelson, R. D. and Adams, R.N. (eds.), N.Y.: Academic Press, 1977.

Amoss, Pamela T. "Strategies of Reorientation: The Contribution of Contemporary Winter Dancing to Coast Salish Identity and Solidarity." In *Blackman, ed.*, 1977.

Amoss, Pamela T. "The Indian Shaker Church." In *Handbook of North American Indians: The Northwest*. Washington, D.C.: Smithsonian Institution.

Amoss, Pamela T. and Stevan Harrell. *Other Ways of Growing Old*. Stanford: Stanford University Press, 1981.

Anderson, Mad Bear. "Traditional Medicine III." In *Indian and Alaska Native Mental Health Seminars: Summarized Proceedings, 1978-1981, Vol. 1*. Seattle: Seattle Indian Health Board, 1982.

Attneave, C.L., "American Indian and Alaska Native Families: Emigrants in Their Own Homeland," Ethnicity and Family Therapy, M. McGoldrich, J.K. Pearce, and J. Giordano (eds.), (New York, NY: Guildord Press, 1982).

Attneave, C. and Beiser, M. "Service Networks and Utilization Patterns, Mental Health Programs, Indian Health Service." Report to the U.S. Public Health Service, Indian Health Service, 1975.

Attneave, C. L. "The American Indian Child." In J. D. Noshpitz (ed.), *Basic Handbook of Child Psychiatry*. N.Y.: Basic, 1979.

Attneave, Carolyn. "Kinship and Family Systems." In *Indian and Alaska Native Mental Health Seminars: Summarized Proceedings 1978-1981, Vol. 1*, Seattle: Seattle Indian Health Board, 1982.

Attneave, Carolyn. "The Wasted Strengths of Indian Families." In Steven Unger, The *Destruction of American Indian Families*. N.Y.: Association of American Indian Affairs, 1977.

Attneave, Carolyn and Kelso, Dianne. *American Indian Annotated Bibliography of Mental Health-Volume I.* Seattle: University of Washington, 1977.

Bergman, Robert. "Developmental Overview of Indian Mental Health." In *Indian and Alaska Native Mental Health Seminars: Summarized Proceedings, Vol. 1*, Seattle: Seattle Indian Health Board, 1982.

Bergman, Robert. "The Human Cost of Removing Indian Children." In Steven Unger, *The Destruction of American Indian Families*. N.Y.: Association of American Indian Affairs, 1977.

Blackshaw, L., Levy, A., & Perciano, J., Listening to High Utilizers of Mental Health Services: Recognizing, Responding to and Recovering From Trauma, State of Oregon, MHDDSD: 1999.

Blanchard, Evelyn L. "Extended Family: Parental Roles and Child Rearing Practices," in *Child Welfare Training: Education for Social Work Practice with American Indian Families*. Washington: DHHS, 1981.

Bourguignon, Erika. "Cross-cultural Perspectives on the Religious Uses of Altered States of Consciousness." In *Religious Movements in Contemporary America*, edited by Irving Zaretsky and Mark P. Leone. Princeton, N.J.: Princeton University Press, 1974.

Brave, Lorraine. "Indians, Courts, and Corrections." In *Indian and Alaska Native Mental Health Seminars: Summarized Proceedings 1978-1981, Vol. 2*, Seattle: Seattle Indian Health Board, 1982.

Clifton, James, (ed.). *Being and Becoming Indian*. Chicago: The Dorsey Press, 1989.

Collins, June McCormick. *Valley of the Spirits: The Upper Skagit Indians of Western Washington*. Seattle: University of Washington Press, 1974.

Cross, T.L., Bazron, B.J., Dennis, K.W., et al., Towards a Culturally Competent System of Care: A Monograph on Effective Services for Minority Children Who Are Severely Emotionally Disturbed (Washington, DC: Child and Adolescent Service System Program (CASSP) Technical Assistance Center, Georgetown University Child Development Center, March 1989).

Crozier-Hogle, Lois et all, Surviving in Two Worlds: Contemporary Native American Voices, Austin: University of Texas Press, 1997.

Culturally Relevant Ethnic Minority Services Coalition. *Multi-Ethnic Mental Health Services: Six Demonstration Programs in Washington State*. Printed by Northwest Graphics in Mount Vernon, WA, 1989.

Danielli, Y. The treatment and prevention of long-term effects and intergenerational transmission of victimization: A lesson from holocaust survivors and their children. In C.R. Figley (Ed.), Trauma and Its Wake (Vol I). New York, Brunner/Mazel, 1985.

Dinges, N., et al. "Social Ecology of Counseling and Psychotherapy with American Indians." In A. J. Marsella and P. Pederson (eds.), *Cross-cultural Counseling and Psychotherapy: Foundations, Evaluation, Cultural Considerations.* Elmsford, N.Y.: Pergamon, 1981.

Dinges, Norman. "Cross-cultural Counseling." In *Indian and Alaska Native Mental Health Seminars: Summarized Proceedings 1978-1981, Vol. 2*, Seattle: Seattle Indian Health Board, 1982.

Ellenberger, H.F. The Discovery of the Unconscious. N.Y.: Basic Books, 1970.

Fitzpatrick, Darlene. "'The Shake': The Indian Shaker Curing Ritual Among the Yakima." M.A. thesis, University of Washington, 1968,

Fleming, C.M., "Substance Abuse Prevention in American Indian and Alaska Native Communities: A Literature Review and OSAP Program Survey," final report submitted to the Office for Substance Abuse Prevention in partial fulfillment of contract no. 88-M-075606501-D, Denver, CO, 1989.

Gallegos, Joseph S., Ph.D. "Ethnic Competence: Practice and Principles." *Beyond Cultural Awareness: Ethnic Competence in Practice*. Multi-Ethnic Mental Health Training Project, 1982.

Gorsline, Jerry, ed: Shadows of Our Ancestors, Port Townsend: Empty Bowl, 1992.

Guilmet, George M., and Whited, David L., The People Who Give More: Health and Mental Health Among the Contemporary Puyallup Indian Tribal Community, American Indian and Alaska Native Mental Health Research, Volume 2, Monograph 2, Winter 1989.

Gunther, Erna. "The Shaker Religion of the Northwest." In *Indians of the Urban Northwest*, edited by Marian Smith. N.Y.: Columbia University Press, 1949.

Hall, R. L. "Alcohol Treatment in American Indian Populations: An Indigenous Treatment Modality Compared with Traditional Approaches," in *Alcohol and Culture: Comparative Perspectives from Europe and America*. Edited by T. F. Babor. Washington, D.C.: U.S. Government Printing Office, 1984.

Hanson, Wynne Dubray and Eisenbise, Margaret Deocampo. *Social Work Methods of Intervention with American Indians*. Rockville: ERIC.

Harris, M. Modification in Service Delivery and Clinical Treatment for Women Diagnosed with Severe Mental Illness Who are Also Survivors of Sexual Abuse Trauma. Special Issue: Women's Mental Health Services, Journal of Mental Health Administration, 21: 397-406: 1994.

Hayes, Susanna Adella. "The Resistance to Education for Assimilation by the Colville Indians." Ph.D. dissertation.

Herman, Judith, Trauma and Recovery, New York: Basic Books, 1992.

Hilbert, Vi. Haboo, *Native American Stories from Puget Sound*. Seattle: University of Washington Press, 1985.

Hilbert, Vi. "The Naming Ceremony." Excerpted from *Ways of the Lushootseed People: Ceremonies and Traditions of Northern Puget Sound Indians*. Seattle: United Indians of All Tribes Foundation, 1980.

Hilbert, Vi and Bierwert. *Ways of the Lushootseed People: Ceremonies and Traditions of Northern Puget Sound Indians*. Seattle: Daybreak Star Press, 1980.

James, William, *The Varieties of Religious Experience.* N.Y., 1902

Jilek, W. *Indian Healing, Shamanic Ceremonialism in the Pacific Northwest Today.* Blaine, WA.: Hancock House, 1982.

Jilek, W. and Jilek-Aall, L. "A Transcultural Approach to Psychotherapy with Canadian Indians: Experiences from the Fraser Valley of British Columbia." In *Psychiatry Part III*, Proceedings of the Fifth World Congress of Psychiatry, pp. 1181-1186, Exerpta Medical International Congress Series, No. 274, Mexico, D.F. 1971.

Kaplan, Bert and Johnson, Dale. "The Social Meaning of Navaho Psychopathology and Psychotherapy." In A. Kiev, *Magic, Faith, and Healing,* 1964.

Kelso, Dianne R. and Attneave, Carolyn L. *Bibliography of North American Indian Mental Health.* Westport CT: Greenwood Press, 1981.

Kew, J. E. Michael. Coast Salish Ceremonial Life: Status and Identity in a Modern Village. *Unpublished Ph.D. dissertation* in anthropology, University of Washington.

Kiev, A. *Magic, Faith and Healing.* N.Y.: Free Press, 1964.

Kiev, A. "The Study of Folk Psychiatry." In *Magic, Faith and Healing,* Ari Kiev, ed. N.Y.: The Free Press, 1964.

Kiev, A. *Transcultural Psychiatry.* N.Y.: McMillan Co., Free Press, 1972.

Kleinman, A. Patients and Healers in the Context of Culture. Berkeley: University of California Press, 1979.

Kleinman, Arthur, M.D. "Indigenous and Traditional Systems of Healing." Paper.

Kluckhohn, Clyde. *Navaho Witchcraft.* Boston: Beacon Press, 1962.

Kulka, R. A., Schlenger, W., & Fairbank, J., Trauma and the Vietnam War Generation, New York, Brunner/Mazel: 1990.

Lake, Medicine Grizzlybear. "A Definition of Shamanism: For Professional and Lay Communities." Indian Education, Resource & Evaluation Center III, School of Education, Gonzaga University, Spokane, WA, 1989.

Lane, Phil Jr. "Healing-A Native Perspective." In *Indian and Alaska Native Mental Health Seminars: Summarized Proceedings, 1978-1981, Vol. 1.* Seattle: Seattle Indian Health Board, 1982.

Lebra, W. P. (ed.). *Culture-bound Syndromes, Ethnopsychiatry and Alternate Therapies.* Honolulu: University Press of Hawaii, 1976.

Manson, S., et al. "The Depressive Experience in American Indian Communities: A Challenge for Psychiatric Theory and Diagnosis," in *Culture and Depression.* Edited by A. Kleinman, et al. Berkeley: University of California Press, 1985.

Manson, S. M. (Ed.) *New Directions in Prevention Among American Indian and Alaska Native Communities.* Denver: University of Colorado Health Science Center, 1988.

Manson, Spero. "Kinship and Family Systems." In *Indian and Alaska Native Mental Health Seminars: Summarized Proceedings 1978-1981, Vol. 1,* Seattle: Seattle Indian Health Board, 1982.

Marsella, A. J. and Pederson, P. (eds.). *Cross-cultural Counseling and Psychotherapy: Foundations, Evaluation, Cultural Considerations.* Elmsford, N.Y.: Permagon,

1981.

Matthiessen, Peter. *Indian Country*. N.Y.: Viking, 1984.

Middleton-Moz, Jane. *Children of Trauma*. Dearfield Beach, Florida: Health Communications.

Miller, Bruce G., A Sociocultural Explanation of the Election of Women to Formal Office: The Upper Skagit Case, Ph.D. Dissertation, Department of Anthropology, Arizona State University, 1989.

Miller, Jay, Lushootseed Culture and the Shamanic Oddyssey, Lincoln and London: University of Nebraska Press, 1999

Moses, Kenneth. "Traditional Philosophy." In *Indian and Alaska Native Mental Health Seminars: Summarized Proceedings 1978-1981, Vol. 1*, Seattle: Seattle Indian Health Board, 1982.

Murphy, Jane M. "Psychotherapeutic Aspects of Shamanism." In A. Kiev, *Magic, Faith, and Healing*, 1964.

National Indian Child Abuse and Neglect Resource Center. "The Indian Extended Family Concept and its Relationship to Parenting." Resource paper. Tulsa, Spring 1980.

Native American Development Corporation, Pass the Word Post-Traumatic Stress: What Some Indian Youth and Vietnam Veterans have in Common Adolescence - A Tough Time for Indian Youth Blue Bay: A Tribal Approach to Fighting Alcohol andDrug AbusePositive Self Esteem Can Protect Native American Youth

Neel, David, The Great Canoes, Reviving a Northwest Coast Tradition, Vancouver, Toronto, Seattle: University of Washington Press, 1995.

Northwest Indian Child Welfare Institute, Inc. *Cross-cultural Skills in Indian Child Welfare: A Guide for the Non-Indian*. Portland, OR, 1987.

Oversight Hearing Before the Senate Committee on Indian Affairs on a Community-based Mental Health Initiative for Indian People. Washington, D.C.: U.S. Government Printing Office, July 1988.

Paul, Patrick. "Alcoholism in the Indian Community." In *Indian and Alaska Native Mental Health Seminars: Summarized Proceedings 1978-1981, Vol. 2*, Seattle: Seattle Indian Health Board, 1982.

Pearlman & Saakvitne. Trauma and the Therapist: Counter Transference and Vicarious Traumatization.

Pederson, P. B., et al, (eds.). *Counseling Across Cultures*. The University Press of Hawaii for the East-West Center, 1981.

Perry, John, The Far Side of Madness, Englewood Cliffs, N.J. : Prentice Hall, 1974

Powell, Peter J. *Sweet Medicine*. The Continuing Role of the Sacred Arrows, the Sun Dance and the Sacred Buffalo Hat in Northern Cheyenne History, Vol. I and II. Norman: University of Oklahoma Press, 1979.

Roman, Abraham and Rubel, Paula. *Feasting with Mine Enemy: Rank and Exchange Among Northwest Coast Societies*. Waveland Press, 1986.

Sampson, Chief Martin J. *Indians of Skagit County*. Mt. Vernon, WA: Skagit County Historical Society, 1972.

Seattle Indian Health Board. *Indian and Alaska Native Mental Health Seminars: Summarized Proceedings 1978-1981, Vols. 1 and 2*, Seattle: Seattle Indian Health Board, 1982. (Set of Vol. 1 and 2 available for purchase price of $30.)

Snyder, Sally. "Skagit Society and Its Existential Basis: An Ethnofolkloristic Reconstruction." Ph.D. dissertation. University of Washington, 1964.

Spence, John. "Indian Community Building." In *Indian and Alaska Native Mental Health Seminars: Summarized Proceedings 1978-1981, Vol. 2*. Seattle: Seattle Indian Health Board, 1982.

Stewart, Hilary, CEDAR, Seattle, London: University of Washington Press, 1984

Suttles, Wayne. *Coast Salish Essays*. Seattle: University of Washington Press, 1987.

Suttles, Wayne. "Spirit Dancing and the Persistence of Native Culture Among the Coast Salish." Paper presented at the Sixth International Congress of Anthropological and Ethnological Sciences, Paris, 1960.

Swinomish Tribal Community, *A Gathering of Wisdoms: Tribal Mental Health, A Cultural Perspective*, ed. Clarke, Jennifer, La Conner, WA, 1991.

Goldie Denney. "Indian Child Welfare." In *Indian and Alaska Native Mental Health Seminars: Summarized Proceedings 1978-1981, Vol. 1*.

Terr, Lenore. *Too Scared to Cry*, Harper & Row, 1990.

Tom, Isadore. "Healing-A Native Perspective." In *Indian and Alaska Native Mental Health Seminars: Summarized Proceedings, 1978-1981, Vol. 1*. Seattle: Seattle Indian Health Board, 1982.

Triandis, H. C. & Draguns, J. C. *Handbook of Cross-cultural Psychology, Vols. 1-6, (Vol. 6 "Psychopathology")*. Boston: Allyn & Bacon, 1980.

Trimble, J. E., et al. "American Indian Concepts of Mental Health: Reflections and Directions."In *Mental Health Services: The Cross-cultural Context*. Edited by Pedersen, P. B., et al. Beverly Hills, CA: Sage, 1984.

Trimble, Joseph. "Cultural Conflict and Self-awareness."In *Indian and Alaska Native Mental Health Seminars: Summarized Proceedings 1978-1981, Vol. 1*. Seattle: Seattle Indian Health Board, 1982.

Twohy, Patrick J. *Finding A Way Home: Indian and Catholic Spiritual Paths of the Plateau Tribes*. Spokane: The University Press, 1983.

Twohy, Patrick J. *Beginnings: A Meditation on Coast Salish Lifeways*. 1999.

Unger, Steven, ed. *The Destruction of American Indian Families*. New York: Association on American Indian Affairs, 1977.

U.S. Congress, Office of Technology Assessment, Indian Adolescent Mental Health, OTA-H-446 (Washington, DC: U.S. Government Printing Office,) January 1990.

van der Kolk, B.A., The Body Keeps the Score: Memory and the Evolving Psychology of Post Traumatic Stress, Harvard Review of Psychiatry, 1, 253-65: 1994.

van der Kolk, B.A. & Fisler, R., Childhood Abuse and Neglect and Loss of Self – Regulation, Bulletin of the Menninger Clinic 58: 145-168: 1994.

van der Kolk, B. A., Peryy, J.C. & Herman, J.L., Childhood Origins of Self Destructive Behavior, American Journal of Psychiatry, 148: 1665-1671: 1991.

van der Kolk, Bessel. *Psychological Trauma*, American Psychiatric Press, 1987.

Walker, P. S., et al. "Alcoholism, Alcohol Abuse and Health in American Indians and Alaska Natives." In S. M. Manson (ed.), *Health and Behavior: A Research Agenda for American Indians and Alaska Natives.*

Washington, Joseph Sr. "Tribal Beliefs and Mental Health." In *Indian and Alaska Native Mental Health Seminars: Summarized Proceedings 1978-1981, Vol. 1.* Seattle: Seattle Indian Health Board, 1982.

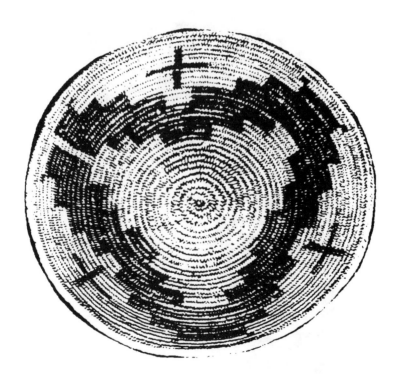

Appendix Two
Journals, Newsletters
and
Journal Articles

JOURNALS and NEWSLETTERS

American Indian and Alaska Native Mental Health Research. The Journal of the National Center. Denver: University of Colorado Health Science Center.

American Indian Culture and Research Journal.

Journal of the National Center for American Indian and Alaska Native Mental Health Research, University of Colorado, Campus Box C249, 4200 East N Avenue, Denver, CO 90062.

ARTICLES FROM JOURNALS

American Psychiatric Association Task Force on Indian Affairs. "A Hazard to Mental Health: Indian Boarding Schools." *American Journal of Psychiatry*, March 1973, 131: No. 3.

Amoss, P. T. "Strategies of Orientation: The Contribution of Contemporary Winter Dancing to Coast Salish Identity and Solidarity." *Arctic Anthropologist*, 1977: 14.

Attneave, C. "Medicine Men and Psychiatrists in the Indian Health Service." *Psychiatric Annals*, 1974, 4: 11.

Bechtold, D.W., "Cluster Suicide in American Indian Adolescents," American Indian and Alaska Native Mental Health Research 1(3):26-35, 1988.

Beiser, Morton. "A Hazard to Mental Health: Indian Boarding Schools." *American Journal of Psychiatry*, 1974, Vol. 131.

Bergman, R. "Learning from Indian Medicine." *Diversion Magazine*, February/March 1975.

Bergman, R. L. "A School for Medicine Men." *American Journal of Psychiatry*, 1973, 130(6).

Bergman, Robert L. "Paraprofessionals in Indian Mental Health Programs." *Psychiatric Annals*, November 1974, Vol. 4: 11.

Collins, June M. "Naming, Continuity, and Social Inheritance Among the Coast Salish of Western Washington." Papers of the Michigan Academy of Science, Arts and Letters, 1966, 51.

Fleming, C. "The Emergence of Culture-based Mental Health Services for Native Americans." *Listening Post*, 1983: 4.

Holm, Tom. "Culture, Ceremonialism, and Stress: American Indian Veterans and the Vietnam War." *Armed Forces and Society*.

Jilek, Wolfgang and Jilek-Aall, Louise. "The Psychiatrist and His Shaman Colleague: Cross-cultural Collaboration with Traditional Amerindian Therapists." *Journal of Operational Psychiatry*, 1978, 9(2).

Jilek, Wolfgang G. and Todd, Norman. "Witchdoctors Succeed Where Doctors Fail: Psychotherapy Among Coast Salish Indians." *Canadian Psychiatric Association Journal*, August 1974, Vol. 19.

Johnson, D. L. and Johnson, C. A. "Totally Discouraged: A Depressive Syndrome of the Dakota Sioux." *Transcultural Psychiatric Research*, 1965, 1.

Johnson, Marilyn. "Ojibwa Soul Traveler." *Shaman's Drum*, Berkeley, No. 15, Midwinter, 1989.

Manson, S.M., Ackerson, L.M., Dick, R.W., et al., "Depressive Symptoms Among American Indian Adolescents: Psychometric Characteristics of the CES-D," Journal of Consulting and Clinical Psychology.

Manson, Spero M. and Pambrun, Audra M. "Social and Psychological Status of the American Indian Elderly: Past Research, Current Advocacy, and Future Inquiry." *White Cloud Journal*, 1979, Vol. 1: 3.

Snyder, Sally. "Quest for the Sacred in Northern Puget Sound: An Interpretation of Potlatch." *Ethnology*, 1975, 14.

Appendix Three
Indian Organizations
and
Other Resources

BUREAU of INDIAN AFFAIRS - AREA OFFICE

Division of Social Services, Aberdeen Area Office, 115 4th Ave., S.E., Aberdeen, SD 57401, (605) 225-0250.

Division of Social Services, Albuquerque Area Office, 5301 Central Ave., N.E., 1000 Indid School, Albuquerque, NM 87103, (505) 766-3038.

Division of Social Services, Anadarko Area Office, P.O. Box 368, Anadarko, OK 73005, (405) 743-7240.

Division of Social Services, Billings Area Office, 316 N. 26th St., Billings, MT 59101, (406) 657-6315.

Division of Social Services, Juneau Area Office, P.O. Box 3-8000, Juneau, AK 99801, (907) 586-7628.

Division of Social Services, Minneapolis Area Office, 813 Second Ave., 15 S. 5th St., Minneapolis, MN 55402, (812) 349-3631.

Division of Social Services, Muskogee Area Office, Federal Bldg., Muskogee, OK 74401, (918) 687-2507.

Division of Social Services, Navajo Area Office, Window Rock, AZ 86515, (602) 871-5505.

Division of Social Services, Phoenix Area Office, P.O. Box 10, Phoenix, AZ 85001, (602) 241-2262.

Division of Social Services, Portland Area Office, 1425 N.E.Irving St., P.O. Box 3785, Portland, OR 97208, (503) 231-6785.

Division of Social Services, Sacramento Area Office, Federal Office Bldg., 2800 Cottage Way, Sacramento, CA 95825.

Division of Social Services, Eastern Area Office, 1951 Constitution Ave., N.W., Washington, D.C. 20245, (703) 235-2794.

Washington State BIA Agencies

Olympic Peninsula Agency, P.O. Box 120, Hoquiam, WA 98550.

Puget Sound Agency, 2707 Colby Ave., Everett, WA 98201, (425) 258-2651.

Spokane Agency, P.O. Box 389, Wellpinit, WA 99040.

Yakima Agency, P. O. Box 632, Toppenish, WA 98948.

FEDERAL ACTS RELEVANT to INDIAN MENTAL HEALTH

American Indian Religious Freedom Act, 1978.

Indian Child Welfare Act, 1978.

Indian Health Care Improvement Act, 1976.

Indian Self-Determination Act, 1975.

(Title 25 Federal Code, Annotated, contains all Federal laws related to Indian affairs.)

INDIAN HEALTH SERVICES

Albuquerque Indian Health Service, 2401 12th St. NW, Albuquerque, NM 87602.

Mental Health Programs Branch, Office of Health Services, Rockville, MD.

The Indian Health Service is divided into a number of area offices, each with several local service units. For example Washington and other Northwestern States are served by the Portland Area Office.

Portland Area Office

Federal Building, Rm. 476, 1220 S.W. 3rd Avenue, Portland, OR 98204.

Washington State Service Units:

Colville Service Unit, P.O. Box 71, Nespelem, WA 99155.

Mental Health/Social Services, Puget Sound Service Unit, Federal Office Building, Room 1300, 909 1st Avenue, Seattle, WA 98174.

Neah Bay Service Unit, P.O. Box 418, Neah Bay, WA 98357.

Northwest Washington Service Unit, 2592 Kwina Road, Bellingham, WA 98226-9297.

Tahola Service Unit, P.O. Box 219, Tahola,, WA 98587.

Wellpinit Service Unit, P.O. Box 357, Wellpinit, WA 99040.

Yakima Service Unit, Route 1, Box 1104, Toppenish, WA 98948.

RESOURCES in WASHINGTON STATE

American Indian Community Center, East 801 Second Avenue, Spokane, WA 99201, (509) 535-0886.

Dept. of Alcohol and Substance Abuse (DASA), Department of Social and Health Services, MS OB-44W, Olympia, WA 98504.

"State of Washington Native American Alcoholism Treatment Facilities Certified and Non-certified and Other Networking Agencies, June, 1988." (List obtainable from DASA.)

Ethnic Minority Mental Health Consortium of Washington State, Tacoma, WA.

Governor's Office of Indian Affairs, 1515 S. Cherry, KE-13, Olympia, WA, www.goia.wa.gov/.

Indian Desk, Department of Social and Health Services, OB 42- F, Olympia, WA 98504.

Kitsap County Indian Center, 3337 NW Byron, Silverdale, WA 98383.

Kwawachee Counseling Center, 2209 E. 32nd St., Tacoma, WA 98404.

Local Indian Child Welfare Committees of Department of Social and Health Services (LICWACs).

Lushootseed Research, 10832 Des Moines Way S., Seattle, WA 98168.

Native American Law Center, University of Washington.

Seattle Indian Center, 121 Stewart St., Seattle, WA 98101, (206) 728-8700.

Seattle Indian Health Board, 611 12 St. S., Seattle, WA 98114, (206) 324-9360, www.sihb.org/.

Small Tribes of Western Washington, P.O. Box 578, Sumner, WA 98390, (206) 593-2894, SCAN 462-3894.

Spokane Urban Indian Health Services, East 801 Second Avenue, P.O. Box 4598, Spokane, WA 99202-0598, (509) 535-0868.

The United Indian Association of Central Washington, 101 Butterfield Road, Yakima, WA 98901-2008, (509) 575-0835.

United Indians of All Tribes Foundation, P.O. Box 99100, Seattle, WA 98199, (206) 285-4425.

Washington State Department of Social and Health Services, Secretary's Indian Affairs Policy Committee

Washington State Governor's Office of Indian Affairs, Mailstop PF-14, Olympia, WA 98504, (206) 753-2411. Email: wamblig@goia.wa.gov

Washington State Regional Indian Child Welfare Advisory Committee (ICWACs).

Indian Studies Programs in Washington State

Eastern Washington State University, Cheney, WA

Evergreen State College, Olympia, WA

Gonzaga University, Spokane, WA

University of Washington, Seattle, WA

Washington State Division of Mental Health

Indian Mental Health Programs Administrator, Division of Mental Health, DSHS, OB-42F, Olympia, WA 98504.

Minority Mental Health Programs Administrator, Division of Mental Health, DSHS, OB-42F, Olympia, WA 98504.

RESOURCES OUTSIDE of WASHINGTON STATE

Aboriginal Mental Health Research team, Affiliated tribes of the Northwest, www.nativeculture.com.

Administration for Native Americans (ANA), HHS-HDS, Hubert Humphrey Bldg., 200 Independence Ave. S.W., Rm. 338-F,Washington, D.C. 20201.

American Indian Heritage Foundation.

American Indian Institute, University of Oklahoma, Norman, OK.

American Indian Law Center, Inc., P.O. Box 4456 Station A, Albuquerque, N.M. 87196, (505) 277-5462.

American Indian Mental Health Research, www.pressuchicago.edu/sm/ncaianmhr.

American Indian Psychology Training Projects, Department of Psychology, Utah State University, Logan, UT 84322-2810.

American Indian Studies Center, 3220 Campbell Hall, University of California, Los Angeles, 405 Hilgard Ave., Los Angeles, CA 90024-1548.

American Indian Training Program, University of Utah School of Social Work.

Association of American Indian Physicians, 10015 S. Pennsylvania, Building D, Oklahoma City, OK 73159.

Association of American Indian Social Workers.

Association on American Indian Affairs, Inc., 95 Madison Ave., New York, N.Y. 10016, (212) 689-8720.

Dept. of the Interior. Email: doi.gov

Four Worlds Development Project, Phil Lane, Coordinator, Faculty of Education, The University of Lethbridge, 4401 University Drive, Lethbridge, Alberta, Canada T1K 3M4.

Linkages for Indian Child Welfare Programs, TCI, Inc., 3410 Garfield Street N.W., Washington, D.C. 20007, (703) 820-4074.

National Center for American Indian and Alaska Native Mental Health Research, University of Colorado Health Sciences Center, Campus Box C 249, 4200 East Ninth Ave., Denver, C 80262, (303) 394-5203.

National Congress of American Indians.

National Indian Health Board, Denver, CO.

National Indian Justice Center, 7 Fourth St. #28, Petaluma, CA 94952.

National Indian Social Worker's Association.

Native American Research Information Service (NARIS), University of Oklahoma, Norman, OK.

North American Bibliography Project at Yale University. Bibliographic Retrieval System. (Collects, indexes, and disseminates information about journal articles, dissertations, professional papers, and research reports on American Indian and Alaska Native mental health.

Northwest Indian Child Welfare Institute, c/o Regional Research Institute, P.O. Box 751, Portland, OR 79207. (503) 229-3038.

Portland Area Indian Health Board, 520 S.W. Harrison, Suite 440, Portland, OR 97201, 1-800-553-9771.

Subcommittee on Indian Affairs, American Psychiatric Association, Washington, D.C.

Veterans Administration Advisory Committee on Native American Veterans.

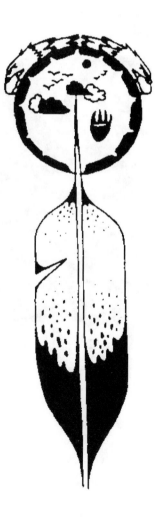

Appendix Four
Native American Tribes

WASHINGTON STATE INDIAN TRIBES
RESERVATION BASED TRIBES

Chehalis Confederated Tribes, Business Council, P.O. Box 536, Oakville, WA 98568, (360) 273-5911, Local 753-3213.

Colville Confederated Tribes, Business Council, P.O. Box 150, Nespelem, WA 99155, (509) 634-4116.

Hoh Tribal Business Committee, HC 80, Box 917, Forks, WA 98331, (360) 374-6582.

Jamestown S'Klallam Indian Tribe, 305 Old Blyn Hwy., Sequim, WA 98382, (360) 683-1109.

Kalispel Tribal Business Committee, P.O. Box 38, Usk, WA 99180, (509) 445-1147.

Lower Elwha Klallam Tribal Council, 1666 Lower Elwha Road, Port Angeles, WA 98362-0298, (360) 452-8471.

Lummi Nation Business Council, 2616 Kwina Road, Bellingham, WA 98225, (360) 384-1489.

Makah Tribal Council, P.O. Box 115, Neah Bay, WA 98357, (36-) 645-2201.

Muckleshoot Tribal Council, 39015 172nd Ave. S.E., Auburn, WA 98002.

Nisqually Tribe, 5820 She-Nah-Num Drive S.E., Olympia, WA 98503, (360) 456-5221.

Nooksack Indian Tribal Council, P.O. Box 157, Deming, WA 98244, (360) 592-5176.

Port Gamble S'Kallam Tribe, Business Committee, P.O. Box 280, Kingston, WA 98436, (360) 297-2646.

Puyallup Tribal Council, 2002 East 28 Street, Tacoma, WA 98404, (253) 573-7800.

Quileute Tribal Council, P.O. Box 279, La Push, WA 98350, (360) 374-6163.

Quinault Nation Business Committee, P.O. Box 189, Taholah, WA 98587, (360) 276-8211.

Samish Nation, Box 217, Anacortes, WA 98221, (360) 293-6404.

Sauk-Suiattle Indian Tribe, 5318 Chief Brown Lane, Darrington, WA 98241, (360) 436-0131.

Shoalwater Bay Tribal Council, P.O. Box 130, Tokeland, WA 98590, (360) 267-6766,

Skokomish Tribal Council, N. 80 Tribal Center Road, Shelton, WA 98584, (360) 426-4232.

Snoqualmie Tribal Council, P.lO. Box 670, Fall City, WA 98024, (425) 222-6900.

Spokane Tribal Business Council, P.O. Box 100, Wellpinit, WA 99040, (509) 258-9243.

Squaxin Island Tribal Council, SE 70 Squaxin Lane, Shelton, WA 98584, (360) 426-9781.

Stillaguamish Tribal Board of Directors, 3439 Stoluckquamish Lane, Arlington, WA 98223, (360) 652-7362.

Suquamish Tribal Council, P.O. Box 498, Suquamish, WA 98392, (360) 598-3311.

Swinomish Tribal Community, P.O. Box 817, La Conner, WA 98257, (360) 466-3163.

Tulalip Tribal Board of Directors, 6700 Totem Beach Road, Marysville, WA 98270, (360) 651-4000.

Upper Skagit Tribal Council, 2284 Community Plaza, Sedro Woolley, WA 98284, (360) 856-5501.

Yakima Nation Tribal Council, P.O. Box 151, Toppenish, WA 98948, (509) 865-5121.

WASHINGTON STATE LANDLESS TRIBES

Chinook Indian Tribe, Inc., Box 228, Chinook, WA 98614, (360) 777-8303.

Cowlitz Tribe, P.O. Box 2547, Longview, WA 98632, (360) 577-8140.

Duwamish Tribe, 14235 Ambaum Blvd. SW, Burien, WA 98166, (206) 431-1582.

Marietta Band of Nooksack Indians, 1827 Marine Dr., Bellingham, WA 98226.

San Juan Indian Tribe, P.O. Box 444, Friday Harbor, WA 98250, (360) 378-4924.

Snohomish Tribe of Indians, 144 Railroad Ave., Suite 201, Edmonds, WA 98020.

Snoqualmoo Tribe, P.O. Box 463, Coupeville, WA 98239.

Steilacoom Tribe, P.O. Box 88419, Steilacoom, WA 98388, (253) 584-6308.

INDIAN TRIBES OUTSIDE OF WASHINGTON STATE

Absentee Shawnee Tribe
Shawnee, OK

Aqua Caliente Band of Cahuilla
Indians
Palm Springs, CA

Ak Chin Indian Community
   of Papago Indians of
   Maricopa
Maricopa, AZ

Alabama & Coushatta Tribes of
Texas
Livingston, TX

Alabama-Quassarte Tribal Town
   Creek Nation
Eufaula, OK

Alturas Indian Rancheria of
Pit River
Alturas, CA

Apache Tribe of Oklahoma
Anadarko, OK

Arapahoe Tribe of Wind River
Ft. Washakie, WY

Assinboine & Sioux Tribe of
Montana
Poplar, MT

Augustine Band of Cahuilla
Mission

Bad River Band of Lake
Superior Chippewa Indians
Odanah, WI

Bay Mills Indian Community
Brimley, MI

Berry Creek Rancheria of
Maidu
Oroville, CA

Big Bend Rancheria of
Pit River
Big Bend, CA

Big Lagoon Rancheria of
Smith River
Trinidad, CA

Big Pine Band of Owens Valley
Paiute Shoshone Indians
Big Pine, CA

Big Sandy Rancheria of Mono
Auberry, CA

Big Valley Rancheria of Pomo
& Pit
Lakeport, CA

Blackfeet Tribe, Montana
Browning, MT

Blue Lake Rancheria of California
Blue Lake, CA

Bridgeport Paiute Indian
Colony
Bridgeport, CA

Buena Vista Rancheria of MeWuk of
California
Ione, CA

Burns Paiute Indian Colony,
Oregon
Burns, OR

Cabazon Band of Cahuilla Mission
Indio, CA

Cachil DeHe Band of Wintun
Indians
Colusa, CA

Caddo Indian Tribe of Oklahoma
Binger, OK

Cahuilla Band of Mission
Indians
Anza, CA

Cahto Indian Tribe of the
Laytonville
Laytonville, CA 95454

Campo Band of Diegueno
Mission
Campo, CA

Capitan Grande Band of Diegueno
Mission Indians of California

Barona Group of Capitan Grande
Band of Mission Indians
Lakeside, CA

Viejas Group of Capitan Grande
Alpine, CA

Cayuga Nation of New York
Versailles, NY

Cedarville Rancheria of Northern
Paiute Indians of California
Cedarville, CA

Chemehuevi Indian Tribe
Chemehuevi, CA

CherAe Heights Indian Community
of the Trinidad Rancheria
Trinidad, CA

Cherokee Nation of Oklahoma
Tahlequah, OK

Cheyenne-Arapaho Tribes
Concho, OK

Cheyenne River Sioux Tribe
Eagle Butte, SD

Chickasaw Nation of Oklahoma
Ada, OK

Chicken Ranch Rancheria of
MeWuk
Jamestown, CA

Chitimacha Tribe of Louisiana
Charenton, LA

Citizen Band Potawatomi
Indians
Shawnee, OK

Coast Indian Community of
Yurok
Klamath, CA

Coeur D'Alene Tribe
Plummer, ID

Colorado River Indian Tribe
Parker, AZ
    Lawton, OK

Confederated Salish &
Kootenai
Pablo, MT
Colville
Nespelem, WA

Confederated Tribes of the
Goshute
Ibapah, UT

Confederated Tribes of the
Siletz
Siletz, OR

Confederated Tribes of
Warm Springs
Warm Springs, OR

Chippewa-Cree Indians of
Rocky Boy
Box Elder, MT

Choktaw Nation of Oklahoma
Durant, OK

Cloverdale Rancheria of Pomo
Cloverdale, CA

Cocopah Tribe of Arizona
Somerton, AZ

Cold Springs Rancheria of Mono
Tollhouse, CA

Comanche Indian Tribe of
Oklahoma

Confederated Tribes of the Coos,
Lower Umpqua & Suislaw
Indians
Coos Bay, OR

Confederated Tribes of the
Grand Ronde
Grand Ronde, OR

Confederated Tribes of the
Umatilla
Pendleton, OR

Cortina Indian Rancheria of
Winton
Sacramento, CA

Coushatta Tribe of Louisiana
Elton, LA

Covelo Indian Community of
Round Valley
Covelo, CA

Cow Creek Bank of Umpqua
Indians
Roseburg, OR

Coyote Valley Band of Pomo
Redwood Valley, CA

Creek Nation of Oklahoma
Okmulgee, OK

Crow Tribe of Montana
Crow Agency, MT

Crow Creek Sioux Tribe of the
Crow Creek Reservation
Fort Thompson, SD

Cuyapaipe Community
Diequeno Mission
Pine Valley, CA

Death Valley TimbiSha Shoshone
Band
Death Valley, CA

Delaware Tribe of Western
Oklahoma
Anadarko, OK

Devils Lake Sioux Tribe
Fort Totten, ND

Dry Creek Rancheria of
Pomo Indians
Geyserville, CA

Duckwater Shoshone Tribe
Duckwater, NV

Eastern Band of Cherokee Indians
of North Carolina
Cherokee, NC

Eastern Shawnee Tribe of
Oklahoma
Seneca, MO

Elem Indian Colony of Pomo
Indians of Sulpher Bank
Clearlake Oaks, CA

Elk Valley Rancheria of
Smith River
Crescent City, CA

Ely Indian Community of Nevada
Ely, NV

Enterprise Rancheria of Maidu
Oroville, CA

Flandreau Santee Sioux
Flandreau, SD

Forest County Potawatomi
Community
Crandon, WI

Fort Belknap Indian Community of
the Fort Belknap Reservation-Montana
Harlem, MT

Fort Bidwell Indian Community
of Paiute Indians
Fort Bidwell, CA

Fort Independence Indian
Community of Paiute Indians
Independence, CA

Fort McDermitt Paiute and
Shoshone
McDermitt, NV

Fort McDowell Mohave-Apache
Fountain Hills, AZ

Fort Mojave Indian Tribe of
Arizona
Needles, CA

Fort Sill Apache Tribe of
Oklahoma
Apache, OK

Gayhead Wampanoag Indians of
Massachusetts
Gay Head, Mass.

Gila River PimaMaricopa Indians
Sacaton, AZ

Grand Traverse Band of Ottawa
& Chippewa Indians of
Michigan
Suttons Bay, MI

Greenville Rancheria of Maidu
Greenville, CA

Grindstone Indian Rancheria
of Wintun Waiulaki
Elk Creek, CA

Hannahville Indian Community
Wilson, MI

Havasupai Tribe of the
Havasupai Reservation
Supai, AZ

Hoopa Valley Tribe of the Hoopa
Hoopa, CA

Hopi Tribe of Arizona
Kykotsmovi, AZ

Hopland Band of Pomo Indians
Hopland, CA

Houlton Band of Maliseet
Indians
Houlton, ME

Hualapai Tribe
Peach Springs, AZ

Inaja Band of
Diequeno Mission
Ramona, CA

Iowa Tribe of Kansas & Nebraska
White Cloud, KS

Iowa Tribe of Oklahoma
Perkins, OK

Jackson Rancheria of MeWuk
Indians
Jackson, CA

Jamul Indian Village of
California
Jamul, CA

Jicarilla Apache Tribe
Dulce, NM

Kaibab Band of Paiute Indians
Pipe Springs, AZ

Karuk Tribe of California
Happy Camp, CA

Kashia Bank of Pomo Indians of
Stwearts Point Rancheria
Stewarts Point, CA

Kaw Indian Tribe of Oklahoma
Kaw City, OK

Keweenaw Bay Indian Community
Baraga, MI

Kialegee Tribal Town of the Creek
Wetumka, OK

Kickapoo Reservation in Kansas
Horton, KS

Kickapoo Tribe of Oklahoma
McLoud, OK

Kiowa Indian Tribe of Oklahoma
Carnegie, OK

Klamath General Council
Chiloquin, OR

Kootenai Tribe of Idaho
Bonners Ferry, ID

Lac Vieux Desert Band
Watersmeet, Michigan

LaJolla Band of Luiseno
    Mission
Valley Center, CA

La Posta Band of Diequeno Mission
Lakeside, CA

Lac Courte Oreilles Band of
Lake Superior Chippewa
Indians
Hayward, WI

Lac du Flambeau Band of Lake
Superior Chippewa Indians
Lac du Flambeau, WI

Las Vegas Tribe of Paiute
Indians
Las Vegas, NV

Lookout Rancheria of Pit River
Lookout, CA

Los Coyotes Band of Cahuilla
Mission
Warner Springs, CA

Lovelock Pauite Tribe of Lovelock
Lovelock, NV

Lower Brule Sioux Tribe
Lower Brule, SD

Lower Sioux Indian Community
Morton, MN

Manchester Band of Pomo
Indians
Point Arena, CA

Manzanita Band of Diequeno
Mission
Boulevard, CA

Mashantucket Pequot Tribe
of Connecticut
Ledyard, CT

Menominee Indian Tribe of
Wisconsin
Keshena, WI

Mesa Grande Band of
Diequeno Mission
Santa Ysabel, CA

Mescalero Apache Tribe
Mescalero, NM

Miami Tribe of Oklahoma
Miami, OK

Miccosukee Tribe of Indians of
Florida
Miami, FL

Middleton Rancheria of
Pomo Indians
Middletown, CA

Minnesota Chippewa Tribe
Cass Lake, MN

Mississippi Band of Choctaw
Philadelphia, Mississippi

Moapa Band of Paiute Indians
Moapa, NV

Modoc Tribe of Oklahoma
Miami, OK

Montgomery Creek Rancheria of
Pit River Indians
Montgomery Creek, CA

Mooretown Rancheria of Maidu
Feather Falls, CA

Morongo Band of Cahuilla Mission
Banning, CA

Naragansett Indian Tribe of
Rhode Island
Kenyon, RI

Navajo Tribe of Arizona, New
Mexico and Utah
Window Rock, AZ

Nez Perce Tribe of Idaho
Lapwai, ID

Northern Cheyenne Tribe
Lame Deer, MT

Northfork Rancheria of
Mono Indians
San Francisco, CA

Northwestern Band of Shoshone
of Utah
Rock Springs, WY

Oglala Sioux Tribe of
Pine Ridge
Pine Ridge, SD

Omaha Tribe of Nebraska
Macy, Nebraska

Oneida Nation of New York
Syracuse, NY

Oneida Tribe of Wisconsin
Oneida, WI

Onondaga Nation of New York
Nedrow, NY

Osage Tribe of Oklahoma
Pawhuska, OK

Ottawa Tribe of Oklahoma
Miami, OK

Otoe-Missouria Tribe of Oklahoma
Red Rock, OK

Paiute Indian Tribe of Utah
Cedar City, UT

Paiute-Shoshone Indians of Bishop
Bishop, CA

Paiute-Shoshone Tribe of
Fallon
Fallon, NV

Paiute-Shoshone Indians of
Lone Pine
Lone Pine, CA

Pala Band of Liuseno
Mission Indians
Pala, CA

Pascua Yaqui Tribe of Arizona
Tucson, AZ

Passamaquoddy Tribe of Maine
Princeton, MA

Pauma Band of Luiseno Mission of
the Pauma & Yuima Reservation
Pauma Valley, CA

Pawnee Indian Tribe of
Oklahoma
Pawnee, OK

Pechanga Band Luiseno Mission
Temecula, CA

Penobscot Tribe of Maine
Old Town, MA

Peoria Tribe of Oklahoma
Miami, OK

Picayne Rancheria of
Chukchansi
Coarsegold, CA

Pinoleville Rancheria of Pomo
Ukiah, CA

Pit River Indian Tribe of the
X-L Ranch Reservation
Burney, CA

Poarch Band of Creek Indians of
Creek Indians of Alabama
Atmore, Alabama

Ponca Tribe of Indians of
Oklahoma
Ponca City, OK

Potter Valley Rancheria of Pomo
Potter Valley, CA

Prairie Band of Potawatomi
Indians
Mayetta, KS

Prairie Island Indian Community
Welch, MN

Pueblo of Acoma, New Mexico
Acomita, NM

Pueblo of Cochiti, New Mexico
Cochiti Pueblo, NM

Pueblo of Jemez, New Mexico
Jemez Pueblo, NM

Pueblo of Isleta, New Mexico
Isleta Pueblo, NM

Pueblo of Laguna, New Mexico
Laguna, NM

Pueblo of Nambe, New Mexico
Santa Fe, NM

Pueblo of Picuris, New Mexico
Penasco, NM

Pueblo of Pojoaque, New Mexico
Santa Fe, NM

Pueblo of San Felipe,
New Mexico
Algondones, NM

Pueblo of San Juan, New Mexico
San Juan Pueblo, NM

Pueblo of San Ildefonso,
New Mexico
Santa Fe, NM

Pueblo of Sandia, New Mexico
Bernalillo, NM

Pueblo of Santa Ana,
New Mexico
Bernalillo, NM

Pueblo of Santa Clara, New Mexico
Espanola, NM

Pueblo of Santo Domingo,
New Mexico
Santo Domingo Pueblo, NM

Pueblo of Taos, New Mexico
Taos, NM

Pueblo of Tesuque, New Mexico
Santa Fe, NM

Pueblo of Zia, New Mexico
San Ysidro, NM

Pyramid Lake Paiute Tribe
Nixon, NV

Quapaw Tribe of Oklahoma
Quapaw, OK

Quartz Valley Rancheria of
Karok, Shasta, and
Upper Klamath
Fort Jones, CA

Quechan Tribe of Fort Yuma
Yuma, AZ

Ramona Band of Village of
Cahuilla Mission
Colton, CA

Red Cliff Band of Lake Superior
Chippewa Indians of Wisconsin
Bayfield, WI

Red Lake Band of Chippewa
Indians
Red Lake, MN

Redding Rancheria of Pomo Indians
Redding, CA

Redwood Valley Rancheria of
Pomo
Redwood Valley, CA

Reno-Sparks Indian Colony Nevada
Reno, NV

Rincon Band of Luiseno Mission
Valley Center, CA

Roaring Creek Rancheria of
Pit River

Robinson Rancheria of Pomo
Indians
Nice, CA

Rohnerville Rancheria of
Bear River
Eureka, CA

Rosebud Sioux Tribe
Rosebud, SD

Rumsey Indian Rancheria of Wintun
Brooks, CA

Sac & Fox of the Mississippi
in Iowa
Tama, Iowa

Sac & Fox Tribe of Missouri in
Kansas and Nebraska
Reserve, KS

Sac & Fox Tribe of Indians
of Oklahoma
Stroud, OK

Saginaw Chippewa Indian Tribe
Mt. Pleasant, MI

Salt River Pima-Maricopa
Indians
Scottsdale, AZ

San Carlos Apache Tribe
San Carlos, AZ

San Manuel Band of Serrano
Mission
Highland, CA

San Pasqual Band of Diequeno
Mission
Valley Center, CA

Santa Rosa Indian Community
of the Santa Rosa Rose
Rancheria
Lemoore, CA

Santa Rosa Band of Cahuilla
Mission
Hemet, CA

Santa Ynez Band of Chumash
Mission
Santa Ynez, CA

Santa Ysabel Band of Diequeno
Mission
Santa Ysabel, CA

Santee Sioux Tribe of Nebraska
Niobrara, Nebraska

Sault Ste Marie Tribe of Chippewa
Sault Ste Marie, MI

Seminole Nation of Oklahoma
Wewoka, OK

Seminole Tribe of Florida, Dania,
Big Cypress & Brighton
Reservation
Hollywood, FL

Seneca Nation of New York
Salamanca, NY

Seneca-Cayuga Tribe of Oklahoma
Miami, OK

Shakopee Mdewakanton Sioux
Community
Prior Lake, MN

Sheep Ranch Rancheria of MeWuk

Sherwood Valley Rancheria
of Pomo
Ukiah, CA

Shingle Springs Band of Miwok
Indians
Shingle Springs, CA

Shoshone Tribe of the
Wind River
Ft. Washakie, WY

Shoshone-Bannock Tribes of
Fort Hall
Fort Hall, ID

Shoshone-Paiute Tribes of
Duck Valley
Owyhee, NV

Sisseton-Wahpeton Sioux of Lake
Traverse Reservation,
South Dakota
Agency Village, SD

Skull Valley Band of Goshute
of Utah
Ft. Duchesne, UT

Smith River Rancheria
Smith River, CA

Soboba Band of Luiseno Mission
San Jacinto, CA

Sokoagon Chippewa (Mole Lake)
Crandon, WI

Southern Ute Reservation,
Colorado
Ignacio, CO

St. Croix Chippewa Indians
Hertel, WI

St. Regis Band of Mohawk,
New York
Hogansburg, NY

Standing Rock Sioux Tribe
Fort Yates, ND

Strockbridge-Munsee Community
Bowler, WI

Summit Lake Paiute Tribe
Denio, NV

Susanville Indian Rancheria
of Paiute, Maidu, Pit
River & Washoe Indians
Susanville, CA

Sycuan Band of Diequeno Mission
Alpine, CA

Table Bluff Rancheria of
Wiyot Indians
Loleta, CA

Table Mountain Rancheria
Friant, CA

Te-Moak Tribe of Western
Shoshone
Elko, NV

Thlopthlocco Tribal Town of Creek
Tulsa, OK

Three Affiliated Tribes of
Fort Berthold Reservation
New Town, ND

Tohono O'odham Nation of Arizona
Sells, AZ

Tonawanda Band of Seneca
Indians
Basom, NY

Tonkawa Tribe of Indians of
Oklahoma
Tonkawa, OK

Tonto Apache Tribe
Payson, AZ

Torres-Martinez Band of Cahuilla
Thermal, CA

Tule River Indian Tribe
Porterville, CA

Tunica-Biloxi Indian Tribe of
Louisiana
Marksville, Louisiana

Tuolumne Band of Me-Wuk
Indians
Tuolumne, CA

Turtle Mountain Band of Chippewa
Belcourt, ND

Tuscarora Nation of New York
Lewiston, NY

Twenty-Nine Palms Band of Luiseno
Palm Springs, CA

United Keetoowah Band of
Cherokee
Tahlequah, OK

Upper Lake Band of Pomo Indians
Sacramento, CA

Upper Sioux Community
Granite Falls, MN

Ute Indian Tribe of Uintah &
Ouray
Fort Duchesne, UT

Ute Mountain Tribe of
Ute Mountain
Towaoc, CO

Utu Utu Gwaiti Paiute of
Benton Paiute Reservation
Benton, CA

Walker River Paiute Tribe
Schurz, NV

Washoe Tribe of Nevada &
California
Gardnerville, NV

White Mountain Apache Tribe
Whiteriver, AZ

Wichita Indian Tribe of Oklahoma
Anadarko, OK

Winnebago Tribe of Nebraska
Winnebago, Nebraska

Winnemucca Indian Colony of
Nevada
Winnemucca, NV

Wisconsin Winnebago Tribe
Toma, WI

Wyandotte Tribe of Oklahoma
Wyandotte, OK

Yankton Sioux Tribe
Marty, SD

Yavapai-Apache Indian Community
of the Camp Verde Reservation
Camp Verde, AZ

Yavapai-Prescott Tribe of
the Yavapai
Prescott, AZ

Yerrington Paiute Tribe
Yerrington, NV

Yomba Shoshone Tribe
Austin, NV

Ysleta Del Sur Pueblo
El Paso, TX

Yurok Tribe of Hoopa Valley
Hoopa, CA

Zuni Tribe of the Zuni
Reservation
Zuni, NM

NOTES

NOTES

NOTES

NOTES

NOTES

NOTES

NOTES

NOTES